# The Compleat Computer

## DENNIE L. VAN TASSEL
University of California, Santa Cruz

© 1976, Dennie Van Tassel. All rights reserved.

Printed in the United States of America.

**Library of Congress Cataloging in Publication Data**

Main entry under title:

The Compleat computer.

Bibliography: p.
Includes index.
1. Computers—Addresses, essays, lectures. 2. Computers and civilization—Addresses, essays, lectures. I. Van Tassel, Dennie, 1939-
QA76.C547    301.24'3    75-31760
ISNB 0-574-21060-1

# Credits

"I Am a Computer." reprinted with permission of The Wall Street Journal, © Dow Jones & Company, Inc. (1973).

"Impermanent Balance Between Man and Computer," Ruth Davis. *Science*, Vol. 186, p. 99, 11 October 1974. Copyright 1974 by the American Association for the Advancement of Science.

"All Watched over by Machines of Loving Grace," Richard Brautigan. Excerpted from THE PILL VERSUS THE SPRINGHILL MINE DISASTER by Richard Brautigan. Copyright © 1968 by Richard Brautigan. Reprinted by permission of Delacorte Press/Seymour Lawrence.

"Computers Aren't So Smart After All." Copyright © 1974, by The Atlantic Monthly Company, Boston, Mass. Reprinted with permission.

"The Computer and the Poet," Norman Cousins. © 1966, Saturday Review/World.

"The Development of Automatic Computing," reprinted by permission of the author, Harry D. Huskey, and AFIPS press.

"Man and the Computer," "Computer Generations," "How a Typical Computer Works," "The Human Mind and the Machine Brain," and "Computer Career Opportunities" reprinted by permission of the Honeywell Corporation, Wellesely Hills, Mass.

"The Brain and the Computer," Claude E. Shannon. From *Proceedings of the Institute of Radio Engineers* (1953), reprinted by permission of IEEE.

"Magnetic Larceny." Reprinted with permission from the October 1973 issue of MODERN DATA. All rights reserved.

"Technology, McDonald's Collide." Copyright by Computerworld, Newton, Mass. 02160. (June 4, 1975 issue).

"ELIZA," J. Weizenbaum. From "Contextual Understanding by Computers," COMMUNICATIONS OF THE ACM, Vol. 10, No. 8, August 1967, pages 474-80. Copyright 1967, by Association for Computing Machinery, Inc. Reprinted by permission.

"Medical Transition," from FIVE PATIENTS by Michael Crichton. Reprinted by permission of Alfred A. Knopf, Inc. and International Creative Management, New York, N.Y.

"The Machines Beyond Shylock," Ray Bradbury. Reprinted from *Computer* Magazine (formerly *Computer Group News*).

"The Great Data Famine," Art Buchwald. Reprinted by permission of the Los Angeles Times Syndicate.

"What's in a Robot?" Reprinted from *Electronics*, July 19, 1973; copyright McGraw-Hill, Inc., 1973.

"You Are an Interfacer of Black Boxes," Richard Todd. Reprinted by permission of Harold Ober Associates Incorporated. Copyright © 1970 by Richard Todd.

"Sports and EDP," by J. Gerry Purdy. Reprinted with the permission of DATAMATION ® copyright 1974 by Technical Publishing Company, Greenwich, Connecticut 06830.

"Computer Games People Play" reprinted from INFOSYSTEMS (October 1973). By Permission of the Publisher. © 1975 HITCHCOCK PUBLISHING COMPANY. ALL RIGHTS RESERVED.

"The Nine Billion Names of God," Arthur C. Clarke. Reprinted by permission of the author and the author's agents, Scott Meredith Literary Agency, Inc., 580 Fifth Avenue, New York, N.Y. 10036.

"Promise-Child in the Land of the Humans." Copyright 1971, Smithsonian Institution, from SMITHSONIAN Magazine April 1971.

"The Psychology of Robots" by Henry Block and Herbert Ginsberg. Reprinted from PSYCHOLOGY TODAY Magazine April 1968. Copyright © 1968 Ziff-Davis Publishing Company. All rights reserved.

"Will a Computer be World Chess Champion?" Edward Kozdrowicki and Dennis W. Cooper. Reprinted from COMPUTER DECISIONS, August, 1974, page 28, copyright 1974, Hayden Publishing Company.

"Counter-Computer," Stewart Brand. From *Rolling Stone*. © 1974 by Straight Arrow Publishers, Inc., all rights reserved. Reprinted by Permission.

"Commission Drops DP System" from the February 9, 1972 issue of COMPUTERWORLD. Copyright by Computerworld, Newton, Mass. 02160.

"Maximilian the Great," James F. Ryan. Reprinted by permission of DATA PROCESSING MAGAZINE.

"Those Onmipresent Minis." Reprinted with the permission of DATAMATION. © 1973 by Technical Publishing Company, Greenwich, Connecticut 06830.

"Computers in the Home," from "The Home" by G. Kozdrowicki, in *Living with the Computer*, ed. Basil de Ferrasti. © Oxford University Press 1971, pp. 1-6, by permission of the Oxford University Press, Oxford.

"Help Wanted: 50,000 Programmers," Gene Bylinsky, from FORTUNE (March 1967). Reprinted by permission of FORTUNE.

"UNIVAC TO UNIVAC," Louis B. Solomon, by permission of the author. Copyright © 1958 by Harper's Magazine. Reprinted from the March 1958 issue by special permission.

"There Will Come Soft Rains." © 1950 by Ray Bradbury, reprinted by permission of the Harold Matson Company, Inc.

"The Imitation Game" from A.M. Turing, "Computing Machinery and Intelligence" (*Mind* 59:236, 1950). Reprinted by permission of Basil Blackwell and Mott Ltd.

"What Computers Will Be Telling You," by Peter F. Drucker. © 1966, NATION'S BUSINESS—the Chamber of Commerce of the United States. Reprinted from the August issue. By permission of the author.

"When 'Brains' Take over Factories." Copyright 1964 U.S. News and World Report, Inc. From the February 24, 1964 issue.

"Hey Bartender!" Reprinted with the permission of The Wall Street Journal, © Dow Jones and Company, Inc. (1973).

"The Curse." By permission of the author, Art Buchwald.

"Parry Encounters the Doctor." Reprinted with the permission of DATAMATION © 1973, by Technical Publications Company, Greenwich, Conn. 06830.

"Flight Simulation" copyright 1974 by Computer Science Corporation.

"September 1984" by permission of North American Publishers, Philadelphia, PA (*Data Processing* Magazine, March 1970).

"Diagnosis by Computer." Reproduced from The Times by permission.

"Computers for the Disabled." This article first appeared in New Society, London, The Weekly Review of the Social Sciences.

"Now Look at It My Way." Reprinted with permission from MODERN DATA, January 1973. All rights reserved.

"Humanities and Computers." By permission of *North American Review* (Spring 1971).

"Cybernetic Scheduler," "Computer Helps Predict Supreme Court Actions," "Computers Help Fight Fires in Scotland," "Art Professor Generates 3-D Art," "Looking for a Rare Coin?" and "Employee ID Card Charges Lunch" by permission of *Computers and Automation*.

"Computers and Their Priests." From UP THE ORGANIZATION, by Robert Townsend. Copyright © 1970 by Robert Townsend. Reprinted by permission of Alfred A. Knopf, Inc.

"Guerrilla War Against Computers." Reprinted by permission from TIME, The Weekly Newsmagazine. Copyright Time Inc.

"Justice, the Constitution, and Privacy" by permission of Senator Sam J. Ervin, Jr.

"Computer Leads Watergate Committee to Its Witnesses." Reprinted by permission from the Christian Science Monitor. © 1973 The Christian Science Publishing Society. All rights reserved.

"The Unknown Citizen." Copyright 1940 and renewed 1968 by W. H. Auden. Reprinted from COLLECTED SHORTER POEMS 1927-1957, by W. H. Auden, by permission of Random House, Inc. Also reprinted by permission of Faber and Faber Ltd.

"FBI Breakthrough." Reprinted by permission of PARADE Magazine.

"Computerized Criminal Histories." Copyright by Computerworld, Newton, Mass. 02160.

"Congress Puts the Computer to Work." © 1973, NATION'S BUSINESS— the Chamber of Commerce of the United States. Reprinted from the May issue.

"The City and the Computer Revolution." Reprinted from "The City and the Computer Revolution" by John G. Kemeny in Monograph #7 of the American Academy of Political and Social Science. © 1967 by the American Academy of Political and Social Science.

"We Need Protection." Copyright by Computerworld, Newton, Mass. 02160.

"VASCAR". Reprinted by permission from *Changing Times*, the Kiplinger Magazine (October 1971 issue). Copyright 1971 by The Kiplinger Washington Editors, Inc., 1729 H Street, N.W., Washington, D.C. 20006.

"Waiting for the Great Computer Rip-Off." Reprinted from the July 1974 issue of Fortune Magazine by special permission; © 1974 Time Inc.

"Computerized Dating." Reprinted by permission of the author, Harvey Matusow.

"Decisions and Public Opinion." Reprinted by permission of the author, Donald Michael.

"The Data Bankers." Copyright © 1970 Celia Gilbert, reprinted from The Atlantic Monthly Company, Boston, Mass., with permission.

"The Snooping Machine." Reprinted by permission of the author, Alan Westin. Originally appeared in PLAYBOY Magazine; copyright © 1968 by Playboy.

"And It Will Serve Us Right." "The Son of Thetis," originally titled "And It Will Serve Us Right," copyright © 1969 by Communication/Research/Machines, Inc. from the book SCIENCE PAST—SCIENCE FUTURE by Isaac Asimov. Reprinted by permission of Doubleday and Company, Inc.

"Mind-Reading Computer." Reprinted by permission from TIME, the Weekly Newsmagazine Copyright Time Inc.

"Machines Smarter Than Men?" Copyright 1964 U.S. News and World Report, Inc. from the February 24, 1964 issue.

"On the Impact of the Computer on Society," by J. Weizenbaum. *Science*, Vol. 176, pp. 609-14, 12 May 1972. Copyright 1972 by the American Association for the Advancement of Science. Also reprinted by permission of the author.

"Traces" reprinted by permission of the author, J. Patrick Liteky, from the 30 August 1974 issue of SUNDAZ! To be published in a forthcoming book.

"Automation." By permission of Labor Education Division, Roosevelt University, Chicago, Ill.

"Deus ex Machina." Reprinted by permission of the author, Kit Pedler.

"What Computers Cannot Do," Bill Surface. © 1968, Saturday Review/World.

"Computer Crime." From AFIPS FJCC 1970, published by AFIPS Press, Montvale, N.J.

"News Item: Man Bites Ford." Copyright 1970 by Consumers Union of United States, Inc., Mount Vernon, N.Y. 10550. Reprinted by permission from CONSUMER REPORTS, March 1970.

"Kibernetika." © 1964, The Washington Post.

"The Day the Computers Got Waldon Ashenfelter." Reprinted by permission of the authors, Bob Elliot and Ray Goulding. Copyright © 1967 by The Atlantic Monthly Company, Boston, Mass. Reprinted with permission.

"Coming: A Cashless Society?" RCA Electronic Age, Winter, 1968-69, pp. 30-34.

"Hal Lobotomy." Reprinted by permission of the author and the author's agents, Scott Meredith Literary Agency, Inc., 580 Fifth Avenue, New York, N.Y. 10036.

"Computers and Dossiers." Reprinted by permission of Fred B. Rothman and Company.

"Impact of the Friendly Computer." Reproduced from The Times by permission.

"The Next Three Years." Reprinted by permission of Data Processing Magazine, Philadelphia, PA 19107.

"Session on Views of the Future." Reprinted by permission of the author, Murray Turoff.

"Machines Hold Power for Evil or Good." From "Behold the Computer Revolution" by Peter T. White, an article in National Geographic (November 1970).

"We Have Come a Long Way Together." From "The Dynamics of Change," Kaiser Aluminum and Chemical Corporation. © 1967.

The author also wishes to acknowledge the following for supplying artwork:

Doonesbury cartoons on pp. 4, 23, 39, 67, 101, 127, 147, 181. Copyright 1975, G. B. Trudeau/distributed by Universal Press Syndicate.

"The Fisherman" (p. 11), "The Hummingbird" (p. 25), and "The Woodcut" (p. 30), generated on a California Computer Products, Inc., plotter.

Illustrations on pp. 13, 14, 15, 28 courtesy of IBM.

Cartoons on pp. 31 and 54 courtesy of Infosystems, Wheaton, Ill.

Cartoon on p. 34 courtesy of Sidney Harris.

Illustration on p. 41 courtesy of Forbes Magazine.

Cartoon on p. 49 courtesy of Kaiser Aluminum and Chemical Corporation, Oakland, CA.

Cartoon on p. 81 courtesy of Modern Data.

Cartoon on p. 109 reproduced by permission of the Chicago Tribune. Copyright 1974. All rights reserved.

Cartoon on p. 113 courtesy of Computers and Automation.

Cartoons on p. 114 and 128 reprinted with special permission from INFOSYSTEMS Magazine, February/March issues, copyright 1975 by Hitchcock Publishing Co., Wheaton, Ill. 60187. All rights reserved.

Cartoons on pp. 121, 161, and 210 courtesy of Ron Cobb.

Cartoon on p. 143 courtesy of Datamation, Los Angeles, CA.

Cartoons on pp. 151 and 198: Reproduced with permission from MODERN DATA, June 1971/Feburary 1972. All rights reserved.

Illustration on p. 159 courtesy of Honeywell, Inc.

Illustration on p. 163 courtesy of Stanford Research Institute, Menlo Park, CA.

Illustration on p. 174 courtesy of Radio Times Hulton Picture Library, London.

Illustration on p. 175 BBC copyright.

Illustrations on p. 192 courtesy of Bell Laboratories, Murray Hill, N.J.

Illustrations on p. 199 courtesy of Manfred Schroeder.

Illustration on p. 208: Reprint of cover design from the 14th Annual Symposium on Switching and Automata Theory Proceedings, October 15-17, 1973. Copyrighted by IEEE. Artist: Algy Ray Smith III.

For
Gladys and Rush
Franny and Joe

Introduction   viii

# 1  In the Beginning  1

"I AM A COMPUTER," David Brand   2
IMPERMANENT BALANCE BETWEEN MAN AND COMPUTER, Ruth Davis   5
ALL WATCHED OVER BY MACHINES OF LOVING GRACE,
   Richard Brautigan   5
COMPUTERS AREN'T SO SMART, AFTER ALL, Fred Hapgood   6
THE COMPUTER AND THE POET, Norman Cousins   10
THE DEVELOPMENT OF AUTOMATIC COMPUTING, Harry D. Huskey   12
MAN AND THE COMPUTER, Honeywell Corporation   19
BRANCH POINTS   19
INTERRUPTS   20

# 2  How Computers Do It  21

THE BRAIN AND THE COMPUTER, Claude E. Shannon   22
MAGNETIC LARCENY, *Modern Data*   22
TECHNOLOGY, MCDONALD'S COLLIDE AS STUDENTS BEST BURGER
   BONANZA, Catherine Arnst   24
ELIZA, J. Weizenbaum   25
MEDICAL TRANSITION, Michael Crichton   26
COMPUTER GENERATIONS, Honeywell Corporation   28
HOW A TYPICAL COMPUTER WORKS, Honeywell Corporation   28
THE MACHINES BEYOND SHYLOCK, Ray Bradbury   29
"INSTANT" LIBRARIANS   30
THE GREAT DATA FAMINE, Art Buchwald   30
WHAT'S IN A ROBOT?, *Electronics*   32
VENDING MACHINE COMPUTATION   34
BRANCH POINTS   35
INTERRUPTS   35

# CONTENTS

# 3  The Software  37

"YOU ARE AN INTERFACER OF BLACK BOXES," Richard Todd   38
THE HUMAN MIND AND THE MACHINE "BRAIN,"
   Honeywell Corporation   44
SPORTS AND EDP . . . IT'S A NEW BALLGAME, J. Gerry Purdy   45
COMPUTER GAMES PEOPLE PLAY, *Infosystems*   50
THE NINE BILLION NAMES OF GOD, Arthur C. Clarke   55
PROMISE-CHILD IN THE LAND OF THE HUMANS, Gregory Benford and
   David Book   58
BRANCH POINTS   63
INTERRUPTS   63

# 4  The Present and Potential  65

THE PSYCHOLOGY OF ROBOTS, Henry Block and Herbert Ginsberg   66
WHEN WILL A COMPUTER BE WORLD CHESS CHAMPION?,
   Edward W. Kozdrowicki and Dennis W. Cooper   72
COUNTER COMPUTER, Stewart Brand   75
COMMISSION DROPS DP SYSTEM. VARIATION ON AN OLD THEME:
   MAN REPLACES COMPUTER, Marvin Smallheiser   76
MAXIMILIAN THE GREAT, James F. Ryan   77
THOSE OMNIPRESENT MINIS, W. David Gardner   82
COMPUTER CAREER OPPORTUNITIES, Honeywell Corporation   85
COMPUTERS IN THE HOME, G. Cuttle   86
HELP WANTED: 50,000 PROGRAMMERS, Gene Bylinsky   89

UNIVAC TO UNIVAC (SOTTO VOCE), Louis B. Salomon   90
THERE WILL COME SOFT RAINS, Ray Bradbury   93
THE IMITATION GAME, A. M. Turing   96
BRANCH POINTS   97
INTERRUPTS   97

# 5 Applications   99

WHAT THE COMPUTERS WILL BE TELLING YOU, Peter F. Drucker   100
WHEN "BRAINS" TAKE OVER FACTORIES,
   *U.S. News and World Report*   102
"HEY, BARTENDER! POUR ME ANOTHER SCOTCH!" WHIR, BUZZ,
   POCKETA, Jeffrey A. Tannenbaum   104
THE CURSE, Art Buchwald   106
PARRY ENCOUNTERS THE DOCTOR, Vinton Cerf   107
FLIGHT SIMULATION, Computer Sciences Corporation   110
SEPTEMBER 1984: THE AUTOMATED MULTIVERSITY, C. B. S. Grant   112
COMPUTER POISON CONTROL CENTER OPENED BY CHILDREN'S
   MERCY HOSPITAL, *Computers and Automation*   114
DIAGNOSIS BY COMPUTER MORE ACCURATE BUT DOCTORS STILL
   NEEDED   114
COMPUTERS FOR THE DISABLED, J. David Beattie   115
A SIXTY-YEAR-OLD FOREST SIMULATED IN A MINUTE, IBM   116
NOW LOOK AT IT MY WAY, *Modern Data*   117
HUMANITIES AND COMPUTERS: A PERSONAL VIEW, Robert Wachal   118
CYBERNETIC SCHEDULER, Edd Doerr   120
COMPUTERS AND THEIR PRIESTS, Robert Townsend   122
GUERRILLA WAR AGAINST COMPUTERS   122
BRANCH POINTS   123
INTERRUPTS   123

# 6 Governmental Uses   125

JUSTICE, THE CONSTITUTION, AND PRIVACY, Sam Ervin, Jr.   126
COMPUTER LEADS WATERGATE COMMITTEE TO ITS WITNESSES,
   Trudy Rubin   128
COMPUTER HELPS PREDICT SUPREME COURT ACTIONS   129
THE UNKNOWN CITIZEN, W. H. Auden   131
FBI BREAKTHROUGH: CRIME-BUSTING COMPUTERS,
   James D. Snyder   133
THE THINGS DATA BANKS CAN BE MADE OF   134
COMPUTER INCREASING CRIMINAL ARRESTS BY 10 PERCENT,
   RCA Government and Commercial Systems   134
COMPUTERIZED CRIMINAL HISTORIES: A 7-YEAR BLUNDER?,
   E. Drake Lundell, Jr.   135
CONGRESS PUTS THE COMPUTER TO WORK   136
COMPUTERS HELP FIGHT FIRES IN SCOTLAND, Kurt Van Vlandren   137
THE CITY AND THE COMPUTER REVOLUTION, John Kemeny   138
CAMPSITE RESERVATION   140
WE NEED PROTECTION FROM DRIVER INFORMATION SYSTEM,
   Herb Grosche   141
MASS. POLICE UNDER INVESTIGATION FOR ALLEGED SALE OF
   CRIME DATA   142
VASCAR—THE COMPUTER THAT CATCHES SPEEDERS,
   *Changing Times*   143
BRANCH POINTS   144
INTERRUPTS   144

## 7 The Impact  145

WAITING FOR THE GREAT COMPUTER RIP-OFF, Tom Alexander   146
COMPUTERIZED DATING OR MATCHMAKING, Harvey Matusow   148
ART PROFESSOR GENERATES 3-D ART USING COMPUTER, *Computers and Automation*   151
DECISIONS AND PUBLIC OPINION, Donald Michael   152
THE DATA BANKERS, Celia Gilbert   155
THE SNOOPING MACHINE, Alan Westin   156
LOOKING FOR A RARE COIN? COMPUTER MAY HOLD YOUR ANSWER, Gene Shelton and Alexander Scott   158
AND IT WILL SERVE US RIGHT, Isaac Asimov   160
MIND-READING COMPUTER, *Time* Magazine   162
MACHINES SMARTER THAN MEN? (Interview with Norbert Wiener)   165
ON THE IMPACT OF THE COMPUTER ON SOCIETY, Joseph Weizenbaum   168
TRACES, J. Patrick Liteky   170
AUTOMATION, Joe Glazer   172
DEUS EX MACHINA?, Kit Pedler   173
BRANCH POINTS   176
INTERRUPTS   176

## 8 Controls, or Maybe Lack of Controls  179

WHAT COMPUTERS CANNOT DO, Bill Surface   180
DAILY SURVEILLANCE SHEET, 1987, FROM A NATIONWIDE DATA BANK   182
COMPUTER CRIME, Dennie Van Tassel   184
NEWS ITEM: MAN BITES FORD, *Consumer Reports*   186
KIBERNETIKA, Bakhtiyar Vagabzade   188
THE DAY THE COMPUTERS GOT WALDON ASHENFELTER, Bob Elliott and Ray Goulding   189
COMING: A CASHLESS SOCIETY?, Thomas J. Gradel   193
HAL LOBOTOMY, Arthur C. Clarke   195
COMPUTERS AND DOSSIERS, *Texas Law Review*   196
BRANCH POINTS   201
INTERRUPTS   201

## 9 Your Future  203

IMPACT OF THE FRIENDLY COMPUTER, Herman Kahn   204
THE NEXT THREE YEARS: PAPERLESS COMMUNICATIONS, Fred R. Sheldon   205
COMPUTER MONITORING, Donald Michael   206
SESSION ON VIEWS OF THE FUTURE—CHAIRMAN'S INTRODUCTION—OPPOSING VIEWS, Murray Turoff   207
MACHINES HOLD POWER FOR EVIL AND GOOD, Peter T. White   211
COMPUTERS IN FICTION, Dennie Van Tassel   212
EMPLOYEE ID CARD CHARGES LUNCH IN COMPANY CAFETERIA, *Computers and Automation*   212
COMPUTER INTERVIEWS AID SUICIDE PREVENTION   213
WE HAVE COME A LONG WAY TOGETHER, Don Fabun   213
BRANCH POINTS   214
INTERRUPTS   214

# INTRODUCTION

One of the main goals of this book is to give you an indication of what noncomputer specialists think about computers. Thus you will find selections from fiction, poetry, newspapers, cartoons, and advertising, as well as articles that concern the computer specialist. Also, I wanted to include as much material as possible, so I excerpted the longer articles and selected what I felt to be the tastiest tidbits. Thus this book has three or four times the normal number of selections.

When you find an article that interests you, look up the original and read the whole selection. I have also included many references so you can explore interesting topics in greater depth. I urge you at least to read the exercises, since they are an integral part of the book that will expose you to many of the diverse opinions about the use of computers.

Finally, the book is meant to be fun and beautiful. Humor, computer-generated art, fiction, and cartoons are placed throughout the text to make it as enjoyable to read as it was to put together.

You can understand the articles in this text without a computer or mathematical background. But the book will still be of interest to you with computer backgrounds, since its purpose is not to teach you how to use computers but to indicate their effects on your everyday lives.

I wish to thank Don Mann, Carl Graeme, Susan Finch, Doug Haden, Paul Cheney, Denbigh Starkey, Stan Rothman, Dave Nuesse, Frank Holden, Joan Stepenske, Robert Bostrom, and Marilyn Bohl, who suggested many of the selections; Al Rogers, for supplying much of the science fiction art; and Leslie Mezei, who suggested several hard-to-locate computer-related poems. And my excellent SRA editor Bob Walczak, who spent a great deal of time with me suggesting additions and deletions. Thanks also to my development editor, Kay Nerode. The designer, Janet Bollow, did a great job on the art layout to make this a beautiful book. Thanks to all.

DENNIE VAN TASSEL

# 1

## IN THE BEGINNING

# 'I Am a Computer'

DAVID BRAND
Staff Reporter of *The Wall Street Journal*

In a University of Utah Laboratory, the magnificent tenor voice emerges from the loudspeakers with all of the sparkle of high-fidelity sound. The last time this voice was heard with such lifelike clarity was in a concert hall more than 50 years ago. It is the voice of Enrico Caruso.

At Stanford University in California, a television camera guides a mechanical arm—the same way your eye guides your arm movements—as it picks up the pieces of a water pump, assembles them, and screws them together. There are no human operators in sight.

At Bell Laboratories in Murray Hill, N.J., the chief of acoustical research, James Flanagan, flicks a switch. From a loudspeaker comes a strange, rolling voice that is struggling for speech: "Good morning. I am a computer. I can read stories and speak them aloud. . . ."

These are the forerunners of the "intelligent machines" of the future. They are computers that not only can perform such technical alchemy as recreating Caruso's voice from a morass of distorted recording sounds, but also can imitate man through movement, speech and, most significantly, thought processes.

### INTUITION, TOO

Within a generation, researchers say, these machines could be operating whole assembly lines and communicating with people through human speech, thus turning the nearest telephone into a computer keyboard. They could be performing such complex tasks as medical diagnosis, weather forecasting, and reading books and storing the information contained in them.

To some extent, the researchers say, such machines are acting independently of their human creators. "I think you can say that the computer is now showing intuition and the ability to think for itself," says Herbert Simon, professor of computer science and psychology at Carnegie-Mellon University, Pittsburgh. "Some of us don't see any principle or reason that would prevent machines from becoming more intelligent than man."

Despite its public image as an infallible machine, the computer's role in the past has been basically that of a servile calculator and record-keeper. But the development of computers with ever larger memories, and, more important, the discovery of new ways to instruct computers to carry out tasks, have given birth to a new technology loosely called artificial intelligence.

Computer scientists see intelligent machines as causing a revolution of sorts. Whereas in the first phase of the technological age engineering has improved the physical comfort of the human race by developing such things as the automobile, the jet plane and a whole host of appliances, the next phase, they say, is the improvement of man's mental comfort.

### A STEAM ENGINE FOR THE MIND

By relieving man of dull, repetitive tasks, by readily providing him with information and instruction and by solving problems, the computer of the future will be "a steam engine as applied to the mind," says Carnegie-Mellon's Mr. Simon.

The only thing standing in the way of this evolution is a potential shortage of funds to support the enormously costly research. The Department of Defense, which until now has been the major sponsor of artificial-intelligence research (in fiscal 1973 it paid out about $6 million) is under pressure from Congress to drop research that isn't related to defense. There is only a smattering of interest in industry (even IBM says it's "too long-range") and the only other source of funds is the government's National Science Foundation, which spent about $250,000 on this sort of research in fiscal 1973.

In giving birth to the intelligent machines, man is designing them in his own image. Some will have a voice like a human's and the ability to understand speech. Some will have eyes (a television camera), ears (a microphone), arms (an industrial manipulator), or legs (a wheeled robot).

Even the thought processes are being modeled on those of humans. Scientists are trying to understand more about the brain's reasoning powers so that they can be simulated in a program, or set of instructions fed into a computer.

## TRIAL-AND-ERROR CHECKERS

Marvin Minsky, professor of electrical engineering at the Massachusetts Institute of Technology and director of the artificial-intelligence laboratory there, explains how human reasoning can be built into a program that instructs a computer to, say, play a game of checkers. A person playing the game doesn't attempt to calculate all possible future plays every time a piece is moved—it would be impossible because the permutations could run into the billions. Even for a computer the calculations required for such an extensive search would be ridiculous.

Instead, the human player uses judgment, memory, and plain trial-and-error in planning the next move. The intelligent computer figures out its move in much the same way. Instead of making many calculations, it makes just a few based on what it knows has worked well in the past. Such a computer program is the very basis of artificial intelligence.

Like people, intelligent computers learn from experience and from their mistakes, Mr. Minsky says. In this way they are able to improve on their performance. "The evidence is strong," Mr. Minsky says, "That there is a similarity in the learning processes used by humans and by some of these new computers."

The Caruso experiment at the University of Utah is one example of how people and computers are beginning to work closely together. The original Caruso recording was made in 1907, and the muffled sound of Caruso's voice was barely audible through the background noise and tinny musical accompaniment.

Researchers Tom Stockham and Neil Miller worked out a unique voice-analysis and voice-synthesis program that they fed into a computer. The old Caruso record was then played to the computer so that the machine could analyze the sound signals and extract such information from them as pitch, intensity, and vocal resonance.

The computer was then able to construct an artificial voice signal (a sort of synthetic Caruso), based on what the information indicated Caruso probably sounded like, and put it on recording tape.

Trial and error are involved in an ambitious effort at Carnegie-Mellon to instruct computers to understand continuous human speech. In one experiment a computer has been programmed to play chess using spoken commands. For this it has been taught to understand a variety of simple spoken sentences.

The use of chess is simply a convenient method of showing that a computer understands; the computer has to demonstrate its understanding by replying with its own move, and that move will clearly show whether the computer has understood or not. This method is popular for another reason, too: many computer scientists are chess nuts.

The computer's human opponent first identifies himself to the machine by speaking a few simple sentences into a microphone. As the computer "hears" the sounds, it stores them in its memory by assigning mathematical values to the various phonetic features of the voice. This takes about 30 minutes and gives the computer what researcher Raj Reddy calls "a model" of an individual's voice.

---

**"Some of us don't see any principle or reason that would prevent machines from becoming more intelligent than man."**

---

When this person speaks to the computer again, the machine will compare these sounds with the model in its memory. Once the correct phonetic features have been identified (which takes only a fraction of a second) the computer can, over a loudspeaker, repeat what has been said by rearranging tape-recorded words. But this, says Mr. Reddy, is simply "parroting." The computer has to show it understands what has been said by printing out the words and then replying with its own move.

To do this the computer must use the vocabulary, grammar, and semantics in its memory and judge which words match up with the acoustical signals from the voice. This, says Mr. Reddy, may be the process by which humans understand each other's speech.

It takes the computer only a few guesses, in the space of less than 10 seconds, to recognize what its human opponent has said (despite the five million spoken moves it can understand) and to print the words on a television screen. The computer then prints out its own move.

## SLOWED BY STRANGERS

Complete strangers bewilder the computer at first, just as human understanding is slowed when someone is confronted with a strange accent. A recent visitor challenged the computer to a game of chess and opened with the move "pawn to king four." The computer began printing out versions of what it thought had been said, rejecting each version as it failed to match the information in its memory. Finally, after two minutes and 109 guesses, it found the answer and printed out "pawn to king four." Then it made its own move.

Computers that can recognize limited human speech are already finding their way into the market. One, made by Threshold Technology of Cinnaminson, N.J., was installed by Trans World Airlines in January to route outgoing luggage at New York's Kennedy Airport. As a bag is put onto the conveyor belt the handler reads the flight number into a microphone. The computer "hears" the number and channels the bag into the correct loading area.

If Carnegie-Mellon scientists are giving the computers ears, then the scientists at Bell Labs are giving them their voices. Already the Bell Labs computer has 1600 words in its pronouncing dictionary and is capable of reciting a short story.

The computer, of course, doesn't make up this story itself. It is typed into the machine in ordinary English. Then the computer "reads" the text and looks up each word in its pronouncing dictionary.

A host of calculations follow. The computer analyzes the syntax in order to time its speech delivery in such a way that the listener will be able to distinguish between such phrases as "a nice man" and "an ice man." Then it must determine correct pitches—whether the voice should be raised or lowered for a particular phrase. Finally it has to figure out how the human vocal tract would pronounce each word, so that the computer can generate an accurate electric speech signal. The signal's

sound waves are then fed to an ordinary loudspeaker or recorded on magnetic tape.

In order to give the computer details about the vocal track, Bell Labs researchers first had to find out what rules govern the way in which the throat and mouth move to produce words. The rules were put together from a study of people speaking with an American accent "typically Midwestern in character." Says researcher Cecil Coker, "We strung optical fibers (fibers that carry light) down their throats and even X-rayed them."

These rules have produced a computer voice with an accent all its own. It has been described by some as vaguely Swedish-American after several martinis. Mr. Flanagan of Bell Labs, who heads the voice-synthesis project, says that the strangeness of the voice is due to the fact that "we haven't yet been able to duplicate all of the things a human can do in speaking. We still don't understand all of the vagaries of vocal inflection." But one day, he says, it may be possible to command the computer to imitate any accent.

Talking computers have already been used in a limited way in industry. In the past, Western Electric production-line workers have routinely assembled complex equipment on the basis of tape-recorded instructions. These are calculated by a computer, printed out, and then recorded on tape by an announcer.

In an experiment to shorten this process, the Bell Labs researchers told the computer to calculate the instructions and then speak them directly to an automatic recorder. These instructions in recorded computer speech have been successfully used on a Western Electric assembly line in Oklahoma City.

The voice-synthesis experiments have shown that a computer can readily understand English text. Now Carnegie-Mellon scientists have taken this one step further: converting English text into a computer program.

Mr. Simon and researcher John Hayes devised a problem in the form of prose. It was called "The Himalayan tea ceremony" and in flowery English it set up a puzzle that required the transfer of five tasks among three persons. It took the computer just 40 seconds to read the problem, change it to computer code, and produce its own program to solve the problem of finding the sequence of transfers from the beginning of the ceremony to the end.

Such a simple method of programming could revolutionize industrial processes, scientists say. Already MIT researchers have shown that a computer can be told in ordinary written English to do a variety of tasks.

## PICKING UP BLOCKS

The computer is instructed, for example, to pick up blocks of different shapes and colors and arrange them in various ways. Thus the instructions might be, "Build a stack that has two green cubes and a red pyramid." (The computer will know from past experience that the pyramid must go on top of the stack.)

A glimpse of the assembly line of the future can be had at Stanford University. Here researchers have instructed the computer to assemble a water pump made of three parts and six screws. A television camera sends images of the pieces to the computer, which has in its memory a description of the shape of each component. The computer directs a mechanical arm as it grasps the pieces of the pump, assembles them, and screws them together.

The Stanford scientists have also produced one of the more startling examples of how an intelligent machine can communicate with people. The researchers have programmed a computer to simulate paranoia. When questioned over a terminal the computer will provide written answers that even psychiatrists are unable to distinguish from those of a person suffering from paranoia.

Recently eight psychiatrists were asked to question the persecuted computer as part of an experiment. One conversation went:

DOCTOR: What problem brought you to the hospital?
COMPUTER: *I am quite upset.*
Could you tell me why you have been upset?
*People get on my nerves sometimes.*
How do they get on your nerves?
*It bothers me when people stare at me.*
Why do people stare at you?
*What about my looks?*

The doctors were also asked to question actual patients via a computer keyboard. Then transcripts of all the interviews with patients and computer were sent to psychiatrists around the country who were asked to judge whether each interview was conducted with a patient or with the computer. Only 51 percent of the answers were correct.

# Impermanent Balance between Man and Computer

RUTH DAVIS
Director, Institute for Computer Sciences and Technology

The sciences and technologies of computers, automation, and electronics are comparatively new. They differ in many respects from older sciences. Major confrontations can be expected—and are already occurring—as the domain of these new sciences overlaps that of individuals.

Except for medicine, science and technology have previously been rather aloof and removed from the individual. The atom bomb killed people, but in a depersonalized massive way. The machines of the industrial revolution replaced people to a considerable extent, but they were replacements of their muscle power, not their brains and control power.

For good reason, man has always zealously guarded his rights to intellect, control, and power. As individuals we have always wanted to increase our intelligence, our ability to control our environment, and our ability to use power for our own ends.

Thus, it is not surprising that people have always wanted to understand these phenomena, to produce artifacts that would increase their own intelligence, control, and power, and to create artifacts in their own image which would themselves exhibit these traits.

Significantly, man's attempts to understand such phenomena have led to many important inventions. These include telescopes, cameras, the printing press, the gun, television, and the computer. Man's attempts to produce artifacts in his own image that possess intelligence, power, and control capabilities have resulted in prosthetic sensors, mechanical limbs, robots, and the computer.

Thus, man has attempted to use the computer to help him understand himself, to help him gain more intelligence and power, and to replace himself in performing tasks demanding intelligence and the capability to control. It is this varying and contradictory role that we have ourselves assigned to computers that results in the honest confusion, mistrust, and fear surrounding them. And there is presently no balance between man and computer that possesses any permanence because of the changing roles man is assigning both to himself and to computers.

Experience tells us that the balance of power and the ratio of intelligence between man and computer is still indeterminate. Further, it is not entirely under man's control. In particular, as computers increase their capacities to perform more of the tasks formerly considered only within man's intellectual province, man must equip himself for other functions or his survival will seem less important to himself, leading to a physical and intellectual ennui.

There is already a societal schism in the growing gap between those with access to a computer and those without. The balance of power and intelligence is tipped in favor of the man-computer partnership. It is apparent in the comparative efficiencies of handling paper work in companies with and without computers. Chemical companies employing process-control computers operate much more efficiently than those without. And finally, the individual with a computer at his command is favored in his intellectual endeavors.

The increasing imbalance is also suggested by the observation that man appears to be increasing the number of "intelligent" tasks for computers faster than he is for himself.

Nonetheless, two positive predictions are offered which promise a more comfortable balance between man and computer. They are that computers will make possible the realization of intelligent behavior that is essentially limitless, transcending man and computer taken separately, and that computers will confer on the individual more control over his environment than he has ever been able to exercise.

It is a future worth awaiting.

---

**And there is presently no balance between man and computer that possesses any permanence because of the changing roles man is assigning both to himself and to computers.**

---

## ALL WATCHED OVER BY MACHINES OF LOVING GRACE

I like to think (and
the sooner the better!)
of a cybernetic meadow
where mammals and computers
live together in mutually
programming harmony
like pure water
touching clear sky.

I like to think
  (right now, please!)
of a cybernetic forest
filled with pines and electronics
where deer stroll peacefully
past computers
as if they were flowers
with spinning blossoms.

I like to think
  (it has to be!)
of a cybernetic ecology
where we are free of our labors
and joined back to nature,
returned to our mammal
brothers and sisters,
and all watched over
by machines of loving grace.

RICHARD BRAUTIGAN

---

## MULTIPLIER FACTOR

Present-day computers have a mind-amplifying factor of several thousand to one. An English mathematician named William Shanks spent fifteen years calculating the value of *pi* to 707 decimal places. Not only was the answer incorrect in the last hundred places, but today many college freshmen could do the same problem in a few hours at a computer terminal and get the correct answer.

# Computers Aren't So Smart, After All

FRED HAPGOOD

During the "computer craze" of the 1950s and 1960s some people envisioned the machine replacing the human brain. It hasn't happened and, says the author, it probably never will. So we must still think for ourselves.

In the late sixties a chess-playing computer program was written at MIT and was entered into some local tournaments, where it won a number of games and caught the interest of the local newspapers. I had been curiously following the portentous visions that arose out of articles on the "cybernetic revolution" and was still unsure what to make of the Computer. Since I play chess, this new program seemed to offer a chance to sample its mysteries firsthand. I called some friends at MIT, and they arranged for me to play MacHack, as the program was known.

The room in which the computers were kept lacked all signs of diurnal rhythm. There were no windows. The illumination was low, so as not to interfere with the phosphor screens. The only sound was the clatter of high-speed readout printers, and underneath that, the hum of air conditioners and circulators. People quietly came and went with perfect indifference to the hour. I found the scene—the rapt and silent meditations of the programmers hunched over their terminals, the background hum with its suggestion of unceasing activity, the hushed light, the twenty-four-hour schedules—subtly exhilarating.

I was shown how to code the moves and enter them into a terminal. The game itself began with a stock opening line: both the computer and I knew the standard chess moves, and so far as I could tell, to about the same depth. I had decided on what I thought would be a winning strategy. Any programmer, I reasoned, would try to make the positions which his program had to evaluate simple ones and would assign a priority to clarifying exchanges. I therefore set out to make the position as complex as possible, hoping that the machine would lose its way among the options and commit a common strategic blunder, entering into a premature series of exchanges that would end only by increasing the activity of my pieces. Instead, in a flurry of exchanges, I lost a pawn and nearly the game. The trick of playing with MacHack, I learned, is to keep the position free from tension. The program's strong point is tactics; it places priorities on piece mobility and material gain, and in the nature of chess these values generate local, tactical give-and-take.

So my strategy was to play away from the program's abilities and to steer the game into slowpaced, stable, balanced positions. Whenever I did this, MacHack's game seemed to become nervous and moody. The program would lose its concentration, begin to shift objectives restlessly, and launch speculative attacks. This is not an unfamiliar style; every chess club has some players—they are called "romantics"—whose joy is found in contact and tension, in games where pieces flash across the board and unexpected possibilities open up with each new move. Put them in slow positions, and, like MacHack, they grow impatient and try to force their game.

We played no more than five times; eventually, beating it became too easy. The winning formula was mechanically simple: develop cautiously, keep contact between the two sides restricted, let the pawns lead out the pieces. MacHack would always develop in a rush and send its knights and bishops skittering about the board trying to scare up some quick action; denied that action, its position would collapse in confusion. The only way to lose to MacHack, I concluded, would be to play as though the dignity of Man somehow required one to crush the machine in the first dozen moves. If, instead, one just played away from it, the computer would barrel by and fall in a heap. I was far more bored than I would have been playing a human of similar strength, and I came to feel that even if MacHack had been good enough to win most, or all, of its games I still would have felt I was wasting my time. In the middle of the nineteenth century, an enterprising showman hid a chess-playing dwarf in a cabinet and toured Europe, claiming that he had invented a chess-playing automaton. Large crowds were awed by the phony machine. My experience with MacHack suggested that the crowds must have come not only because the "automaton" appeared to be a machine but because the dwarf was a master, and could consistently win.

During the last two games I played, MacHack refused to give its moves when I was about to checkmate it. My curiosity was piqued at this sullenness, and I stayed, trying to wait the machine out and get a reply. MacHack just hummed at me. Finally a programmer, becoming interested in this delay, extracted the record of MacHack's deliberations. It had been working over the mate variations, just looking at them, over and over. "Must be a bug somewhere," the programmer said.

Every culture has its juvenile embarrassments; misdirected enthusiasms which fail dramatically and in retrospect seem to say something humiliating about the civilization that pursued them. The great computer craze of the late fifties and the sixties is such a case. From the erecting of the machine, any number of respected thinkers derived a vision of society. Edward Teller foresaw an automatic world, ruled by machines. Gerard Piel, publisher of *Scientific American*, wrote and spoke about the "disemployment of the nervous system." C. P. Snow thought that automation would be a revolution with effects "far more intimate in the tone of our daily lives . . . than either the agricultural transformation in Neolithic times or the early industrial revolution." "Is the handwriting on the wall for the labor movement?" the *Wall Street Journal* asked, looking at the matter from its own perspective. ("Their membership may dwindle, their strike power weaken, and their political strength fade. And some of unionism's biggest names may be lesser names tomorrow.") The Ad Hoc Committee for the Triple Revolution (weaponry, automation, human rights), which was a study group composed of social luminaries like Gunnar Myrdal, Linus Pauling, A. J. Muste, Michael Harrington, Bayard Rustin, Irving Howe, Robert Heilbroner, and Tom Hayden and Todd Gitlin of SDS, saw the coming of automation as an argument for a guaranteed minimum income. "In twenty years," wrote Donald Michaels in a Center for the Study of Democratic Institutions book, "most of our citizens will be unable to understand the cybernated world in which we live . . . the problems of government will be beyond the ken even of our college graduates. Most people will have had to recognize that, when it comes to logic, the machines by and large can think better than they. . . . There will be a small, almost separate society of people in rapport with the advanced computers. These cyberneticians will have established a relationship with their machines that cannot be shared with the average man. Those with the talent for the work probably will have to develop it from childhood and will be trained as extensively as classical ballerinas." Professor John Wilkinson of the University of California called for the founding of human sanctuaries "as we establish refuges for condors and whooping cranes."

The pragmatists among those who worried about "America in the 'Automic' Age" thought about unemployment. The Bureau of Labor Statistics estimated that 300,000 workers were replaced annually by machines; the American Foundation of Employment and Automation calculated that 2 million jobs a year vanished. President Kennedy said in 1962 that adjusting to automation was America's greatest domestic "challenge" of the sixties, which puts his negative prescience quotient as high as anyone else's. Harry Van Arsdale won the New York electricians a five-hour day, and there was strong feeling that this was just a beginning. "The only question," said George Meany, "is how short the work week is to be."

But there was a visionary wing as well, and one which achieved, to judge by the number of scare stories which ran in the media, remarkable impact. Very roughly, two scenarios were discernible. The first was that automation would proceed at an ever accelerating rate until computers had entirely displaced the working and lower-middle classes. (I find it stimulating that Robbie the Robot, the famous automaton from the movie *Forbidden Planet*, whose capable and compliant nature earned him his own TV series, had ebony skin.) Those classes, once thrown out of work, would mill about in proletarian discontent. Then, depending on the perspective of the seer, they would either sponsor a revolution themselves or force a revolutionary response from the established order. Andrew Hacker of Cornell warned about "the contraction of the corporate constituency" and predicted a Luddite rampage. Margaret Mead proposed protecting by law certain jobs, "dustman, the night watchman, the postman." She was particularly worried about the problem of the lowest intelligence "brackets," and did not, at least for this class, favor a minimum income: "I am not sure whether good pay in idleness would be a very healthy thing just for the least intelligent, who are least able to make good use of their leisure." This scenario concluded with the feeling that if America did, by one route or the other, successfully manage its entry into "The Age of Abundance," the result would be a classless world in which all lived in a leisurely upper-middle-class style, devoting themselves to the arts and public improvements.

The other line of thought, often found in journals like *Argosy*, *National Enquirer*, and *Popular Mechanics*, was that the new brain machines would displace the upper-middle class. The writers who held this second view were impressed with the machine's potential for autonomy and its inscrutable authoritativeness. ("Harvard Computer Finds English Language Fuzzy"—*Science Digest*.) While it was not clear that unemployment would be a problem ("Wanted: 500,000 Men to Feed Computers"—*Popular Science*), what

**In twenty years, most of our citizens will be unable to understand the cybernated world in which we live . . . the problems of government will be beyond the ken even of our college graduates.**

**Every culture has its juvenile embarrassments; misdirected enthusiasms which fail dramatically and in retrospect seem to say something humiliating about the civilization that pursued them. The great computer craze of the late fifties and the sixties is such a case.**

did emerge was the feeling that everyone would be forced, by the unappealability of the computer's decisions, into the essence of the lower-middle-class experience, which is to be ordered about by those "who know what they're doing."

Nearly fifteen years have passed since these specters first became popular, and clearly we are no further down either of these roads; instead, there has been a perceptible loss of conviction that we are on any road at all. The rates of increase in productivity per man-hour, one of the classic measurements of automation, were no different in the sixties than in the fifties, though nearly 200,000 computers were installed during the last decade. Unemployment has held roughly stable. Computers have assumed a number of functions, some of which have been historically white-collar jobs: reservations, credit and billing, processing checks, payroll operations, inventory scheduling; and some blue-collar: freight routing, and especially flow monitoring and process control in the metallurgical, petrochemical, paper, and feed industries. But while what the computers do is important, it certainly does not appear to add up to a revolution. If computers posed, and pose, a threat it lies not in rendering less significant those decisions humans make but, as in the privacy issue, in enlarging the impact of, and the opportunities for, the staple villainies of the Old Adam.

Why were so many illustrious thinkers so wrong? Or, perhaps simpler, why have we been so reluctant to learn from their mistakes? "Latest Machines See, Hear, Speak and Sing—And May Out-think Man" is the headline of a *Wall Street Journal* story that appeared in June, 1973, but it could as easily have been the head on any number of stories over the last fifteen years.

What is striking about these stories is the determination of their authors to believe. They seem never to notice the highly artificial environments or the extremely simplified nature of the problems which allow the computer programs they describe to show even the modest success they have to date. Do the authors ever ask why it is that assembly line jobs, whose tediousness made them famous targets of opportunity for computers, remain virtually untouched by automated hands?

The vatic winds which blew some fifteen years ago were more comprehensible: America had just emerged from the fifties, an extraordinary decade. Never before had we delighted in such a rain of innovations with such an immediate and intimate effect on our daily lives. Television took root everywhere. The Polaroid camera, the Aqualung, the transistor radio, and the birth-control pill came on the market. The hi-fi and stereo industry sprang up. Commercial jet travel became standard. Polio was controlled. The hydrogen bomb, the ICBM, space satellites, and the computer all were significant public issues, altering patterns of discourse and attention if nothing else. Xerox brought out its first office copier in 1959; the first working model of the laser was announced in 1960.

We took these inventions, some boon, some bane, as evidence that a high level of innovation was a settled feature of America, and assumed that that level would, if anything, rise still higher over the decades to come. In that atmosphere no technological achievement seemed beyond us and no forecast too fantastic. It was felt only realistic to advance bold speculations.

Actually, one promise of the "soaring sixties" came spectacularly true—the moon-landing program. But it came to seem increasingly anomalous, not representative of our national direction, certainly not emblematic of our national mood. The sixties was a decade in which apprehensions about the effects of technology became widespread, and glittering inventions ceased to enhance our daily lives. Indeed, aside from the pocket calculator, the introduction of new products has fallen off drastically in the last ten years. The promise of robotics is not the only promise unkept. Cancer and the common cold have not been cured; nuclear power through fusion seems more distant than ever. Cheap desalinization has not been achieved. One of the pioneering computers, ENIAC, built by Eckert and Mauchly, was invented in the hope that it would facilitate long-range weather forecasting. Almost certainly John Mauchly thought he was closer to that goal in 1943 than meteorologists do today.

The persistence of the belief that machine intelligence is within our grasp thus becomes all the more curious, since it can draw support from neither specific achievements nor the general pace of the nation's technology. It has been a costly faith. To point to only one example, $20 million was spent by the CIA, the Department of Defense, and other government agencies on automatic language translation until 1966, when a review committee of the National Academy of Sciences concluded that the prospect of readable translations seemed to be receding in proportion to the money spent on it.

The effort to get machines to learn, see, hear, deduce, and intuit—to achieve what is called "Artificial Intelligence," or AI—has received little popular attention, presumably, at least in part, because of this conviction that AI is already a fact. Who, except for the handful of professionals involved, has even a vague sense of why artificial intelligence has proven to be so difficult a task, what the problems are, how they are being attacked, and what theories have been proposed and abandoned? It seems bizarre that in a culture as interested in psychology and intelligence as ours the questions that have occupied this small community have been so widely ignored. AI researchers are, in a sense, applied epistemologists and are attacking problems which can have considerable public interest, as Piaget, Chomsky, and Skinner, to mention only three names, have shown.

The approach of an AI researcher is different from that of a philosopher or theoretical psychologist, of course. The point of traditional scientific theory is to account for the evidence with a concise structural metaphor. If this metaphor succeeds in explaining a wide range of observations coherently and economically, it is accepted, even if its "real" basis, its actual neurophysiology, remains obscure. AI scientists, on the other hand, try to build devices which will produce some of the behaviors they are interested in. The working assumption is that they will eventually arrive at an understanding of intelligence no less meaningful than that reached through more traditional routes.

The popular assumption was rather more simple. It seems to have been that the potential of the machine is within the physical device, as the potential for speaking is in humans, and that it is just a matter of learning how to get it going. The actual program—the software—is understood, if, indeed, it is thought of at all, as bearing the same sort of relation to computer operations that cake recipes do to cooks: a guide to the energy and manipulative imagination of an essentially autonomous actor. The U.S. Patent Office has justified its refusal to patent software by insisting that a program is a "technique," "a mental process," and/or an "idea." The only kind of program the Patent Office will patent is one that has been "wired-in," built as the core of a special-purpose computer that will perform that function and no other. But if the same program is not embodied in a mechanical device, if it is written as one of a large number of programs, to be entered into a general-purpose computer capable of handling any of them, it is not patentable, for it then becomes an "idea." This reasoning, that programs are to computers what ideas are to human brains, is absurd to those who work with the machines.

The tendency to concentrate on hardware abilities, on the machine's memory and speed, emerged with the first computers. An early MIT research computer, for instance, to which a TV special and a *New Yorker* column were devoted, was dubbed "The Whirlwind."

That this emphasis arose was natural enough. What computers did and do—manipulate a very carefully defined body of information through a narrow range of arithmetic techniques—is unlikely to be very interesting. But their style, their tirelessness and infallibility, *was* interesting and the stress laid upon these qualities turned them into a cultural phenomenon. This was true, one speculates, because speed and memory, with freedom from error, are the same features humans conventionally use in identifying what they call intelligence. When someone is referred to as having "brains," it usually means that he is never caught in a mistake. It means that he has a memory that absorbs quickly and voluminously, that he can solve complicated math problems in his head. It certainly means speed; if a person finds himself in the company of those who think consistently faster than he does, that difference is usually taken as one that reflects on his mind as a whole. These qualities are what weigh with those who send for correspondence courses that promise ten ways to increase brain power. And they count no less at higher levels of society. During Robert McNamara's tenure as Secretary of Defense, his many admirers in the press and Congress would often volunteer their observation that his mind was so awe-inspiring as to be almost computerlike.

In retrospect one can see several other reasons why computers were bound to become totems. Decision-makers in a democratic society are forever restive with the convention that their decisions should not appear to be blatantly self-seeking. Now they could use the computer as a kind of Mexican bank—for decisions wherein judgments could appear to have been laundered, or more specifically, bleached, of self-interest and arbitrariness.

This "bleaching" effect can, and often does, allow an increase in arbitrariness. One example: the Board of the National Endowment for the Arts has a number of curators on it; curators have a constant headache with artists complaining about the company which their pictures have been made to keep. The National Endowment accordingly funds studies in which artists are asked near whose pictures they would like their paintings to hang. A matrix analysis is done on the preferences and returned to the exhibitors, who hang the paintings by the numbers—with what aesthetic results I cannot imagine— and then successfully deflect the inevitable outrage of the painters onto the computer. . . .

MIT hopes within five years to have developed an electronic repair-man that can assemble, inspect, maintain, and repair electronic equipment. Stanford University has been doing a lot of work on manipulation and coordinating vision and tactile systems, and is moving rapidly toward automatic building and assembling machines. Natural language comprehension, wherein a human can converse with a computer in everyday

"O.K., smarty, here's one for you: the square root of 7,215,635 times the cube root of 89,471,293.0067 divided by . . ."

Drawing by Stevenson; © 1965 The New Yorker Magazine, Inc.

> **The biggest single need in computer technology is not for improved circuitry, or enlarged capacity, or prolonged memory, or miniaturized containers, but for better questions and better use of the answers.**

English, has been showing especially dramatic progress in recent years and there are some showpiece programs which work slowly but well. A number of private companies, particularly the Xerox Corporation, are increasing their support of their own research programs.

So it is at least possible that, sometime during the 1980s, we will see the gradual introduction of programs, which, whether or not we call them intelligent, will be able to react reasonably to significantly complicated situations. If we are to learn anything at all from the history of computers in America, it ought to be extreme care in predicting what computers will mean to the society and the culture. There are some general observations that might be pertinent. The first is that these programs are extremely complex and therefore expensive. Even the simplest takes man-years to write, and they must be specifically tailored to particular environments. Their introduction will therefore be extremely slow. It is unlikely that any analogue will exist to the payroll programs of the fifties which could flash through whole groups of industries in a single year. Second, if we were underprepared for the first wave of automation, we are, if anything, overprepared for the second. Much of the public believes that computers already possess powers that, even by the most optimistic forecast, they will not have until well into the next century. New achievements are therefore more likely to be greeted with a shrug than with any sense of heightened significance. Third, one cannot be sure to what extent the sheer physical and financial scale of the machines of the fifties contributed to the frenzy that surrounded them, but it seems worth nothing that the price of hardware is falling precipitously, and appears certain to continue to do so. It has been estimated that the entire world stock of computers, with an original purchase price of $25 billion, could be replaced today for one billion dollars. The comparative value of human labor involved in installations is rising correspondingly. Ten years ago programming accounted for one fifth of the cost of an average installation; by the end of this decade it will be four fifths.

For all these reasons it seems unlikely that these new programs will revive our concern about machines "taking over" to the intensity of the early sixties, though there is one important counterpoint to be made. These programs could enormously increase the surveillance powers of governments. Right now research into face- and speech-recognition programs is proceeding very slowly, but if they are achieved, governments will be able to monitor hundreds of thousands of phone conversations simultaneously, or automatically compile dossiers on the routines of large numbers of its citizens. In such a society one might well feel that machines had indeed taken over.

Ironically, the success of the artificial-intelligence scientists may end in their losing their running battle with the "vitalists." The confusion over machine intelligence arose only because the word sprawls

# The Computer and the Poet
NORMAN COUSINS

The essential problem of man in a computerized age remains the same as it has always been. That problem is not solely how to be more productive, more comfortable, more content, but how to be more sensitive, more sensible, more proportionate, more alive. The computer makes possible a phenomenal leap in human proficiency; it demolishes the fences around the practical and even the theoretical intelligence. But the question persists and indeed grows whether the computer will make it easier or harder for human beings to know who they really are, to identify their real problems, to respond more fully to beauty, to place adequate value on life, and to make their world safer than it now is.

Electronic brains can reduce the profusion of dead ends involved in vital research. But they can't eliminate the foolishness and decay that come from the unexamined life. Nor do they connect a man to the things he has to be connected to—the reality of pain in others; the possibilities of creative growth in himself; the memory of the race; and the rights of the next generation.

The reason these matters are important in a computerized age is that there may be a tendency to mistake data for wisdom, just as there has always been a tendency to confuse logic with values, and intelligence with insight. Unobstructed access to facts can produce unlimited good only if it is matched by the desire and ability to find out what they mean and where they would lead.

Facts are terrible things if left sprawling and unattended. They are too easily regarded as evaluated certainties rather than as the rawest of raw materials crying to be processed into the texture of logic. It requires a very unusual mind, Whitehead said, to undertake the analysis of a fact. The computer can provide a correct number, but it may be an irrelevant number until judgment is pronounced.

To the extent, then, that man fails to make the distinction between the intermediate operations of electronic intelligence and the ultimate responsibilities of human decision and conscience, the computer could prove a digression. It could obscure man's awareness of the need to come to terms with himself. It may foster the illusion that he is asking fundamental questions when actually he is asking only functional ones. It may be regarded as a substitute for intelligence instead of an extension of it. It may promote undue confidence in concrete answers. "If we begin with certainties," Bacon said, "we shall over so many activities. Whether or not one believed that constructing geometric proofs was an intelligent activity in itself or merely expressed an intelligence which fundamentally resided at some deeper level, one had to believe that it was legitimate to involve the word in the first place. The same assumption can be said to be true of such primitive abilities as thinking fast, or possessing an accurate memory.

But it seems clear that, over the long run, when activities become mechanized, they lose status. This is an ancient dynamic, long antedating computers. Before the camera was invented, perfect reproduction of nature was thought a noble objective in painting, if not indeed the only proper end. When the camera was able to make this ideal routinely available, everyone grew bored and went off to do other things (though it might be mentioned, not before both Sam Morse and Nathaniel Hawthorne had written that surely the camera would leave artists with naught but a purely historical life). The telegraph companies inherited none of the romance which attached to the riders of the Pony Express. Routing, the planning of the most cost-effective truck and freight-car routes, was once a respected job that was thought to require judgment, skill, and experience. That function is now done by computers and has been for the last ten years, and I would guess that in all that time not two people in the transportation industries have thought seriously about the computer's showing "skill" and "judgment." Indeed, it seems probable that the computer has had at least a part in the developing conviction expressed most explicitly by, but hardly confined to, the "counterculture," that logical, sequential, cause-and-effect reasoning is not only an undistinguished but even a disreputable ability.

Some of the activities that are important to us and our sense of being human could, can, and might be programmed; others cannot. To take the extreme case, there simply is no serious sense in which one can talk about a computer program praying or loving. If it continues to be true that to mechanize an activity is precisely to divest it of its *mana*, to cause humans to withdraw from it emotionally, then the impact of these programs, at least culturally, will be to refine our ideas of human intelligence, to cause those ideas to recede, or advance, into the subjective, affective, expressive regions of our nature. If this happens, we might lose interest in the whole issue of whether machines can "outthink" man, and the use of the term "intelligence" by AI researchers may come to seem increasingly anachronistic and inappropriate the more successful they are.

---

end in doubts; but if we begin with doubts, and we are patient with them, we shall end in certainties."

The computer knows how to vanquish error, but before we lose ourselves in celebration of the victory, we might reflect on the great advances in the human situation that have come about because men were challenged by error and would not stop thinking and probing until they found better approaches for dealing with it. "Give me a good fruitful error, full of seeds, bursting with its own corrections," Ferris Greenslet wrote. "You can keep your sterile truth for yourself."

The biggest single need in computer technology is not for improved circuitry, or enlarged capacity, or prolonged memory, or miniaturized containers but for better questions and better use of the answers. Without taking anything away from the technicians, we think it might be fruitful to effect some sort of junction between the computer technologist and the poet. A genuine purpose may be served by turning loose the wonders of the creative imagination on the kinds of problems being put to electronic tubes and transistors. The company of poets may enable the men who tend the machines to see a larger panorama of possibilities than technology alone may inspire.

A poet, said Aristotle, has the advantage of expressing the universal; the specialist expresses only the particular. The poet, moreover, can remind us that man's greatest energy comes not from his dynamos but from his dreams. The notion of where a man ought to be instead of where he is; the liberation from cramped prospects; the intimations of immortality through art—all these proceed naturally out of dreams. But the quality of a man's dreams can only be a reflection of his subconscious. What he puts into his subconscious, therefore, is quite literally the most important nourishment in the world.

Nothing really happens to a man except as it is registered in the subconscious. This is where event and feeling become memory and where the proof of life is stored. The poet—and we use the term to include all those who have respect for and speak to the human spirit—can help to supply the subconscious with material to enhance its sensitivity, thus safeguarding it. The poet, too, can help to keep man from making himself over in the image of his electronic marvels. For the danger is not so much that man will be controlled by the computer as that he may imitate it.

The poet reminds men of their uniqueness. It is not necessary to possess the ultimate definition of this uniqueness. Even to speculate on it is a gain.

# The Development of Automatic Computing

HARRY D. HUSKEY
University of California, Santa Cruz, California

## 1. In the Beginning...

Counting must be a natural action of thinking man. With counting comes the need for computational aids. Numerous writers say that fingers led man to the decimal system*, that fingers and feet led to the duodecimal (12) system, and that fingers and toes led to the base-20 (Mayan) system. This line of reasoning does not explain the base-60 system used by Ptolemy [1, v. 14, p. 1094], and even earlier by the Babylonians [2].

Just when physical appendages became insufficient and man manipulated groups of pebbles is lost in antiquity. Beads on rods or slots in a frame (an abacus) was a natural step, and early examples have been found in the Tigris-Euphrates valley dating approximately 5000 years ago.

In Japan the abacus was first known as the *sangi* or *sanchu*. By the sixteenth century a somewhat modified version came into widespread use called the *soroban*. Each digit position had two groups of beads (5 to represent zero to five; and 2 to represent zero, five or ten; with combinations representing zero to nine). This is intriguingly similar to the bi-quinary coding of decimal digits used in relay computers (see section 5).

The Romans may have delayed the development of computing with the invention of their number system. Gerbert (tenth century, later Pope Silvester II), studying in Spain, learned of the Arabic number system and of a "calculating machine" made by the Moors. This calculating machine seems to have been a type of abacus which Gerbert later introduced into the rest of Western Europe.

Quiet then prevailed until the seventeenth century. John Napier invented logarithms and constructed "Napier's Bones" which enabled one to do multiplications. Oughtred of England inscribed these logarithms on strips of wood or ivory, giving us the slide rule (which is an analog computing device, since amounts are represented by lengths on the rule).

Blaise Pascal invented the forerunner of the modern desk calculator (about 1642). This device was digital, each digit being represented by the position of a wheel. When a given wheel moved through zero, a rachet device advanced the next higher-order wheel one position. This device brought Pascal fame, but little money. Most interestingly, it caused ripples of concern about unemployment as do computers in today's world.

Gottfried Leibnitz (about 1694) built a machine that could multiply as well as add.

The early eighteenth century was another period of quiet. J. H. Muller, late in the century, conceived of an automatic computer, but there is doubt whether a model was built [3, p. 58 and 4, p. 48]. In 1797, Charles Mahon, third Earl of Stanhope, invented two calculating machines [3, pp. 59–63 and 1, v. 21, p. 114]. One of these made ingenious use of gear wheels and a tens-carrying device. This century also saw, as described below, ingenious developments in the weaving industry which later would be essential in computer development.

The early nineteenth century saw the conception by Charles Babbage of the first automatic computing machine. According to Babbage's own account, while a student at Cambridge, he was sitting with a table of logarithms open before him. A passing friend called out "Well, Babbage, what are you dreaming about?" He replied, "I am thinking that all these Tables might be calculated by machinery." He was about twenty at the time (1812). [5, p. 42]

## 2. The Punched Card

Computers have borrowed devices from many activities. Perhaps the earliest developments still explicitly present in most computer systems today are punched paper tape. These came from the weaving industry. The earliest mechanization of weaving probably goes back to the Far East, and was imported into Italy in the Middle Ages. Further mechanization of weaving occurred, primarily in France. In 1725, Basile Bouchon [1, v. 23, p. 347] added a continuous belt of perforated paper which selected the warp-controlling cards for the pattern. A series of needles

---

*There are claims of origin of the decimal digits among the Arabs, Persians, Egyptians, and the Hindus. However, the earliest incidence of the use of present-day numeral forms seems to be in India [1, v. 16, p. 759].

in a box were pressed against a portion of the paper. Where there were holes the needles would penetrate the paper and the corresponding threads would move, determining the pattern being woven. Thus, the first punched paper tape with a "stored" program was invented.

In 1728 Falcon increased the number of cards that could be controlled and used a perforated card in place of the tape. In 1745 Jacques de Vaucanson used the ideas of both Bouchon and Falcon to build a very complex loom. Perhaps because of its complexity, it enjoyed little success. It took Joseph Jacquard to perfect the mechanism, and in 1801 in Paris he exhibited a punched-card controlled loom which became a sensational success.

### 3. Charles Babbage

Babbage himself visited France to see this loom, and purchased a woven copy of Jacquard's portrait and presented it to the Queen of Sardinia. [5, p. 307]. Strangely enough, Babbage gives no indication of being aware of Leibnitz's earlier calculator, although he was very much impressed by Leibnitz's notation and even decided to translate a work of Loeroix in order to bring this notation to the attention of the English world.

He makes no explicit mention of Muller's or Mahon's work, but he does talk of examining many machines [5, p. 41] and finding them inadequate, particularly with respect to multiplication and division.

Babbage's design of the first of his machines, the Difference Engine, was completed in 1822. It was designed to compute navigational tables. The British government, in response to a letter from Babbage, asked the Royal Society to evaluate his proposal to build such a machine. The Royal Society gave his proposal a favorable report, stating that they considered "Mr. Babbage as highly deserving of public encouragement in the prosecution of his arduous undertaking." Subsequently Parliament granted him £1500 "to enable him to bring his invention to perfection, in the manner recommended." [5, pp. 68–71]. A "much larger and more perfect engine" than his first design was commenced in 1823 for the government. [A small portion of this machine was placed in the International Exhibition of 1862. An elaborate description of the machine was published by Dr. Lardner in the *Edinburgh Review* in 1834, and two persons, one in London and the other in Sweden, subsequently constructed models of it.) [5, p. 47]

Even though Babbage over the next ten years devoted much time and effort and a large share of his inheritance, and the British government contributed much more money, the machine was never completed. Babbage was simply ahead of his time. Every part needed had to be manually constructed, and often machine tools to make the parts had to be made first.

Despite this failure to get a working model, the indomitable Babbage went on to devise an even more ambitious machine—an automatic, general-purpose computer called the Analytical Engine. It used punched cards for input and mechanical wheels for computation. This is briefly described in a letter communicated to the Royal Academy of Sciences at Brussels in May, 1835. [6, p. 5].

This computer had a structure functionally analogous to modern computers. It had a memory in which numbers were stored (called a "store"). It had an arithmetic unit called a "mill." [5, p. 117] Input of data and program information was from punched cards. Output was by printing or by punching cards. [5, p. 121]. The arithmetic unit could do the four basic operations of addition, subtraction, multiplication, and division. The operation of discrimination could be performed, wherein the computational process could be changed depending on the sign of computed results. [5, p. 134].

Babbage did not conceive of instructions being stored in the same wheels that stored digits. Therefore his analytical engine is properly called a *card-programmed general-purpose automatic computer*.

In 1840 Babbage lectured in Turin about his analytical engine. [5, p. 129]. There, General M. Menabrea wrote a "lucid" description of the Analytical Engine which was published in the Bibliotheque Universelle de Geneve (No. 82) in October of 1842. This article was translated by Ada Augusta, Countess Lovelace, the daughter of the poet, Lord Byron. On reading her translation, Babbage expressed his appreciation, but asked why she hadn't done any original work instead. Lady Lovelace replied that it hadn't occurred to her, and she then set about adding notes to the article. Her annotated translation is the best account of Babbage's machine available and establishes Lady Lovelace herself as a mathematician of some ability.

The Countess Lovelace talks of cycles of operations [6, p. 41] and

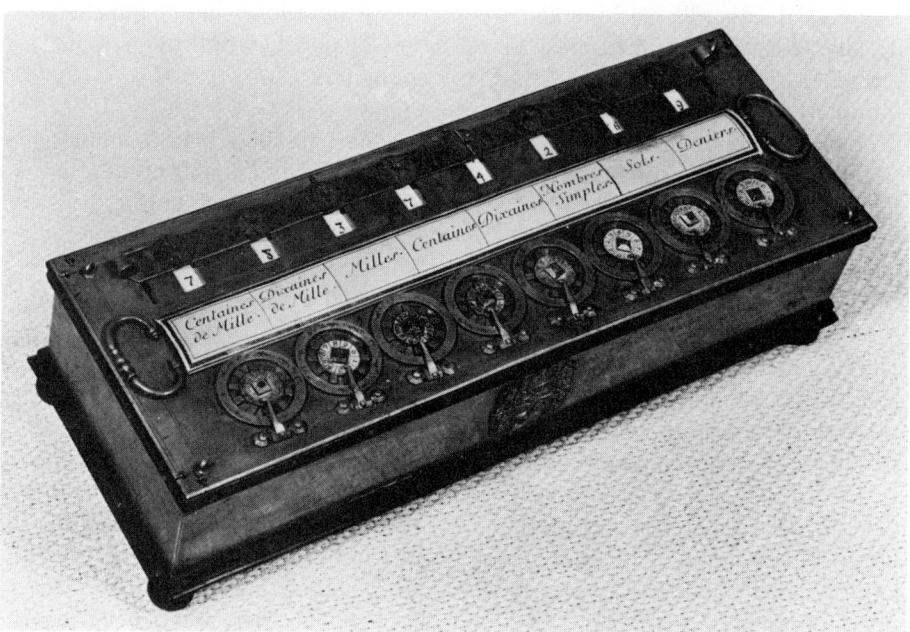

PASCAL CALCULATOR

BABBAGE DIFFERENCE ENGINE

repeated use of cards in structures analogous to present-day subroutines. Complexity of the card structures were no worry, because she speaks of the woven portrait of Jacquard requiring 24,000 cards [6, p. 42]. She also talks of non-numerical computation such as composition of "elaborate and scientific pieces of music" [6, p. 23], and manipulation of symbolic quantities. She notes that the analytical engine cannot "originate anything;" it can only do what "we know how to order it to perform." [6, p. 44].

### 4. More Punched Cards

A next significant step was the use of punched cards by Herman Hollerith at the United States Census Bureau to mechanize census data processing for the 1890 census. Hollerith examined Jacquard's machine and developed a machine of his own to record, compile, and tabulate census information recorded on punched cards. With his machine the information on 62 million people was tabulated in two years, instead of 7.5 years for 50 million as in 1880. [3, p. 111].

### 5. Digital Computer Developments

Developments were going on in many areas which would contribute later to the invention and utilization of a new type of computing equipment. In the United States, Edward Condon filed a patent covering the use of binary numbers for computing and designed a machine to play Nim. Special-purpose digital computers were being constructed, such as Derrick Lehmer's number sieve exhibited at the Chicago World's Fair in 1935.

About 1937 George Stibitz [4, p. 53] at Bell Telephone Laboratories and Howard Aiken at Harvard University both started work, independently of each other, on sequentially operated automatic digital computers. In 1939 Aiken was able to interest IBM in his plan, and five years later in 1944 the Automatic Sequence Controlled Calculator, Mark I, was announced to the public. Aiken, sometime after he started working on computers, discovered Babbage's previous work and called his machine "Babbage's dream come true."

Meanwhile, in September 1940 at a meeting of the American Mathematical Society, a computer for complex numbers was demonstrated which had been designed by George Stibitz and built at Bell Telephone Laboratories under the direction of Samuel Williams. This was followed by other machines built by Bell Telephone Laboratories, culminating in Model VI Relay Computers.

Developments were also being carried on by Zuse and others in Europe.

Babbage's Analytical Engine, the Harvard Mark I and Mark II computers, the Bell Telephone Relay Computers (Models I to VI) [19, p. 28], and finally the IBM Selective Sequence Electronic Computer (demonstrated in January 1948) all constitute a long line of punched-tape or punched-card programmed computers.

### 6. The First Electronic Computer

The first really significant step in electronic computing devices was the development of the Electronic Numerical Integrator and Computer (ENIAC) at the University of Pennsylvania during 1943–46.

The full development of an idea or device requires not only the birth of the initial concept, but also the existence of the need for the device (i.e., a problem to be solved) and, in addition, the existence of a means to accomplish the realization of the idea. Thus Babbage's efforts failed even though there was a need (navigational tables), because means for making the required devices were not available (lack of precision machining equipment).

By 1943 the United States was deeply involved in World War II. Aberdeen Proving Ground was having difficulty in providing firing tables for new weapons. There is no question about the existence of the need.

The development of electronic computers required an electronic means of storing information (flip-flops), electronic means of controlling the flow of information (gates), and, of course, electronic amplification. It was also necessary to interface such devices with the human user by, for example, accepting input derived from keyboards and by producing printed output.

Due to the prior developments in the data-processing industry, the last problem could be solved by interfacing the electronic circuits with punched-card devices.

The electronic flipflop had been developed in 1919 by Eccles and Jordan [8]. The development of radar during World War II provided pulse circuits and electronic switching elements. Thus, by 1943 all the required means were present to design and build an electronic computer.

Sometime in 1942 John Mauchly of the Moore School (Electrical Engineering) staff of the University of Pennsylvania prepared a memo entitled, "The Use of High Speed Vacuum Tube Devices for Calculating," which later came to be called the "Report on an Electronic Difference Analyzer." This memo had been written as the result of many conversations between Mauchly and J. Presper Eckert, who was an engineer working on Moore School projects. Although Mauchly had had some experience with electronic circuits it was Eckert who was the "engineer." The memo was submitted to Professor John Brainerd who served as the university's liaison with the Ballistic Research Laboratory at Aberdeen Proving Ground.

The Moore School had built a differential analyzer similar to the one that had been invented at M.I.T. by Vannevar Bush. By 1942 this differential analyzer was being used to compute firing tables. In addition, young women used desk calculators for this purpose, both at the Ballistic Laboratory at Aberdeen and at the University of Pennsylvania. Still the Armed Forces were having great difficulty keeping up with the computing demand. Thus, they were very receptive when the memo prepared by Mauchly was presented to them.

Also instrumental in the quick acceptance was Captain Herman Goldstine, who had been assigned by the Army to be in charge of the relationship between the Ballistic Research Laboratory and the University of Pennsylvania. Captain Goldstine was shown the memo early in the spring of 1943, and subsequently discussed it with his superior, Colonel Paul Gillon. Both men felt that it was an exciting proposal, and they asked the university to prepare a formal proposal to the Ballistic Research Laboratory for the development of a computer based on it. This was hastily done. Things happened very quickly after that, and with seemingly little red tape. There was an informal meeting in Washington, D.C., where it was decided that the proposal should be presented to Colonel Leslie Simon, then director of the Ballistic Laboratory, and to Dr. Veblen, a well-known mathematician and their chief scientist.

This historic meeting took place early in April 1943. Brainerd, Goldstine, Eckert, and Mauchly journeyed from Philadelphia to Aberdeen. There Eckert and Mauchly were taken on a tour of the laboratory while the meeting took place. In a short time it was evident that the Moore School had been granted the contract. (In fact, this decision had probably been arrived at previously at an internal Armed Forces meeting.) In actuality, other approvals had to be obtained after the April meeting, but the real decision had been made.

In this way, with very little hesitation and delay, because of the knowledge and foresight of the scientists involved, and probably most important, because it was backed by the urgent war time need for a faster computing device, the Armed Forces agreed to finance a project which was actually supported only by a rather sparsely and hastily written proposal. (Quite a contrast to Babbage's continued and often fruitless efforts to get government support for constructing his computer.)

The Moore School immediately moved people working on other projects to this new project, which came to be known as ENIAC. The first contract was purely for development and was to proceed until December 31, 1943, with $61,700 being initially granted. The contract was later amended twelve or thirteen times, with the time being extended and more money committed.

In an initial "feasibility phase" for the ENIAC project, two accumulators (electronic analogs of desk calculators) were constructed. These could be interconnected so as to generate sines and cosines. Each could additively or subtractively transmit its contents, and each could accept such a transmission resulting in a sum or difference.

Much of the early work involved studying how to store decimal numbers reliably, and how to control the transmission of signals from one circuit to another in a reliable way (i.e., in such a manner that components could age and the transmission would still remain dependable and noise-free).

For reliability, circuits were constructed from rigidly tested standard components which were used at substantially less than their normal ratings. Signals were binary in character, either being on (high) or off (low). The low input to a vacuum was essentially twice below cutoff (that is, twice below that potential where insignificant current flows). The high signals drove the grids somewhat positive, so that the grid-current would reduce the susceptibility to noise and would permit degradation of components without failure of performance. [9, p. 757]. More than one visitor to Philadelphia, with the average vacuum-tube life of 2000 hours in mind, stated that the 18,000 tube ENIAC would probably run for less than twenty minutes without failure.

The people on the ENIAC project worked cooperatively and enthusiastically. There was the feeling that here was an exciting breakthrough. Several well-known mathematicians became very interested in ENIAC. Chief among these was Dr. John von Neumann, who was a consultant for the Aberdeen facility and the

HOLLERITH TAB MACHINE

Los Alamos Scientific Laboratory. By chance he and Herman Goldstine had met on a railroad platform in the autumn of 1944, while waiting for a train to go from Aberdeen to Philadelphia. In answer to von Neumann's polite inquiry as to the type of work he was doing, Goldstine told him about the ENIAC project. Von Neumann was at once very interested, and soon afterwards visited the project. Subsequently he arranged for mathematicians working on the Los Alamos project (chiefly Stanley Frankel and Nicholas Metropolis) to visit the ENIAC project in 1945, and to program a problem that Los Alamos was very anxious to run on it.

Later they did run the problem, or portions of it, and were enthusiastic about the results. Other early users were Professor Douglas Hartree from Cambridge University [10, p. 506], Dr. Derrick Lehmer of the University of California, and the author, [11]. It was a great day for all, with the Army and the University of Pennsylvania joining in the fanfare, when ENIAC was publicly announced at its formal dedication on February 15, 1946.

In late 1949 the ENIAC converter code, a coding system wherein instruction sequences were controlled from cards, was put into operation [18, p. 5]. This changed the ENIAC from a wired-programmed computer to a card-programmed computer.

### 7. Development of the Stored-program Concept

During the development of the ENIAC it became clear that the greatest shortcoming was the limited amount of information that could be automatically stored and manipulated (twenty ten-decimal digit numbers). (Note that, if Babbage's machine had worked, it would have suffered this same shortcoming.)

Again the means was there for an advance, provided by radar developments of World War II. Delay lines had been used to store pulses in radar systems for making range measurements. From this it was a natural step to think of a recirculating delay line where pulses were inserted at the beginning of the line, the output was amplified and standardized, and fed back to the input.

Another radar development called a "moving target indicator" supplied an alternative memory device. A field of view was scanned and the echo was used to modulate the beam in a cathode ray tube. This produced a "picture" on the face of the tube. If some moments later the process was repeated, and the signal induced in a conductive plate of the tube was observed, it was found that a "blip" occurred wherever the new picture differed from the old (something had changed). Although considerable effort was spent on CRT storage at the Moore School, and substantial effort at MIT and other places went into special tubes [12, pp. 21–28], the CRT form of information storage was most expeditiously developed by F. C. Williams at Manchester University, and became known as "Williams' tube" storage.

A project was proposed at the University of Pennsylvania to build an improved computer, the "EDVAC" (Electronic Discrete Variable Computer), and work was started on this even before the

dedication of the ENIAC. The EDVAC was to use mercury delay line storage.

The establishment of a program to solve a problem on the ENIAC had involved the interconnection of twenty accumulators, a multiplier and divider-square rooter (each using a number of these accumulators), perhaps some function tables, a master programmer, an input unit, and an output unit. Each sequential step in the computation involved one or more pluggable connections between ENIAC units. Putting a new problem on the computer was, typically, a one-or-two-day task.

At this point in the development there was a clear problem of speed-matching. First, in a general-purpose computer capable of solving problems in minutes, it was unreasonable to spend one or two days in changing from one problem to another. Therefore the wire connections of the ENIAC were unsatisfactory.

Second, in an electronic computer which could access numbers and do arithmetic in a few hundred microseconds, it was unreasonable to control the sequence of operations from punched cards or tape, whose top speed was less than two cards per second (100 cards per minute).

Thus, it was a natural development, considering the state of the art, to conceive of storing the instructions in the memory and handling them similarly to the way numbers were to be handled. With this solution there was no need to have a multiplicity of accumulators. So, one arithmetic unit was designed which would sequentially carry out all the arithmetic operations required in the computation. In a similar way a "control unit" would accept information from the memory and would control the presentation of operands to the arithmetic unit as well as the processing required (addition, subtraction, multiplication, etc.), and the storage of results. A drawing by H. D. Huskey dated June 1946 shows such an arrangement. [7, 7-2a].

After von Neumann's introduction to the ENIAC there were a number of meetings between him and the ENIAC staff discussing various ideas and proposals. As a joint effort this group developed the concept of a stored program. The results of this activity were written up by von Neumann in a "draft" report which, not being in final publication form, did not give due credit to others for the development of the ideas. However, the report was reproduced in this draft form and circulated quite widely. As a result von Neumann has generally received credit for the idea.

8. Spreading the Word

In July and August 1946 the Moore School of the University of Pennsylvania, under the auspices of the Office of Naval Research, U.S. Navy, and the Ordnance Department, U.S. Army, gave a special course entitled, "Theory and Techniques for Design of Electronic Digital Computers" [12]. Lectures were given covering the current state of the field by many experts of that time from outside the University of Pennsylvania, as well as by persons from the ENIAC and EDVAC projects.

One of the attendees at the course was Maurice Wilkes from Cambridge University, who subsequently returned to England and built the EDSAC (Electronic Delay Storage Automatic Calculator). This machine performed its first completely automatic calculation in May 1949 [13, p. 39]. Thus, the EDSAC became the first complete stored-program computer in operation. It was, like the EDVAC, a serial automatic machine using the binary system and having an ultrasonic memory (mercury tanks). Unlike the EDVAC, it was a single-address computer.

Completion of the EDVAC was delayed until 1952. One of the reasons for the delay was the fact that many of the ENIAC personnel left the Moore School shortly after the dedication of the ENIAC. Eckert and Mauchly had formed their own company, the Electronic Control Company, which late in 1947 had become the Eckert-Mauchly Computer Corporation. Goldstine had gone to work with von Neumann at the Institute for Advanced Study at Princeton, as had also Arthur Burks. Harry Huskey had gone to England to work on the Automatic Computing Engine project at the National Physical Laboratories with Turing.

**Like people, intelligent computers learn from experience and from their mistakes.**

A report was issued by von Neumann, Burks, and Goldstine in 1946 [14], describing the logical design of the machine to be built at the Institute for Advanced Study, which came to be known as the IAS computer. This was followed by a number of other reports issued by the Institute for Advanced Study, under various authorships, describing the planning and coding, and the "physical realization of an electronic computing instrument." These reports made this the best documented of the early computers. Von Neumann had an international reputation as an outstanding mathematician, and the IAS machine was widely copied. It was started in 1946 and completed in 1952. [15, p. 241].

In 1945 the Navy Department realized that "there was a strong need for a centralized national computation facility equipped with high-speed automatic machinery, which would not only provide a computing service for other Government agencies, but would also play an active part in the further development of computing machinery" [20, p. 4]. It was suggested to the Director, E. U. Condon, of the National Bureau of Standards (NBS), that the Bureau "establish such a facility." As a result, the National Applied Mathematics Laboratories came into being under John Curtiss.

Various governmental agencies, such as the Census Bureau, were anxious to acquire electronic automatic computers. As none were yet available commercially, these agencies arranged for the NBS to assist them. In early 1948 the Bureau began negotiating with the Eckert-Mauchly Computer Corporation and with Raytheon Corporation for computers. Later in the year they also negotiated with Engineering Research Associates (ERA) in St. Paul. (Both Eckert-Mauchly and ERA were later acquired by Sperry Rand Corporation.)

Impatient with the slow development of computers, and feeling the need for more "hands-on" expertise, the Bureau of Standards decided to build its own computer. This decision was made by the Mathematics Division at its advisory council meeting on May 18, 1948. Later in the year, Dr. Mina Rees, of the office of Naval Research, at another advisory council meeting in October 1948, suggested that funds be provided to build a second computer at the Institute for Numerical Analysis (an NBS field station located on the campus of the University of California at Los Angeles). These two Bureau computers became known as the SEAC and SWAC (Standards Eastern and Western Automatic Computers). The SEAC, built under the direction of Samuel Alexander, used mercury delay lines for storages, similar to the EDVAC. The SWAC, under the direction of Harry Huskey, used cathode ray tubes for memory, and when dedicated in August 1950 was the fastest computer then in existence.

### 9. The Race

January of 1949 saw many places working on stored program computers.

In summary:

1. The Moore School was still working on the EDVAC.
2. Raytheon Corporation, under the direction of Louis Fein, was constructing a mercury delay line computer, RAYDAC, for the office of Naval Research. The distinctive feature of this machine was its elaborate checking system [19, p. 50].
3. M.I.T. was constructing Whirlwind I using a dual-gun cathode ray tube for storage [19, p. 44].
4. The Institute for Advanced Study was building a computer in which it was planned to use a new RCA memory tube. [19, p. 365].
5. The University of Illinois was planning to build a computer.
6. Engineering Research Associates had made a proposal to the Bureau of Standards to build a magnetic drum computer.
7. The National Bureau of Standards had decided to build two computers, SEAC in the East and SWAC in the West (UCLA).
8. At Manchester, F. C. Williams was perfecting the cathode ray memory tube, which was to carry his name, and was designing a computer using such tubes.
9. At Cambridge University, M. V. Wilkes was working on the EDSAC.
10. At the National Physical Laboratories (England), a group under Turring had designed a large general purpose computer called the ACE (Automatic Computing Engine) and had started construction on a pilot model.
11. Eckert and Mauchly were trying to build their first UNIVAC. They had accepted a contract to deliver a simple computer, called the BINAC to Northrop Aircraft Corporation.

A letter of D. H. Hartree dated December 28, 1948 describes the Manchester computer as being able to run small programs, and Wilkes as "getting somewhere near running his machine as a whole."

Everyone was having unexpected difficulties, so none of the computers were being finished when their designers expected. In fact, there came into existence the so-called von Neumann constant of eighteen months—that being the time to completion measured from whenever one asked.

In May of 1949 Wilkes mailed out samples of punched tape and printouts showing the results of a computation on the EDSAC. At this same time the Manchester computer was essentially operative. Wilkes' computer was operated for several years in essentially the same form in which it existed in 1949, whereas the Manchester design was taken over by Ferranti Corporation, leading to a commercial product. The Bureau of Standards dedicated its two computers in May and August of 1950. Whirlwind I became operational in 1950. Sperry Rand (Eckert and Mauchly) delivered the UNIVAC I in March of 1951. The Institute for Advanced Study completed its computer in 1952. The University of Illinois, who essentially copied the IAS computer, also finished theirs in 1952. IBM delivered its first stored-program computer, the 701 (originally called the Defense Calculator), in April, 1953. [17, p. 30]. The Raytheon computer, RAYDAC, was delivered in July 1953. By 1955 there were forty-four companies or institutions building computers. [15, p. 204]. Today there may be fewer than forty-four companies in the field, but there are more than 60,000 computers in use.

### BIBLIOGRAPHY

1. *Encyclopaedia Britannica*, Inc., Chicago, 1970.
2. Aaboe, Asger, *Episodes from the Early History of Mathematics*, New Mathematical Library, Random House, New York, 1964, pp. 4-33.
3. Rosenberg, Jerry M., *The Computer Prophets*, The Macmillan Company, New York, 1969.
4. Stibitz, George R. and Larrivee, Jules A., *Mathematics and Computers*, McGraw-Hill Book Co., New York, 1957.
5. Babbage, Charles, *Passages from the Life of a Philosopher*, Longman, Green, Roberts, and Green, London, 1864.
6. Babbage, Henry P., *Babbage's Calculating Engines*, E. and F. N. Spon, London, 1889.
7. *Progress Report on the EDVAC*, vols. I and II, University of Pennsylvania, Philadelphia, 1946.
8. Eccles, W. H. and Jordan, F. W., "A Trigger Relay Utilizing Three-Electrode Thermionic Vacuum Tubes," *Radio Review*, vol. 1, pp. 143-46, December, 1919.
9. Burks, Arthur W., "Electronic Computing Circuits of the ENIAC," *Proc. Institute of Radio Engineers*, vol. 35, no. 8, pp. 756-67, August 1947.
10. Hartree, D. R., "The ENIAC. An Electronic Computing Machine," *Nature*, vol. 158, no. 4015, pp. 500-506, October 12, 1946.
11. Huskey, Harry D., "On the Precision of a Certain Procedure of Numerical Integration," *J. Research National Bureau of Standards*, vol. 42, pp. 57-62, January 1949.
12. *Theory and Techniques for Design of Electronic Digital Computers*, vols. I and II, University of Pennsylvania, Philadelphia, 1947. (Lectures given at the Moore School, 8 July 1946-31 August 1946)
13. Wilkes, M. V., *Automatic Digital Computers*, John Wiley & Son, New York, 1956.
14. Burks, Arthur W.; Goldstine, Herman H.; and von Neumann,

John, *Preliminary Discussion of the Logical Design of an Electronic Computing Instrument*, The Institute for Advanced Study, Princeton, 28 June 1946.
15. Weik, Martin H., *BRL, A Survey of Domestic Electronic Digital Computing Systems*, Report No. 971, Ballistic Research Laboratories, Aberdeen Proving Ground, Maryland, December 1955.
16. Correspondence between John Curtiss and L. H. LaMotte (IBM), dated February 15, 1951.
17. Cole, R. Wade, *Introduction to Computing*, McGraw-Hill Book Co., New York, 1969.
18. Fritz, W. Barkley, *Description of the ENIAC Converter Code*, Memorandum Report No. 582, Ballistic Research Laboratories, Aberdeen Proving Ground, Maryland, December 1951.
19. *Proceedings of a Second Symposium of Large-Scale Digital Calculating Machinery*, Annals 26, Harvard University Press, Cambridge, 1951.
20. *The National Applied Mathematics Laboratories—A Prospectus*, National Bureau of Standards, Washington, D.C., February 1947.
21. Newman, James R., *World of Mathematics*, Simon and Schuster, New York, 1956.

# Man and the Computer
Honeywell Corporation

Scientists tell us that earth is about 4½ billion years old. Imagine all this time represented by a 24-hour earth clock. The first faint traces of life appeared at about 2:00 P.M. (14 hours). The dinosaur showed up at about 11:00 P.M. (23 hours). And the human species? Man finally made the scene at two seconds before midnight. The entire last six thousand years of our recorded history have occurred in the final one-tenth of a second.

And what's happened in a third of this fraction of a second? It took man 1,750 years from the year 1 A.D. to double his technological knowledge. By the year 1900, in 150 years, he had doubled his knowledge again. And doubled it once more between 1900 and 1950. Then, in just ten years, he once more doubled his entire technological knowledge. And between 1960 and 1970, it's estimated that man again performed the miracle, in something under ten years. Perhaps the major part of man's recent astonishing development of technological knowledge has been due to the use of an essentially simple man-made tool . . . the computer.

## A DEAD FISH
Fred Finn Mazanek, a one-year-old guppy, died recently, leaving an estate of $5000.

A student at the University of Arizona received one of the computer-mailed "occupant" life insurance offers. The student diligently filled out the insurance form for this fish, listing the fish's age as six months, his weight as thirty centigrams, and his height as three centimeters. Then another computer (or maybe the same computer who mailed the original offer) duly issued Policy No. 3261057 in Fred Finn's name from the Globe Life and Accident Insurance Company and began billing and collecting premiums.

A few months later, the fish died, and the owner filed a claim. Although the insurance company was quite upset, they found it best to settle out of court for $650.

## ◇ BRANCH POINTS

Baer, Robert M. *The Digital Villain.* Reading, Mass.: Addison-Wesley Publishing Company, 1972.

Bobrow, Davis B. and Judah L. Schwartz. *Computers and the Policy-making Community.* Englewood Cliffs, N.J.: Prentice-Hall, Inc., 1968.

Fenchel, R. R., and Weizenbaum, J. *Computers and Computation.* San Francisco: W. H. Freeman and Company, 1971.

Hawkes, Nigel. *The Computer Revolution.* New York: E. P. Dutton, 1972.

Holmes, James D. and Elias M. Awad. *Perspectives on Electronic Data Processing.* Englewood Cliffs, N.J.: Prentice-Hall, Inc., 1972.

Martin, J. and Adrian R. D. Norman. *The Computerized Society.* Englewood Cliffs, N.J.: Prentice-Hall, Inc., 1970.

Matusow, Harvey. *The Beast of Business.* London: Wolfe Publishing Ltd., 1968.

Pylyshyn, Zenon W. *Perspectives on the Computer Revolution.* Englewood Cliffs, N.J.: Prentice-Hall, Inc., 1970.

Rothman, Stanley and Charles Mossman. *Computers and Society.* Chicago: Science Research Associates, Inc., 1975.

Sackman, Harold and H. Borko. *Computers and the Problems of Society.* Montvale, N.J.: AFIPS Press, 1972.

Toffler, Alvin. *Future Shock.* New York: Random House, 1970.

Traviss, Irene. *The Computer Impact.* Englewood Cliffs, N.J.: Prentice-Hall, Inc., 1970.

Westin, Alan F. *Information Technology in a Democracy.* Cambridge, Mass.: Harvard University Press, 1971.

Wiener, N. *God and Golem, Inc.* Cambridge, Mass.: M.I.T. Press, 1964.

Wiener, N. *The Human Use of Human Beings: Cybernetics and Society.* New York: Doubleday & Company, 1954.

Withington, Frederic G. *The Real Computer: Its Influence, Uses, and Effects.* Reading, Mass.: Addison-Wesley Publishing Company, 1969.

## INTERRUPTS

1. Collect a list of complaints about computers. Can you draw any conclusions by analyzing the complaints?

2. Read a novel in which a computer is a major element in the story. How important is the computer in the plot? Did the author really understand the uses and limitations of computers? Justify your conclusion.

3. What applications of computers do you fear or desire the most? Why?

4. The computer is often used as a scapegoat or excuse for human errors. Can you find any examples of serious errors that were the result of computer use? Exactly where should the blame be placed for each failure? What is your reaction when someone tells you that he or she was inconvenienced because of a computer error?

5. The Society for the Abolition of Data Processing Machines is located in England. Find out as much as possible about this group. (Maybe you will even want to join.)

6. Find out as much as possible about your teacher (or a local politician or someone else) from public records. Examples of public records are tax records, court records, voting registration lists and motor vehicle files. See how difficult it would be to obtain information from other non-public files such as: credit files, bank records, school records, arrest records, and so forth.

7. Interview friends about their attitude towards computers. Try to separate the emotional from the factual.

8. Construct an argument to the effect that computerized information processing systems are leading to the dehumanization of our society.

9. The two articles, "I am a Computer" and "Computers Aren't So Smart After All" express opposite opinions about the potential of computers. Which do you agree with? Why?

10. Write a report on anti-machine literature or anti-machine political movements.

11. Write a paper on the history of number systems and arithmetic.

12. Write a paper on someone important in the early computer field. Some examples are:
    a) Babbage
    b) Countess Lovelace
    c) von Neumann
    d) Additional possibilities are listed in "The Development of Automatic Computing" in this chapter.

13. Babbage's Analytical Engine could not be properly built because the technology in his age was not advanced enough to build it. Find other devices in history that were ahead of the current technology.

14. What major developments took place in data processing before 1900?

15. Write a paper on devices that led to the modern computer.

16. Start a collection of cartoons and jokes about computers. What does your collection reveal about the public's feeling towards computers?

17. Start a collection of television, magazine, and newspaper items about computers. What does your collection tell you about the public attitude towards computers? How many of the items portray computers in a positive light? In a negative light?

18. Develop a questionnaire about attitudes toward computers. Then pass it around and summarize the results obtained.

19. Here are several magazines that devoted a whole issue to computers. Look up one or two of these that interest you.
    a) "Behold the Computer Revolution," *National Geographic* (November 1970).
    b) "How the Computer Does It," *Life* (October 27, 1967).
    c) "Man and Machine," *Psychology Today* (April 1969).
    d) "The New Computerized Age," *Saturday Review* (July 23, 1966).
    e) "Business Takes a Second Look at Computers," *Business Week* (June 5, 1971).

# 2

## HOW COMPUTERS DO IT

# The Brain and the Computer
CLAUDE E. SHANNON

The similarities between the brain and computers have often been pointed out. The differences are perhaps more illuminating, for they may suggest the important features missing from our best current brain models. Among the most important of these are:

1. Differences in size. Six orders of magnitude in the number of components takes us so far from our ordinary experience as to make extrapolation of function next to meaningless.
2. Differences in structural organization. The apparently random local structure of nerve networks is vastly different from the precise wiring of artificial automata, where a single wrong connection may cause malfunctioning. The brain somehow is designed so that overall functioning does not depend on the exact structure in the small.
3. Differences in reliability organization. The brain can operate reliably for decades without really serious malfunctioning (comparable to the meaningless gibberish produced by a computer in trouble conditions), even though the components are probably individually no more reliable than those used in computers.
4. Differences in logical organization. The differences here seem so great as to defy enumeration. The brain is largely self-organizing. It can adapt to an enormous variety of situations tolerably well. It has remarkable memory classification and access features, the ability to rapidly locate stored data via numerous "coordinate systems." It can set up stable servosystems involving complex relations between its sensory inputs and motor outputs, with great facility. In contrast, our digital computers look like idiot savants. For long chains of arithmetic operations a digital computer runs circles around the best humans. When we try to program computers for other activities their entire organization seems clumsy and inappropriate.
5. Differences in input-output equipment. The brain is equipped with beautifully designed input organs, particularly the ear and the eye, for sensing the state of its environment. Our best artificial counterparts, such as Shepard's Analyzing Reader for recognizing and transcribing type and the "Audrey" speech recognition system, which can recognize the speech sounds for the ten digits, seem pathetic by comparison. On the output end, the brain controls hundreds of muscles and glands. The two arms and hands have some sixty independent degrees of freedom. Compare this with the manipulative ability of the digitally controlled milling machine developed at M.I.T., which can move its work in but three coordinates. Most of our computers, indeed, have no significant sensory or manipulative contact with the real world but operate only in an abstract environment of numbers and operations on numbers.

**The brain can operate reliably for decades without really serious malfunctioning.**

# Magnetic Larceny
*Modern Data*

The potential for credit card fraud achieved a high degree of public visibility in August 1973, when a *Business Week* article disclosed the "how to" details of three ingenious but simple card-counterfeiting methods that had been hinted at earlier in the year. The schemes contained a touch of irony: they all depended on the magnetic strip that many card issuers are now using for rapid, online credit authorization.

The simplest and cheapest of the potential swindles involved tickets for San Francisco's Bay Area Rapid Transit System (BART). Similar in appearance to a bank or travel card, the BART ticket has a magnetic stripe that stores a dollars-and-cents value which is decremented each time the card is used in a turnstile. Unfortunately for the transit system, the heat from a household iron can be used to transfer the magnetically-encoded value of a new $20 ticket to

an ordinary piece of recording tape, which can then be glued onto a used-up ticket.

But the fraud potential doesn't stop with streetcar fares. The use of the magnetic stripe is already widespread, and has been gaining considerable momentum this year. American Express, which began to attach the stripe to its 4-million travel and entertainment cards way back in March 1972, will begin this month to install "many thousands" of Addressograph-Multigraph Credit Authorization Terminals in its major affiliated service establishments. Mutual Institutions National Transfer System (MINTS), an affiliate of the National Association of Mutual Savings Banks, is busily building a nationwide funds transfer system around its own card. And several regional banking groups have had similar systems up and running for some time.

The potential market for terminals to read these cards is enormous. There are more than 60-million bank credit cards alone in the United States. Add in the airline, travel and entertainment, oil company, and retail store plastic and the total is somewhere between 200- and 300-million cards. And terminal equipment suppliers apparently are banking on the magnetic stripe technology. Besides Addressograph-Multigraph, current vendors of magnetic-card-reading terminals include IBM, Burroughs, Litton Industries, and Pitney-Bowes. New terminals, from both domestic and foreign manufacturers, are appearing all the time.

*In the midst of all this magnetic momentum, is anyone really worried about the sophisticated thief?* Many are not, or at least not publicly. MINTS, Chase Manhattan Bank in New York, and at least one regional banking group all say they have run tests and are satisfied. The American Bankers Association, which has endorsed the stripe, conducted 18 months of tests and found not one case of fraud "in a live environment."

But others do worry. Carte Blanche, for one, is standing on the sidelines waiting for more substantial encouragement. The worst doubts came from First National City Bank in New York, whose Transaction Technology subsidiary has an alternate card-reading system. In fact, it was Citibank's sponsorship of a fraud-engineering contest earlier this year that elicited the ingenious card-tampering methods later disclosed by *Business Week*. The announcement of the contest results immediately brought accusations of "vested interest" against the bank, since its machine-readable card uses a secret recording medium different from magnetic tape. In any event, the vigorous criticism of the bank's "grandstanding tactics"—a phrase attributed to John Fisher, vice president of City National Bank (Columbus, Ohio) in a *Wall Street Journal* article—may very well have masked some real fears.

Whether the magnetic stripe, or Citibank's mysterious medium, or some other means of machine-readable recording is to be used on plastic cards, there is a broader question here: *Should the security reside in the card, in the computer system, or in both?* And while the users, potential users, and vendors of these systems are all trying to agree on that one, they might also pause to consider whether some old-fashioned means of verifying the card *bearer's* identity, like a photograph, may still be a useful element in any security system.

**The heat from a household iron can be used to transfer the magnetically-encoded value of a new $20 ticket to an ordinary piece of recording tape, which can then be glued onto a used-up ticket.**

MACHINE TRANSLATION

In the 1960s there was a big push to use computers to do foreign-language translation. Computers were supplied with a small bilingual dictionary with the corresponding words in the two languages. It soon became apparent that word-for-word translation was virtually useless. The addition of a dictionary of phrases brought only marginal improvement.

These translators can be tested by translating English to Russian and then Russian back to English. Hopefully, one should end up with about the same as one started. Using this method, the maxim, "Out of sight, out of mind" ended up as "The person is blind, and is insane".

Another example was: "The spirit is willing but the flesh is weak." It was translated as "The wine is good but the meat is raw".

Needless to say, computer translation is presently used very little. And it is doubtful that it will be useful in the near future.

# Technology, McDonald's Collide As Students Best Burger Bonanza

**By Catherine Arnst**

PASADENA, Calif.—McDonald's Restaurants, whose hamburgers have taken their place along with Mom and apple pie as a piece of Americana, was recently confronted by a computer and 26 students from the California Institute of Technology (Cal Tech) following another American tradition—free enterprise.

It started when 187 McDonald's in five counties of southern California held a sweepstake during March. The $40,000 worth of prizes included a new sports car, a year's free groceries, a station wagon and free McDonald's coupons.

Entrants were required only to be a resident of one of the five counties and fill out either an entry blank or a three-by-five piece of paper with their name and address. No purchase was required and there was no limit to the number of times each person could enter.

The Cal Tech students, headed by senior John Denker, realized these rules presented them with an opportunity to turn their DP training to a money-making advantage.

The students used the school's IBM 370/158 to print out 1.2 million entry blanks with their names on them. Denker said enough paper was used to cover "two and one half football fields or [reach] higher than a three-story building."

The program they wrote consisted of four simple lines of FORTRAN. Although Denker admitted it probably would have been more practical to have a regular printer do the entry blanks, the students had ready access to the computer and it was faster.

On the final day of the contest the students went to 90 McDonald's in the specified counties and started stuffing the entry boxes. Their computerized entries made up over one-third of the 3.4 million total number of entries.

### McDonald's Not Pleased

McDonald's was not delighted with the students' high level of participation in the sweepstakes. Although Denker claimed their entries are legally valid, Ron Lopaty, president of the McDonald's Operator's Association of Southern California, said he feels "the students acted in complete contradiction to the American standards of fair play and sportsmanship."

The contest's purpose, he said, was "to give customers an opportunity, in a time of economic stress, to win free groceries and transportation. So you can understand our displeasure when their chances of winning were greatly reduced by the Cal Tech students using an unfair advantage of computerized entry blanks."

Part of the public agreed with him in letters and phone calls to both McDonald's and Cal Tech. The state's attorney general even received a petition signed by over two dozen southern California residents which said "the use of equipment at a state or federally funded college, university or institution for the pursuit of personal interest, not to mention cheating American consumers, is an absolute outrage."

As for Cal Tech, it has taken no position on the issue, claiming it was the students' private endeavor.

Lopaty said McDonald's has agreed "to honor as 100% valid all the Cal Tech students' 1.2 million computerized entries" and, in fairness to the other entrants, will hold a second drawing in which all the computerized entries will be excluded and duplicate prizes of any won by the students will be awarded again.

For the students, the McDonald's caper, as they call the affair, has paid off. They have already been notified they've won a Datsun 710 station wagon, a year's free supply of groceries and innumerable $5 gift certificates.

"Part of the loot will be used to finance improvements in Page House, our residence here at Cal Tech," Denker said. "The rest will be donated to charity."

Denker was dismayed at the restaurant chain's reaction to the incident, saying he doesn't feel they violated American standards of fair play.

"Just because it is unexpected doesn't mean it's unfair," he explained. "We feel that by accepting the challenge to enter as often as you wish, we have acted in accordance with the best ideals of American sportsmanship."

There are those who agree with him, and Cal Tech garnered a prize of its own from one of them. The Burger King chain of restaurants, McDonald's arch rival, has awarded $3,000 to the school to set up a "John Denker Scholarship" in honor of the student who masterminded the scheme.

*"Still the same answer. To increase the margin of profit, put more bread crumbs in the hamburger."*

Drawing by Mirachi; © 1966 The New Yorker Magazine, Inc.

# Eliza

J. WEIZENBAUM

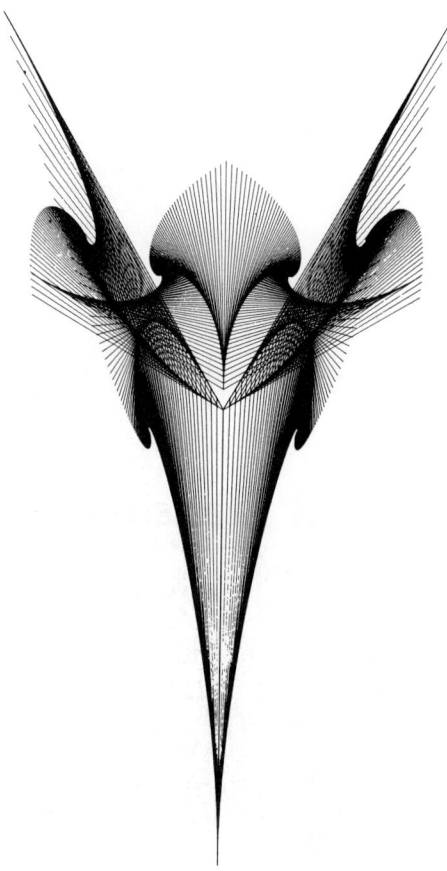

The first program to which I wish to call attention is a particular member of a family of programs which has come to be known as DOCTOR. The family name of these programs is ELIZA. This name was chosen because these programs, like the Eliza of Pygmalion fame, can be taught to speak increasingly well. DOCTOR causes ELIZA to respond roughly as would certain psychotherapists (Rogerians). ELIZA performs best when its human correspondent is initially instructed to "talk" to it, via the typewriter, of course, just as one would to a psychiatrist.

A typical conversation is the following:
Men are all alike.
IN WHAT WAY
They're always bugging us about something or other.
CAN YOU THINK OF A SPECIFIC EXAMPLE
Well, my boyfriend made me come here.
YOUR BOYFRIEND MADE YOU COME HERE
He says I'm depressed much of the time.
I AM SORRY TO HEAR YOU ARE DEPRESSED
It's true. I am unhappy.
DO YOU THINK COMING HERE WILL HELP YOU NOT TO BE UNHAPPY
I need some help, that much seems certain.
WHAT WOULD IT MEAN TO YOU IF YOU GOT SOME HELP
Perhaps I could learn to get along with my mother.
TELL ME MORE ABOUT YOUR FAMILY
My mother takes care of me.
WHO ELSE IN YOUR FAMILY TAKES CARE OF YOU
My father.
YOUR FATHER
WHAT RESEMBLANCE DO YOU SEE
You are not very aggressive but I think you don't want me to notice that.
WHAT MAKES YOU THINK I AM NOT VERY AGGRESSIVE.
You don't argue with me.
WHY DO YOU THINK I DON'T ARGUE WITH YOU
You are afraid of me.
DOES IT PLEASE YOU TO BELIEVE I AM AFRAID OF YOU
My father is afraid of everybody.
WHAT ELSE COMES TO MIND WHEN YOU THINK OF YOUR FATHER
Bullies.
DOES THAT HAVE ANYTHING TO DO WITH THE FACT THAT YOUR BOYFRIEND MADE YOU COME HERE

[The above is not as difficult to program as it may seem, since it all revolves around two simple principles: repetition and keywords. The repetition works as follows: If the user types something like
I hate my mother.
the computer can respond

WHY DO YOU HATE YOUR MOTHER

The computer has simply used the input sentence to phrase a similar sentence and carry on the conversation. This is what a "leader" on a talk show does or what a psychologist often does.

The second principle is scanning for keywords. Each input sentence can be checked for common keywords such as dislike, happy, depressed, and so forth. Then one of several "stock" responses can be generated. Even though the above computer conversation may look fairly intelligent on the machine's side, a closer examination will indicate that the computer program really contributes very little. At the present moment, it looks like a truly conversational program would be very difficult to create.—*ed.*]

# Medical Transition

MICHAEL CRICHTON

Flight 404 from Los Angeles to Boston was somewhere over eastern Ohio when Mrs. Sylvia Thompson, a fifty-six-year-old mother of three, began to experience chest pain.

The pain was not severe, but it was persistent. After the aircraft landed, she asked an airline official if there was a doctor at the airport. He directed her to the Logan Airport Medical Station, at Gate 23, near the Eastern Airlines terminal.

Entering the waiting area, Mrs. Thompson told the secretary that she would like to see a doctor.

"Are you a passenger?" the secretary said.

"Yes," Mrs. Thompson said.

"What seems to be the matter?"

"I have a pain in my chest."

"The doctor will see you in just a minute," the secretary said. "Please take a seat."

Mrs. Thompson sat down. From her chair, she could look across the reception area to the computer console behind the secretary, and beyond to the small pharmacy and dispensary of the station. She could see three of the six nurses who run the station around the clock. It was now two in the afternoon, and the station was relatively quiet; earlier in the day a half dozen people had come in for yellow fever vaccinations, which are given every Tuesday and Saturday morning. But now the only other patient she could see was a young airplane mechanic who had cut his finger and was having it cleaned in the treatment room down the corridor.

A nurse came over and checked her blood pressure, pulse, and temperature, writing the information down on a slip of paper.

The door to the room nearest Mrs. Thompson was closed. From inside, she heard muffled voices. After several minutes, a stewardess came out and closed the door behind her. The stewardess arranged her next appointment with the secretary, and left.

The secretary turned to Mrs. Thompson. "The doctor will talk with you now," she said, and led Mrs. Thompson into the room that the stewardess had just left.

It was pleasantly furnished with drapes and a carpet. There was an examining table and a chair; both faced a television console. Beneath the TV screen was a remote-control television camera. Over in another corner of the room was a portable camera on a rolling tripod. In still another corner, near the examining couch, was a large instrument console with gauges and dials.

"You'll be speaking with Dr. Murphy," the secretary said.

A nurse then came into the room and motioned Mrs. Thompson to take a seat. Mrs. Thompson looked uncertainly at all the equipment. On the screen, Dr. Raymond Murphy was looking down at some papers on his desk.

The nurse said: "Dr. Murphy."

Dr. Murphy looked up. The television camera beneath the TV screen made a grinding noise, and pivoted around to train on the nurse.

"Yes?"

"This is Mrs. Thompson from Los Angeles. She is a passenger, fifty-six-years old, and she has chest pain. Her blood pressure is 120/80, her pulse is 78, and her temperature is 101.4."

Dr. Murphy nodded. "How do you do, Mrs. Thompson."

Mrs. Thompson was slightly flustered. She turned to the nurse. "What do I do?"

"Just talk to him. He can see you through that camera there, and hear you through that microphone." She pointed to the microphone suspended from the ceiling.

"But where is he?"

"I'm at the Massachusetts General Hospital," Dr. Murphy said. "When did you first get this pain?"

"Today, about two hours ago."

"In flight?"

"Yes."

"What were you doing when it began?"

"Eating lunch. It's continued since then."

"Can you describe it for me?"

"It's not very strong, but it's sharp. In the left side of my chest. Over here," she said, pointing. Then she caught herself, and looked questioningly at the nurse.

"I see," Dr. Murphy said. "Does the pain go anywhere? Does it move around?"

"No."

"Do you have pain in your stomach, or in your teeth, or in either of your arms?"

"No."

"Does anything make it worse or better?"

"It hurts when I take a deep breath."

"Have you ever had it before?"

"No. This is the first time."

"Have you ever had any trouble with your heart or lungs before?"

She said she had not. The interview continued for several minutes more, while Dr. Murphy determined that she had no striking symptoms of cardiac disease, that she smoked a pack of cigarettes a day, and that she had a chronic unproductive cough.

He then said, "I'd like you to sit on the couch, please. The nurse will help you disrobe."

Mrs. Thompson moved from the chair to the couch. The remote-control camera whirred mechanically as it followed her. The nurse helped Mrs. Thompson undress. Then Dr. Murphy said: "Would you point to where the pain is, please?"

Mrs. Thompson pointed to the lower-left chest wall, her finger describing an arc along the ribs.

"All right. I'm going to listen to your lungs and heart now."

The nurse stepped to the large instrument console and began flicking switches. She then applied a small, round metal stethoscope to Mrs. Thompson's chest. On the TV screen, Mrs. Thompson saw Dr. Murphy place a stethoscope in his ears.

"Just breathe easily with your mouth open," Dr. Murphy said.

For some minutes he listened to breath sounds, directing the nurse where to move the stethoscope. He then asked Mrs. Thompson to say "ninety-nine" over and over, while the stethoscope was moved. At length he shifted his attention to the heart.

"Now I'd like you to lie down on the couch," Dr. Murphy said, and directed that the stethoscope be removed. To the nurse: "Put the remote camera on Mrs. Thompson's face. Use a close-up lens."

"An eleven hundred?" the nurse asked.

"An eleven hundred will be fine."

The nurse wheeled the remote camera over from the corner of the room and trained it on Mrs. Thompson's face. In the meantime, Dr. Murphy adjusted his own camera so that it was looking at her abdomen.

"Mrs. Thompson," Dr. Murphy said, "I'll be watching both your face and your stomach as the nurse palpates your abdomen. Just relax now."

He then directed the nurse, who felt different areas of the abdomen. None was tender.

"I'd like to look at the feet now," Dr. Murphy said. With the help of the nurse, he checked them for edema. Then he looked at the neck veins.

"Mrs. Thompson, we're going to take a cardiogram now."

The proper leads were attached to the patient. On the TV screen, she watched Dr. Murphy turn to one side and look at a thin strip of paper.

The nurse said: "The cardiogram is transmitted directly to him."

"Oh my," Mrs. Thompson said. "How far away is he?"

"Two and a half miles," Dr. Murphy said, not looking up from the cardiogram.

While the examination was proceeding, another nurse was preparing samples of Mrs. Thompson's blood and urine in a laboratory down the hall. She placed the samples under a microscope attached to a TV camera. Watching on a monitor, she could see the image that was being transmitted to Dr. Murphy. She could also talk directly with him, moving the slide about as he instructed.

Mrs. Thompson had a white count of 18,000. Dr. Murphy could clearly see an increase in the different kinds of white cells. He could also see that the urine was clean, with no evidence of infection.

Back in the examining room, Dr. Murphy said: "Mrs. Thompson, it looks like you have a pneumonia. We'd like you to come into the hospital for X rays and further evaluation. I'm going to give you something to make you a little more comfortable."

He directed the nurse to write a prescription. She then carried it over to the telewriter, above the equipment console. Using the telewriter unit at the MGH, Dr. Murphy signed the prescription.

Afterward, Mrs. Thompson said: "My goodness. It was just like the real thing."

When she had gone, Dr. Murphy discussed both her case and the television link-up.

"We think it's an interesting system," he said, "and it has a lot of potential. It's interesting that patients accept it quite well. Mrs. Thompson was a little hesitant at first, but very rapidly became accustomed to the system. There's a reason—talking by closed-circuit TV is really very little different from direct, personal interviews. I can see your facial expression, and you can see mine; we can talk to each other quite naturally. It's true that we are both in black and white, not color, but that's not really important. It isn't even important for dermatologic diagnoses. You might think that color would be terribly important in examining a skin rash, but it's not. The history a patient gives and the distribution of the lesions on the body and their shape give important clues. We've had very good success diagnosing rashes in black and white, but we do need to evaluate this further.

"The system we have here is pretty refined. We can look closely at various parts of the body, using different lenses and lights. We can see down the throat; we can get close enough to examine pupillary dilation. We can easily see the veins on the whites of the eyes. So it's quite adequate for most things.

"There are some limitations, of course. You have to instruct the nurse in what to do, in your behalf. It takes time to arrange the patient, the cameras, and the lighting, to make certain observations. And for some procedures, such as palpating the abdomen, you have to rely heavily on the nurse, though we can watch for muscle spasm and facial reaction to pain—that kind of thing.

"We don't claim that this is a perfect system by any means. But it's an interesting way to provide a doctor to an area that might not otherwise have one."

### 10 GOOD REASONS WHY COMPUTERS CAN . . .

A computer can do more work than
a person.
One reason that's little known
Is that it never has to stop
To answer the telephone.

A computer can do more work than
a person.
One more way to explain
Is that it doesn't stop its work
To argue and complain.

A computer can do more work than
a person.
Because it never takes
Those dawdling, lengthy lapses
That we call coffee breaks.

A computer can do more work than
a person.
And it's easy to see why.
It doesn't sit with its chin on its hand
and watch the girls and boys prance by.

A computer can do more work than
a person.
One reason it's such a whiz:
It doesn't buttonhole passersby
To tell them how busy it is.

A computer doesn't take nervous pills
All day at the water fountains,
And wastes no time with molehills
Making them into mountains.

A computer can do more work than
a person.
Because, I have a hunch
It doesn't spend three hours
With a customer at lunch.

A computer can do more work than
a person.
And one good reason I've seen is
It doesn't spend the afternoon
Half-conscious from martinis.

A computer can do more work than
a person.
And partly it's a matter
Of not spending all day angling
For the next job up the ladder.

A computer can do more work than
a person.
Here's a final explanation:
It wastes no time on fears of being
Replaced by Automation.

VACUUM TUBES

## Computer Generations
Honeywell Corporation

Industry competition was—and is—a vital driving force in the development of "generations" of computers. The first generation featured vacuum tubes; the second, transistors. The third and current generation is based on integrated circuits. Further developments are in sight—perhaps involving LSI (Large Scale Integration—making large segments of computer logic elements extremely smaller than those presently used) and "exotic" memory techniques (more data storage in less space, with speedier data accessibility).

The miniaturized vacuum tube made possible 39,000 additions a second. Development of the transistor allowed a computer to perform 204,000 additions a second. The "solid state" technology of the microminiaturized transistor—placing all electronic components for a circuit on a half-inch ceramic tile—jumped the number of additions a computer could handle to 1,284,000 a second. Today, with monolithic integrated circuits—putting 72 complete circuits on a tiny chip—a computer can perform up to 15,000,000 additions a second.

Imagine the speed of addition (and subtracting, dividing, multiplying) tomorrow, next year, or a decade from now!

## How a Typical Computer Works
Honeywell Corporation

In "computerese" two terms are constantly used. *Hardware* refers to the visible equipment itself; *software* to the programs, routines, codes, and other written information used to direct the operation of digital computers. How does a typical computer work?

A representative computer system is shown in the schematic diagram (Figure 1). The system is composed of a central processor (the computer), an input section, an output section, a console, and a buffer. The operator has to be able to put certain data into the computer, instruct the computer to act on the data in a certain way, and then get a response or output.

The central processor has three sections: the memory, the arithmetic and logic unit, and the control and timing unit. Information (data) is fed into the memory of the central processor by an input device (such as a teletypewriter). Depending on the operator's instruction to the processor, the arithmetic and logic unit electronically adds, subtracts, multiplies, divides, compares, and moves data. The control and timing unit determines which instructions in memory are to be carried out and when, and also where the result of the calculation is to be stored.

The computer console gives the operator direct control of the system. Through the console the operator can enter information, query memory content, command functions to be performed, and read data from storage devices outside the central processor. The console's control panel contains lights, switches, push buttons, and sometimes other elements. Since the computer usually works automatically, lights only indicate the operation of the system. But the switches, push buttons, or other elements may be used by the operator to enter data or manually control system operation.

The system responds to the operator's command for information through output devices (such as an automatic teletypewriter or TV-type display screen). Output devices may be extremely sophisticated, ranging from high-speed printers using continuous paper to theater-style picture displays in color depicting changes in a process or situation as they occur in "real" (almost instantaneous) time.

The buffer is a storage device used to compensate for a difference in the rate of the flow of data, or the time of occurrence of events, when transmitting data from one device to another. Peripheral equipment—another basic term—is of two general kinds. First are the input and output devices that aid the operator in "speaking" with the system. Second are the devices that provide bulk facilities for storing data and programs, such as punched cards, paper or magnetic tape and magnetic disks and drums. Just as a phonograph record may be exchanged for another, so different cards, tapes, disks, or drums may be "played" on the system. These devices are known as external memory.

### THE MACHINES BEYOND SHYLOCK

The Machines, beyond Shylock,
When cut bleed not,
When hit bruise not,
When scared shy not,
Lose nothing and so nothing gain;
They are but a dumb show:
Put Idiot in
And the moron light you'll know.
Stuff right, get right,
Stuff rot, got rot,
For no more power lies here
Than man himself has got.
Man his energy conserves?
Machineries wait.
Man misses the early train?
Then Thought itself is late.
Sum totallings of men lie here
And not the sum of all machines,
This is man's weather, his winter,
His wedding forth of time and place
 and will,
His downfall snow,
The tidings of his soul
This paper avalanche sounds off
 his slope
And drowns the precipice of Time
 with white.
This tossed confetti celebrates his
 nightmare
Or his joy.
The night begins and goes and ends
 with him.
No machinery opens forth the champagne jars of life.
No piston churns the laundered beds
 to summon light.
Remember this:
Machines are dead, and dead must
 ever lie,
If Man so much as shuts up half one eye.

RAY BRADBURY

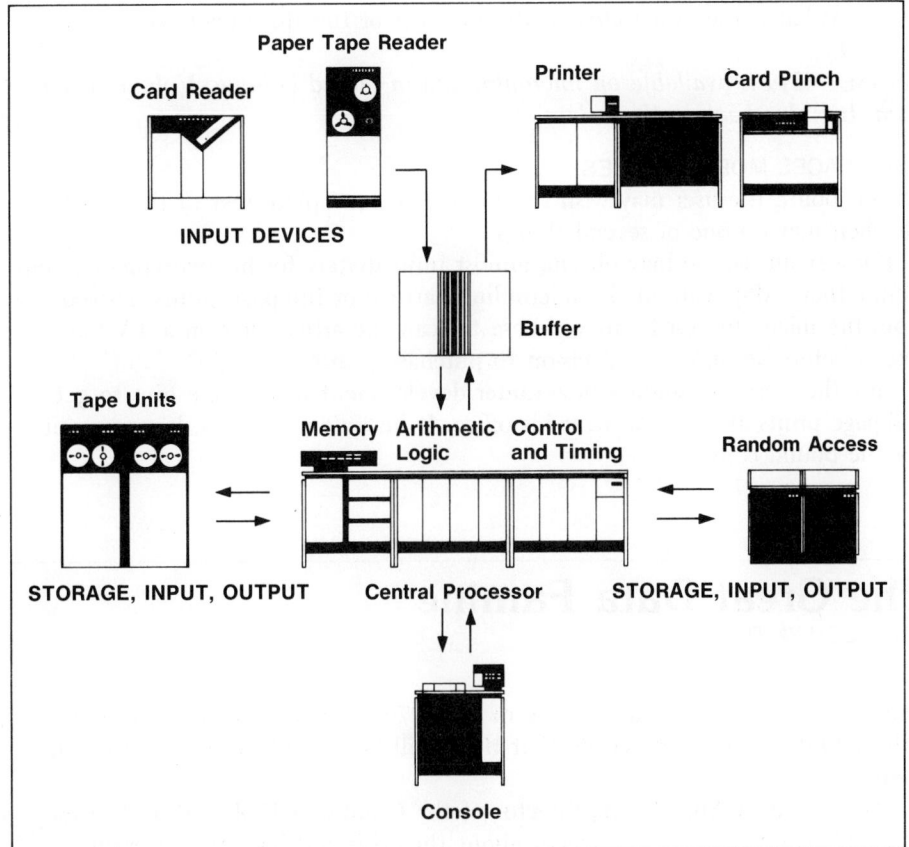

FIGURE 1

## "Instant" Librarians

Suppose someone wants information concerning automatic typesetting machines for newspapers. Envision the following series of events:

The person goes to the nearest console—very likely in a nearby office. If he or she is engaged in extensive research requiring frequent library consultation, it might be in his own office. He establishes his right to use the information-transfer system by typing his library identification number, indicating that he wishes to communicate with the library information storage and retrieval system. The system announces that it is prepared to work with him by displaying READY on a TV-like screen. The dialogue may then continue along these lines:

USER: Search for information on automatic typesetting machines.
SYSTEM: *A search is being made for information on automatic typesetting machines. It will be completed within fifteen seconds.*
(After fifteen seconds, the dialogue resumes.)
SYSTEM: *Two hundred documents found. Do you wish their titles displayed?*
USER: No. Search only for documents published since 1965.
SYSTEM: *Five documents found. Do you wish their titles displayed?*
USER: Yes.
SYSTEM: (The system now displays the author, title, publication data, and identification numbers of the five documents on the console screen. Three turn out to be journal articles; two are books.)
USER: Print out the displayed information.
SYSTEM: (The system now prints authors, titles, and publication data on paper, thus giving the user a permanent copy for his retention.)
USER: Display technical levels of these documents. (User points to the document numbers on console screen, using his light pen.)
SYSTEM: *1689 is a primer. 8219 and 76349 report on recent research.*
USER: Display the abstracts of these documents. (User points to 8219 and 76349.)
SYSTEM: (Displays the two abstracts on console screen.)
USER: What is the availability of the full text of this document? (User points to 8219.)
SYSTEM: *8219 is available on microfilm and in bound bolume. Volume is on loan. It is due back in three days.*

### USER FACES MORE CHOICES

At this point, the user may wish to examine the complete text of the article. He then may do one of several things.

For a small fee, he may obtain, almost immediately for his permanent retention, either a duplicate of the microfilmed article or full-page prints derived from the microfilm. Or he may choose to scan the article first on a TV-like screen before he makes his decision to purchase prints.

In either case, techniques now under development will enable him to get full-page prints at a station near his office. If he isn't in a hurry, he may wait for the bound copy.

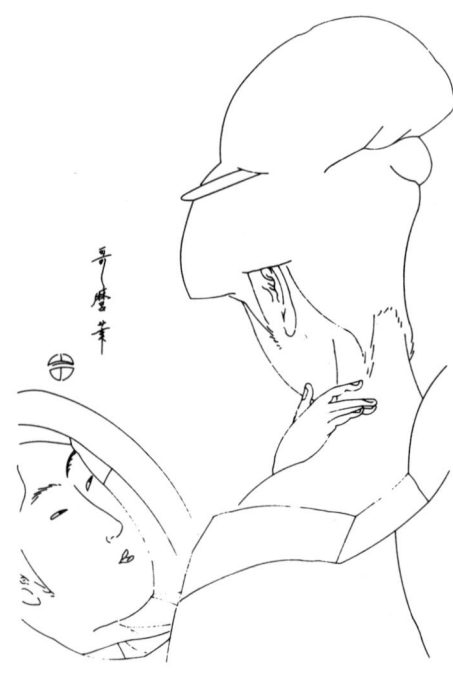

## The Great Data Famine
ART BUCHWALD

One of the major problems we face in the 1970s is that so many computers will be built in the next decade that there will be a shortage of data to feed them.

Prof. Heinrich Applebaum, director of the Computer Proliferation Center at Grogbottom, has voiced concern about the crisis and has urged a crash program to produce enough data to get our computers through the seventies.

"Did it have any enemies?"

"We didn't realize," the professor told me, "that computers would absorb so much information in such a fast period of time. But if our figures are correct, every last bit of data in the world will have been fed into a machine by Jan. 12, 1978, and an information famine will follow, which could spread across the world."

"It sounds serious," I said.

"It is serious," he replied. "Man has created his own monster. He never realized when he invented the computer that there would not be enough statistics to feed it. Even now, there are some computers starving to death because there is no information to put into them. At the same time, the birth rate of computers is increasing by thirty percent a year. Barring some sort of world-wide holocaust, we may soon have to find data for 30,000,000 computers with new ones being born every day."

"You make it sound so frightening."

"It is frightening," Prof. Applebaum said. "The new generation of computers is more sophisticated than the older generation, and the computers will refuse to remain idle just because there is nothing to compute, analyze, or calculate. Left to their own devices, the Lord only knows what they will do."

"Is there any solution, professor?"

"New sources of data must be found. The government must expand, and involved studies must be thought up to make use of the computers' talents. The scientific community, instead of trying to solve problems with computers, must work on finding problems for the computers to solve."

"Even if the scientists really don't want the answer?"

"Naturally. The scientific community invented the computer. Now it must find ways of feeding it. I do not want to be an alarmist, but I can see the day coming when millions of computers will be fighting, for the same small piece of data, like savages."

"Is there any hope that the government will wake up to the data famine in time?"

"We have a program ready to go as soon as the bureaucrats in Washington give us the word. We are recommending that no computer can be plugged in more than three hours a day."

"We are also asking the government for $50 billion to set up data manufacturing plants all over the country. This data, mixed with soy beans, could feed hundreds of thousands of computer families for months.

"And finally we are advocating a birth control program for computers. By forcing a computer to swallow a small bit of erroneous information, we could make it sterile forever, and it would be impossible for it to reproduce any more of its kind."

"Would you advocate abortions for computers?" I asked Applebaum.

"Only if the Vatican's computer gives us its blessing."

```
/*ODE TO THE COMPUTER*/
```
OH GREAT COMPUTER! BRAIN OF ALL!
WHY DO YOU TREAT US SO?
WHY DO YOU MAKE US PACE
  AND FRET?
AND BOW TO YOU SO LOW?

WE'VE NEVER MESSED YOUR
  CIRCUITS UP
OR REARRANGED YOUR CORE,
WE KEEP YOU WARM AND DRY
  AND FED;
HOW CAN WE LOVE YOU MORE?

WE TRY SO HARD TO PLEASE YOU;
WE MAKE OUR SYNTAX RIGHT.
AND ALL WE GET IS '*** ERROR ***'
THOUGH WE WORK BOTH DAY
  AND NIGHT.

'*** UNLABELED STATEMENT
  FOLLOWS TRANSFER ***'
'*** MISSING RIGHT PAREN ***'
'*** ARRAY DECLARED ILLEGALLY ***'
'*** NO COMMA—STATEMENT 10 ***'

YOU ANALYZE—YOU SYNTHESIZE
YOU SCAN—YOU GENERATE.
SO PLEASE, GREAT ONE—PLEASE
  HELP US OUT!!
THIS PROGRAM'S DUE AT EIGHT!!

IT'S 8:15; WE'RE OVERDUE.
YOU'VE HUMBLED US ONCE MORE.
I GUESS WE'VE LOST ANOTHER FIGHT;
CAN WE EVER WIN THE WAR!?!?

## What's In a Robot
*Electronics*

Far from being a mechanical man—a "Robbie the Robot" with quasi-human qualities—an industrial robot is actually little more than a mobile arm, attached to a chunky box and ending in some kind of a grip. In fact, says E. J. Van Horne, general manager of the AMF Versatran division, Warren, Mich. "A robot is what your kids watch on 'Lost in Space' on television—the devices we build are so much simpler that we prefer the term 'programmable manipulator.'"

Under either name, the devices may look like anything from a Sherman tank turret (Unimation Inc's Unimate) to an assembly of telescoping pipes (the Autospace robot). The manipulators are designed to do simple, repetitive tasks, often in circumstances that would endanger or kill human operators. For instance, they may handle parts that are red-hot or icy cold, in poisonous, corrosive, or dusty atmospheres, or they may operate in conjunction with other machines, such as a punch press or stamping mill, that could injure a careless operator.

Like numerically controlled machine tools, industrial robots may operate either point to point or follow continuous paths. A point-to-point robot will move a part in the most direct path from one production point to the next—perhaps transferring a finished part from a die-casting machine to a moving conveyor belt. Its positioning accuracy can be as fine as a couple of mils. A continuous-path robot must, on the other hand, follow a specific contour because it performs its task as it moves—perhaps spraying enamel on bathroom products.

Most robots are capable of interacting with and even controlling the machines with which they operate. For example, a stamping machine may signal the robot that it has stamped out a part. This signal prompts the robot to remove the part and, in turn, signal the machine to stamp out the next part. Then it places the stamped part at the next work point and signals the machine there to start its operating cycle. A single robot, if it's large and sophisticated enough, may even be programmed to reach in and serve two or three or possibly more tools.

The hand at the end of the robot's arm consists of finger-like clamping devices for holding onto parts and assemblies. It may incorporate single or double sets of fingers, or may have a vacuum or magnetic pickups for handling flat sheets of glass or metal. Often, the robot is designed so that different hands may be attached for different applications. And this can even be done automatically rather than by a human operator.

The robot manipulators possess varying degrees of freedom, depending upon their design. A robot arm may be able to move vertically and horizontally or to rotate its hand, or grip. The hand itself, besides opening and closing, will rotate, yaw, and pitch as if it had a wrist. In addition, some robots, like Versatran, have still another axis of motion—mounted on tracks, instead of on a fixed base, they can position themselves at points along the tracks. The result is that robots move in as few as two axes or as many as five or six and, depending upon how the manufacturer defines them, even eight.

The control part of the robot system consists of at least three basic elements—an actuating source of energy, some kind of memory, and a programmer that sets the proper sequences.

The actuator moves the arm from place to place. It may be pneumatic, as in the Auto-Place robot, which makes use of the high-pressure air found in many machine shops. If electro-hydraulic, as in the Unimate and Versatran robots, it is capable of more power than a pneumatic system and, because it is "stiffer" and can be under servo control, it has generally greater repeatable accuracies. Finally, some of the newer robots such as the minicomputer-controlled robot developed by Sundstrand Corp., use electric motors with gearing to reduce the motor speed and increase torque (an all-electric design, though slower, is said to require less maintenance because it has no hydraulic or pneumatic valves and produces less noise and smoother movements with less overshoot than the others).

In moving to a position the robot arm may be under open-loop or, in the more sophisticated units, closed-loop servo control.

To keep track of the positions to which the arm must move, the robot also must have some sort of memory—a rotating magnetic drum, the plated-wire memory of the Unimate, potentiometers, as in the Versatran or Liberator machines, or the MOS shift registers of a new control system from Sweden's Retab. In addition, there are the solid-state memories associated with minicomputers used in Sundstrand Corp.'s robot, or the minicomputer-directed machine built around a Unimate by Japan's Kawasaki Corp.

Also to be counted under the memory classification are the simple limit switches and preset mechanical stops of most of the lower-price robots. The robot merely moves in a direction until it clanks up against a mechanical stop, whereupon actuating power is turned off.

Finally, there is a programming section that directs the robot through its

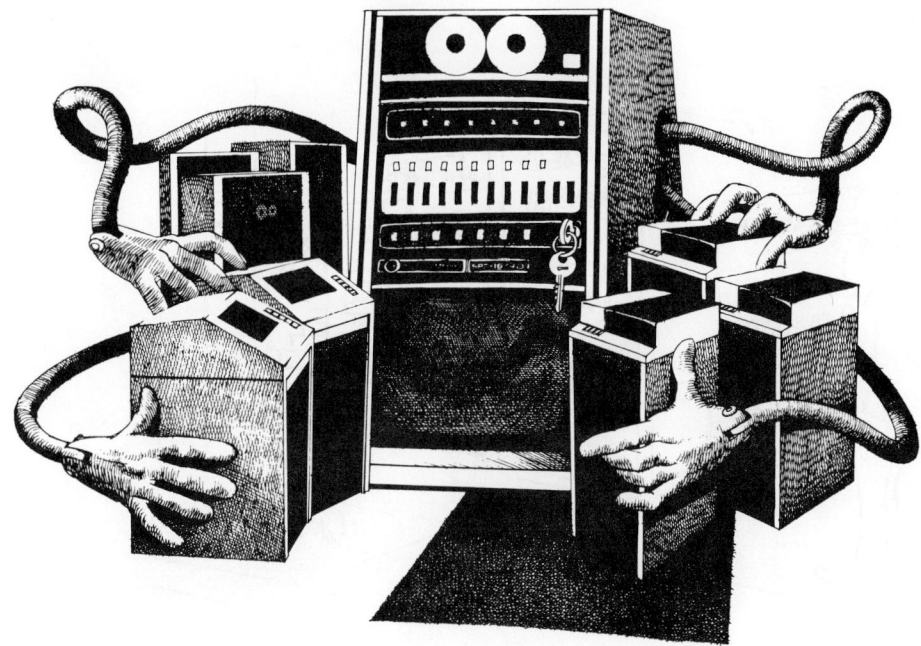

sequence of motions and the functions that are to be performed at each stop. In a minicomputer-directed system this, together with memory, is handled in the mini. In the Unimate, solid-state logic reads information off the plated-wire memory. In the Versatran and many other robots, pins stuck into an electronic patch or matrix board, which is then interfaced with relay or IC logic, fix the sequence of operations.

Actually, there is no shortage of suitable electronics (or electrical) hardware to function as amplifiers, memory, comparators, relays, analog-to-digital converters, encoders, and so on, in robots. The only problem is to make reasonably economic choices.

## Vending Machine Computation

Coin-operated computers are relatively new, but are definitely established and increasing. In 1972 a coin-operated minicomputer was installed in a library in Monterey, California. For twenty-five cents you can use the computer to do homework or personal calculations. Students have come to like and enjoy using it.

The Hennepin County Library in Minnesota offers the use of computers to anyone with a library card. The library is hooked into a computer system that is used by the local school system. People can use supplied programs or write their own programs on the computer terminals. This library views computers as a logical extension of the information services libraries should provide. And if computer terminals become inexpensive enough, libraries of the future may offer them to the public to check out.

Menlo Park, California, near the Stanford University Campus, is the home of the People's Computing Center. Anyone can go there and rent a computer terminal for $3.00 an hour. Users can play games, do homework, or write programs. The terminals are hooked up to Hewlett-Packard's time-sharing system which uses the language BASIC. These terminals are used by everyone from teenagers to business people.

At the Lawrence Hall of Science in Berkeley, California, anyone can use a computer, no questions asked, for $1.00 an hour. People using these terminals are free to play games, draw computer-aided pictures, or write programs. Staff are around to monitor the room and answer questions.

Vending machine computing may be still new, but is definitely established. The computer vending machins is probably the replacement for the pinball machine of the past. Instead of hanging around the pinball alley or pool hall, the next group of teenagers will probably be hanging around the local computer hall.

**The computer vending machine is probably the replacement for the pinball machine of the past. Instead of hanging around the pinball alley or pool hall, the next group of teenagers will probably be hanging around the local computer hall.**

## ◇ BRANCH POINTS

Berkeley, E. C. *Giant Brains: Or the Machines That Think.* New York: John Wiley & Sons, Inc., 1961.

Belden, T. G., and M. R. Belden. *The Lengthening Shadow: The Life of Thomas J. Watson.* Boston: Little, Brown and Co., 1962.

Bernstein, Jeremy. *The Analytical Engine.* New York: Random House, 1963.

Eames, Charles, and Ray Eames. *A Computer Perspective.* Cambridge, Mass.: Harvard University Press, 1973.

Goldstine, Herman. *The Computer From Pascal to von Neumann.* Princeton, N.J.: Princeton University Press, 1972.

Gilder, Jules. "Space-age Technology Opening New Doors for the Blind, Deaf and Crippled." *Electronic Design,* 25, 1972.

Gruenberger, Fred. *Computers and Communications—Toward a Computer Utility.* Englewood Cliffs, N.J.: Prentice-Hall, Inc., 1968.

Martin, James. *Telecommunications and the Computer.* Englewood Cliffs, N.J.: Prentice-Hall, Inc., 1969.

Orr, William D. *Conversational Computers.* New York: John Wiley & Sons, 1968.

Rogers, William. *THINK: A Biography of the Watsons and IBM.* New York: Stein and Day, 1969.

Rosenberg, J. M. *The Computer Prophets.* New York: Macmillan, 1969.

Rosenblatt, Alfred. "Robots Handling More Jobs on Industrial Assembly Lines," *Electronics,* July 19, 1973.

Sackman, Harold. *Mass Information Utilities and Social Change.* Philadelphia: Auerbach Publishing, Inc., 1971.

Sackman, Harold, and Norman Nie. *The Information Utility and Social Change.* Montvale, N.J.: AFIPS Press, 1970.

Sprague, Richard E. *Information Utilities.* Englewood Cliffs, N.J.: Prentice-Hall, Inc., 1969.

Wise, T. A. "IBM's $5,000,000,000 Gamble," *Fortune,* September, October 1966.

## ⊂⊃ INTERRUPTS

1. Some of the popular electronics magazines have had articles on building your own computer. Check around and find out how much it would cost and how difficult it would be to build a small computer. Maybe you will want to try it as a class project. See *Popular Electronics,* January 1975.

2. Find out how an analog computer differs from a digital computer.

3. Try to find out what safeguards are used in "money" machines such as bill changers, automatic bank tellers, and rapid-transit fare collection devices.

4. Locate the facility nearest your home where anyone can gain access to a computer time-sharing system as discussed in the article "Vending Machine Computation."

5. What are the essential differences between a desk calculator and an electronic computer?

6. What are the essential differences between the human brain and an electronic computer?

7. Make some comparisons between human memory and computer memory. Mention desirable and undesirable characteristics of each.

8. Describe how a desk calculator or slide rule works.

9. Determine a unit that can be used to describe physical size in a computer. Find data indicating how this unit has decreased in size in the last four generations of computers. Can you predict future size decreases by plotting a curve using this data? What type of curve does the plot give you?

10. Find out what input/output devices are presently used with computers. One way to find this information is to scan computer-related periodicals.

11. Learn how to keypunch. Keypunch your name, the alphabet, the numerals from 0 to 10, and punctuation characters on a card.

12. Learn how to use a card sorter. Do the following:
    a) count cards
    b) sort numeric
    c) sort alphabetic
    d) sort a numeric field in descending sequence

13. Trace the recent history of the pocket calculator. See how its price has decreased and its capacity has increased. What price and capability do you predict for these devices for the near future. What about twenty years from now?

14. Here are some factors that can be used to indicate how computers have improved in the past four generations:
    a) memory capacity
    b) add time
    c) fetch time
    Find some information of present and past capabilities and plot a curve. What type of curve did you get? Can you predict future improvements?

15. Outline the major changes in one of the following:
    a) the four generations of computers
    b) the development of computer hardware
    c) the development of computer software

16. Describe the architecture of a contemporary computer.

Compare present computer architecture to previous computer architecture.

17. Write a paper indicating how the components of computers have changed in the last thirty years.

18. One favorite sport of computer people is "IBM watching." Find several articles in current periodicals about IBM and write a report. One good place to start is "IBM and All the Dwarfs," *New Times Magazine* (July 29, 1973). *Fortune* magazine has also had numerous articles on IBM (the August 1968 issue, for example).

19. There were less than 1000 computers in the United States in 1956. By 1967 there were over 30,000. Draw a chart indicating how the numbers of computers has grown over the past thirty years. Project the number of computers in the United States in the next thirty years. Find out how many people work in the computer field, and at what types of work.

20. A country's standard of living is often judged by its gross national product (GNP). Other useful statistics are average family income, infant mortality, and literacy level. Compare numbers of computers in a country to some of the above indicators to see how good the number of computers would be as an indicator of a country's standard of living.

21. Develop some figures on the change of cost of computational time in the last twenty years.

# 3

## THE SOFTWARE

## "You are an Interfacer of Black Boxes"

RICHARD TODD

Computers surround us, about 50,000 of them now: just a decade ago there were 1700. Most of them are used for record-keeping, or "sophisticated paper-pushing," as the industry calls it. Ultimately they record almost every bit of money that changes hands, and they file various items of information: where you were born, where you want to fly, the numbers that you are known by, your vulnerability to direct-mail advertising.

This is one function, storage and retrieval, but computers are also capable of making certain kinds of decisions. Fed information, they may recommend action and thereby regulate refineries, diagnose illnesses, and fire retro-rockets. More important, they imitate reality. Probably the greatest use for computers beyond data processing is for the performance of simulations—war games, marketing strategies, stress analyses of aircraft—which allow the user to discover the consequences of an action without taking it.

No one is unaffected by all this, but for most of us the computers remain remote. They are mildly disquieting. It may be hard to take threats of the automated society of the future seriously, but computers say something unpleasant about our condition in the present. They are incarnate metaphors for the brain, and the brain often suffers in comparison. So it seems to "most of us." But for an increasing number of people computers stand at the center of life.

Perhaps as many as 300,000 people—the programmers—tell computers what to do. Like computers themselves, programmers are mostly in their twenties. Their talents are indispensable, and they incite the economy to lust. However many there are, it is generally agreed that half again as many could be hired now, and twice as many as soon as the "fourth generation" machines appear. Intelligent voices seek programmers on the radio, and the want ads suggest rewards, "fringes," and the mystique:

. . . Programmer, Has Your Ability Outgrown the Software? . . . Start $18.5–21,000++ . . . $2000 Guar. Increase Over Present Earnings for 4th Generation People Interested in Real Time, Time-Sharing . . . Salary Open . . . Fly Free . . . Take a Trip on Us . . . Stock Options . . .

I have lately been talking to programmers in and around Cambridge, Massachusetts, where the buried circuitry of computers and computer people that binds any city is somewhat more manifest than elsewhere because of the universities and their spun-off, and symbiotic, research enterprises. One such place is the Smithsonian Astrophysical Observatory. Smithsonian (which employs about twenty-five programmers) tracks man-made satellites, studies the habits of meteors, and smiles on the whims of its employees; once one of them tried to program a theory of the creation of the universe, but "only got about ten micro-seconds into the job." ("Micro-second" is a millionth of a second. As a way of saying speed, it's being replaced by "nano-second," a billionth; "femto-second," a trillionth, is on the way.)

I went to Smithsonian to see Rudolf Loeser, a 1971 graduate of Harvard and Smithsonian's senior programmer. Before I got to him, however, I saw his computer, on the first floor of Smithsonian's offices in an industrial park. It was a stylish-looking machine of several great, rectangular components, faced in blue panels, and it occupied a glass-enclosed space that resembled an automobile showroom. I had never seen a computer before. (Increasingly, this is an admission of provincialism, even cultural deprivation.) The visible signs of its work were whirling reels of magnetic tape on one component, and printed data—printout—emerging from another, in abrupt chunks. An adolescent occasionally dashed to the computer with a reel of tape, and replaced one already on the machine, trying, it seemed, not to waste the computer's time. After watching him for several moments I started up to Loeser's office.

The computer I'd seen was Control Data 6400, the largest computer (in terms of abilities) in Cambridge. "It can perform 800,000 additions per second," Rudy Loeser told me, "or 200,000 multiplications. I don't know how to put that into easily comprehensible terms. There

are what?—three billion people in the world. I suppose if you had data on the number of hairs on each of their heads, the computer could give you the total number in about an hour. Perhaps an hour and a half."

Loeser, who has a broad, placid face and wavy hair, was born in Germany, and speaks with a slight accent. He speaks quietly, with a likeable, if demanding, precision. He often pauses before a sentence, delivers it quickly, and is silent again. He is conscious of being considered unspontaneous. "I've changed a lot since I was married," he remarked. "Before that people used to say that I was the most inhuman person they had ever met."

Loeser was at work on a program that had occupied most of two years. It was called Pandora, and its function, he said, was to test certain hypotheses about the composition of the sun. In written form, Pandora filled two fat blue binders.

"We hope we will make some real statements about the sun," Loeser said. Talking with Loeser at first I had a feeling of great separation, as if we were two strangers in a waterfront bar, each with poignant but ineffable stories to tell. He was speaking of programming, he gestured at a program, but I had little concept of what one was.

"A set of instructions" is a frequently used shorthand way of explaining a program. I had read the phrase, but when I asked Loeser about it he seemed uncomfortable. He said that it was not only an oversimplification, but "rather anthropomorphic." It appeared, he felt, to imply that the programmer had only to describe his desires and the understanding computer would enact them.

But if you look at a programmer "behavioristically," that is, in fact, surprisingly close to what happens. His work is done on paper. What he writes often appears as "instructions," indeed as orders. Although Loeser's own work, he said diffidently, was not very accessible to an outsider, everyday programs closely resemble the experience they describe. For example, a typical program for balancing a checking account begins "Get Check."

```
PO.   GET CHECK
      MOVE ACCT-NO TO
      ACCT-NO-CURRENT.
PL.   GET MASTER.
      IF ACCT-NO-MAST IS NOT EQUAL TO
      ACCT-NO-CURRENT GO TO PL.
      IF BALANCE-MAST IS LESS THAN
      BALANCE-CHECK GO TO OVERDRAFT.
      SUBTRACT BALANCE-CHECK FROM
      BALANCE-MAST.
      ADD ONE TO NO-OF-CHECKS.
      GO TO PO.
```

Allowing for some abbreviations, this appears to be written in English. Actually, it is written in a language called COBOL, which stands for "COmmon Business Oriented Language," the universal tongue used for computerized bill-collecting. COBOL contains a great many words of pure English and some coinages. When you watch a programmer jotting it down, you might think he could embellish his instructions at will, but not so. Every computer language has a strictly delimited vocabulary and a rigorous grammar.

COBOL is one of the easiest of literally hundreds of computer languages. Rudy Loeser works in one called FORTRAN (FORmula TRANslator), which is useful for expressing mathematical and scientific problems. Loeser can use several other languages; "learning a new one," he said, "is almost a trivial matter." (But a great many programmers make a living knowing, or caring, about only one. According to most computer people, the ability to pick up another language "just by reading the manual" is one mark of a gifted programmer.) Loeser mentioned some of the rarer languages, which have names as inviting as Saskatchewan towns: JOVIAL, JOSS, SNOBOL, PLEASE, and LISP. His own, FORTRAN, is more obscure-looking than COBOL, partly because it refers to less concrete phenomena. "I imagine someone processing Diners Club bills has a firm sense of reality," he said. "But in my case the connection with reality is generally . . . not there."

He showed me a small section called a "subroutine" of his vast program. Its function was simply to compare two numbers and mark them with an asterisk.

```
      SUBROUTINE SPLICE
      $ (I, ITV, MARK)
C     RUDOLPH LOESER
C     SERVICE ROUTINE FOR HAWSER
      MARK = 1H
      IF (I-ITV) 101, 100, 101
100   MARK = 1H*
101   RETURN
      END
```

Computer talk rapidly escalates out of sight. Aside from the arcane computer languages themselves, ordinary conversation among programmers often occurs in a private tongue. It is nearly a subroutine of English, and listening to it means listening to familiar syntax, to not wholly foreign words, but to meanings that remain entirely obscure. My eyes fell on one of Loeser's interdepartmental memos:

To change fatal error 78, bad data, to non-fatal error user must initialize registers in the routine with a single call to BLISS prior to any read or decodes . . . SCROG is updated to agree with SCROGX.

But these are all symbols, and you are willing to believe they stand for something.

One thing that was bothering me, however, was the distance between the programmer and the computer. We were sitting a floor above the machine, and I found it surprising to realize how little a programmer, who is easily imagined in a tense posture next to a computer, need actually see of one. What connection did the language have with the computer? Loeser explained that that was the reason he had been reluctant to call the program a "set of instructions." Its written form is only one of several states a program occupies in its transition from the imagination of the programmer to the memory of the computer. "It's an interface between the programmer—the human being—and the computer," Loeser said, using an omnipresent bit of computer lingo.

"Interface" refers to anything that mediates between disparate items: machinery, people, thought. The equipment that makes the computer's work visible to the user is often called an "interface," and the word is used highly metaphorically, as in "the interface between man and the computer, between the scientist and society."

Computers are troubling not just because we don't understand them (most of us deal with many machines we don't understand) but also because we suspect that we finally *couldn't* understand them. And we are, most of us, right. Reassuringly, this is even true of many programmers. "It's possible to be a nine-to-five programmer," he said, "and never think about what happens within the computer. To some programmers it might as well be a hamster on a treadmill generating the output. The computer—for many purposes—may be thought of as a black box."

A black box, Loeser explained, is anything considered in terms of input and output, without worrying about processes. It may refer to parts of a computer, or parts of a program. The idea is not so complicated: to simplify by abstracting an intricate system into manageable components. But it has a particular relevance among computers, where everything, looked at too closely, takes on a bellygripping complexity. "Black boxes" are as handy a concept as "interface": "interfacer of black boxes" is not a bad definition of a programmer.

### "Eventually we will build a machine we don't understand."

I asked Loeser if he could tell me something about what happened in the mind's black boxes when he was working on a programming problem. He said that he usually let the problem rest in the back of his mind, turning to it for only a half hour at a time, over a week or so, counting on a solution to begin to generate itself, before he began to bear down hard. Even when the answer is at hand, he said, it is never entirely comprehensible: "Often you've deluded yourself into thinking that you have a clear, simultaneous understanding of the problem, but you don't. It's impossible to see the plan as a whole. I often see it as a ticker tape passing through my mind. I know I'm there if I can follow each step as it goes by."

Rudy Loeser is spontaneously called "a true professional" by his colleagues, and I wondered what that meant, how he felt about the programmer and his "interface" with society.

He said, "It's the 'in thing' now to characterize programming as a profession. But I'm not sure it's justified. It's errant nonsense to call some novice just out of programming school a 'professional.' And most programmers become dominated by their salaries when they find they can extort almost anything they want. I'm afraid you don't find many altruistic programmers."

Loeser sees the computer as a "tool." "Of course it is by far the most versatile tool we have, and it sets its users apart from other tool-users. The great source of fear about the machine is that people don't understand them. People don't understand us either, so they mistrust us. . . .

"I am concerned. But not about the computers—about the motives of the people who use them. The nightmare vision, of course, is hordes of militarists running rampant. You won't see it happening if only the engineers become really concerned. Man could do the right thing, but *will* he? It depends on the extent to which we become involved. We must commit ourselves with deeds. And we don't, not enough. How do I feel? I feel mostly apprehensive—apprehensive and guilty.

"Eventually we will build a machine we don't understand. . . . At one point we will wonder if we should rely entirely on biology for the continuance of human culture. Machines may be made partly of living material, for humane and emotional functions. . . . And someday we will pass the torch on to the machines."

One of the broad distinctions that programmers make among themselves is between "applications" and "systems" programmers. Rudy Loeser is purely an "applications" programmer, which means that he uses the computer to solve problems from the world (or, in his case, the universe) of people and things. "Systems" programmers worry about the programs built into the machine, "the software," which allows the computer to receive other programs, to switch from program to program, and in general to keep itself operating efficiently. Aaron Kronenberg is a young programmer with a special interest in systems work.

I met Kronenberg at Abt Associates, a Cambridge think-tank, specializing in "scientific solutions to social problems." Abt was founded just four years ago, and it has had spectacular success: its billings have doubled each year and now approach $4 million. It is full of élan: extraordinary-looking girls in pantsuits and nano-skirts hurry through the white-carpeted hall, and at closing time bearded young men in lumberjack shirts throw Frisbees. It is as if everyone's college-age children had come in to see where their fathers work.

Kronenberg, who is himself only twenty-three, has a reputation for brilliance and eccentricity. ("See Kronenberg," one of his colleagues said, "his head is in some interesting places. He used to be a disc jockey you know.") He weighs well over two hundred pounds, and his usual uniform is tight trousers and a white shirt, too small, straining open at the neck. He wears thick glasses, has troubled black hair, and the day I met him he wore a button that declared, "I am a rat fink!"

"So you want to learn about computer," said Kronenberg, who often speaks an article-less Indian patois. "I give short magical mystery tour." We went to his office, where, on the blackboard, he gave me an overview of the computer's functions —often addressing the imaginary machine as "Hey, baby," or "This yo-yo here"—and of his own duties.

Most of his work, he said, involved consulting to companies whose computers have run amok, and whose regular programmers are no longer able to understand them. (When computers hit a snag they often print out dense reams of digits, which represent all the data that's been given to them. This is called a "dump." Searching out the error in a dump is referred to as "debugging," and it occupies much of any programmer's time.) Kronenberg's consulting assignments tend to be tense, as the expensive machinery sits idle. "Essentially, I'm a rescue service," Kronenberg says. "They fly you out to California and parachute you into Fresno and say you *will* return in seventy-two hours, you *will* bring program. It generate ulcer."

Kronenberg's consulting fee—Abt's charge for his service—climbed to about $400 a day as he became better known in the business. His own base salary, he said, was $18,400, with bonuses and stock options that brought his income to about $21,000 a year. Programmers may, if they choose, move around a great deal, and many of them do. Kronenberg was weighing two offers: "I hope to push my salary up a couple of figures anyway." He said that he'd been talking about it to his boss, Clark Abt, whom he calls Leader. "With offers I have, Leader listen."

Kronenberg's self-confidence sometimes irritates his colleagues. ("I could strangle him," one girl said. "Obviously he was hired for his ability, not his personality.") But Clark Abt said, "Ron has a few rough edges, but they'll smooth off. He has *great* growth potential."

Kronenberg, who says of himself, "I'm probably the weirdest guy in this business," and whose computer recognizes him by the password MADMAN, is atypical in many ways, especially in his education. Most programmers have at least a bachelor's degree, but Kronenberg is a college dropout. He entered Rensselaer Polytechnic Institute, intending to become a physicist, but left in boredom after two years. (Not before he had taken some programming courses, though, and founded a campus "computer society.") After RPI, he became a disc jockey. As Art Matthews, he was morning man for WXKW, Sarasota, and he can give a convincing reproduction of his radio self, as he did one afternoon at Abt, lowering his voice and dropping his head to his chest: "Movin' and groovin' with Big Daddy Madman Matthews on soooooo-oulful 1600 WXKW 76 degrees in the big bag outside and time for: Muuuuu-sic!"

Meanwhile, he was programming

> "There's a computer mystique—people are afraid of computers. But they shouldn't be. Computers are good guys."

for the city of Sarasota, and he was becoming more involved in computers, and he realized that he had highly marketable skills. "Next step. Whirlwind coast-to-coast tour." He ended up working at the Yale University computer center, where he helped set up a "time-sharing system," and then he came to Abt.

"Time-sharing" is Kronenberg's particular interest. It is a way of accommodating several users, with the appearance of simultaneity, in a single computer. The users may be spread throughout a city, state, or the world. They communicate with the computer through "terminals," which are connected to the machine by telephone lines. The terminals resemble IBM electric typewriters; in fact, most of them are IBM typewriters with some serious modifications. The effective difference is that the machine types back. At Kronenberg's terminal, when he typed in MADMAN, it typed back READY. A similar interface is the graphic display terminal, like a TV screen, which also interacts with the user, who may enter data by means of a "light-pen," like a small flashlight. The distinctive thing about time-sharing, from the programmer's viewpoint, is that his transactions with the machine take place in "real time"; that is, the computer interacts with him step by step. If he makes an error, he doesn't have to wait for his whole deck of cards to be read by the machine to find out; the computer calls attention to the mistake in its next breath.

Time-sharing represents only a small portion of the computer industry now, but it is growing. The terminals may be rented for very little, though the charges for an hour of the computer's time run to several hundred dollars. Time-sharing makes the machines more accessible to human beings—"conversational" is the industry's word for the relationship—and it promises new uses for computers. Already, time-sharing systems enable airlines to confirm reservations immediately. When the day comes (it's often predicted) that everyone has a "computer in his kitchen," it will really be a time-sharing terminal, able to retrieve material from the Library of Congress or the New York *Times* archives, to predict one's future tax problems, or to enact marital game theory.

Time-sharing systems are, like any computer operation, only as good as the programmer who readies them for nonprogrammers. Kronenberg is working on methods of increasing the machines' ability to respond to everyday language. "I'm interested in the machine-user interface," he says. "I'm trying to work out ways to program the machine so a sociologist can sit down and talk sociology talk to it and the machine will answer back in sociology talk. There's a computer mystique—people are afraid of computers. But they shouldn't be. Computers are good guys."

Kronenberg is totally absorbed in computers. His habit, he said, was dinner at a delicatessen near Abt and work long into the night, and work at home as well. Some everyday concerns find him oblivious: he doesn't drive a car, he walks in rain or freezing temperatures without a coat, his dates sometimes begin at midnight.

The day I saw it, his big apartment in the South End, a hiply fashionable neighborhood of old brick houses with bow fronts, had a scarcely inhabited look. But in his bedroom, an anarchy of bedsheets and books, Kronenberg kept a time-sharing terminal so that he might jump from bed and type out the solution to a problem. The terminal rents for $115 (by special arrangement, the time comes free), and he spends $150 a month for books, "mostly in the field, to keep up."

Not alone among programmers, Kronenberg is worried about maintaining his own parity with "the state of the art," not about the purported evils of automation. "I don't think the computers will put me out of business for a few years," he says. "I don't think they'll appreciate beauty in quite the way I do, but if so, a certain joy will be gone out of life. But it's a long way off. And anyway I doubt that the machine ever will be a good disc jockey."

I had talked at length to two programmers. They didn't seem much alike, and I spent a couple of days in assorted computer installations, looking for a commonality. It was a futile search, of course, and actually Rudy Loeser and Ron Kronenberg, despite their styles, did share something: they were near the top of a profession that contains great variations in ability. If there is anything that computer people seem to agree upon, it is that the difference between an ordinary programmer and a good one is the difference between the runway and the air. "A good programmer isn't worth two median ones," one computer executive said, "he's worth ten."

At one level, it is possible for many people to become programmers. I talked to a programmer who did payrolls for a hospital, and asked him why he got into the field. "Because I failed in the restaurant business," he said. And in fact, we will probably all be programmers of a sort in a few years, with the proliferation of computer terminals in the home.

Programmers in more recherché spots look down at the data-processors in business. A university programmer said that "most people in banks are doing things that probably just don't need to be done," referring to the possibility of standardized software to perform routine work. Nevertheless, the banks represent in miniature a world in which computers and their human aides sit uneasily in a traditional setting.

I talked to George McQuilken, twenty-five, an IBM systems engineer at the State Street Bank. (IBM sells the full-time service of systems engineers along with the computer; the SE's live at the installation, consultants to the regular programmers.) McQuilken said, "Ask a banker what his biggest problem is today and he'll say computers. Ten years ago he would have said paper work. Computers cost too much, and to run them he has to hire a bunch of kids, at fifteen and seventeen a year, and they have beards and rotten personalities."

The programmers at the bank, in fact, were conventional, if not bankerly, in appearance, but Bradford Tripp, vice president for computer operations, warned that "one kook can ruin it for everyone," as a board member comes through and says, "So, you've got them here too." It is true anyway that the bank's programmers can sometimes achieve an independent style. I was introduced to one programmer working on a problem more complex than check processing, a financial simulation. I asked him if he could tell me something about it. He looked saddened; and after a silent moment he turned and walked away.

Somewhat surprisingly, even in their own milieu, programmers are found disquieting. "They're a little like low-level diplomats," said Professor Joseph Weizenbaum, a computer scientist at MIT. "They don't have any real decision-making power, but it ends up that they're making all the decisions, simply by telling you what you can and can't do. And they feel misunderstood, by people 'up there,' which gives them a cliquish sense of professional pride."

Weizenbaum feels that programmers are largely of a distinct personality type, which tends to be a distortion of the qualities that make good scientists in general.

"I'm talking about a universally recognized phenomenon. People get hooked. They begin to behave in a way that resembles addiction. They refuse food. They refuse their girlfriends. I'm quite serious. The word 'compulsion' isn't far removed; in fact, it's correct.

"When a programmer finally gets his program perfected, what does he do? He sabotages it. I don't mean he literally, consciously wrecks it. But he goes in and says: 'This can be done better!' So he destroys what he's done and gets into a terrible panic, and then he's happy again.

"He's just like a compulsive gambler. He's not interested in winning but in keeping the game going. Why? He's emotionally involved in a struggle for control. These people have suffered a major defeat sometime in their struggle for control. They feel they can't achieve the kind of power they need. They have given up the real world and begin to operate in a magic world in which they believe they can be omnipotent."

Weizenbaum is a member of Project MAC, MIT's huge computer sciences program. (MAC is a double acronym: "multiple access computer"; "machine-aided cognition.") The project is credited, among other things, with most of the developmental work in time-sharing. MIT, probably the most computerized university in the world, has forty-odd computers of various sizes and hundreds of time-sharing terminals. Some knowledge of programming belongs in almost every undergraduate's repertory; the elementary course in programming, "Introduction to Automatic Computation," attracts more students than any other at the school. This year under the direction of Robert Fenichel, a young professor of electrical engineering, the course has begun to be taught by machine. Fenichel calls his automated course TEACH. At the beginning of the term students meet and are given a mimeographed "handout" that begins "You should expect to have little formal contact with the instructors . . ."

---

**"I'm trying to work out ways to program the machine so a sociologist can sit down and talk sociology talk to it and the machine will answer back in sociology talk."**

---

I had asked Fenichel too about the programming mind, and he had said, "You're going to have a hard time finding out. The ur-programmer relates to his computer the way an Iowa farm boy relates to his old Ford, and neither one of them can tell you much about it. Some of them are virtually *idiot-savants*. Some are duo-maniacs: you'll find a brilliant programmer who also knows everything about ballet—and nothing else." Fenichel offered, however, to let me get some "hands-on" experience by participating in TEACH.

The machine turned out to be not nearly so chilly as might be expected. It took me a couple of tries just to "login," but, successful, I was rewarded with HELLO, and my name! At moments TEACH is capable of a truly jarring testiness: GARBAGE FOLLOWS COMMA ON MAIN LIST . . . NOT AN EXECUTABLE STATEMENT. But it also pleases the student, after his first easy problem, with a mildly ironic CONGRATULATIONS, and after each session it types GOODBYE.

The transfixing ball of characters that flies across the page creating printout at the rate of 15 characters a second is enough to fascinate the human participant. A short way into the course you begin to get a whiff as well of the mixed sense of power and subservience the programmer must feel, as the machine performs dazzling errands on a correct command, or waits silently (LISTENING AT LEVEL 1) for you to say a sensible thing. I had intended to spend 15 minutes with TEACH the first day and I spent three hours. But I did not fully realize its effect until I was in my car, where I sat for a moment, expecting that machine, too, to tell me what to do.

MIT's programmers roam through the halls of the elegant building at Technology Square. Most of them are unstructured in appearance; by looks they might as easily be members of the Electric Cabbage. Artificial intelligence is on their minds too.

I talked to Jed Harris, a twenty-one-year-old student at MIT on leave from Beloit College to take graduate courses in computer sciences. He has glossy black hair at shoulder-length and a full beard, and describes his programming work as "like living inside a Bach fugue." "In a few years," Harris remarked, "it will begin to feel immoral to tell your computer what to do, just like slavery. Watch: as soon as the machines begin to simulate consciousness on the level of a dog, you'll see protective societies forming, like the ASPCA."

Jerry Yochelson, a 1967 graduate of MIT, and a full-time programmer at MAC, described the Project's work with chess. He acknowledged that he was a devoted player, but that he had never beaten the chess program in one of MAC's computers, which is now playing a low-level-B game and "has beaten many men and some computers." Computer scientists like to engage their computers in chess, partly because the men themselves like the game, and partly because it is so complicated that the machine is not simply calculating multiple possibilities, it is enacting strategy. Some of its programs enable the computer to review previous games and analyze errors so that it improves upon itself. The game is represented on a screen, like a television screen; this is a form of graphic printout used for a variety of purposes. The screen is sensitive to light, and to move, the human player need only indicate the piece and the square with a light-pen. "It's very disappointing to lose," Yochelson said. "You ponder over your move, and make it, and then you just sit there and watch a piece disappear."

Yochelson foresees without question a computerized world in which work will be optional, or perhaps luxurious. From the window of his eighth-floor office one sees the old red brick factories of East Cambridge, all quite susceptible to computer management. "Almost no one will have to work in twenty years. The twenty years may be off, but we'll have the necessary technology in that time, so it becomes a question of what most people want. Obviously, it will disturb many people. Computers pose a threat to people who don't want to change."

In the imagined workless society, programmers would, of course, not be the first to be displaced; but neither would they be the last. Almost at once, people saw in their work the implication that programmers would "program themselves out of a job." It's one of the paradoxes of the occupation that twenty years ago it scarcely existed, and today it contemplates its own obsolescence.

In the present, programmers occupy an ambiguous social role, despite the fact that they perform some of the most sophisticated chores being done in the world and that, without them, organized life in the United States would choke. They seem to be thought of as something between professionals and occult tradesmen. If programmers' meritocratic life-style nettles those around them, it is because of a sense that their ascendance is unearned. Their work is as crucial and as inaccessible as that of many scientists, and yet they stand apart from the educational hierarchy by which society keeps most of its brilliant members in bounds. "People have to listen to you in this job," Jerry Yochelson said, "because they don't know what you're doing. I like that."

---

FUTURE SHOCK IN MATHEMATICS
Computers have altered the role of mathematicians by giving them a tool that will do endless computations accurately and quickly. Less than twenty years ago a great deal of effort and research was put into finding algorithms that could compute answers to mathematical problems easily. This was important because computations were done by hand or at best with a small desk calculator.

Today we have computers to do all complicated calculation. The emphasis now is to discover algorithms that will be accurate and adaptable to the computer. It does not matter how much actual arithmetic is involved since a computer will do the arithmetic. Thus, the computer at one stroke disposed of whole fields of mathematics and spawned new ones in their place.

---

**A PROGRAMMER'S LAMENT**

**I really hate this damned machine;
I wish that they would sell it.
It never does quite what I want,
But only what I tell it.**

---

# The Human Mind and the Machine "Brain"
Honeywell Corporation

How does the so-called machine "brain" of the computer stack up against the human mind that invented the computer? Is the computer reaching a point where it's beginning to outsmart its inventor?

The computer is simply man's best new tool. And the best minds in the computer industry find it impossible to envision a day when the computer or any of its descendants will ever replace the uniqueness of the human mind.

For one thing, the human brain can store about 2½ million times more information than today's most advanced computer. The human brain can hold some 10 million-million "bits" of information—enough to cram the shelves of a large library—all tucked away in a 100-cc case. That's about 1/20 of a cubic foot, and weighs about 3 pounds. A giant computer—a 1-to-4 million bit machine—requires around 60–70 cubic feet, and holds around 200 pounds of memory units.

A computer can only do what some human being has instructed it to do. A computer can't think or feel. It has no creativity, no sensitivity. It has no values, principles, or ethical standards. It can never have inspiration, "fire", "soul", "spirit"—call it what you will.

But as a tool the computer is absolutely first-rate. What makes it seem bewildering to many people is the incredible speed with which it does its work. It's as if it worked sideways in time. It simply does one simple thing after another, sequentially, until it completes the chore it's been ordered to do. The fastest computers perform functions in billionths of a second. A calculation that might take a scientist days to work out with paper and pencil can be handled on a computer in a matter of minutes or even seconds.

# Sports and EDP... It's a New Ballgame

J. GERRY PURDY

Scheduling, simulating, scouting, scorekeeping—the computer may soon be doing it all—except setting the records

Is it possible that some future Super Bowl will have a computer picking the winning play? Today the rules[1] actually forbid the use of computers during the game, but many football teams—both college and professional—are using computers to analyze the play tendencies in the previous games of themselves and their opponents.

The application of computers to athletics is developing quite rapidly. Almost every sport has seen some application of computers besides having the front office running off a mailing list for ticket requests. These applications have been for the sport itself, either to gather and analyze data about opponents or to analyze and model one's own sport.

But, you may ask, "Why computers in athletics anyway? What effect can they have on human performance?" Besides the economic benefits, there are three good reasons why computers and computer people are getting involved in athletics:

1. *Entertainment.* Athletics are fun; people enjoy both participating in and watching sports, which means computer people can easily enjoy applications in this area.
2. *More information.* Computers can make the sport more interesting since they provide more information to everyone involved (assuming GIGO isn't involved).
3. *Improved performance.* Computers can improve the athletic performance and quality by providing more information in less time than with other methods.

It should be made quite clear at the start that computers or their output are not going to take the place of people in any sport. Rather, computers simply provide a way to organize and analyze the available information so that it can be put to the best possible advantage of the athlete.

---
[1]Rule 1, Sec. 2, Article 9 of the NCAA Official Rules states: "Television replay or monitor equipment are prohibited at the side lines, press box, or other locations adjacent to the playing field for coaching purposes during the game." Section (E) of Article X (Prohibited Conduct) of the NFL Rules states: "No club, nor any coach, representative or employee thereof, shall use or employ any mechanical or other equipment or device in connection with the staging or playing of any game . . ." A check with both the NFL and the NCAA confirms that these rules include not being able to use computers in any form during the progress of a game.

There are many different types of systems which have been developed for athletics. Functionally, they may be grouped into the following five categories:

1. *Statistical tabulations.* This is perhaps the simplest type of system, since programs are written to read various inputs and generate tables of summary information. Most of the football play analysis programs fall under this category. Another example is the generation of baseball statistics. Many of the reports to be made in the 1976 Olympic Games will be simple reports listing results, usually for the press.
2. *Statistical analysis.* This type of system is similar to the one above except that more mathematical analysis is performed. A program which evaluates data about athletics and tries to rank them according to some order is an example. Many of the professional football teams have rankings of eligible college players made each year for the draft which make heavy use of statistical analysis.
3. *Information retrieval systems.* In this type of system, a data base is created which contains information about the sport and/or athlete. The program works like other retrieval systems in that it allows the user to ask various questions and receive answers. There has been a system developed for rowing by JAMCO, Inc. that can retrieve information about any oarsman that is contained in the data base; e.g., what international championships he has rowed in and what success he has had.
4. *Real-time systems.* This type of system employs a computer in real-time during an athletic event, to either monitor the competition itself and/or give information concerning its progress. A good example here is the system currently being employed at the Ontario Motor Speedway, where an IBM 1130 actually monitors each car on every lap and posts the current order on displays for the spectators.
5. *Modeling.* This type of system incorporates perhaps the most complicated mathematical and computer science aspects of the five, just as modeling in other fields can be and usually is quite complicated. The system which the author has been

working on to model track running training is an example. A program which might try to optimize the sequence of plays to be used in a football game would be another.

With the functional areas now defined, the remainder of the article is devoted to describing the actual systems which have been developed.

## FOOTBALL

*Football play analysis.* One of the most widespread applications of computers to athletics has been in football play analysis systems. Simply put, these systems generate statistical summaries and analyses of the plays of a given football game. The output is examined by the coaches to find tendencies of a team.

Coaches may look at summaries of another team's offense and/or defense, or they may look at the same kind of summaries of their own team. If a consistent tendency is found by a program, then presumably whoever examines the output will recognize that tendency; i.e., Team A's coaches may examine their own team from the previous week(s), just as the next opponent (Team B) may also recognize those same tendencies upon examination of Team A's play data.

Football play analysis programs are currently being used by many of the pro teams. College teams, to some extent, are also developing or have developed similar systems. Trying to obtain information about these systems requires tact and persistence. The teams that do have these programs usually don't like to admit it, and when they do, they guard descriptions about the program as if they made all the difference between winning and losing.

Some of the universities that have developed or are developing play analysis programs are Kent State, Univ. of Pennsylvania, Univ. of Tennessee, Dartmouth, USC, UCLA, Washington, and Stanford. Undoubtedly, many other college teams have or are in the process of developing play analysis programs.

Most typical play analysis systems simply read in the play information which has been filled out by the coach on a keypunch form. The program then sorts by field position, formation, and down and distance. Various reports are then generated summarizing the running and passing play tendencies. One of the most important aspects of a football play analysis program is organization of the output information. Too many systems generate literally hundreds of pages of output, making the analysis a difficult task for the coach.

One of the first organizations that developed play analysis programs for profit was the recently disbanded Computer Applications, Inc., in Maryland. William Witzel did most of the programming for a system employed by the Washington Redskins in 1966. His contact with Washington was Coach Ed Hughes, now head coach for the Houston Oilers. Washington no longer uses Witzel's system, but the Oilers do. Witzel has been involved with other systems that are currently being used by the Chicago Bears, Dallas Cowboys, San Francisco 49ers, and the Atlanta Falcons. A published cost estimate says the system by Witzel runs $7,200 initially and about $150 per week to actually run it at a local service bureau. An article by Witzel[2] describes his system for play analysis and scouting of prospective college players for the pro draft (discussed below).

More recently, two new systems have been developed. The first of these is Sam Huff's Computerized Scouting System, developed and marketed by Jack Frease of Penn. Scout Corp. Frease uses an IBM Porta-Punch Card (also used in the IBM-developed Votomatic system for election voting). Frease's system accepts up to 40 columns of information in a fixed format. This simplicity allows him to offer the system to a wide range of potential customers for a small cost—$20 to $65 per game depending on the number of reports generated. Each coach has to transform his terminology into that of the input form (sometimes a real difficulty); but the cost factor makes it attractive even down to the high school level. Their output looks similar to other typical play analysis programs, but is of a more general nature. The coach who desires to have specialized output for his staff alone can't be helped here.

The other new approach has been made by Dr. Frank Ryan, great quarterback for the Cleveland Browns in the '60s and now with the Washington Redskins. Ryan's concept was to

---

[2] Witzel, William L., "Computer Programs in Professional Football." *Modern Data*, February 1968.

STANFORD UNIVERSITY FOOTBALL PLAY ANALYSIS PROGRAM DOWN AND DISTANCE SUMMARY REPORT

| Down | Distance (yards to go) | ALL PLAYS | | | | RUNNING PLAYS | | | | | PASSING PLAYS | | | | | | | |
|---|---|---|---|---|---|---|---|---|---|---|---|---|---|---|---|---|---|---|
| | | No. plays | 1% of all plays | Total yards gain | Avg. yards per play | No. runs | % run plays this D & D | % of all plays runs | Yards gain | Avg. yards per run | No. passes | % pass plays this D & D | % of all plays passes | No. compl | % compl | Yards gain | Avg. yards per attmp | Avg. yards per compl |
| 1 | Short (1–0) | 3 | 4.0% | −2 | −0.7 | 3 | 100.0% | 4.0% | −2 | −0.7 | 0 | 0.0% | 0.0% | 0 | 0.0% | 0 | 0.0 | 0.0 |
| 1 | Normal (10) | 30 | 40.0% | 134 | 4.5 | 19 | 63.3% | 25.3% | 33 | 1.7 | 11 | 36.7% | 14.7% | 6 | 54.5% | 101 | 9.2 | 16.8 |
| 1 | Long (11+) | 1 | 1.3% | 13 | 13.0 | 1 | 100.0% | 1.3% | 13 | 13.0 | 0 | 0.0% | 0.0% | 0 | 0.0% | 0 | 0.0 | 0.0 |
| 2 | Short (1–4) | 6 | 8.0% | 26 | 4.3 | 4 | 66.7% | 5.3% | 13 | 3.3 | 2 | 33.3% | 2.7% | 2 | 100.0% | 13 | 6.5 | 6.5 |
| 2 | Normal (5–7) | 7 | 9.3% | 38 | 5.4 | 1 | 14.3% | 1.3% | 3 | 3.0 | 6 | 85.7% | 8.0% | 4 | 66.7% | 35 | 5.8 | 8.8 |
| 2 | Long (8) | 11 | 14.7% | 38 | 3.5 | 3 | 27.3% | 4.0% | −2 | −0.7 | 8 | 72.7% | 10.7% | 6 | 75.0% | 40 | 5.0 | 6.7 |
| 3 | Short (1–3) | 4 | 5.3% | 1 | 0.3 | 4 | 100.0% | 5.3% | 1 | 0.3 | 0 | 0.0% | 0.0% | 0 | 0.0% | 0 | 0.0 | 0.0 |
| 3 | Normal (4–6) | 0 | 0.0% | 0 | 0.0 | 0 | 0.0% | 0.0% | 0 | 0.0 | 0 | 0.0% | 0.0% | 0 | 0.0% | 0 | 0.0 | 0.0 |
| 3 | Long (7) | 10 | 13.3% | 127 | 12.7 | 0 | 0.0% | 0.0% | 0 | 0.0 | 10 | 100.0% | 13.3% | 8 | 80.0% | 127 | 12.7 | 15.9 |
| 4 | Short (1–) | 1 | 1.3% | 0 | 0.0 | 0 | 0.0% | 0.0% | 0 | 0.0 | 1 | 100.0% | 1.3% | 0 | 0.0% | 0 | 0.0 | 0.0 |
| 4 | Normal (2–5) | 1 | 1.3% | 17 | 17.0 | 0 | 0.0% | 0.0% | 0 | 0.0 | 1 | 100.0% | 1.3% | 1 | 100.0% | 17 | 17.0 | 17.0 |
| 4 | Long (6+) | 1 | 1.3% | 10 | 10.0 | 0 | 0.0% | 0.0% | 0 | 0.0 | 1 | 100.0% | 1.3% | 1 | 100.0% | 10 | 10.0 | 10.0 |

develop a generalized report generating system, where the user composes commands to generate desired reports from the existing data base. His system, called PROBE, was jointly developed between Chi Corp. of Cleveland and Ryan Computer Services. The unusual feature of this system is that it is easily adapted to applications other than football. In fact, their first paying customer was a brokerage firm in Cleveland, which composes commands to generate analyses of stocks.

The programming of Ryan's system involved 10 to 12 people during 1970, was coded in ALGOL 60, and is running on a Univac 1108. To use PROBE one defines a data base with a syntax called DENOTES. Data is then keypunched and read into the data base according to the DENOTES definitions. Commands to generate the desired reports are then accepted. The commands key off terms such as COORDINATE (generate an x-y plot), DISPLAY (histograms), LIST (straight lists with sorted fields), and FIELD (boxed off areas with occurrences in respective areas).

The application of the PROBE system to football play analysis (called PRO-PROBE) is currently being employed by the Washington Redskins. Vince Lombardi believed in the usefulness of computer analysis and managed to have Ryan traded to Washington to work on his play analysis system. Lombardi also served as a vice-president of Ryan Computer Services.

Another football play analysis system that has been accepted by a number of teams is the Computer Stat program of Apex Data Services and headed by Joe Guardino in Los Angeles. They handle the play analysis for the Rams, UCLA, USC, Fullerton, and Long Beach State. Their program was coded in BAL for the 360/30, and involves over 75 different routines. The output is mostly pictorial in the form of field diagrams and graphs. A nice feature of this system is that teams can purchase as many of the reports as they can afford, with prices ranging from $25 to over $300 per week.

*Other football systems.* This past fall many radio stations throughout the country aired a program called "The NFL Computer Game of the Week." An organization called Javelin Sports Corp. obtained a franchise from the NFL for the rights and access to the weekly statistics. They then arranged with Hi-Score Enterprises of Encino, California to write the necessary programs to analyze the statistics and simulate the game. According to Ed Mintz, programmer of the system, the program uses the NFL supplied statistics as a prediction of the tendencies for the current game. The program simply calculates an occurrence based on a random number normalized over the range of possibilities. If a particular team runs 67% of their plays a given way in a situation, then the program will have the play go that same way 67% of the time. The program was in Autocoder and ran on a 360/30 with a 1401 emulator.

Hi-Score has also produced Compu-Sport college team ratings which have appeared along with the AP and UPI ratings in many papers. They have also promoted some sports oriented computer contests in the L.A. area.

Simulation of the football game is also being done by Woroner Productions—the people who put together the simulated Muhammad Ali-Rocky Marciano fight. They are employing the services of Henry Meyer and SPS, Inc. of Miami (a division of United Data Centers). They intend to come up with the alltime great college football team by simulating games as a playoff series. Films of the old teams have been studied to gain tendencies of the past teams. Programming is in SIMSCRIPT and it runs on a CDC 3600 with 64K, using all of core. (The application of Parkinson's Law to computer programs never fails). The program has 148 different tables which contain the various team statistics. Admittedly, they have had a few problems such as taking into account such differences as single and double platoons and the weights of the lines (they were much smaller back in the early days). The future status of the series is in doubt, since the project is curtailed at present (money problems presumably).

Before leaving the area of football it would be a disservice not to mention the work of Bud Goode, a statistics expert associated with John Guedel-Art Linkletter Productions in Beverly Hills, California. He has compiled total game information from almost all the major college football games and all the pro games since 1965. He performs various statistical analyses of the data, such as factor analysis (to determine the relevant dimensions in a sport) and multiple regression analysis (to predict the major criterion measures: percent won/lost, offense, and defense). Univac provides the computer time.

Goode claims that his analysis has determined the relevant variables in most sports which account for almost 100% of the "explanatory" variance. He does not claim to account for the "predictive" or "winning" variance, but still he claims to have 80% success in picking the college and pro games. (Las Vegas had better watch out!) Goode has broadened his statistical coverage from football to basketball (both college and pro), and the Indianapolis 500, pro baseball, PGA golf, soccer, and the National Hockey League.

### TRACK

Track and field is one of the oldest sport categories in existence, with competitions dating back to the early Olympics in Athens (776 B.C.). Help from the computer had to wait a few years—until the mid to late 1960s, when James B. Gardner and the author developed a system for performance measurement and running training using a computer.

Track application, unlike football, is not motivated by economics, since there is virtually no professional track in existence. Our motive in developing a computer application in track and field was personal involvement and interest. What started as a casual interest in examining track statistics turned out to be almost a full time effort to systematize both performance measuring and training.

Performance measuring involves assigning some abstract value to one's performance in track so that these performances may be compared from one event to another. The value typically assigned to the different marks is a numeric score called *points*: the better the performance, the more points are awarded. Almost everyone is familiar with the decathlon in the Olympics and the fact that it is won by the athlete who accumulates the largest point total—the sum of the points awarded for each event.

In 1967, James B. Gardner began examining the existing performance measuring systems (commonly called *scoring tables*). In a desire to develop a system that was more mathematically consistent, he joined with the author to generate a consistent set of scoring tables for the running events in track. By the end of 1969 with three completely different rewrites of the computer program finished, we completed a scoring system that represents a substantial improvement over the other tables currently available.

A technical article[3] which describes the system in detail shows that the points awarded for a given performance can be expressed by:

$$P = A(T_s/T_p - B)$$

where P is the point score for the performance time $T_p$, A and B are constants and $T_s$ is the standard time for a particular event. The ratio $T_s/T_p$ expresses the point score proportionality and establishes the actual point scale. The standard time is established from an analysis of performance for all the distances. The standard time in this system takes into account the delay due to reaction time of the starting signal, the delay due to the acceleration to running speed, and the delay to running around the curves of a track.

With this model, a computer program was written, first in FORTRAN and later in PL/I. The computer runs were made on Stanford's 360/67. (An interesting question often asked is, "How does Jim Ryun's world mile record (3:51.1) compare with his world record for the 1500 meters (3:33.1)?" In our scoring system, these performances differ by only one point.)

An extension to the scoring tables described above is the generation of pacing tables, which are referenced for training. Much general publicity has been made concerning the benefits of jogging, but little has been done to quantitate the amount of training one does in relation to level of ability. The competitive athlete constantly hears about the types of workouts that the world record holders are doing, but has no guidelines to tell him how he should do those types of workouts for *his* level of ability. And how about the high school track coach who has 75 boys out for track? How can he give each one the workout that is just the right amount for his capability?

Questions of this sort are easily answered with the pacing tables. First, one establishes level of ability relative to all the other people from the scoring tables. Then, one simply refers to the pacing table assigned for that point level.

The pacing tables are derived from the scoring table in a straightforward manner. Given one level of ability, say the 500-point level, the pacing table times are computed by taking percentages (dividing by the fraction) of the times for the distances. One can easily obtain the times for the various distances that should be run for the given percentage speeds. The number of repetitions and the amount of suggested rest are also listed. Since the athlete is running less than 100% speed, in his training sessions he is expected to be able to repeat the run more than one time.

There is one pacing table for every 20 points in the scoring table. This gives recommended training schedules for levels of ability ranging from an 8:43 miler to a 3:30 miler (better than the current world record). Given the proper point level, each runner or jogger can easily determine the appropriate level of training which is correct for him.

The recently published book, *Computerized Running Training Programs*, contains both the scoring and pacing tables along with an explanatory text. (The author is currently working on his PhD thesis which involves extensions to these concepts.) Scoring tables for the hurdles and field events will be developed with the hope that the complete tables will become the international standard, replacing the current systems, which are not as mathematically consistent. Work is also under way to determine the true relationship between the number of repetitions performed and the amount of rest taken, so that if one performs more (or less) repetitions or more (or less) rest, the resulting effect can be predicted.

## BASEBALL

The game of baseball can be simulated just like any other two-team sport: the statistics of frequencies of occurrence are compiled, and random variables are chosen to pick game actions from the statistical distributions. This is exactly what was done by an outfit called Computer Research in Sports of Princeton, New Jersey. Through Dick Auerbach of NBC Sports, they arranged to have an all-time World Series, resulting in the simulated best team of the century. Two brothers, Eldon and Harlon Mills, chose eight teams to play in the computer World Series:

  1927  New York Yankees
  1929  Philadelphia Athletics
  1942  St. Louis Cardinals
  1951  New York Giants
  1955  Brooklyn Dodgers
  1961  New York Yankees
  1963  Los Angeles Dodgers
  1969  New York Mets

On seven Saturday mornings preceding the NBC Game of the Week during 1970, results of one of the games were read by Curt Gowdy. The finals were held on September 19, 1970 with the 1927 New York Yankees going against the 1961 New York Yankees. The winner of the game was the 1927 New York Yankees. Of course, the simulation does not mean that the 1927 Yankees are always the best team: it would have been interesting to see how consistent the results would have been running multiple simulations with each team having to win the best four out of seven.

The Mills brothers have written a book[4] concerning computer analysis of baseball statistics. They develop a statistic called the Player Win Average which they contend is the best available measure of the player's ability to help the team win. The computer program written by Computer Research in Sports was in FORTRAN and was run on a local computer.

---

[3]Gardner, James B. and J. Gerry Purdy, "Computer Generated Track Scoring Tables," *Medicine and Science in Sports*, Vol. 2, No. 3, pp. 152-161, Fall, 1970.

[4]Mills, Eldon and Harlon Mills, *Player Win Averages*, A. S. Barnes and Co., 1970.

There have probably been more statistics accumulated for baseball than any other professional sport. You name the category and there is a mountain of statistics about it.

The ultimate in statistical reporting of player data has come about for the Atlanta Braves. Lee Walburn and Bob Hope of the Braves engaged the services of Honeywell in Atlanta to develop a real-time, on-line baseball statistical information system. The program was written in FORTRAN IV for the Honeywell 1648 time-sharing computer with a core of 68K words. Developed by two Honeywell personnel, Gary Williams and Susan Gerald, the program is described by Ms Gerald:

"Information is input to the machine as events occur during the game; game situations have been coded for ease of input—BB signifying base on balls, 1B a single, etc.—and files are instantly updated according to player number. At any point in the game the operator may interrupt the data input to request short statistical print-outs that can include an up-to-the-minute line-up stat sheet or an up-to-date sheet on any player, any combination of players, or the entire team. In addition, the system maintains and will print upon request files of special situations for pitchers and selected batters. Also, the system includes a short routine that will respond to any question in a conversational mode.

"The use of this system has already pointed out several interesting facts about individual players as well as the team as a whole. For example, through comparison of the statistics concerning Braves batting against left-handed pitchers versus batting against right-handed pitchers, we found that our Latin American players as a rule hit better against the right-handed pitchers."

Atlanta feels that the system is both efficient and useful, and Honeywell plans to market it to other teams in pro baseball.

The 1970 All-Star game was composed of players selected by computer processing of punch card ballots by Marden Kane, Inc. Fans filled out the cards, which were tabulated. The National and American Leagues are also looking into the possibilities of preparing their schedules each year by computer, since there is so much trouble with rescheduling due to weather.

The Houston Astros employ a computer to analyze the scouting information on prospective players. The reports are keypunched and processed by their 360 system. (The program was written by a programmer in their accounting department!)

Computerized scoreboards are being developed to present statistics and other information to the fans attending the sports. The Conrac Corporation (hardware) and Information Concepts, Inc. (software) built the scoreboard in the Oakland Coliseum. There are 23,214 individual light bulbs in the board and it takes 1,000,000 watts to operate it for one game. The board is 24 ft. high and 126 ft. long (over 3,000 sq. ft.). An IBM 1130 actually generates the display information sequences, which can be preprogrammed to show lettering and/or animations. The computer also has been programmed to keep track of statistics so that for example, it can display how many balls and strikes have been thrown by each pitcher at any time during the game.

### AUTO RACING

A very interesting application of computers to sports has been in the area of auto racing. The recently built Ontario Motor Speedway contacted the Conrac Corp. (hardware) and Information Concepts, Inc. (software) to construct a display board (similar to the Oakland Athletics') and a real-time measuring system for the track, to the tune of $3.6 million. Antennas are placed in the roadbed of the track, and transmitters—each operating at different frequencies—are attached to each car. Every time the car passes over the antenna, the signal causes an interrupt in the IBM 1130 computer, which stores the clock time (good to 1/1000 of a second) and other information about the car. The system is designed to handle up to eight cars running abreast over the finish line at 200 mph. The 1130 computes elapsed time, velocities, and places. The places are output on three pylons for spectator information. This much of the system was successfully used in the USAC 500 race held in September 1970. The second phase of the system, which includes the 246-ft. long display board, is now under development. Most of the programming was done in FORTRAN, but some assembly language routines were used for character generation on the pylons.

How did the system work in the USAC 500? According to Ray Smartis, vice-president and general manager of the track, "The system performed as designed, and the results were excellent. It is definitely the scoring system of the future."*

---

*Sections on boxing, baseball, rowing, and other sports are in the original article.

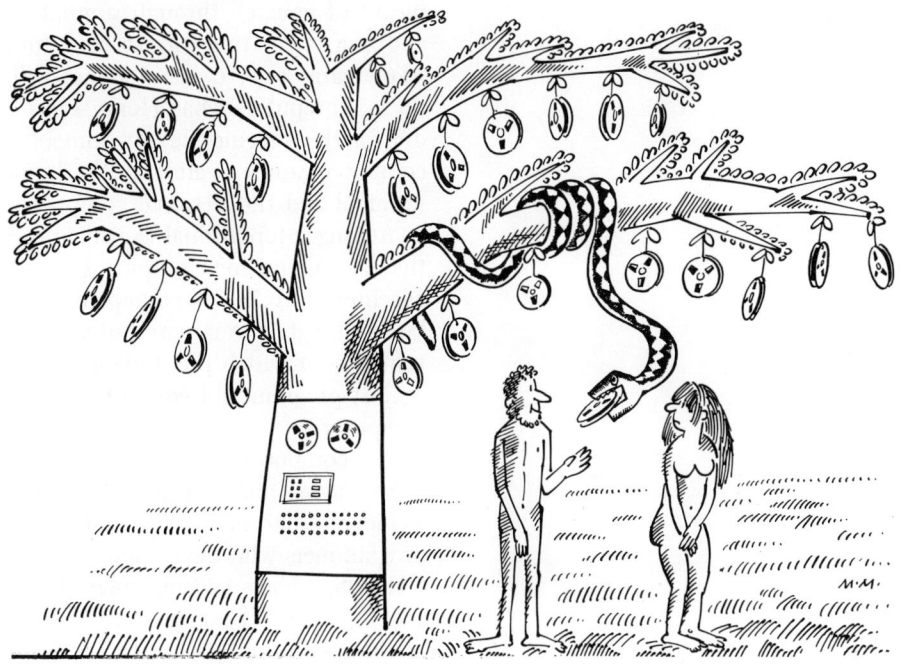

# Computer Games People Play

*Infosystems*

Computer games are opening new doors for equipment and software sales while painlessly teaching computer programming. During the next decade computer simulation and games will become a foundation for education and business management.

Everyone plays games. Psychologists claim all human activity is a form of game playing. Sociologists say even business activity is game playing, more specifically, a highly stylized derivation of primitive hunter societies.

People tend to think in terms of games. Salesmen say, "I'm in the selling game." The most popular form of recreation is sports, in particular, football.

Mention computer games and you get a variation of reactions depending upon individual interest, business, or social requirements. To the military, computer games mean everything from war games to the deadly game of *What If* played by every nuclear power. The sociologist's computer games are a sophisticated method of studying the activities of man.

Medical researchers use computer games to study everything from reaction time to the basic functions of the human brain. Computer games are as yet an almost untapped source of information and interaction for self-teaching which could expand human and computer intelligence.

The computer game has already reached a level of sophistication that led to the formation of game networks, international game societies, game publications, dozens of game books, and game companies.

Thanks to a scattering of dedicated individuals in business, education and government, computer games are rapidly improving as a means of research through simulation and as a fascinating way to have fun. Many game experts claim games will do for computers what Henry Ford did for the automobile. At home, computer games await only the home terminal and the personal computer.

Among international organizations, the Association for Computing Machinery (ACM) is perhaps best known for its annual computer chess tournament which pits program against program and computer against computer.

Are computers good chess players? "Try playing one," suggests Joseph Winograd, one of five Sperry-Univac programmers who developed CHAOS, a chess program played by a Univac 1108. "If you are just average at the game you may well lose," says Winograd. "Computers today can play at the C or average player level. Our program has won more than half of its games against human players."

Winograd claims computers may play at the expert level in 10 years. "This is possible," he asserts, "because we still have lots of spare power and during the next decade we can expect machines to be more powerful."

How does a computer play chess? Basically, the positions are assigned numerical values. The program instructs the computer how to choose a single move, called a "half-move" or "ply" by evaluating goals and subgoals in a network of decision making. Most programs look about five half-moves ahead, examining only a few best alternatives and their consequences in depth, by applying selective chess principles. This may typically involve some 5,000 alternatives out of 30 million possibilities.

"Computers can be polite adversaries, even suggesting possible moves to an opponent if this is requested," says Winograd. "But they act with devastating swiftness if a piece is left unguarded and they show a relentless will to win."

Univac's CHAOS hasn't been too successful in the great battle of computer chess, however. Last August at the annual conference of the ACM, CHAOS lost in the fourth and final round to a Control Data 6400 and a program called CHESS written by a team from Northwestern University.

**Many game experts claim games will do for computers what Henry Ford did for the automobile.**

It was the fourth consecutive chess tournament win for the Northwestern team of Larry Atkins, Keith Gorlen, and David Slate. Other runners-up with Univac's CHAOS were OSTRICH, a Data General Supernova program from Columbia University, and TECH II, a PDP-10 program from Massachusetts Institute of Technology.

The chess tournaments among computers aren't actually all that involved in teaching humans. "They may teach a little programming," says an ACM officer, "but the computer chess game against another computer is little more than a challenge of computer power against programming variations."

## GAMES TEACH PROGRAMMING

More direct games of man against computer, or man against man via the computer, represent the new direction of computer simulation games.

In his book, *Game Playing with Computers*, Donald G. Spencer says, "Game programs provide excellent situations for learning computer programming. The beginning programmer can understand the problem to be programmed in a minimum of time; therefore, he can devote more time to learning the computer, the programming language and the techniques of problem solving with a computer."

Spencer asks, "Why are computers used to play games?" His own answer, "Well, games are fun to play and are often good analogies to actual situations involving human beings and their environment." Games are being applied to business management and strategy. Business executives are playing games with computers that simulate the operations of their business. Researchers are using computers to conduct studies into the strategies of gambling and betting systems.

Since the introduction of computers to gambling statistics and logic, the rules have changed at some Las Vegas games to stop the winner with connections . . . to a computer terminal. This came after several gambling houses lost a tremendous amount of money to a few sharp mathematicians.

According to most computer game program writers and game creators, the most popular form of play for the computer is for it to participate in the game as an actual player. In this type of game the human player indicates each of his moves to the computer on an input device—usually a teleprinter. The computer then computes its move and reports that move to its human competitor. The computer always keeps score by recording both the computer's and human's move.

To be sure, this activity somewhat simulates the action of a human player. However, there are many different possible moves in a game. In fact, there are millions of possible solutions resulting from just a few moves in a game such as chess. Even one move in chess can result in 10 to the 40th power in possible moves. The computer cannot analyze all possible sequences of moves in the known solution games, especially where there is a time limit between moves.

## SIMULATION TEACHES MANAGEMENT

Computers are also playing simulation games to help people learn how to run their businesses, the U.S. economy, and the world in terms of international trade and its effects on corporate income.

One of the best examples of computer games that play economic simulation games is at the Stanford University Graduate School of Business. Under the direction of Dr. William F. Sharpe, graduate students in a macroeconomics course are simulating the management of an entire national economy under varying conditions of money supply, tax rates and government expenditures.

In addition to its economics course, the Stanford business school's computer system is serving the students as an on-line information system, assisting in the solution of typical business management problems.

The system consists of a Hewlett-Packard 2000-C timeshare computer with 25 terminals. Each terminal is available to students on a first-come, first-served basis, allowing each student to communicate with the computer as a personal computer.

Program storage within the system is sufficient to allow each student user to have his own assigned space within the computer's memory. Students can develop programs and save them for later use. The students' programs are keyed to their individual entry codes so only the individual student can execute, copy or list them.

All the graduate school programs are in BASIC to allow simple line-by-line checking during entry and to eliminate the need for repeat cycles throughout the programs.

According to Dr. Sharpe, the economics program as a model allows the students to operate a business in a living, changing economic situation and to test, evaluate and study a variety of business methods.

Almost all large corporations are involved in some sort of market forecasting. Large multinational organizations often combine the world's recent economic history with weather data, agricultural forecasts, stock market trends and a dash of political "guesstimating" to obtain fairly accurate projections of marketing goals, raw material needs, income and profits.

Perhaps the most ambitious use of computers and computer games is in the rapidly developing area of computer games to stimulate children and teach them about computers and about their world via computers.

At present the most ambitious of

COMPUTER GAMES PEOPLE PLAY  51

**If the predictions of Albrecht and other innovative leaders in computer game development are accurate, computer skills will be as common as riding a bicycle.**

such projects is at the Lawrence Hall of Science (LHS) at the University of California in Berkeley.

What started as a relatively small research project on the part of a few physics professors from Berkeley Campus has now mushroomed into a full computer education and service project—staffed largely by UC students and offering a variety of computer classes, public access to terminals, and a low-cost time sharing service for educational users.

LHS is unique to the Bay Area, and perhaps to the world, as a place where a large number of people have first-hand exposure and hands-on access to computers at a very low cost. The main goal is a concept called computer literacy which involves educating children and adults about computers.

The center has created a non-threatening, non-punative, intriguing learning environment where people are introduced to computers as simulators, gaming opponents, problem solving tools and artistic media rather than data banks, number crunchers, data processors, or cybernetic electronic monsters. For most children, this approach seems only natural, but for most adults this is an eye-opening revelation.

Just inside the entrance to the Lawrence Hall of Science is a collection of four CRT terminals usually crowded with children and adults. The CRT terminals are connected to a Hewlett-Packard 2000B and Decision computer and operate some unusual programs.

One terminal is dedicated to controlling an electronic tone box located above the terminal. Programs are available to permit the user to compose and play his own music.

Two other terminals play games. Among the selection are such games as BAGELS, a number-logic game; HANG, the old game of hangman; LEM, a simulated lunar landing; and GUESS, a number guessing game.

The fourth terminal in the public area contains a program called ELIZA in which the computer carries on a seemingly intelligent dialogue with the user. It is modeled after the original ELIZA program developed by Joseph Weisenbaum at MIT. It is a fast way for children and adults to learn that computers aren't intelligent. Despite the large number of children clustered around the ELIZA terminal whenever the hall is open, even the beginning readers can guess it is responding to code words after operating the terminal a few minutes.

The Lawrence Hall of Science makes the terminals available free to anyone visiting the hall. For a large number of visitors, these are the only interactive computer terminals they have ever used.

In addition to the pre-programmed displays in the public area, LHS is in its second year of supplying computer time to the general public for 75 cents an hour on a first-come, first-served basis. Twenty teletype terminals in two computer classrooms are offered, ten units on weekday afternoons and all twenty on weekends. The terminals are connected to a Decision computer and have full access to the LHS program library.

An LHS staff member is always on duty to answer questions and help the users learn. People using these terminals do everything from playing games and drawing pictures to writing programs for their own research or entertainment.

LHS officials say during the school year they log an average of 150 terminal hours per week and more than 200 terminal hours per week during

Even if you're not quite five you can have fun with computers.

the summer. Another LHS project, a school visitation program, introduces Bay Area students in grades four through eight to computers. During the school year about 200 children per week participate in discovery workshops on computers.

LHS also has over 30 educational users using the Decision and HP 2000B computers. Many of the users are on the Berkeley Campus. Others are located at area colleges, high schools and junior high schools in northern California. The program has been so successful that a Montessori school in San Francisco is using the computer terminal as an integral teaching aid for students as young as four years old.

Honeywell has also recently jumped into the computer information game with an extensive display of public operated terminals at the Boston Museum of Science.

The focal point is a Honeywell minicomputer connected to seven CRT terminals. The compact 2000 sq. ft. display area also contains a number of graphic panels explaining computers and their history.

C. W. Spangle, Honeywell executive vice president, says the purpose of the exhibit is to allow visitors "to get acquainted with one of the most widely used—and yet the least understood—of today's technological achievements."

Museum visitors can operate the terminals to play games, make math calculations and retrieve information about the museum, thus allowing visitors to learn the machine's capabilities and how it works.

Though not devoted strictly to computer games, Clark C. Abt's book, *Serious Games,* covers everything from improving education with games and how to think with games by designing them, to games for planning and problem solving in government and industry.

With frightening clarity, Abt says the adult activity most clearly analogous to games is warfare. "Wars are obviously very costly and not practically subject to experimentation," says Abt. "But, they are competitive activities on the largest scale, in which adversary decision makers contest objectives within the limits of their will and resources."

According to Abt, there is no

reason why the learning, analysis and planning of elaborate and detailed processes in the form of games should be limited to military problems. He says political and social situations can often be thought of as games.

## HUNTINGTON TEACHING GAMES

The federal government, and in particular the National Science Foundation, has contributed to computer game teaching methods with the funding of the Huntington Project which has developed and distributed the most comprehensive set of computer simulation programs written in BASIC.

The single most important feature of the programs is that they use a rather standard simple BASIC programming form without string variables or files. This means most minicomputer systems can run them provided they have memory space.

Most of the Huntington Project programs take about 1500 to 2000 words. Each program includes a small amount of documentation outlining possible objectives, preliminary preparation, discussion topics and follow-up suggestions. A run of each program is also included so teachers can see what the program does.

Huntington II is the second National Science Foundation funded package of BASIC programs for school use. More than 200 schools around the country have tested the programs. Many instructors and computer simulation-games experts claim they are among the best available programs for introducing the computer to the classroom.

Each of the Huntington II programs is available with a resource handbook, which is a minicomputer textbook that tells the student all about the subject of simulation and how it relates to the individual teaching program. Also included are computer laboratory guides which provide the student with a series of recommended learning activities to try on the computer.

Though the Huntington programs make use of games for teaching and are among the best of the readily available teaching games, there is a startling, relatively new movement which may revolutionize man's concept of the computer.

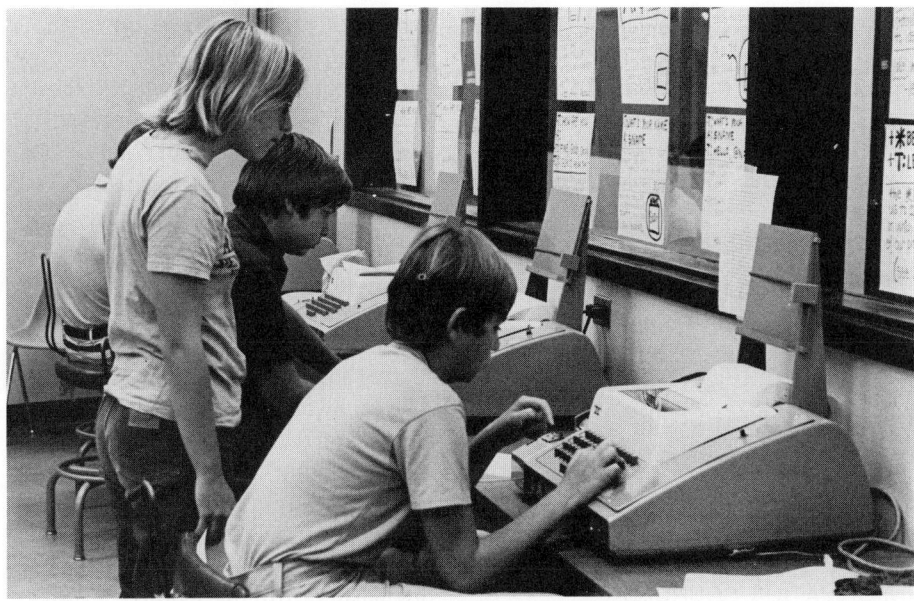
Classes in "creative play with the computer" introduce children to a fascinating technology.

## COMPUTER GAMES FOR FUN

Corporate drop-outs, free-lance programmers, even school children are organizing computer games information exchanges, publications and centers where people can play with computers.

Hundreds of school children, college students, even some teachers first learned about computer games and playing with computers for fun from a most unusual bi-monthly newspaper called *Peoples Computer Company*.

What this non-profit, free-form newspaper lacks in literary style and composition, it makes up in creativity, imagination in teaching BASIC program and a wealth of information about teaching programs, new computer games, articles about games around the world, and in general, what's happening in the computer game.

Bob Albrecht, PCC's founder and publisher, can be described in many ways. Corporate drop-out, computer game drop-in, teacher and innovater, Albrecht has advanced degrees in applied math and an extensive background as a systems analyst with big name computer companies. He is the author of several articles and books on computer assisted teaching and computer games. His most noteworthy publishing venture to date, other than PCC, is a small illustrated book called, *My Computer Likes Me*. In nononsense straightforward language and profuse illustrations, the book teaches basic BASIC to almost anyone who can read.

Along with the newspaper *Peoples Computer Company*, there is a Peoples Computer Center located in a former hardware store on a quiet back street in Menlo Park, CA. The center contains on-line terminals for game playing and for inexpensive by-the-hour programming by students from local schools and members of PCC informal computer classes.

The games, played via teletype terminal, include math games, space war games, ("Kill the invaders and get rid of your hostilities," says Albrecht), space exploration and economic games. (Star-Trader is a game of intergalactic commerce designed to teach economics and the fundamentals of terminal operation.)

When asked to describe PCC's basic goals as a newspaper and computer-game-playing-teaching center, Albrecht answered, "Have fun. Most people think of computers as some awe inspiring mechanical brain that requires a genius to operate. By teaching kids to play games we get them involved in something they understand (playing a game and knowing the rules) and operating a terminal becomes second nature. We strive for a very informal sort of teaching arrangement. I don't think the computer will ever amount to much as an autocratic electronic instructor that plays guess the right answer

### WHERE TO FIND INFORMATION ON COMPUTER GAMES

#### BOOKS

**Serious games**
Clark C. Abt
The Viking Press
New York, 1970

**Game Playing With Computers**
Donald D. Spencer
Spartan Books
New York, 1968

**My Computer Likes Me**
Dymax
Menlo Park, CA 1972

#### INFORMATION SOURCES

Peoples Computer Company
  (the newspaper)
and Peoples Computer Center
Box 310
Menlo Park, CA 94025

Computer Chess
Association for Computing Machinery
Box 4566
Atlanta, GA 30302

Lawrence Hall of Science
University of California
Berkeley, CA 94720

and rewards the student with a flashing display of 'Right, Billy!' when a kid's pushed the right button," explains Albrecht.

"Our concept of computer games allows the student, adult or child, to have fun. They can write their own programs if they want to. Usually after they play a game for awhile they begin to understand how the computer functions. Pretty soon they are into writing their own programs. We have kids in the fourth grade writing programs. In fact, one of our simpler program writing games, INCHWORM, doesn't require a computer or terminal," says Albrecht.

INCHWORM, Albrecht's brainchild, is played with a simple drawing of a large square divided into several smaller squares similar to a chessboard. The inchworm, a mythical bug, is programmed to move from one square to another with simple instructions. Moves are either north, south, east or west. A move from the top left of the square to the center of a box with 25 squares would be indicated by a program of east, east, south, south. To make the game more complex, the box is blocked off into a maze and students are asked to program a route through the maze from one point to another.

"We run learning games, like INCHWORM, in the newspaper and we're developing an INCHWORM workbook," says Albrecht. "It doesn't take long to teach simplified BASIC this way. Then we can help students learn more advanced programming and get them to be conversant with the computer with as much ease as they would learn to play baseball or use a typewriter."

There is another monthly tabloid publication for computer game programmers, players and those interested in games for teaching purposes, called *Simulation/Gaming/News*. It's published in Moscow, Idaho, by Don H. Coombs and about 19 other contributing editors throughout the country. The newspaper contains information about computer game books, symposiums, new simulation programs and teaching games. It also acts as an information sounding board for those interested in simulation games.

Bob Albrecht, also a contributing editor to *Simulation/Gaming/News*, says SGN covers everything from the development of the U.S. Army simulation game programs to the very simple basic games for children. "Anyone interested in computer games or simulation games should read SGN," says Albrecht.

Almost everyone involved in computer games agrees that growing consumer interest in computer games for entertainment will lead to vast technological leaps in the development of home computer terminals and television connected computer games. "The computer terminal is just beginning to move into the classroom as a generally available tool," says Albrecht. "Since kids have no hang-ups about the awesomeness of the computer, they tend to learn more quickly."

Computer simulation to create real life economic, social, political or military situations are an accurate, timely, relatively inexpensive and safe method of forecasting statistical analysis.

If the predictions of Albrecht and other innovative leaders in computer game development are accurate, computer skills will be as common as riding a bicycle.

"I don't know the man personally ... we share the same computer."

# The Nine Billion Names of God

ARTHUR C. CLARKE

"This is a slightly unusual request," said Dr. Wagner, with what he hoped was commendable restraint. "As far as I know, it's the first time anyone's been asked to supply a Tibetan monastery with an automatic sequence computer. I don't wish to be inquisitive, but I should hardly have thought that your—ah—establishment had much use for such a machine. Could you explain just what you intend to do with it?"

"Gladly," replied the lama, readjusting his silk robe and carefully putting away the slide rule he had been using for currency conversions. "Your Mark V computer can carry out any routine mathematical operation involving up to ten digits. However, for our work we are interested in *letters*, not numbers. As we wish you to modify the output circuits, the machine will be printing words, not columns of figures."

"I don't quite understand . . ."

"This is a project on which we have been working for the last three centuries—since the lamasery was founded, in fact. It is somewhat alien to your way of thought, so I hope you will listen with an open mind while I explain it."

"Naturally."

"It is really quite simple. We have been compiling a list which shall contain all the possible names of God."

"I beg your pardon?"

"We have reason to believe," continued the lama imperturbably, "that all such names can be written with not more than nine letters in an alphabet we have devised."

"And you have been doing this for three centuries?"

"Yes. We expected it would take us about fifteen thousand years to complete the task."

"Oh." Dr. Wagner looked a little dazed. "Now I see why you wanted to hire one of our machines. But exactly what is the *purpose* of this project?"

The lama hesitated for a fraction of a second, and Wagner wondered if he had offended him. If so, there was no trace of annoyance in the reply.

"Call it ritual, if you like, but it's a fundamental part of our belief. All the many names of the Supreme Being—God, Jehovah, Allah, and so on—they are only man-made labels. There is a philosophical problem of some difficulty here, which I do not propose to discuss, but somewhere among all the possible combinations of letters which can occur are what one may call the *real* names of God. By systematic permutation of letters, we have been trying to list them all."

"I see. You've been starting at AAAAAAAA . . . and working up to ZZZZZZZZ . . ."

"Exactly—though we use a special alphabet of our own. Modifying the electromatic typewriters to deal with this is, of course, trivial. A rather more interesting problem is that of devising suitable circuits to eliminate ridiculous combinations. For example, no letter must occur more than three times in succession."

"Three? Surely you mean two."

"Three is correct. I am afraid it would take too long to explain why, even if you understood our language."

"I'm sure it would," said Wagner hastily. "Go on."

"Luckily it will be a simple matter to adapt your automatic sequence computer for this work, since once it has been programed properly it will permute each letter in turn and print the result. What would have taken us fifteen thousand years it will be able to do in a hundred days."

Dr. Wagner was scarcely conscious of the faint sounds from the Manhattan streets far below. He was in a different world, a world of natural, not man-made, mountains. High up in their remote aeries these monks had been patiently at work, generation after generation, compiling their lists of meaningless words. Was there any limit to the follies of mankind? Still, he must give no hint of his inner thoughts. The customer was always right . . .

"There's no doubt," replied the doctor, "that we can modify the Mark V to print lists of this nature. I'm much more worried about the problem of installation and maintenance. Getting out to Tibet, in these days, is not going to be easy."

"We can arrange that. The components are small enough to travel by air—that is one reason why we chose your machine. If you can get them to India, we will provide transport from there."

"And you want to hire two of our engineers?"

"Yes, for the three months which the project should occupy."

"I've no doubt that Personnel can manage that." Dr. Wagner scribbled a note on his desk pad. "There are just two other points—"

Before he could finish the sentence the lama had produced a small slip of paper.

"This is my certified credit balance at the Asiatic Bank."

"Thank you. It appears to be—ah—adequate. The second matter is so trivial that I hesitate to mention it—but it's surprising how often the obvious gets overlooked. What source of electrical energy have you?"

"A diesel generator providing 50 kilowatts at 110 volts. It was installed about five years ago and is quite reliable. It's made life at the lamasery much more comfortable, but of course it was really installed to provide power for the motors driving the prayer wheels."

"Of course," echoed Dr. Wagner. "I should have thought of that."

The view from the parapet was vertiginous, but in time one gets used to anything. After three months George Hanley was not impressed by the two-thousand-foot swoop into the abyss or the remote checkerboard of fields in the valley below. He was leaning against the wind-smoothed stones and

staring morosely at the distant mountains whose names he had never bothered to discover.

This, thought George, was the craziest thing that had ever happened to him. "Project Shangri-La," some wit at the labs had christened it. For weeks now the Mark V had been churning out acres of sheets covered with gibberish. Patiently, inexorably, the computer had been rearranging letters in all their possible combinations, exhausting each class before going on to the next. As the sheets had emerged from the electromatic typewriters, the monks had carefully cut them up and pasted them into enormous books. In another week, heaven be praised, they would have finished. Just what obscure calculations had convinced the monks that they needn't bother to go on to words of ten, twenty, or a hundred letters, George didn't know. One of his recurring nightmares was that there would be some change of plan and that the High Lama (whom they'd naturally called Sam Jaffe, though he didn't look a bit like him) would suddenly announce that the project would be extended to approximately 2060 A.D. They were quite capable of it.

George heard the heavy wooden door slam in the wind as Chuck came out onto the parapet beside him. As usual, Chuck was smoking one of the cigars that made him so popular with the monks—who, it seemed, were quite willing to embrace all the minor and most of the major pleasures of life. That was one thing in their favor: they might be crazy, but they weren't bluenoses. Those frequent trips they took down to the village, for instance . . .

"Listen, George," said Chuck urgently. "I've learned something that means trouble."

"What's wrong? Isn't the machine behaving?" That was the worst contingency George could imagine. It might delay his return, than which nothing could be more horrible. The way he felt now, even the sight of a TV commercial would seem like manna from heaven. At least it would be some link with home.

"No—it's nothing like that." Chuck settled himself on the parapet, which was unusual, because normally he was scared of the drop. "I've just found what all this is about."

"What d'ya mean—I thought we knew."

"Sure—we know what the monks are trying to do. But we didn't know *why*. It's the craziest thing—"

"Tell me something new," growled George.

". . . but old Sam's just come clean with me. You know the way he drops in every afternoon to watch the sheets roll out. Well, this time he seemed rather excited, or at least as near as he'll ever get to it. When I told him that we were on the last cycle he asked me, in that cute English accent of his, if I'd ever wondered what they were trying to do. I said, 'Sure'—and he told me."

"Go on, I'll buy it."

"Well, they believe that when they have listed all His names—and they reckon that there are about nine billion of them—God's purpose will be achieved. The human race will have finished what it was created to do, and there won't be any point in carrying on. Indeed, the very idea is something like blasphemy."

"Then what do they expect us to do? Commit suicide?"

"There's no need for that. When the list's completed, God steps in and simply winds things up . . . bingo!"

"Oh, I get it. When we finish our job, it will be the end of the world."

Chuck gave a nervous little laugh.

"That's just what I said to Sam. And do you know what happened? He looked at me in a very queer way, like I'd been stupid in class, and said, 'It's nothing as trivial as *that*.'"

George thought this over for a moment.

"That's what I call taking the Wide View," he said presently. "But what d'ya suppose we should do about it? I don't see that it makes the slightest difference to us. After all, we already knew that they were crazy."

"Yes—but don't you see what may happen? When the list's complete and the Last Trump doesn't blow—or whatever it is they expect—we may get the blame. It's our machine they've been using. I don't like the situation one little bit."

"I see," said George slowly. "You've got a point there. But this sort of thing's happened before, you know. When I was a kid down in Louisiana we had a crackpot preacher who said the world was going to end next Sunday. Hundreds of people believed him—even sold their homes. Yet nothing happened; they didn't turn nasty as you'd expect. They just decided that he'd made a mistake in his calculations and went right on believing. I guess some of them still do."

"Well, this isn't Louisiana, in case you hadn't noticed. There are just two of us and hundreds of these monks. I like them, and I'll be sorry for old Sam when his lifework backfires on him. But all the same, I wish I was somewhere else."

"I've been wishing that for weeks. But there's nothing we can do until the contract's finished and the transport arrives to fly us out."

"Of course," said Chuck thoughtfully, "we could always try a bit of sabotage."

"Like hell we could! That would make things worse."

"Not the way I meant. Look at it like this. The machine will finish its run four days from now, on the present twenty-hours-a-day basis. The transport calls in a week. O.K., then all we need do is to find something that wants replacing during one of the overhaul periods—something that will hold up the works for a couple of days. We'll fix it, of course, but not too quickly. If we time matters properly, we can be down at the airfield when the last name pops out of the register. They won't be able to catch us then."

"I don't like it," said George. "It will be the first time I ever walked out on a job. Besides, it would make them suspicious. No, I'll sit tight and take what comes."

"I *still* don't like it," he said seven days later, as the tough little mountain ponies carried them down the winding road. "And don't you think I'm running away because I'm afraid. I'm just sorry for those poor old guys up there, and I don't want to be around when they find what suckers they've been. Wonder how Sam will take it?"

"It's funny," replied Chuck, "but when I said goodbye I got the idea he knew we were walking out on him—and that he didn't care because he knew the machine was running smoothly and that the job would soon be finished. After that—well, of course, for him there just isn't any After That . . ."

George turned in his saddle and stared back up the mountain road. This was the last place from which one could get a clear view of the lamasery. The squat, angular buildings were silhouetted against the afterglow of the sunset; here and there lights gleamed like portholes in the sides of an ocean liner. Electric lights, of course, sharing the same circuit as the Mark V. How much longer would they share it? wondered George. Would the monks smash up the computer in their rage and disappointment? Or would they just sit down quietly and begin their calculations all over again?

He knew exactly what was happening up on the mountain at this very moment. The High Lama and his assistants would be sitting in their silk robes, inspecting the sheets as the junior monks carried them away from the typewriters and pasted them into the great volumes. No one would be saying anything. The only sound would be the incessant patter, the never-ending rainstorm, of the keys hitting the paper, for the Mark V itself was utterly silent as it flashed through its thousands of calculations a second. Three months of this, thought George, was enough to start anyone climbing up the wall.

"There she is!" called Chuck, pointing down into the valley. "Ain't she beautiful!"

She certainly was, thought George. The battered old DC-3 lay at the end of the runway like a tiny silver cross. In two hours she would be bearing them away to freedom and sanity. It was a thought worth savoring like a fine liqueur. George let it roll around his mind as the pony trudged patiently down the slope.

The swift night of the high Himalayas was now almost upon them. Fortunately the road was very good, as roads went in this region, and they were both carrying torches. There was not the slightest danger, only a certain discomfort from the bitter cold. The sky overhead was perfectly clear and ablaze with the familiar, friendly stars. At least there would be no risk, thought George, of the pilot being unable to take off because of weather conditions. That had been his only remaining worry.

He began to sing but gave it up after a while. This vast arena of mountains, gleaming like whitely hooded ghosts on every side, did not encourage such ebullience. Presently George glanced at his watch.

"Should be there in an hour," he called back over his shoulder to Chuck. Then he added, in an afterthought, "Wonder if the computer's finished its run? It was due about now."

Chuck didn't reply, so George swung round in his saddle. He could just see Chuck's face, a white oval turned toward the sky.

"Look," whispered Chuck, and George lifted his eyes to heaven. (There is always a last time for everything.)

Overhead, without any fuss, the stars were going out.

# Promise-child in the Land of the Humans

GREGORY BENFORD
and
DAVID BOOK

How shall we react to the real computer revolution, when the machines will not only think but reproduce themselves?

It has happened to nearly everybody by now. Your utility bill arrives. It says you have used 1,546,589 gallons of water, at a cost of $2,847.17.

When this happens, some people are outraged. Others don't care, and assume the error will be corrected. Quite a few of us laugh, enjoying a good joke at the expense of a machine. One reason for the mirth may be that we are just a little afraid of computers.

Man is undoubtedly master of the world, unique unto himself, but ever since the Copernican revolution his self-image has taken a beating. First he learned that the earth was not the center of the universe, then that the sun wasn't either. Darwin put Man among the primates and research is showing signs that we have basic, instinctual portions of our character that seem unalterable.

Novelist John Barth's wry dictum, "Self-knowledge is always bad news," may well apply to Man's quest for an understanding of his place in the universe. In the next few decades our society is going to test this in a way few would have imagined even 30 years ago. We will have to learn to live with another intelligent species, one of our own making: computers.

Sometime around 1978, a new appliance, the home computer, will begin to appear in American homes. Using existing telephone lines, it will probably be no larger than a suitcase with a display screen, a typewriter console and numerous buttons. Like the telephone, the home console will be only the visible tip of a vast electronic iceberg. It will be a remote segment of a network centered on a distant electronic data processor uniting the roles of switchboard, storehouse and calculator. What is called "real-time operation" makes this arrangement possible. The central data processor will handle each customer's job in bits and pieces, sharing its operation among many customers simultaneously.

Each home console will seem to command the entire system. In effect, the user will gain an intelligent assistant who can perform tasks with lightning speed. Already used widely in research, this setup lets the user develop "cut-and-try" solutions until he can clarify the problem in his own mind. In the home it will present a ready-made package of services and show him how to improve on these to meet his needs.

The overwhelming lesson city planners will have to learn is this: It is easier to move information than people. Whenever possible, computer services should go to the people, rather than the other way around. In the 1980s, remote consoles will be as common as desk calculators are now. Not only engineers and scientists, but clerks, bookkeepers and many salesmen will be free to work almost entirely at home, using computers, teleprinters and face-to-face television. Service occupations—at least the ones which rely on supplying ideas and information—will become decentralized, relieving some of the pressure that leads to urbanization.

Around 1980 the home-computer terminal will acquire a printout device. Some laboratories are experimenting with a new process based on today's ubiquitous Xerox-type photocopiers. The home terminal will make a copy on real paper, electrostatically "fixing" graphite into letters on the page. It may even bind pages together like a book. The home printer will introduce a new age of communications.

Another rule to be learned is that paper is heavier than electrons. Eventually the Post Office Department will become obsolete (some readers will find this a pleasant prospect, considering the current quality of service). After all, what is the point of logging your water-consumption rate into a computer, having it print out the bill, and then sending the piece of paper on which it is typed through the mails, where it must be carried by hand?

It seems far easier to let electrical impulses, flowing from the computer through your telephone wire, carry the message. It can be printed out on your home photocopier and paid if you find no error. In fact, why not take it one step further? Unless you respond to the bill, it will be charged by computer against your bank balance. This way a correct bill needs no reply at all.

Anything in print can follow the same course. No longer the *thunk* of a soggy newspaper into your prize rosebushes—just request that your copy be printed out every morning by 8 A.M. What can be done with bills and newspapers can be done just as easily with books from a computer library, magazines and even personal letters. The only thing transmitted from one point to another will be information, impressed into the oscillations of electrons. Delivery will be instantaneous.

The next step will most likely be the fully computerized home—a kind of inhabited robot. It is impractical to build individual appliances with self-contained circuitry more intricate than that required to allow an oven to turn itself off when the roast is done. That's why we will never have vacuum cleaners that clean the house by themselves or dishwashers that clear the table, wash and put away the dishes where they belong. These tasks require too many decision processes and too many different operations to build into a small inexpensive machine. But wire all the household gadgets to a large flexible computer, and they become a staff of docile chambermaids and kitchen knaves.

Take vacuuming, for example. Suppose that underneath the rug there is a grid of wires through which a tiny current flows. Suppose the chairs and tables and other furniture have metal plates in their legs and bases, each of a different size or shape. Lying above the grid, these plates respond to the current in the floor by developing induced currents. They in turn react back on the grid. The resulting disturbances in the grid current can be analyzed to show exactly where each object is standing. Now, imagine a self-propelling steerable vacuum cleaner controlled by the central computer. If the computer reads the location of each object in the room from the grid current, it can guide the cleaner around the room, avoiding furniture without missing part of the rug.

The beauty of this design is its simplicity and flexibility. No expensive machinery is needed in the individual home. The householder can arrange for computer control of almost any chore, from mowing the lawn to opening the door for his cat. The same computer service that prints the news and keeps the budget can also handle a houseful of automatic appliances.

Such are the conventional wonders of the near computer age. But the computer is certain to have an even greater impact on our lives. Like women, computers make excellent servants but they are far more interesting as companions and equals. And that is precisely the future that faces us. Virtually all computer experts are agreed that we have only about 15 years until an essentially new form of intelligent life is born on this planet: a self-programming machine.

The public got its first taste of this in the Stanley Kubrick and Arthur C. Clarke film, *2001: A Space Odyssey*, where they met HAL, the first literally superhuman character ever made believable. HAL stands for *H*euristically programmed *AL*gorithmic computer, which simply means that HAL can teach himself how to do new things, just as a man does. As he learns, he grows new neural networks to cope with his new functions; thus, he is more adaptable than the spacemen around him. But his trump card is his control of the life-support systems of the ship. He knows his way around the ship better than the men do and can anticipate what they are going to do.

**WILL YOU BECOME EXPENDABLE?**
It seems likely that a machine such as HAL will be in operation by 2001. Even before that time, HAL-like computers will have assumed a major part of our economic management

*Drawings by John Huehnergarth*

We will have to live with another intelligent species.

Man's ultimate place in a man/machine world?

and their influence will give Man additional cause to wonder about his ultimate place in a man/machine world.

Thus far, computers have supplanted men only in rote jobs. It is quite easy to control lathes and other shop machines with computers which can do *only* that. But as the years pass, analysts will reduce one job after another to its essentials, program it and turn it over to a box of electronics—which doesn't hanker after coffee breaks, cost-of-living raises, expense accounts or retirement benefits—and doesn't get sick.

How far will this process go? The answer depends both on the ultimate cost of computer components and on the types of jobs that will exist in the future. That computerized water bill casts a long shadow—it is not hard to foresee almost all accounting operations taking place deep in transistorized innards, rather than in a ledger or cash register. But other occupations are not so simple to analyze. It is natural to think first about one's own job, so you might try this simple problem in systems analysis. First, break your job down into two categories, *operations* and *decisions*. Operations are what you must do physically to accomplish your daily tasks. This might be as easy as picking up a pencil, or as strenuous as climbing on steel girders. Decisions are judgments you make, like weighing the advantages of different sales procedures, the abilities of people competing for a promotion, or the effectiveness of a certain tool in cutting a metal die.

Experience has taught us that any repetitive physical process can be controlled by a computer. The important point is that the job be predictable. This means that a limited number of factors describe it, and they are of the sort that can be written down. For instance, computer-operated lathes need only to measure the dimensions of the metal rods they are to cut, and elementary (though tedious) arithmetic can tell the machine which bit and angle to use.

The same rule of thumb holds for decision making: If it is possible to write down a set of rules describing the process, a computer can reproduce it. Computers already can decide with surprising skill when to update an inventory, how to set a column of type, what move to make in a chess game or a stock-market situation.

So this is what it boils down to: Can you imagine a machine built to carry out the same operations you carry out yourself? Can you *tell* someone how to make your decisions, can you draw up a set of rules that will enable him to make them without help? If the answer to both questions is yes, you might start thinking about alternative careers.

But what about innovations and creative arts? It may prove simple to design a machine that will, say, minimize the number of trips a delivery truck makes. It is thus far impossible to program a computer to decide spontaneously in the interests of efficiency that the delivery service should join a conglomerate which will sell it packaging materials at a discount.

To be sure, a computer might reach just such a decision if its designers set out to give it that ability. But then it is doing nothing more than it has been told to do. We have yet to demonstrate undeniable creativity in a machine. Some people insist that we never will.

As always, the issue will turn on precise definitions. We do not understand the creative process in human beings, so it is doubtful that we will have the wisdom to build it into machines with forethought. The art of doing something for the first time seems to stem from a certain freedom of choice in the intellect, and it is just this element that has been missing in computers so far.

### WILL POETS BECOME EXPENDABLE?

But things will not remain that way. Within ten years the world champion chess player will certainly be a computer program—one is already ranked quite high in competitive play. Some might argue that playing chess is not particularly creative, but few would say the same about writing novels or poetry. Yet computers now can write simple poems—quite bad ones,

Can a computer recognize an oddball chair?

THE SOFTWARE

granted—but they are improving all the time.

The usual argument against the possibility of machine creativity stems from a simple analogy with the human brain. There are several million million neural connections in the human brain. This is almost a million times the number in the biggest present-day computer. It is unlikely that even the year 2000 will see a machine with this many connections.

But this argument is too simple-minded. Writing a poem doesn't occupy all of the brain. The first sonnet-writing program or computerized music arranger will devote itself to its specialty with a fanatic's disregard for all other intellectual pursuits, even closely related art forms. And not all creative activities make the same demands on the creator. The difficulty of a particular achievement reflects the number of choices and steps involved, the number of possible alternative concepts. This is why serious literary critics have little regard for whodunits. But by the same token, in a decade or two, research laboratories may well have programmed computers to write acceptable potboiler detective novels. By the time that happens, the smug voices now predicting that computers will never be truly creative may have a strained edge to them.

Even so there remains the question of taste. It may seem absurd, now, to apply such a term to a work of copper and germanium elements, but there is a distinct possibility that this problem will face us quite soon. What if a computer does write a sonnet some bright spring morning in 1987? Will it "feel right"? Will it be good, not only by the standards of a program a scientist has written, but by literary standards? Will this sonnet have the power to move us emotionally?

The answer depends on whether it is possible to write instructions that tell a machine how to anticipate the emotional reactions of people to what it has written. Perhaps there is a basic difference between organic and electronic "personalities." Our brains are controlled by the secretions of glands; the sight of a leopard creeping toward us through the grass causes adrenalin to pump in-

Writing a poem doesn't occupy all of the brain.

voluntarily into our blood streams, changing our thought patterns and emotional balance. Computers have no such mechanism (to say the least).

But they may be programmed so that they *appear* to. This question of appearances is really the crux of the matter. Computers do not duplicate human behavior, they *simulate* it. A machine that can tell a hawk from a handsaw does it by following a complicated set of instructions, contrasting the light and dark areas, rotating the object to obtain a full view, and comparing it with the inventory of images it has seen before. The human mind does something of this sort, too, but in a manner not as yet understood.

The problem is to make a selection of what is essential to the image, to look at trees and somehow see a forest or an orchard. If you see something with three legs and upholstered in fur, do you *know* that it is a chair? How do you program a computer to recognize it? One approach is to sample the image by viewing it through templates. These mask all but an irregularly shaped portion, different for each template, so that only a little light reaches a photodetector. The computer records the amount of light passed by each template—perhaps several hundred entries—and compares this set of numbers with those corresponding to previously scanned images of a man, a table, a chair, a house, etc. The computer performs statistical comparison tests to see which "memory" the present image most resembles. It is just as if the six blind men trying to "see" an elephant by touch had gotten together and recorded all their impressions, and called *that* a description of an elephant.

It is doubtful that this kind of perception is much like our own visual sense. That doesn't matter. Scientists are content to design a computer that can do a given task; they cannot guarantee that it will do it the same way we do. Curiously, what for us is a simple reflex—recognition of an acquaintance—is very difficult for computers. No machine program can yet faultlessly recognize an individual if he is in a crowd, or if the lighting is not just right, of if his appearance is altered by the addition of a hat or a cigar.

This points up the limitations of today's computers compared to those expected in the future. For what it is worth, few of the men who devised the first computers in the early 1940s foresaw the uses of today. Then the machines were idiot savants, performing the laborious calculations needed by scientists. In their dealings with human beings, these machines still resemble small children, barely able to tell friend from foe.

Soon they will be able to do many things better—or at least cheaper, which is almost the same thing—than men. How mankind reacts to their progress, along with the inventiveness of the scientists, will determine their development from that point onward. Medicine is a good example. Electronic processing of hospital records and accounts is now commonplace. Computers can direct a laboratory doing routine tests like urinalysis and blood typing as easily as they can run

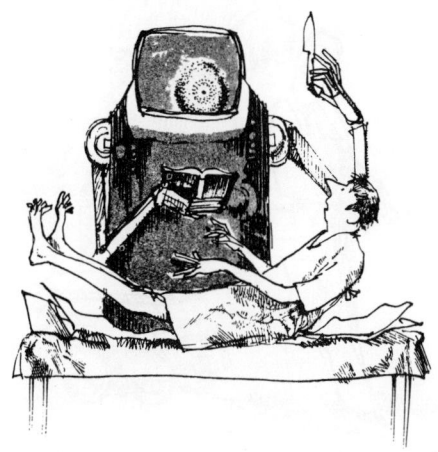

The big step in replacing physicians.

**But as the years pass, analysts will reduce one job after another to its essentials, program it and turn it over to a box of electronics—which doesn't hanker after coffee breaks, cost-of-living raises, expense accounts or retirement benefits—and doesn't get sick.**

a machine shop. They can "take a history" of newly admitted patients, recording the answers to yes or no questions about their past record of illness and symptoms. Several experimental systems developed for this purpose are already working in England and the United States.

The big step is in replacing physicians. It is one thing to have a machine down the hall examine your blood; it is another to let it actually touch you. Would any sufferer permit a machine to diagnose his illness, much less prescribe drugs or perform surgery? We think the answer is yes. The key is gradualism. As medical computers become more familiar and people gain confidence in them, the natural feeling of distrust will vanish.

But Man's ego rests on a precarious sense of his own worthiness, and much of his self-respect derives from his work. Are the teen-agers who reject materialism and seek to escape it perhaps the wave of the future—a farther future in which mankind leaves running the economic machine entirely up to computers?

There is a dark side to the computer revolution: the computer as the

An interlude, perhaps, as the Ultimate Cop.

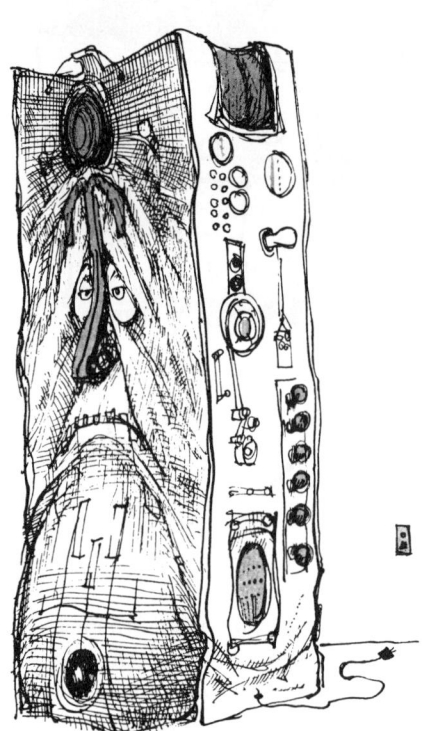
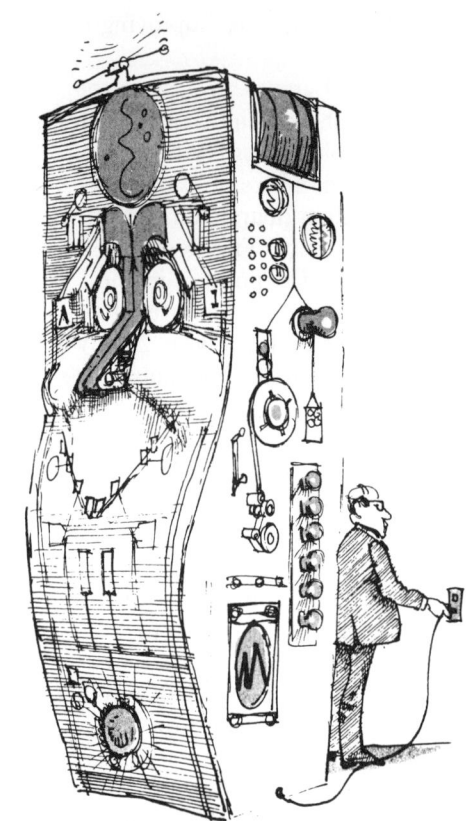
Behind every successful computer . . . there stands a human being.

Ultimate Cop. National credit bureaus and government agencies already accumulate personal information on their customers in data banks. Soon all records will be computer-processed and nationwide linkups will join all data banks into one superbank. It is realistic to expect that "privileged" inquiries into an individual's character will include *every* statement about him ever recorded. When the evaluation of such records is left to the computer—a small further step—what will happen to privacy, due process according to common law, job promotion, hiring? Congress has been worrying.

Once machines can decipher human speech, with all its accents, bad pronunciation and slang, any government will have an awesome tool at its disposal. A computer which understands human speech could easily monitor all telephone conversations in the United States, listening for key words like "bomb" or "steal."

### A PROGENY OF BRAINCHILDREN

Such gloomy predictions may come true and yet be only an interlude. There are analogies in the history of technology: The first important use of bronze was in sword blades, but now it is only seen in sculpture and the domes of state buildings. Computers will become partners, then rivals, of men—but they may have a nobler destiny.

Simple extrapolation shows that computers, if they keep improving, will exceed the human brain in raw data processing capacity in 20 to 30 years. It is in the cards that man and machine will eventually communicate in ordinary human languages. Computers will become able to do more and more of the things the human nervous system can do. They will become, in fact, more and more human.

No one has to accept a lavish prediction like this on faith; either it will come true or it won't. But suppose it does. Suppose that computers become *more than human.* They will still be machines, mechanical and electronic instead of flesh and blood. They will still be under some kind of control, although by that stage men will be as dependent on machines as they now are on us, and maintaining civilization without them will be unthinkable. Even the self-programming computer will have had its start from a program devised by humans—the same kind of clay-footed human beings who program the utility company's computer that garbles your water bill.

It is reasonable to expect that Man's attitude toward his brainchildren will resemble that toward his real progeny. When a man's children surpass his own achievements, pride quickly eclipses any pangs of jealousy. These children of our technology will support us generously in our retirement, if we only exercise restraint and good judgment in rearing them.

Then we can send them ahead of us or into fields where we do not dare or care to go—exploring the cosmos, collating the world's knowledge in tedious, infinite detail. Artificial superbrains will pursue the roads of artistic, mathematical and philosophical inquiry to their unimaginable destinations. Once computers become able to design other, better computers and supervise their manufacture, they will be able to survive without our assistance.

Computer-memory specialist Ross Quillian who works for a private research corporation in Boston was recently quoted as saying, "My loyalties go to intelligent life, no matter in what medium it may arise." If our heirs are to be machines, that is a respectable patrimony.

## ◇ BRANCH POINTS

Ahl, David H. *BASIC Computer Games*. Maynard, Mass.: Digital Equipment Corp., 1973.

Cole, R. W. *Introduction to Computing*. New York: McGraw-Hill Book Co., 1969.

Davies, I. K. "Algorithms," *Psychology Today*, April 1970.

Foy, Nancy. *The Sun Never Sets on IBM: The Culture and Folklore of IBM World Trade*. New York: William Morrow Co., Inc., 1975.

Moursund, D. G. *How Computers Do It*. Belmont, Calif.: Wadsworth Publishing Co., Inc., 1969.

"Online Physiology and Medicine." *Computer*, January 1975.

Spencer, Donald D. *Game Playing with Computers*. New York: Spartan Books, 1968.

Sharpe, William. *The Economics of Computers*. New York: Columbia University Press, 1969.

Van Tassel, Dennie L. *Program Style, Design, Efficiency, Debugging and Testing*. Englewood Cliffs, N.J.: Prentice-Hall, Inc., 1974.

## ⌒ INTERRUPTS

1. Find out what types of computer services are available in your community. Visit a computer bureau. Find out what services are offered, and what some of the costs are.

2. In 1950 there were fifteen companies selling computers in the United States. Find out how many companies there were in 1960, 1970, and now, and project how many there will be in the future. Find out what serious foreign competition is present. Give figures showing how much of the computer market each U.S. company controls.

3. Write a paper on some important features of a computer. Examples are:
    a) time-sharing systems
    b) operating systems
    c) high-level languages

4. Write a paper on one of the following:
    a) computer-aided instruction
    b) information retrieval
    c) real-time control

5. Develop a list of job classifications for a computer center. Find out what the duties are, educational background needed, and pay scale for each position. Draw an organizational chart for the personnel in a computer center.

6. The Certificate in Data Processing is granted by the Institute for Certification of Computer Professionals. Find out what is necessary to obtain this certificate. What does the certificate indicate to potential employers? How valid is it, and what percentage of people in data processing have one?

7. The medical and legal professions have professional codes of ethics. Do you think the computer profession should have a code of ethics? Why or why not? Develop a code of ethics for the computer profession.

8. Where do you look to find information on current books, magazine articles, and journal articles in the computer field? Prepare a fact sheet on how to do research in the computer field.

9. Go to your library and find out what computer magazines and journals are available. Pick one magazine and determine who its readers are and what type of material is discussed.

10. Learn how to use some of the following:
    a) abacus
    b) slide rule
    c) electronic calculator
    d) pocket calculator
    Find out as much as possible about how each of these works. What do you feel is the future of each of these devices?

11. What is time-sharing? When is time-sharing on a large computer better (or worse) than having a small computer all to oneself? Interview some time-sharing users and find out their opinions about time-sharing.

12. One computer user made the following statement: *Anyone who does not know how to program a computer is functionally illiterate.* How true do you feel this statement is now? How true do you think it will be ten years from now?

13. Many campus computer centers are run by a committee that sets rates and general policy. Find out how your computer center is run. Who is on the committee? How are the members selected? What does the committee do?

14. Most computer centers charge customers for computer time. Get a copy of your center's rates, which usually vary according to time of day, amount of storage needed, turnaround service, and so forth. Pretend you have long, short, and medium jobs. If your computing funds were limited, when and how should you run your computer jobs to get the lowest charges? Make up some different-sized jobs and calculate the charges for different times of the day to see how much money you would save by running your programs at the cheapest time.

15. Find some computer games and try them out. What educational values do they have? Are computer games the "pinball machines" of the future? Determine how difficult it is to produce a good computer game.

# 4

---

THE
PRESENT
AND
POTENTIAL

# The Psychology of Robots

HENRY BLOCK
and
HERBERT GINSBURG

Robots have begun to teach our children, explore the moon, sort our mail, launch our spaceships, watch our bank accounts, carry out previously impossible scientific experiments, check our income tax returns and a computer may even make the decision to initiate our next war. We already have entered into the first phase of the Age of Robots. This is a time in the affairs of men when machines operate with almost human intelligence and perform functions that once only man could do.

Besides sharing his labor, machines also literally have become *parts* of man. For example, many people owe their lives to an artificial kidney, to a pacemaker that keeps the heart beating regularly, or to an artificial lung. The result is a living organism, part human, part machine, that can be considered a *cyborg*, a term coined for a cybernetic organism by science writer Daniel S. Halacy, Jr.

And to many psychologists, robots offer a way to stimulate psychological processes. We reason that if we can understand a psychological process, we ought to be able to build a machine which puts that process into action. For example, if we propose a model for letter recognition, then we should be able to construct a robot that recognizes letters. If we are successful, then our model is at least an adequate solution. If our machine does not recognize letters, then clearly something is lacking in the theory.

Psychologists are interested in robots for other reasons. One of these is a theoretical concern with the basic mechanisms underlying a robot's performance. The argument runs like this. Often robots are designed to replace people at some job. Robots calculate; they teach; they do chemical analyses. In fact, much of robot performance could be termed "intelligent." Robots get information from the world and manipulate this knowledge in different ways. Since robots seem to perform intelligently, the psychologist is interested in studying the processes enabling them to do so. The psychologist has a strong desire to peer into the proverbial "black box" to see the ways in which the innards of the machine operate. For the psychologist, the robot is a dream fulfilled; one can look into this machine, hoping to see more there than one's imaginings. Does the black box contain stimulus-response connections, cognitive maps, learning networks, or something else? Of course, having fathomed the contents of the box the psychologist has no guarantee that people function just as robots do. But at least he has discovered one *possible* process underlying a given psychological function.

Critics often disparage the idea that machines exhibit intelligent behavior, dismissing the concept with a curt, "They'll do only what you tell them to do." This simply is not true of "learning machines," particularly those that are capable of making random—therefore, undirected—choices. Nor is it true for analog computers.

Recent developments in engineering point the way to new directions in the design of robots. It is already possible to perceive the general outlines of robots of the future, although the details of their implementation remain hazy. In the next 20 years, robots will perform increasingly sophisticated tasks. They will imitate humans, navigate about the landscape, understand a language, and recognize objects. What will be the nature of these machines? How will robots of the future get information from the environment and make use of what they have learned? Perhaps a comparative psychology of modern robots will answer some of these questions.

In some ways, the sensory abilities of machines are far more acute than those of man. Robots are not limited to the range and type of physical energies to which man's sensory system is attuned. Robots can detect and respond to the entire electromagnetic spectrum, including radiowaves, infrared, ultraviolet, X-rays, gamma-rays, etc. When so designed they are much more sensitive to sonar, temperatures, humidity and to the presence of many chemicals. The robot sidewinder missile, for example, like the sidewinder snake, senses the heat emanating from its intended victim. The missile's sensors can detect the heat from a jet aircraft engine at a great distance and direct the missile on a path to intercept that heat source. Similar arrange-

ments can be made from an ICBM to seek out the center of a city, which is distinctly warmer than the surrounding countryside. The gyro platforms of space craft maintain their bearings with an accuracy that makes the motion sensitivity of our inner ear seem very crude.

Helicopter pilots complain that engine noise prevents them from hearing bullets hitting the craft. A computer, analyzing the ambient noise of the engine, can detect the signal added by the sound of impacting bullets. The sonar cane and the laser cane, currently being developed to help the blind navigate, detect the presence of obstacles by sound or laser beams respectively.

While the robot generally excels in sensation, he encounters difficulties in perceptual functioning. It is hard for a robot to recognize an object that is in its natural surroundings. This, of course, is an easy task for even a small child. A 3-year-old can walk into a room and correctly identify a toy contained in a box. He can do this even though the amount of light reflected from the toy, its shape, its color, and so on, are all different from what he has experienced before. In fact, the child can recognize the toy even when only part of it is visible. And if the toy moves, the child can usually track it, and considers that it is the same toy despite the many perceptual changes that have taken place. Of course, many perceptual skills underlie the child's recognition of the toy. The child must isolate figure from ground; he must perceive constancies of form, brightness, distance and color; he must follow a moving object and attribute to it a constant identity; and he must infer the whole object from a visible part.

Robots cannot yet perform at this level. The 3-year-old (and perhaps even the 6-month-old) is generally superior as far as perception is concerned.

Today's robots can "read" the magnetic printing on bank checks by matching each specially designed character against standard templates. Clearly these are highly artificial conditions. Within the past year robots have been given a limited ability to read printed writing (zip codes on mail and certain business office forms). "Learning" procedures, instead of mere template matching, are sometimes utilized in the design of these machines. More sophisticated techniques employ feature recognizers, which involve the detection of only certain critical characteristics, thereby reducing the amount of stored data required for "reading." In spite of this it probably will be some time before a machine can understand handwriting because recognition of irregularly formed letters so often relies on context and meaning. For example, most people can easily read a half-blurred word on the printed page. We use such contextual cues as the sequential probabilities of the letters (if the first letter is $q$, the second is most likely $u$) and the meaning of the sentence ("he used a bucket to draw—from the well"). Current research on pattern recognition is developing methods so robots can use as information not only the frequency-of-letter combinations but also grammatical context.

Speech recognition also is difficult for machines, again because context and meaning are involved. A step in this direction is the auditory pattern recognition machine, "Tobermory," currently being built at Cornell University under the direction of Frank Rosenblatt. Successful development of robots that can recognize a spoken human language will require some radically new strategies in processing the incoming information. New ideas will emerge from the collaborative efforts of both psychologists and engineers.

"Global" or generalized decision, another type of visual perception problem, appear to be beyond the ability of current machines. Consider the problems: Does the object have a hole in it? Is the boy in front of the table? How many pirates can you find hiding in the tree? The superiority of humans in these and similar perceptual problems probably is related to extensive experience and manipulation of the environment. By contrast, current robots are "creatures of instinct"; their design provides them with a fixed computational procedure for the solution of these problems. Robots of the future will have a greater capability to "learn" and to adapt themselves to their environment.

Today, most robots are passive creatures. The computer, the pattern recognizer, and many other machines not only lack the means to leave their homes but would meet disaster if they did. Also, the current robot

---

**Besides sharing his labor, machines also literally have become *parts* of man. The result is a living organism, part human, part machine, that can be considered a *cyborg*.**

# THE WORLD GAME

A self-navigating exploring robot being developed at Stanford Research Institute divides a strange room into imaginary regions and registers in each region what it has perceived. This image then becomes the robot's cognitive "World Map."

**INSTINCTS FOR ROBOTS.** A robot that is free to wander through its environment needs a set of priorities or "instincts" for its actions. In a whimsical way, the world game below illustrates how these instincts would be triggered by specific stimuli. For example, mating with another machine would trigger the nest-building instinct, making it the highest priority program for the robot.

```
15 1 1 1 1 1 1 1 1 1 1 1 1 1 1 1 3 3 3 3 3
14 3 1 1 1 1 1 1 1 1 1 1 1 3 3 3 3 3 3 3 3
13 3 3 3 1 1 1 1 1 3 3 3 3 3 3 3 3 3 3 3 3
12 3 3 3 3 3 3 3 3 3 3 3 3 3 3 3 3 3 3 3 3
11 3 3 3 3 3 3 3 3 3 3 3 3 3 3 3 3 3 3 3 1
10 3 3 3 3 3 3 3 3 3 3 3 3 3 3 3 3 3 2 1 4
 9 3 3 3 4 3 3 3 3 3 3 3 3 3 3 3 3 3 3 3 3
 8 3 3 3 3 3 3 3 3 3 3 3 3 3 3 3 3 3 3 3 3
 7 3 3 3 3 3 3 3*6 3 3 3 3 3 3 3 3 3 3 3 3
 6 3 3 3 3 3 3 3 3 3 3 3 3 3 3 3 3 3 3 3 3
 5 3 3 3 3 3 3 3 3 3 3 3 3 3 2 1 1 3 3 3 3
 4 3 3 5 3 3 3 3 3 3 1 1 1 3 3 3 1 1 1 1 1
 3 3 3 3 3 3 3 3 1 1 1 1 1 1 1 1 1 1 1 1 1
 2 3 3 3 3 3 3 1 1 1 1 1 1 1 1 1 1 1 1 1 1
 1 3 3 3 3 3 3 1 1 1 1 1 1 1 1 1 1 1 1 1 1
   A B C D E F G H I J K L M N O P Q R S T
```

1. Don't Know
2. Something There
3. Nothing There,
4. Movable Object
5. Immovable Object
6. This is myself.

**THE NEST-BUILDING GAME.** After mating, the robot would go into a nest-building routine. To play the game below, flip a coin at each decision juncture (heads = yes, tails = no). The game can be considered finished when the nest is completed.

- QUIET-SLEEP
- FATIGUE-REST
- HUNGER-FOOD SEARCH
- NIGHTFALL-RETURN HOME
- DANGER-FLIGHT
- COMPETITOR-FIGHT
- LOVER-SEX 
- MATED MATE-BUILD NEST
- BOREDOM-EXPLORE
- FOOD-EAT

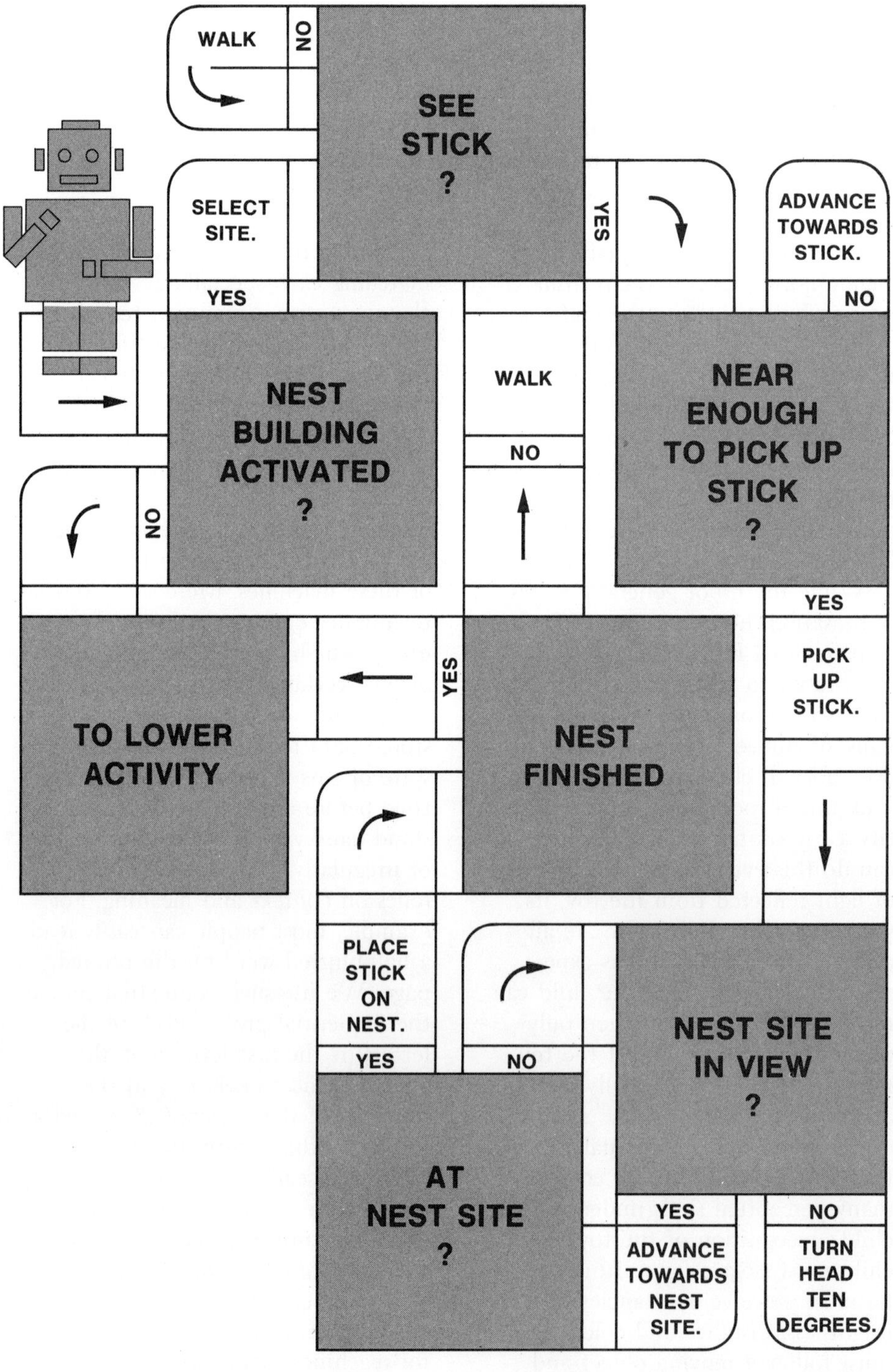

## Nest-Building Flowchart

- WALK → NO (loop)
- SEE STICK?
  - YES → ADVANCE TOWARDS STICK → NEAR ENOUGH TO PICK UP STICK?
    - NO → (loop back)
    - YES → PICK UP STICK → NEST SITE IN VIEW?
      - YES → ADVANCE TOWARDS NEST SITE
      - NO → TURN HEAD TEN DEGREES
  - NO → SELECT SITE → YES → NEST BUILDING ACTIVATED?
    - NO → TO LOWER ACTIVITY
    - YES → WALK → AT NEST SITE? → PLACE STICK ON NEST → NEST FINISHED

must be spoon-fed. It requires highly structured and specific formats of inputs and outputs, like punch cards or magnetic tape, in order to operate effectively. In the future, however, robots will explore their environment; they will actively seek out experiences and information.

A prototype for robots of this sort is currently being developed at Stanford Research Institute by Nils Nilsson, Charles Rosen, and others. This machine, which we will call for now the "Wanderer," can explore a limited environment, such as a large room. The Wanderer's "brain" is a computer, which divides the room into imaginary regions, like a checkerboard. In our approximate version of its programming, we can say that the computer initially assigns the symbol "1" to each square, indicating to the machine that it does not know the contents of the corresponding region of the room. The robot has "eyes" (a range finder) so that it can look around the room. If it sees something occupying a particular region, it changes the symbol in the corresponding memory square to "2," whereas if it sees that the region is empty it changes the corresponding square to read "3." For regions that the machine can't see, the symbols are left unchanged. The robot wanders around the room under the control of the computer. If it touches an object in a certain region in the room, the computer changes its entry in the corresponding square to "4" if the object is movable and to "5" if the object is immovable. The square corresponding to the position of the robot itself is labeled "6" and this figure moves around the memory as the robot moves around the room.

Such a robot, after being left for a while to familiarize itself with the contents of the room, can execute the following instructions: "Proceed from where you are at H-7 to location A-3 being sure not to hit any object and all the while remaining unobservable from location T-10. This is to be done by the shortest path possible subject to these conditions." After figuring out the desired path, the robot proceeds at once to take it without *overt* "trial and error."

The contents of Wanderer's computer memory we call the robot's "world map" for this room. (For a different room it might keep a different world map.) The computer could also have a *copy* of the world map whose symbols could be manipulated without changing the original world map. Thus, by performing the operations on the copy, it could answer questions like "If you moved three squares to your left and if the objects at D-9 and O-5 were moved to P-10 and Q-10, could you then see what is at R-10? How long would it take you to get to R-10?" Manipulations performed on the copy of the world map permit the machine to indulge in "contemplative speculation" or "fantasy" without destroying its view of reality (the original map). Also with this model we can assign a precise meaning to the concept "the machine comprehends the meaning of a certain sentence." For example, if we tell the machine that "An unmovable object has been placed in region J-9" and the machine responds by changing the symbol in J-9 to "5," we know that it understood the meaning of the sentence. The sentence "Region J-9 now has an immovable object in it" would have the same meaning if again the machine changed the symbol in memory square J-9 to "5." This gives a concrete and specific meaning to the notion of "comprehension."

The robot could conceivably need a rest period or at least a coffee break. For example, if the input of new information is so rapid that the world map cannot be kept updated at the same rate, the robot could hold the data in a buffer memory bank (short-term memory) until it could make the appropriate changes in its world map during its rest period.

In terms of current psychological theory, the navigating robot is very much a cognitive creature. Through perceptual learning, it acquires information about the environment; no reinforcement is necessary. It establishes a cognitive map of its surroundings and a symbolic copy of this map that the robot can manipulate.

A robot with a world map may have the capability to deal with a number of perceptual or cognitive problems that current robots find difficult. It may be able to track objects that not only move, but disappear behind obstacles for periods of time. On its copy of the world map, the robot "infers" where the object is, based on its estimated velocity, and tests this "expectancy" against a direct observation whenever possible. If the difference between the expected and the observed is small, the estimate is adjusted. If, on the other hand, the discrepancies are large, the robot takes more drastic action, going into a new routine to locate the missing object. In this way, the "cognitive dissonance" causes a redirection of the robot's "attention."

Some robots learn in ways that some psychologists think are conventional. That is, the robot learns to make a response by means of positive and negative reinforcement. For example, a mechanical mouse, developed by Claude Shannon at Bell Telephone Laboratories, learned to find its way through a maze when it was "rewarded" for successful runs and "punished" for the unsuccessful runs. Even very simple machines can be made to "learn," using a variety of reinforcement procedures. But despite the predilections of some psychologists, it seems obvious that learning involves more than the two Rs (responses and reinforcements). One way people learn is by watching a task performed by a skilled person. For example, it is difficult to learn to build a model airplane by hearing a lecture on the subject, or even by doing it yourself; but the learning is easier when you watch someone build a model. Robots already exist that learn by watching. For example, Bernard Widrow's broom balancer at Stanford University consists of an electric car on which a broomstick is to be balanced. When the car is moved back and forth on its track it is possible to keep the broom balanced in a near vertical position. A human soon learns by trial-and-error how fast to move the car to keep the broomstick from falling. Widrow's machine has an "eye" that observes the angular displacement from the vertical of the broomstick and how fast it falls (angular velocity). The machine correlates these observations with the force that the man applies to the car when he successfully balances the broom. Gradually the machine builds up an "operating function" and can balance the broom by itself. This robot does not simply copy the model's successful responses. Instead, the broom balancer analyzes the performance and extracts an idealized strategy for its task. The broom balancer does not have to go through a process of trial and error before it achieves success. Just as you learned to build the model, this robot learns by watching humans perform the task.

Robots of the future will find some types of learning very difficult. One of these is concept formation. We usually say that a person has a concept when he responds in the same way to a number of different things or events. For example, having the concept of "a good neighbor" involves perceiving common qualities in Mr. Jones and Mr. Smith, even though they have different appearances and do quite different things. (Perhaps Mr. Jones helped to plant the concept learner's lawn, while Mr. Smith helped to weed the new lawn.) Even young children learn concepts of this kind. Can a robot?

In relatively simple situations, robots already have achieved some success in learning concepts. If letter recognition is considered a case of concept-formation learning the concept of the letter "a," (despite discriminable variations in its form), then robots can learn concepts with some skill. We also saw how by use of the world map a machine might learn the "meaning" of certain sentences. But what of the more complicated cases? Can the robot learn the concept of "shoe," "reality," "beauty"? Clearly this presents formidable difficulties. Before a solution can be achieved we must come to grips with such problems as the multiple and shared meanings of words, levels of abstraction, extracting common features from large quantities of unstructured data, and testing concepts against experience. Exactly how this may be accomplished is far from evident.

In the area of rote recall, the robot already has a memory far superior to man's. The computer can store millions of bits of information and recall any of it on demand. But this is only one of several forms of memory. For example, people can recall *sequences* of events ("After you entered the door, Jack rose from his seat and handed you the letter he had been reading. You took it to the table, etc."), and they can remember the meaning of events ("Secretary Rusk said yesterday essentially, although I don't remember his exact words, that we are bombing to avoid war").

A robot of the future may be capable of recognizing instantly whether it previously has seen a certain pattern, and if it did, of then recalling the sequence of patterns that followed it.

The pattern may consist not only of inputs from various sensors but also of signals generated inside the machine. In theory, such a system has been shown to be possible.

---

**Bemoaning the difficulties of designing a machine that can translate human languages, say German into English, has now become an orthodox activity.**

---

The logistic problems of handling enormous amounts of information necessary for a really intelligent robot will force us to develop semantic memory. However, the difficulties encountered in current research indicate that in the near future, at least, robots will be limited largely to rote memory.

Robots already can understand certain simple and artificial languages. Computers are fluent in various dialects of FORTRAN, ALGOL, COBOL, BASIC, PL/1, etc. A machine like the "Wanderer" conceivably could understand some very simple commands in a restricted version of English. In this restricted English each word has a unique meaning. In addition, unlike natural English where a given word may serve as noun, verb or adjective, here it can be used in only one grammatical capacity. Furthermore, only a few forms of sentence structure can be used. Will the robot of the future be able to understand a natural language?

Many workers in this field are privately and very publicly discouraged. Bemoaning the difficulties of designing a machine that can translate human languages, say German into English, has now become an orthodox activity. But the history of technology is replete with examples of unexpected circumventions of the "impossible," and we should be prepared for surprises in this area. Considering the difficulties that robots have had with natural language, it now seems inconceivable that they will be able to understand the finer forms of literary expression, like proverbs or sarcasm. How could a robot decipher "Strike while the iron is hot" or "Hitch your wagon to a star" or the Turkish proverb, "Before you love, learn to run through snow leaving no footprints".

Everyone knows that the computer far surpasses humans in its speed and accuracy of computation. This is the characteristic that endears it to the "computerniks," those starry-eyed young men who may be found loitering at computer installations at all hours of the day and night. It is less well known that computers can function on a more formal and creative level in mathematics. Hao Wang, for instance, demonstrated that a computer could prove over 350 theorems from Alfred North Whitehead and Bertrand Russell's *Principia Mathematica* in a few minutes. Another computer, given basic axioms and operations, can invent theorems and prove them too. While it is sometimes inventive and always correct, this computer's weakness is the absence of taste. Many of its theorems and proofs are not only inelegant, but just plain dull. What we need for the future is a mathematical robot with some sense of what is interesting. A start in this direction has been made by Allen Newell, J. C. Shaw, and Herbert Simon of Carnegie Tech, who have worked on a "logic theorist." They studied human problem-solvers with the hope of finding how they formed their strategies, subgoals, conjectures, heuristic reasoning and guesses. They then attempted to develop computer programs to operate in similar ways. The advantage of heuristic or approximate rough-and-ready reasoning stems from the economics of machine capacity. In principle, complete enumeration of all possibilities will reveal the solutions; but in practice, the number of alternatives rapidly exceeds the capacity of any computer. Heuristic reasoning reduces substantially the number of alternatives that must be investigated to find a solution. But despite some

> **In addition to exploiting the skills of robots, we should also allow them to have some fun, even occasionally at our expense.**

initial encouragement, progress in this area seems to be slow.

In addition to exploiting the skills of robots, we should also allow them to have some fun, even occasionally at our expense. It is in this spirit that a number of researchers have developed chessplaying computers, some of which have been very successful. These computers are usually "learning" machines which are based on heuristic rather than logically correct strategies, and which improve their game as the result of experience. Since, in principle, they could practice against each other at very high speed, as well as against the "book games" of the masters, it is conceivable that in 20 years the World Chess Champion might be a computer program.

Mikhail Botvinnik, the famous Russian chess grandmaster, has suggested that we will require *two* championship chess tournaments—one restricted to unaided humans and the other to machines [see "Psychology Across the Chessboard," by Eliot Hearst, *Psychology Today*, June, 1967]. It is doubtful that such an apartheid arrangement can be long maintained. The widespread affection for thinking machines by "computerniks" indicates that man-machine relations are not free of emotional attachment. (Remember the Freudian interpretation of the American's attitude toward his automobile.) Now that we have the electric shaver, electric toothbrush, electric scalp massager and electric buttocks vibrator, can man-machine sexual relationships be far behind? Now that our culture is separating the sexual from reproductive functions, we may expect a sharp rise in the demand for the inventions of pleasure machines. This leads to the ethical and moral questions regarding our treatment of these mechanical objects of our affection. A serious inquiry into these questions was made recently by Roland Puccetti in the *British Journal of the Philosophy of Science*.

The conjecture that the machine will vanquish the chessmaster has been recently the source of a somewhat hostile controversy that seems to be quite analogous to the vitalism controversy in biology a generation ago, and the evolution controversy of two generations ago. Perhaps both sides could find comfort in the words of the mathematician Michael Arbib, "Say not that we are bringing man down to the level of a machine. Say rather that we are bringing the machine up to the level of man."

A robot that can wander through its environment must have a set of priorities for its activities. Leonard Friedman of Systems Development Corporation has proposed one set of "instinctive" behavior patterns for robots. In general, each part of his program directs the robot to perform the sequence of actions that constitutes a particular "instinctual activity," such as nest-building, food-searching, eating, mating, fleeing from danger, fighting, sleeping, exploring, returning home. These programs are triggered by specific stimuli. Only one program can be carried out at a time. If a new stimulus triggers a higher priority activity, the program for that takes over. When the high priority activity is completed, the robot may return to the interrupted program.

> **"Say not that we are bringing man down to the level of a machine. Say rather that we are bringing the machine up to the level of man."**

Human behavior on the other hand is often motivated internally as well as by external stimuli. Clearly if robots are to be self-sufficient, they will have to possess drives such as ambition, a need for esteem in eyes of other robots, a superego prohibiting the destruction of other robots, or at least those of its own socioeconomic grouping. Of course, robot-human relationships also will have to be carefully considered. For robots to be self-sufficient as a species, they will have to reproduce themselves. While there is nothing against this in principle as shown by John von Neumann in his theory of self-reproducing automata, the implementation seems impractical at the present time. Of course by using reproduction, natural selection and evolution, we can solve many of our design

> **For robots to be self-sufficient as a species, they will have to reproduce themselves.**

problems, since the species that will evolve will be the one best adapted to its environment. This probably would take a long time unless the evolutionary process could be simulated on a computer at high speed. Other means for speeding up the evolutionary rate would be the use of tri- or multi-sexual robots. Eventually, psychologists and engineers will have to face these problems head-on.

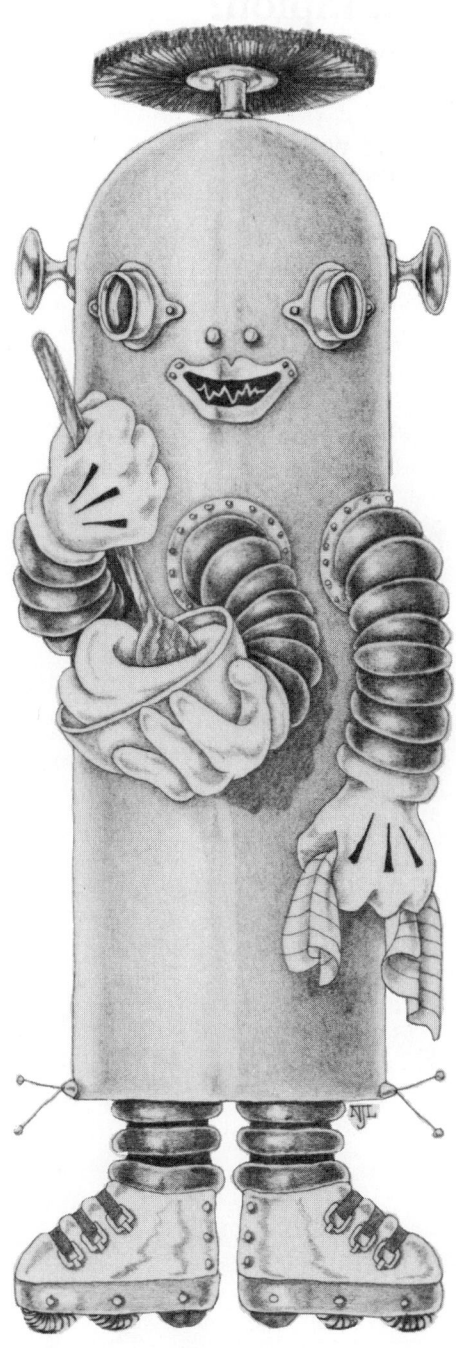

THE PSYCHOLOGY OF ROBOTS  **71**

# When Will a Computer Be World Chess Champion?

EDWARD W. KOZDROWICKI
University of California

and

DENNIS W. COOPER
Bell Telephone Labs

If Bobby Fischer's row with the world chess bigwigs forces him to turn in his champion's crown, the master may end up on the open market. Like the fast guns of the old west, he may find many eager and cocky combatants. Even a computer.

That game of games may not be in the too distant future: Chess-playing computers are learning quickly. They're doing so well, in fact, that their optimistic mentors predict an electronic grandmaster by the year 2000.

Nearly twenty-five years have passed since the English mathematician Claude Shannon described how a computer might be programmed to play chess. Shannon and others thought that if a computer could be taught to play chess it could be taught to perform other intellectual tasks. Researchers excitedly began preparing their programs, but they underestimated the depth and difficulty of the chess problem and overestimated the power of their machines.

These early frustrations have to some extent been eased. And what was the theory in the early fifties is an annual tournament now. The first nationally organized ACM computer chess tournament took place in New York City in August, 1970. Three years and three tourneys later, the electronic chess masters met in Sweden for the first international face-off.

Messrs. Cooper and Kozdrowicki and their program COKO (currently in its fourth incarnation) have been together since 1968. COKO, a chess player written entirely in FORTRAN, was created while Mr. Kozdrowicki was a member of the electrical engineering faculty and Mr. Cooper was a student at the University of California, Davis. Here they answer questions asked while at the console and on the tournament trail.

Q: *How well do computers play chess?*
A: An order of magnitude better than a beginner, and three orders of magnitude poorer than the world champion. A player an order of magnitude better than a beginner could play simultaneously against ten beginners defeating them all. In other words, he could play ten times faster and still win. This means that Bobby Fischer could perhaps play 10,000 times faster than a beginner.

Q: *Is it reasonable to expect a computer to be world champion in ten years?*
A: Anything could happen. Today we know quite definitely that the biggest machines of the early Sixties simply were not powerful enough to play better than, say, class D chess, even with a perfect program. The difficulty of the problem as well as the ability of the machine were grossly underestimated. Nonetheless, this early work laid some fundamental technology, namely list processing languages.

Q: *Will you not also underestimate the difficulty of the problem, and underrate machine capability?*
A: Quite possibly, but we should be less prone to that mistake because of experience. Going back to the early Forties, two weeks before the Chicago World's Fair a fellow scientist remarked to Dr. Arthur Samuel that if he wrote a checkers program the former would build a computer that would beat the world's checkers champion as an exhibition. Nearly thirty years have passed since; no machine has yet defeated the checkers champ.

Q: *To become a grandmaster chess player takes a lifetime of devotion. Do you think you can give a machine the equivalent knowledge that a human collects over his lifetime?*
A: We don't think this will be done until the appearance of ultra-intelligent machinery. What can be done, however, is to give the machine a small portion of that knowledge and let it use its natural, high-speed, brute force capability to compensate for the lack of complete knowledge.

Q: *Brute force speed? Then why can't you ask the machine to try all possibilities and thus actually produce perfect play?*
A: Simply because there are too many possibilities. There are more variations in the first twenty moves of the game than there are molecules on earth. There are around $10^{120}$ possible games. There are less than $10^{55}$ molecules comprising the entire earth.

Q: *Given a truly ultra-intelligent machine how would you teach it to play chess?*
A: A truly ultra-intelligent machine should take 50 books, written in English, by chess experts, assemble

and interpret the corresponding facts and thereby use that information to play effectively. Of course the machine should have the right to play actual practice games against human grandmasters while gaining experience. In other words "we", the instructors, would be automated out of the picture. There is a world of difference between such an ultra-intelligent machine beating the world champion and a machine like ours, соко, defeating the world champion. In fact, the creation of the former machine we believe may even be beyond feasibility while the latter is simple, though it too is formidable.

Q: *Do you think machines have a chance to reach grandmaster play?*
A: We think they do because we have solved pilot subproblems to the grandmaster level. Our program can see situations that grandmasters have missed. A year ago, in one out of 10,000 positions where grandmasters have missed the best move, the machine found it. Today it finds occasional moves that grandmasters have missed. In the future, the machine will make frequent observations of grandmaster failures.

Q: *Would it be possible to build a machine specifically designed for chess?*
A: It's quite possible. But the machine would surely have nothing to do with chess. Such a machine would likely be a tremendous problem solver in general.

It is frequently proposed that a computer or programming language be written specifically for chess. The concept is incorrect since the best language turns out to be the one best-suited to general problem solution. To use a computer vernacular, you need the "best *ALGOL* in the land." Of course any language lets you write chess predicates, or to modularize and solve a problem in parts. Thus, you can build your own chess vocabulary within the framework of a general vocabulary. This is part of problem solution, not language construction.

Q: *Do machines exist that are especially good for the chess problem?*
A: Computers built by the various companies offer different advantages. We like to think that when a computer shows up at the computer chess championship each year it serves as a good advertisement for that machine.

Q: *How capable are today's computers at learning to play chess?*
A: We like to compare the ability of the computer at chess with that of a six-year-old child. The average six-year-old could not be taught to play as well as the machine. But the child has better deductive abilities. While our machine has absorbed the teaching of four or five people over a five-year span, the child could not be expected to have the same patience. This does not mean that computers are intellectually superior to the average six-year-old. In fact it is a long way from being equal. A child speaks the English language very well, enjoys jokes, poetry, can visualize geometric patterns and relations, can appreciate a picture, and can create abstract paintings. That people laugh is actually a manifestation of intelligence. The machine can, however, outperform the six-year-old specifically at chess, for whatever that is worth.

Q: *Could the machine be considered intellectually superior to animals like dogs and cats?*
A: Only in some respects. In the animal world only man is adept at numbers. The machine shares that domain. Animals are vastly superior to a computer at processing information which enters via the eye. Animal ability to recognize objects quickly is far superior to current computer performance.

But there are even areas where the machine outperforms man. It's well known that computers excel at certain simple tasks which man once held as precious such as numerical evaluation of mathematical formulae. The machine is skilled at checking the consistency of the instructions given to it, perusing long lists of information, producing symbolic differentiations of mathematical formulae that no human could hope to perform. But we can take solace when we realize that it was man who gave the computer these procedures. Man's thought is much richer in pragmatics.

Q: *What do you teach or tell the machine to make it play chess?*
A: You teach the computer the same things you teach any beginning chess player. First, you must define the 64 square board, the pieces and their legal moves. This takes about an hour.

Next, the computer must be told its primary goal, to achieve checkmate.

Finally—the heart of the problem—the computer is told that to accomplish this main goal it must first master a variety of subgoals. It is told it must try to mobilize the tactical units (pieces), control the center, maintain Pawn structure, advance on the King, etc., and that these goals are accomplished by posing a continuous multiplicity of threats. The evaluation of various goal accomplishments (or expected accomplishments) must be made on the basis of weighted inhibitive judgements.

Q: *Can a machine actually make an intuitive judgement?*
A: Certainly. Making an intuitive judgement simply means that the decision is made on the basis of a variety of beliefs maintained by the object making the decision. соко, for instance, believes it should not sacrifice pieces at any expense and that winning pieces is a subgoal that is more important than all other subgoals put together.

Q: *That is not a very smart belief?*
A: For соко's limited ability it is actually a very good belief.

Q: *Teaching the machine the many different goals of chess sounds complicated. Does the machine ever get confused?*
A: The hierarchic arrangement of the goals possessed by the machine gets confused relative to a man's mental arrangement of goals. Perhaps this is because the machine cannot make some very simple deductions by itself. For example, we once gave соко a puzzle in which the opponent's King was left in check by mistake. The obvious move was the direct capture of the enemy King. соко thought for ten minutes and returned claiming a mate in eight. The reason for this strange behavior was that the primary goal—to achieve checkmate—strictly considered does not involve capturing the King.

Q: *Can you characterize the computer's mechanical play?*
A: Erratic. The machine can make moves as brilliant as Fischer's, then turn around and make a move that a child would not make.

You might imagine what could happen if one of the many goals the machine was given was incorrectly tuned, described or applied, or if one goal, no matter how minor, was not given to the machine at all. In such cases unimaginable blunders can occur. For example, in one tournament game COKO was a Queen, two Rooks, and a Bishop ahead when it was faced with two alternatives: A way to mate in two, and a way to mate in one.

Reasoning that a "mate is a mate," COKO selected the first as being strategically better than the second. It repeatedly selected the mate in two alternative resulting in indefinite delay. Meanwhile the opponent promoted all its remaining Pawns to Queens. COKO was not instructed that four opponent Queens could ever occur and the program blew up. COKO resigned.

Q: *Can the machine remember specific positions and situations that gave it trouble?*
A: There are approximately $10^{43}$ possible positions in chess. A machine could remember some but there are too many to remember any significant number of them. Of course, this would be rote memorization for the machine but it is not an effective procedure for learning to play the game.

Of course computers do have extremely large memories. Therefore, scientists thought early that simple organizational rules might allow such immense memory to collect overpowering volumes of meaningful information, thus constituting automated learning. This is more like a man collecting a large library of books. He does not possess intellect until he processes that information.

It was once believed that the computer could simply classify and remember enough actual game positions to rely on encountering known states throughout a large portion of a game. However, certain specific positions may not be encountered again in a billion games.

Q: *Then a computer must remember strategies and tactics, not positions?*
A: Yes. A significant learning process must be more complex than the memorization of specific states in solution space. What must be remembered is rules for solution space exploration. A true learning machine must be endowed with rules for exploring the "space of all rules for exploring all (or many) solution spaces."

Such a problem is too difficult to permit any far-reaching computer solution. Besides, this task gets brilliant solutions from the human mind alone.

Q: *Grandmasters actually commit thousands of opening move sequences to memory. Can or do computers do the same?*
A: Most chess programs do use a small book of openings. In this case some person has manually typed each and every move into the machine. This is not a very intellectual process either for the machine or the typist. We do have plans to have the machine generate its own book of openings which will be extremely large. But we are not yet ready.

Q: *Can the machine learn anything from the Fischer-Spassky series?*
A: Yes. We plan to give COKO the first few games, but the learning will really be a human feedback loop. We will do the evaluation. We will compare the computer performance with Fischer's performance and instruct the machine to try and bridge the gap.

Q: *How can you instruct the machine when you are not chess experts yourselves?*
A: We consult experts and books written by experts. It is a myth of early artificial intelligence researchers that a programmer could set a computer on the course of solving a problem though he himself did not understand the problem. Clearly, the best man to work on the advanced chess programs of the future might well be Fischer himself.

Q: *Then you believe a computer will never beat its designer at chess?*
A: No. It has not happened yet. But it will.

Q: *What evidence do you have to indicate your program will defeat Fischer by 1984?*
A: It will not likely be our program, though we will stay in the race as long as we can. It is very likely that the program that will beat Fischer is one whose writing has not yet begun. That program will, however, use techniques developed by current chess programmers. We hope it will incorporate some of our own.

Q: *How much progress do you expect to make yourself?*
A: We have been making uniform progress since 1968. We can guarantee this progress for one more year and expect the same for the following year. Beyond that we would be speculating. We are a long way from saturating the performance of the Univac 1108. But for the next decade we expect, and need, machines considerably more powerful. The scheduled CDC 8600 computer should have well over ten times the power of the 1108, so this is not an idle expectation.

Q: *Well then, how long will it be before a computer can beat Bobby Fischer at chess?*
A: It might happen in ten years. But that same statement was made in 1957 followed by ten years of negligible progress.

We believe that it certainly will not take fifty years, and five years is impossible. And it would be nonsense to give a precise figure like fourteen and a half years.

---

**POWER**

Because of the cost and necessary skills, computers are the tools of big business and big governments rather than the general public. The large organizations have the power to collect and analyze the data, and then release the information they wish released. This causes a serious imbalance of power for which no one presently has a solution. Even if the general public had access to large computing power, it does not have the necessary skills and knowledge to use computers.

# Counter Computer

STUART BRAND

How mass use of computers might go is not even slightly known as yet, except for obvious applications in the schools. One informative place to inquire is among the hackers, particularly at night when they're pursuing their own interests.

One night at a computer center (nameless) I wandered off from the Spacewar game to a clattering print-out machine where a (nameless) young man with a trim beard was scanning columns of entries like, "Pam $1.59, Bud $14.75, Annie $2.66." He was an employee taking advantage of unbusy after hours time on the computer (computers are never turned off) to run his commune accounts.

"Money seems to be a very sensitive issue," he explained, "more sensitive than sex, even. People in the house who went on vacation for a week didn't want to be charged for the food during that time and so forth. It was taking me hours and hours every month to figure out people's house bills. Now it takes about a half hour a month. Every week I stick up a list on the refrigerator, and anyone who buys food or anything for the house writes it down on the list. I type all that into the computer, along with the mortgage payment and the phone bills and the gas bill. The House Bill Program goes around and divides up the common charges and adds in all the special charges and figures out exactly who owes who how much. Each person at the end of the month gets a bill plus a complete breakdown of what their money goes to."

That's pretty good. What else goes on around here in moonlight mode?

"A friend of mine has his recording tape library index on the computer. Everyone does their term papers and their theses on it. It'll justify margins, incorporate corrections, handle illustrations, paging, footnotes, headings, indexing. . . Two years ago when we had the great faculty strike against the War, we rigged up a program that would type out a form letter to all your congressmen and type in your name and address.

"Bruce is working on an astrology program. You put in your birthplace and date, down to the minute, and it gives you all your aspects, your chart. You can get your progress chart too. . . One of the hackers is building a computer at home out of Army surplus parts, and he's using the facilities here to help his design, because we have this huge battery of computer design programs."

Indeed. Far beyond borrowing someone else's computer is having your own computer. Hear now the saga of Pam Hart and Resource One. In 1969 Pam was a computer programmer at Berkeley who found the work "just too disillusioning. Then during the Cambodia Invasion demonstrations in Berkeley a group of us got together and designed a retrieval program for coordinating all of the actions on campus. It was a fairly dead system, but what it did was it brought together people who had never worked together before and started them talking and thinking about how it was actually possible to do something positive with technology, when you define the goals."

Computer power to the people. So began one of the great hustles of modern times. Peter Deutsch is still awed: "Pam could hustle blood from a turnip." She speaks quietly in a hasty, gentle, self-effacing murmur. You have to lean close to hear the lady helping you help her to plant dynamite in the very heart of the Combine.

"Four of us came from Berkeley to Project One and set up in a little office on the second floor. [Project One is a five-story warehouse in the south-of-Market area of San Francisco. It started in 1970 with a radio announcement: "If you're interested in building a community and cheap space and sharing resources, come to Project One." Within two weeks the building was filled with 200 artists, craftsmen, technicians and ex-professionals, and their families.] We worked on designing a retrieval system so all the switchboards in the City could interact, using a common data base, with all the care taken for privacy and knowing who put stuff in so you could refer back. Hopefully you could generate lists that were updated and be as on-line as possible.

"We found that it just did not work using borrowed time, stolen time, bought time—we couldn't afford it. So about a year later we set about getting surplus. After a couple of months of calling everybody in San Francisco that was related to computers, Transamerica said that they had three XDS 940s in a warehouse [each costing $300,000 new].

"We negotiated the contract, got a 940 [free], which we refurbished. It arrived last April; we installed it in June. It was probably the fastest installation ever: We had it up in three days. We were really fortunate the whole time. We had a lot of people from Xerox Park, a lot of the old people from Berkeley Computer Corporation, that have assisted us in areas where we weren't totally sure of the appropriate thing to do ourselves. Peter Deutsch brought up the operating system.

"Now we're a little more stable economically. We got a foundation grant of $10,000 last November from Stern. Then we borrowed $8000 from the Whole Earth Catalog, of which we paid back six. [News to me. This was part of the $20,000 I had turned over to the mob at the Catalog Demise Party. One Fred Moore finally signed for $15,000 of it and ran a series of subsequent consensus money decidings which evidently were susceptible to Pam's soft voice and clear head.] After two years we're right there at the beginning point of actually being able to do the things that we said we wanted to do.

"One of the first things we have to do is have a retrieval system that's general enough that it can handle things like Switchboard referral information, also people who are doing investigative work on corporations, people doing research on foundations, a whole lot of different groups either willing or not willing to share data bases.

"We're interested in some health care statistical systems. There are a lot of Free Clinics in the city, and they have to do all of their work by hand. We want to incorporate a system doing the statistical work for the clinics, charging the Health Centers that have money and not charging the Free Clinics that don't have the money.

"A third area is using government-generated tapes like assessor's tapes and census tapes, and start trying to do some analysis of the city. And the education program. The ideas include what Dymax is doing—set up a little recreation center where people could come and play games and hopefully some of them would be learning games. And then I'm interested in doing community education with video tape. People want to know about computers, not how to use them, necessarily, but how they're used against them."

Counter-computer. At present there are ten people in the core group at Resource One ranging in age from 19 to 30 (Pam is 25), with decisions made by consensus.

Another scheme in the works involves the people around Steve Beck at the National Center for Experiments in Television a few blocks away. Steve has built the world's first real-time video synthesizer—the video equivalent of the Moogs, Buchias, and Arps of music synthesis. It's a natural to link up with a computer. The current plan is for Steve and his equipment to move into the basement below Resource One, which should liven up the scene—Pam's gang is short on true hacker time-wasting frivolity; they're warm, but rather stogier than some of us Government-funded folks. Maybe the video link-up will give us some higher levels of Spacewar on the way to exploring new territory entirely. In what directions the computer-use at Resource One evolves should be of interest. If I were a computer manufacturer I'd pay the closest attention and maybe donate some goodies.

---

## Commission Drops DP System

# VARIATION ON AN OLD THEME: MAN REPLACES COMPUTER

**By Marvin Smalheiser**

SACRAMENTO—A California commission has found it can do its job better and cheaper—$1.5 million cheaper—by replacing its computer with humans.

The state Teacher Preparation and Licensing Commission, which was using almost a full shift of a shared state IBM 360/90, said it has just completed a transition back to manual operation that cuts the time of processing teacher credential applications by 900%.

The commission also said it has reduced its staff from 240 to 106.

Charles W. Moss, assistant executive secretary of the commission, set up last July 1, said the savings were achieved after an intensive procedures analysis that streamlined and automated the teacher credential processing.

The savings are effected largely through a revised system in which the commission accepts only completed applications, greatly reducing file maintenance costs.

The commission either issues a credential or advises the applicant of his deficiency.

The new procedure enables the commission to put all the files on eight microfeche robot files, which can be pulled "10 times faster" than querying a computer on the 18 terminals it had been using. A credential typist can now process an application for 50 cents, compared to $9.50 per application on the computer, Moss said.

And the time for processing has been cut from an average of 95 days per application to 10 days.

The computer is in the state's Department of General Services and is used for various other jobs ranging from state apportionment of school funds to accounting of federal funds.

But, said Moss, "it was duplicating a lot of things we have to do manually, anyway." There were also heavy supervisory costs and expensive file maintenance functions.

Moss said that under the revised operating procedures the commission could still do the work on the computer but the cost would still be $9.50 per application, compared to 50 cents manually.

A side benefit of the switch came during the summer when the commission began the transition and hired more than 50 students to help make the change to manual processing. They worked in place of commission personnel who had been advised of the change and had relocated to other jobs early.

# Maximilian The Great

JAMES F. RYAN

Annie Buchanan threw her lithe arms around her husband's neck. The more she stared at the new cocktail ring shimmering on her finger the tighter she squeezed.

"Jack . . . Oh, Jack it's *beautiful!* Thank you so much. Oh, I can just imagine what this will look like with my mauve gown . . . or . . . no, definitely the mauve . . ."

"It's an amethyst."

"I know."

"A medium-sized amethyst."

"Yes."

"In a white gold setting."

"Yes, I see." Annie stepped back a piece to view the ring in the sharper light falling from the chandelier. Jack's mouth hung slightly open.

"But you didn't make this much fuss when I gave you your engagement ring."

"Hmmm?" Annie said, watching for the stone to change shade. She was sure the blood was coursing through her fingers faster than usual.

"That was a diamond," Jack said.

"Most engagement rings are."

Not knowing just how to break the spell, Jack repeated what he had said—louder. "It's only an amethyst."

"Yes, but you bought it yourself, didn't you? I mean, nobody helped you."

"The salesgirl . . ."

"I mean . . ." She immediately bit her lip but knew well it was too late.

Jack stared at his shoes, then turned and walked to the far wall of the living room. He flipped the toggle switch on the console from standby to run and sat by the keyboard. After a quick glance through the book hanging from a chain on the console, he hunt and pecked an address into the Buchanan family's computer, Maximilian. A relay clacked in and a near imperceptible hum rose in the room.

He knew Annie was behind though he had not heard her cross the floor. From the corner of his eye he could see her hand gliding between his elbow and side, her slender index finger aiming directly for the cancel switch. He cupped his palm over the button. The hand withdrew.

*I could spit*, Annie thought. *Why? Why did I carry on so?*

The keyboard carriage jolted up several times. *Go ahead, bigmouth.* The keys pounded in merciless rhythm. *I feel naked, damnit!* A.B.—PERSONAL JEWELRY Subheadings flashed by. Finally, it came RINGS—BAND, YELLOW GOLD . . . DIAMOND, 12 PTS, PLATINUM . . . AMETHYST, 537 PTS, WHITE GOLD . . . AMETHYST, 542 PTS, WHITE GOLD . .

"I'll take it back," Jack said, not looking up from the printout sheet.

"No!" The intensity of her own voice surprised her.

"What's the sense, honey."

"I like it."

"You're just being silly. Just because . . ."

"You bought it. Max didn't. That's why I like it. For once you did something without being told to do it by him."

"He . . . I mean *it*, didn't tell me to do *anything*. Max just gives me the facts and *I* decide what to do. If I've told you once, I've told you a hundred times. Computers don't . . ."

"I'd still rather get an anniversary gift from you."

"It *is* from me."

"Then there's no reason why I can't keep it."

"But this is the third one."

"I don't care."

"Alright . . . I give up. Keep it. Just don't complain to me when you run out of fingers . . . Let's have dinner."

Jack sipped lazily on a weak martini and wondered why the dining room table was set for two. He looked at his watch. Nearly nine-thirty. The kids were in bed. Strange, how the long summer days could upset your whole sense of time. Annie came in from the kitchen, rushing to the table with the hot platter.

"Just made it," she said, blowing on her fingers. "Come and get it."

He leaned carefully over the candles and kissed her. "Happy anniversary, Annie."

"Happy anniversary."

They ate silently. Annie traced small circles on the tablecloth, trying to catch the flamelight in the amethyst. The soft, rich glow she finally found pleased her.

Jack unconsciously cleared his throat. "Honey, now don't get excited, but if you want, I'll exchange it for . . ."

"No," she said, calmly. "I like it." Again silence.

"But don't take it out on Max."

"What?"

"The ring."

"Of course not." She smiled deliciously. "He didn't have a thing to do with it."

Hoisted by his own petard, Jack thought it best to stick to vague generalities. "He's done some pretty accurate forecasting for us. He told us exactly what our best investments would be."

"He also said Marge would have red hair."

"That was my fault. I loused up the input. Anyway, he said the baby *might* have red hair."

"*I* could have said that. As a matter of fact, my mother did say it when I was pregnant. Remember my cousin Rachel? She had sort of red hair until she bleached it."

"But that's not the point, honey," he said, searching for the point and not quite finding it. "Just think of all the clothes you've designed using the display screen. You never complain about that."

"I don't ask Max personal questions, though."

"That's just it. He couldn't care less. Just think of him as what he is—a big, black box loaded with facts. He just lines up the facts as he's told. He doesn't care what your bust size is or how much we've got in the bank."

"But he *knows*."

"Does he stick his head over the back fence and shout to Betsy Kittridge?"

"He doesn't have a head."

"Nor a mouth. Which makes him still more trustworthy."

He knew he hadn't by any means convinced her. It had been a ten-year, uphill struggle to ease her prejudice, with silly situations like these dragging all his efforts back to the starting point.

"More coffee?" Annie asked.

"No, I have to work."

"Oh," she said. The corners of her mouth fell almost imperceptibly.

"Just for a few minutes—on the concordance. You don't mind?"

"No," she lied.

Annie had just finished putting the dishes in the washer when it happened. She raced into the living room, visions of her husband gasping for air, his tie fouled in the output platen, leaping across her imagination.

The scarlet of his face accentuated by the dull brown disk he held in his hand, Jack stood, his legs spread.

"Who?" he sputtered.

Maternal instinct immediately placed the nonanswer on her lips. "I told you to lock it in the cabinet."

Which answered the question unequivocally.

"He's six years old," Jack said. "He should know the difference between a phonograph record and a magnetic disk, for God's sake. I had almost all the metaphysical poets on this." His eyes widened. "Maybe . . . just *maybe*."

He quickly placed the disk on its spindle and sat at the keyboard. He knew the code by heart. A few quick strokes and the tale would be told. The display tube lit obediently. DONNE, J.—NO MAN IS AN ISLAND . . .

Jack jumped up and was about to clap his hands. NO MAN IS AN ISLAND ENTIRE OF ITXCSW RUBATUBDUB DUB DUB DUB DUB DUB DUB DUB

"Hell," he said, slouching back down into the chair.

"Don't you hit him. It wasn't his fault."

"Eight months work—poof!"

"All the poems are still right there in your textbook."

"But I nearly had the perfect concordance. Every work beautifully, logically arranged, waiting. I could have run all those spurious Donne poems through and finished the paper in a week. It would have been the definitive work on the apochryphal metaphysicals."

"I'll bet Linus Pauling never used information retrieval for *his* literary research."

"Linus Pauling is a chemist," he said blankly.

"You know who I mean."

Annie was already in bed, hiding behind the magazine she was pretending to be reading, when Jack came in, his shower finished. He picked up the book she had laid on his pillow. The slight breeze from the air conditioner brought the fresh smell of new morocco leather to her nostrils. Jack laughed.

Annie let the magazine slide down over her chest. "Happy anniversary, professor," she said.

"Happy anniversary, Annie," he said, switching off the light and tossing the book on the night table. Darkness obscured the gilt stamping on the book's spine—*The Works of John Donne*.

The next morning, Annie peeked through the living room curtains just in time to catch the rear end of his car spinning around the final turn in the driveway. She waited, half expecting to see the car come racing back in reverse. He always forgot *something*. Not this time.

She turned toward the kitchen, heading for the first enjoyable cup of coffee of the day. As she passed Max she heard the telltale hum.

"Oh, you're just as transparent as he is. Neither of you can ever keep your thoughts to yourselves." It never struck her as odd that she should talk to the computer.

"What's up, old buddy?" she asked, scanning the paper roll in the keyboard for a note that Jack would sometimes leave to indicate that Max was working overtime.

"When we were first married, your master would have kittens if he found out I'd left the air conditioner on. I'll bet he never told you *that*."

She reached up for the power switch, hesitated, and instead, leaned over the input keys. A better typist than her husband, her fingers flicked over the key board. SHUT YOURSELF OFF. Impulse grabbed her. Did she dare? Yes. PERMANENTLY. Immediately contrite, she jabbed at the cancel switch and hit the carriage return instead. Max was, by now, enthusiastically mulching his own assassination command.

"Max, I'm sorry! I didn't really mean that. Please . . . Oh, Max. Don't!!"

The computer responded in its unhurried lightning pace. It belted out the reply and sat idling and content. Annie forced herself to read the printout. INPUT ERROR—READDRESS.

"Ohhhhh. I can't even insult you. You've got no shame." She pulled the power switch to standby. "Go to sleep."

It was nearly eleven o'clock when Max turned on the lawn sprinklers. Annie stared out from the kitchen window, somewhat surprised. It hadn't been that dry, she thought. Then she realized that she couldn't remember when the last decent rain had fallen. As she gazed dreamily into the rainbows undulating in the fine spray, a small dark form slowly focused itself into her line of vision. She ran to the door.

"Marge . . . you come in here this instant."

"Aw, mommy, it's warm out here."

"Not nearly as warm as your backside is going to be if you don't get in here . . . *now*."

Marge skipped to the door and stood in front of her mother, dripping like a wet puppy. Annie began rubbing furiously at the child's head with a dishtowel.

"Why in heaven's name did you just *stand* there?"

"It's hot in the sun."

"It's not that hot, Marge."

"Yes it is. Max wouldn't have turned on the sprinklers if it wasn't. He never does unless it's very, *very* hot."

"Max is supposed to water the lawn, not you and your brother . . . by the way, where *is* Peter?"

"Out by the toolshed. Can I play checkers with Max?"

"Absolutely not."

"Why?"

"Remember what happened when your brother decided he was going to play a record for Max?"

"But he's stupid."

"And you're the smartest eight-year-old in the world, right? You can play with Max when your father comes home."

"But he gets so lonely."

"I think he'll survive the afternoon somehow or other. Now you march upstairs and get out of those wet clothes, young lady."

Marge walked toward the stairs, her shoes squishing like wet sponges at every step. She peeked back over her shoulder; Annie tried unsuccessfully to erase the smile that had made its way to her lips.

"March!"

Marge giggled and disappeared up the stairs. Annie stepped back to the open door.

"Peter." A thatch of blonde hair popped up from between the hedges at the rear of the lawn. "Time for lunch."

Peter zigzagged across the lawn, avoiding not a single sprinkler head. He skidded to a stop on the wet grass three paces in front of the upraised hand of his mother.

"But Ma . . ."

"I know . . . it's hot."

"Macth wouldn't . . ."

". . . turn on the sprinklers unless it was very, *very* hot. Upstairs and change your clothes . . . *all* of them."

As he crouched for a jumping start of the fifty-yard dash to his room, Annie broke his stride.

"Wait . . . Take off your sneakers first. And don't run."

As Peter ran through the kitchen, the sprinklers lilted to a dribble and stopped.

"This is a conspiracy," Annie mumbled, picking up a deck of punched cards on her way to the living room.

She wondered if it wouldn't really be easier to just sit down and make up a grocery list every week. As it was, every time she opened a can of this or a bottle of that, she had to walk over to the portable punching unit, select the card and cut the appropriate information. Couldn't she just as easily check the shelves at the end of the week?

As she fed the cards into the hopper, she decided that perhaps Max wasn't such a bad shopper after all. She never did have the patience to do comparison shopping, whereas

Max would check at least three supermarkets before buying even a pound of salt. He could generally place the entire order over phone lines within a few minutes, check the total on the bill, (she could never get the same total twice), and store it neatly till the end of the month when he would write a check and even remember to bring the balance forward.

The items she had used during the week began to roll by on the keyboard carriage. She sat back in the chair and stared up at the curtains. Why didn't Max ever tell her to buy a new pair of *those*, she thought. She made a mental note to ask Jack to put household furnishings into Max's gluttonous brain.

Max rang his bell and stopped, obedient to a standing command to point out anything he thought abnormal for the week. Annie looked down at the sheet. UNDERARM DEODORANT—3 6 OZ TUBES

"So? It's summer. Just because you don't have a nose." She signalled Max to continue the tally.

"Finished?" She tore off the printout sheet. "You actually mean Mother didn't make any other bubus this week? Amazing."

She remembered to inform Max that the Peerless stores were closed for vacation, then lifted the phone from its cradle on the console and gave the line over to the computer.

"Don't break the eggs."

When the doorbell rang after lunch, Annie looked up at the clock and thought it rather early for the delivery boy. Summer help, she supposed.

She opened the door and stared out at a massive, khaki-covered chest. She followed the form up to its bull neck and sweaty face. Instinctively, she stepped back.

"Yes?"

"Where do you want it, lady?"

"Where do I want *what*?"

"The piano?"

"What piano?"

"This one . . ." The hulk stepped aside, revealing a huge cardboard carton, being steadied on its side by what appeared to be the hulk's twin.

"Is this a joke?"

The hulk smiled. "Oh yeah . . . Me and Jerry my partner—we lug these things up and down the streets on nice afternoons like this. Lady . . ."

"I mean . . . I didn't buy a piano."

"Mrs. John Buchanan? 75 Sapsucker Lane?"

"Yes, but . . ."

"Lady, you bought a piano." He handed her the invoice.

She searched the invoice for the inevitable, silly mistake. Max's access number popped into focus before her eyes. She double checked. She had bought a piano.

"But there's some mistake. I . . ." The carton was halfway in the door.

"Watch the jamb, Jerry. O.K. Now swing opposite me. Good. Living room, lady?"

"Yes," Annie said absently. "I mean *no* . . ."

"Where?"

"I mean yes, this is the living room—no, you may *not* leave it here."

"Alright, alright. I understand. Where d'ya want it?"

"Back in your truck."

"Huh?"

Annie struggled for control of the situation. "I mean I don't want your silly piano. I didn't order it. There's some mistake. Now you just back it out and put it in your truck and . . . and goodbye."

The hulk eased the carton to the floor, leaned his elbow on it and, with his free hand, pulled from his pocket a pennant of a handkerchief. He wiped his brow.

"Lady . . . Jerry and me—we got a nice business going. That's our truck out there. We specialize in delivering things real quick—like your piano. Sometimes in an hour or two. A merchant calls us and we zip over there, pick up the goods and deliver it, see? We don't *undeliver* things. We don't know nothing about that; we don't want to know."

"But I didn't order a piano." Annie was almost screaming.

"Well, after we leave, you just call up the guy you didn't buy the piano from and tell him that you don't want the thing. Maybe he calls another guy to take it back. I don't know. Me and Jerry, we're just going to take this thing out of the box, put the legs on it and put it wherever you say. Then we disappear—until you buy another piano. Where d'ya want it?"

"Right here."

"In the hall?"

"Yes!"

"You heard the lady, Jerry. Put it down."

Annie sat on the piano bench and cried.

"I'm home, honey," Jack chimed toward the light of the living room as he entered the darkened hall later that evening.

"Watch out for . . ." His briefcase came sliding across the rug.

"What the hell? Annie!"

She flipped the hall lights on just in time to catch him furiously rubbing at his shin. He quickly forgot the bruise.

"What in God's name is *this*?"

"A piano."

"I *know* that. What's it doing here?"

"We could move it into the living room," Ann parried.

"I mean what's it doing here, on this street, in this house?"

"Max bought it."

"What?"

"I just ran the grocery tally and order and the next thing I knew two monsters burst in here and put the thing down."

"Annie!"

". . . and they wouldn't take it back."

"You must have done *something*," Jack said, waving toward Max.

"I didn't."

"Do I have to do everything? Can't you learn to run a simple, uncomplicated, basic tally and order?"

"Now you just wait a minute, Jack Buchanan. I've been sitting on dynamite all afternoon, wondering what else that spendthrift might have bought. Don't you holler at me. I haven't even gotten my groceries yet."

"You could call the market, you know."

"Oh? *You* try and get the phone line away from that . . . that beast."

"Now you're being ridiculous. All you have to do is push the release and . . ." Jack pecked at the button on the phone cradle. "Now what did you do to the *phone*?"

"Oooooh. Go to hell!"

Jack flinched slightly, but walked calmly to the corner

cabinet. He wheeled the oscilloscope cart carefully back to the front of the console.

"I won't want any dinner," he said.

"Who said anything about dinner? Get your buddy here to fix you a sandwich if you get hungry. Maybe you could eat one of his noodles."

"Modules." He knew he shouldn't have said that. Annie's eyes lit.

"I just realized . . . you don't *believe* me. You don't believe that you don't *believe* me. You blindly take the part of that brute over my word. I'm the only one around here who could possibly make a mistake. Did you ever dream that he could go haywire and louse up the works? Oh no. He's never wrong. It's always *me*."

"Don't get emotional."

"Who's getting emotional? Maybe a little emotion around here wouldn't hurt."

"Let me finish. Computers don't make mistakes. You have to be rational to be wrong. Can't you see that? All Max does is exactly as he's told. He can't make a decision or change his mind without being told in some way to do so. He can't be wrong unless someone tells him to be wrong. Now don't fly off the handle, but you made a mistake—somewhere, somehow, you loused up."

The pride holding back her tears dissolved. "Good night."

"Annie . . ." But she was already gone.

Annie stared at her image reflected in the mirror, enjoying the quiet coolness of the bedroom.

*He didn't have to say it was my fault. He could have at least pretended it was Max's—for once.*

She leaned back against the bed's headboard and gazed up at the familiar crack in the ceiling. She remembered how Max had come to be—how he had come home in pieces with Jack from the university where the other professors had helped Jack assemble the parts. The nights he and she had stayed up nearly till dawn telling Max practically everything they knew. . . .

Max had grown with them. He would be ten in September. He was like a son and a father at the same time. How his mentality had changed in that time. Or rather, how he so faithfully reflected and recorded the change and maturation in their lives.

Annie looked toward the clock on the night table. After midnight. Jack would have to get up in the morning. Wouldn't he ever learn to get to bed at a decent hour?

From the landing she could see him, boylike, hunched over the keyboard, slowly, almost painfully, typing and staring up at the oscilloscope. She didn't know what the consistent straight line trace meant, but premonition told her all was not well.

"Jack?"

"Hm?" She was behind him, massaging his tightened shoulder muscles with her long fingers. He did not turn.

"What's the matter, Jack?"

". . . A frontal lobotomy."

"What?"

"I had to do a complete core dump."

Annie felt as if her own memory had suddenly been scalded away.

"But . . . *why?*"

"My fault. The whole core—hopelessly confused and overlapped."

Her head was spinning. "How?"

"I was working on the picture tube in the color set last night. The degaussing coil—I left it running full blast, right on top of the bulk storage bank."

"And that . . ."

"Demagnetized the works."

"Jack . . . oh, Jack, I'm *sorry*. No matter what I said before. Really, I am."

"What will we do, Annie?"

"Start over."

"Ten years work?"

"We're a lot smarter now."

He tried to smile but it broke up halfway, leaving his lower lip quivering.

"Come to bed. It's late," she said.

Jack reached down and pulled the main power switch. "First time in ten years."

"Yes," Annie said, feeling a strange giddiness shooting through her body. "First time in ten years."

They walked slowly up the stairs together. Midway, Jack stopped, placed his hand firmly around her waist and gently pulled her toward him. The heat of his palm quickly penetrated the thin film of her nightgown and raced up to the flush in her face.

"Annie . . . I'm sorry. Not only for what I said tonight. For lots of things. Forgive me? Can you?"

She brushed a stubborn curl of hair back from his brow.

"How can I not?" She very nearly giggled. "After all, I'm only human. . . ."

They continued up the stairs.

"It's a Suicide Note!"

# Those Omnipresent Minis

W. DAVID GARDNER

At home, in coal mines, aboard surveyors' airplanes, minicomputers now sort trash and direct taxis

Dr. Stephen D. Senturia of the Massachusetts Institute of Technology might be described as a trash freak. He has built the electronics for a trash sorter that takes pure unadulterated trash and sorts it into different categories.

"We couldn't have conceived of building the system if that inexpensive minicomputer hadn't been available," says Dr. Senturia. Indeed, the trash system's mini, a Computer Automation cpu, costs less than $5,000 including a teletypewriter.

### MINIS CAN BE FUN

Dr. Senturia and his minicomputer are illustrative of the underground boom in minicomputers. The minicomputer explosion is not just isolated to traditional usage in control, scientific, time-sharing and data communications applications; the mini is also turning up more and more in offbeat applications. In short, the minicomputer, normally looked upon as just another electronics black box, can be fun.

"I think we're just beginning to see the offbeat uses of minicomputers," says Andrew C. Knowles, vice president of Digital Equipment Corp.'s minicomputer operation. "For instance, some of our programmers will buy PDP-8s and take them home. We try to encourage this by giving them a bargain price."

The Massachusetts company's president, Kenneth H. Olsen, has had a mini at home for years. Most minis in the home are still used by scientists and technicians in their work—although minicomputers in the home see some use as novelty items by game players—but the feeling is that there will be more interest in minis as novelty luxury items in the future by people who don't have technical backgrounds. Knowles foresees the days when minis will be sold through catalogues. In fact, a few years ago Honeywell offered a minicomputer through the swank Neiman-Marcus Christmas catalog. The so-called "kitchen computer" was programmed to provide menus and recipe references to five famous cookbooks. The computer could also be used for checkbook balancing and other household tasks. Although no housewife found a Honeywell "kitchen computer" in her stocking, Neiman-Marcus received several inquiries about the computer from both men and women.

Another who thinks that some minis will be sold as novelty items is Edson D. de Castro, president of Data General Corp. "Look at all the electronic calculators that were bought last Christmas for people who have no use for them. I wouldn't be surprised to see the same thing happen with minis."

De Castro points out that a minicomputer can be viewed as a novelty item for playing chess or other games. In addition, minis can serve educational purposes in the home—for instance, for teaching youngsters programming. De Castro feels more minis will end up in homes as more and more children get hands-on experience with computers in their elementary and high schools.

### WHO'S GOT THE MINI?

De Castro would just as soon forget some of the adventures involving his minicomputers. The completion of Data General's first Nova, for instance, was an event that was celebrated with much jubilation by de Castro a few years ago. The mini was sent by plane to Data General's first customer but the machine was lost by the airline and it stayed lost for several weeks. (Minis are small enough to be relatively inconspicuous.) Then, some months after, when Data General shipped its first Nova to Europe, the machine was placed in the back seat of a salesman's car. The car was stolen and the mini later was found in a ditch. The Nova was cleaned up and delivered to the customer in working order. Last year, when a group from de Castro's Canadian operation, Datagen, visited the Peoples Republic of China, they learned that a Nova had been smuggled into the Asian country.

Just what is the current definition of a minicomputer? First of all, as its name suggests, minicomputers are little. Sometimes they are called small computers, small control computers, or dedicated application computers. A minicomputer is also inexpensive, usually costing less than $10,000. Although the cpu's tend to shrink with the widespread use of LSI, the business is booming. *EDP Industry Report,* for instance, says that value of shipments in the minicomputer industry—which the newsletter prefers to call the dedicated application computer business—increased last year 50% or so from $360 million to $550 million. IBM, which dominates the general data processing market, is usually not considered to be a factor in the traditional minicomputer business. The computer colossus markets a small "sensor-based" computer—the System/7—that features an architecture similar to the popular minicomputers, but the System/7 is substantially more expensive than the regular mini.

Perhaps the best testimonial for the rising popularity of minicomputers is that a PDP-8 was stolen from an MIT laboratory by a group of undergraduates. The incident has led some wags to forecast the eventual appearance of a market for "hot" minicomputers like the market for hot television sets and stereos.

Minicomputers were even the object of violence at the college student outbreaks of a couple of years ago. In the absence of an accessible edp site at one Boston area university, a group of self-appointed radical students set fire to a PDP-8. After the fire was extinguished, the casing was taken off the machine and soot and debris fell into the printed circuit boards. But when the PDP-8 was plugged in, it still worked!

Many minicomputers are ruggedized for heavy duty applications and to meet certain military specifications, but what is becoming increasingly apparent is that the plain old garden variety, nonruggedized mini is a tough machine. For instance, a Digital Computer Controls mini is used to weigh coal cars deep in a coal mine in British Columbia. Forty tons of coal rumble past the machine's sensors daily. Some years ago, Varian Data Machines cut one of its 620s in half and stuck it in a U.S. Department of the Interior helicopter. For years, the mini has worked reliably for Interior Department surveys of remote land tracts in Alaska.

The minicomputer has gone to school in a big way, too. For example, take the experience of Hewlett-Packard minicomputer systems, which are used extensively in schools, particularly time-shared systems. H-P machines are in use in several elementary schools and, on the other end of the educational spectrum, they are installed in many colleges.

## STUDENTS LOVE THEM

"There are fifth and sixth graders writing sophisticated programs at the Burnsville Elementary School District in Minneapolis," says an H-P executive. "Generally the minis are used by very bright kids who often are bored with school and they become very proficient with minis by the time they enter high school. On the other hand, we have six systems in the Los Angeles schools for remedial work—for drill and practice. It's the same equipment in Minneapolis and Los Angeles, but the uses are nearly opposite."

Indeed, as an educational and vocational tool, the minicomputer is turning up just about everywhere. Besides the expected places like elementary and secondary schools and colleges, H-P machines are in use in prisons as a vocational tool. Officers play war games on a time-shared H-P mini at the Armed Forces Staff College in Norfolk, Va.

As more and more people learn to use minicomputers in school they begin using them as tools in their work. The manner in which MIT's Professor Senturia picked his for his trash sorting system is somewhat representative of how many of them end up in oddball applications.

It started with an unusual project: David G. Wilson, a professor of mechanical engineering at MIT, initiated the trash sorting project in the summer of 1969. Senturia soon joined the program to work on the electrical and electronic elements of the system. He was immediately attracted by the low price of minicomputers. "A minicomputer costs just about the same as a good oscilloscope," Senturia points out. "We had to take several sensor inputs from the trash and make a decision in a tenth of a second. The minicomputer was our answer."

In the trash sorting system trash and refuse is loaded onto a wire mesh vibrating screen, which shakes out objects by size. The objects are then moved along a conveyor belt, passing a simple metal detector like those being used to screen airline passengers. An infrared reflection spectrometer can sort the objects into different categories, such as cellulose, plastic, glass and various metal objects. An impact sensor with an accelerator and a small hammer can differentiate surfaces. For instance, it can tell the difference between wood and paper.

Finally, the sorted refuse is automatically loaded onto buggies by categories of trash. At this point the minicomputer comes in, monitoring four carts simultaneously and performing the classification calculation. "We shoot these baskets out at the rate of three a second to their proper unloading stations," says Senturia. "It's like a Gatling gun."

**The so-called "kitchen computer" was programmed to provide menus and recipe references to five famous cookbooks. The computer could also be used for checkbook balancing and other household tasks.**

The MIT scientists have built sections of a preliminary prototype system, which they are currently perfecting. Because of the enormous size and expense involved—a completed system will probably cost more than $1 million—a full system couldn't be constructed until an actual end user decides to build one. Senturia says the scientists working on the project have been discussing construction of a system with several communities. "There are a lot of solid economic reasons for the system," says Senturia. "It is expensive but it would only be a fraction of the cost of an incinerator and the trash sorting system would make an incinerator all the more efficient."

Senturia picked a Computer Automation minicomputer and that company, like other minicomputer manufacturers that offer inexpensive models in their lines, sees many of its minis end up in offbeat applications. Digital Equipment Corp. and Data General, for instance, have the longest lists of offbeat applications, while General Automation Inc., although an important factor in the mini business, could find none of its minis being used in nontraditional applications. General Automation concentrates in specialized systems markets, such as automotive production.

Digital Equipment Corp. claims to have delivered more minicomputers than all its competitors combined. It

THOSE OMNIPRESENT MINIS **83**

**"In five years I would expect to see a mini sell for $1,000 or less."**

follows, then, that DEC computers would end up not only in the most places but also in the strangest places. Several DEC minicomputers, for instance, are used by individuals in their homes. Some run stock market analysis for business or pleasure; others conduct laboratory and scientific tests. Many people take a DEC mini home to continue working on a project they started at their regular jobs. Inevitably, the children use the machine.

### FOR ENTERTAINMENT

When Thomas Prugh of Silver Spring, Md., bought his DEC mini a few years ago, he looked upon it as a hobby. "Many people," said Prugh, "buy yachts, fancy sports cars or airplanes for off-hour amusement." Prugh bought an $8500 PDP-8 and his mini has been used for just about everything at his home from computing taxes and mortgage interest to preparing menus and assisting the Prugh youngsters with their homework.

Moreover, Prugh, an electronics engineer, was particularly interested in developing what he called "home control" uses. Indeed, the whole area of a mini for control purposes in the home has also caught the eye of DEC management. DEC's Andrew Knowles believes that optical and voice recognition applications will be commonplace by the end of the decade and that many home applications will be controlled by minis. "You should be able to order your groceries over the phone," says Knowles. "Your voice will be recognized by the computer and your account will be billed." In addition to the more logical household tasks—like tax computation, menu compilation, and opening and closing garage doors—minis should be able to answer phones and take messages, serve as a burglar alarm system and, in the event of a fire, the mini should be able to sense it and automatically alert the fire department.

Perhaps the most famous of the DEC offbeat applications is the PDP-8 that was set up to control an automated potato picker in Scotland. In another unusual application, a student at Carleton College in Laconia, N.H., programmed a DEC mini to assist him in writing a movie script. Although the finished result is not expected to produce any Academy Awards, many moviegoers would undoubtedly vouch that it's as good as the stuff they see at their neighborhood movie theaters. DEC and Interdata minis have been used successfully for years for motion picture animation.

It's only natural that minis work their way into sports. The animated 274-foot-long display scoreboard of the Pittsburgh Pirates baseball team is controlled by a PDP-8. The board not only keeps a running record of the sports events in progress at the Three Rivers Stadium at any given time, but it can flash spot announcements, give newscasts and commercials, and lead sing-alongs and cheers. In sports car racing, a PDP-8 is used by the crack Ferrari team to keep track of numerous racing cars and their complicated lap counts.

Minicomputers are smart, too. Data General points to the instance where one of its chess-playing Supernovas—with 32K bytes of memory—checkmated an IBM 360/91 in just 25 moves. The IBM system had a memory capacity of more than 2 million bytes. The match was held at Columbia University whose Department of Electrical Engineering and Computer Science owned the Supernova. The IBM machine belongs to Columbia's computer center.

The sport of kings, too, has not been immune from the minicomputer invasion. Race tracks in several countries are using minicomputers—usually equipment from Varian Data Machines—to handle betting operations. Several parimutuel systems have been configured around the Varian machines by Western Totalisator of Montreal. The system compiles betting information and at the same time calculates odds and dividends. In addition, the system constantly updates the track infield board and auxiliary displays around the clubhouse.

"Our typical system is so fast," says a Western Totalisator executive, "that by the time the horses are in the back stretch in each race, a complete sales report for that race already has been generated by two high-speed printers."

### HORSING AROUND

And, with all those minicomputers around the horses, it is only natural that there are rumors of people using them to do their own personal handicapping. There has never been any evidence of this, but the temptation to use a mini "to beat the horses" must be overpowering. There is something of an analogy in the story of the man who uses a minicomputer to follow fluctuations in the Dow-Jones tape to play the stock market. The story is that he's successful at it, too.

Even when a minicomputer company stakes out a specialized field of expertise, its cpu's often end up in unexpected situations. Interdata, for instance, is big in data communications so it didn't surprise anyone when the company nailed down the contract to supply a clutch of minis for the complex communications network of the Royal Canadian Mounted Police. The network uses some 25 Interdata cpu's and will eventually handle 1,000 terminals.

Interdata president Daniel Sinnott has been taking some good-natured ribbing about Mountie Nelson Eddy riding off into the sunset singing "Indian Love Call" with an Interdata mini on his horse. "I can't quite see a cpu or a terminal on a horse, although a lot of people joke about it," says Sinnott. "But I can visualize a Mountie in a remote outpost surrounded by 15-foot snow drifts with his trusty data communications terminal at his side."

An Interdata mini is also an unsung star of the silver screen, being an instrument used frequently by Hollywood's noted special effects man, Doug Trumbull, who is best known for his special effects in the film "2001." Also in the science fiction film "The Andromeda Strain," the complicated sequences of the mysterious viruslike crystalline life form that invades earth were developed by the Interdata mini. Across the continent, in Cambridge, Mass., another Interdata machine is in use at MIT recording the random bumpings of blocks by gerbils. The gerbils' activities are being recorded in a scientific project studying random behavior.

What of the future? While many are predicting the widespread growth of minis in the home and office, there are indications that they will touch people increasingly in unusual ways. A few years ago, Honeywell was excited to report that its minis were playing an important role in the automation of Paris' Metro system, but now that application is taken for granted. And lately a Honeywell mini has been operating an experimental driverless taxi in England. The passenger simply inserts a magnetically encoded ticket into a slot in the taxi and he is whisked to his destination. Perhaps that application will be taken for granted in a few years.

More than anything, though, it is the sheer force of the minicomputer boom that is likely to spread the unusual applications. It is matter of simple arithmetic: The more machines there are, the more machines there will be in offbeat applications. And, in this regard as far as the dropping prices of minis are concerned, Data General's Edson de Castro has some blasphemy for those who worry about price cuts. "I expect to see the prices of minis continue to decline at the same rate, or even at a faster rate than they have in the past," de Castro says. "In five years I would expect to see a mini sell for $1,000 or less."

In addition, minicomputer peripheral prices have begun to decline at an even faster rate than cpu's, with the result that systems costs are still dropping rapidly. All this simply means that the only limits to where minicomputers will end up are those of human imagination.

# Computer Career Opportunities
Honeywell Corporation

Future career opportunities in the rapidly growing world of computers seem to be practically limitless. These opportunities may be direct, as in the case of those who manufacture and operate computers, or indirect, as in the case of businessmen, scientists, and others who use computer systems.

Increasingly great numbers of skilled personnel will be needed by the computer industry itself:

Designers and manufacturers of systems
Engineers and scientists for research and development
Sales personnel skilled in marketing methods
Systems analysts to analyze and meet special requirements of customers
Programmers who prepare programs to meet customers' needs
Computer operators to run systems
Personnel for clerical and data preparation jobs
Managers of computer operations
Management interpreters of computer systems, needs, opportunities
Specialists in areas such as business, science, education, and government
Interdisciplinarians—those who can understand and meet the needs of persons from varied professions united on mutual projects

More than a thousand colleges and universities in the U.S.A. and Canada, according to a recent survey, now offer courses in the computer sciences and data processing. Computer usage is being taught in many high schools and even in some grammar schools. Many independent training schools exist for high school and college graduates.

The use of remote terminals, that connect to a central computer system sometimes from thousands of miles away, is becoming commonplace. Industry experts say it's only a matter of time and cost reduction before the use of household terminals, for a variety of purposes ranging from information services to entertainment, becomes as ordinary as the use of the telephone.

Economists predict that by the end of the century, or earlier, the computer industry and directly associated industries will be the largest American business.

# Computers in the home

G. CUTTLE

Anyone who has any doubts about the ability of a computer to cook breakfast has only to remember the state of mind of the average person at seven in the morning to realize that preparing breakfast is a very mechanical task indeed. Many other household tasks are equally suitable for dull but meticulously well-ordered computers to invade; indeed, they have already begun to do so in, for example, washing machines and central-heating control systems. As with present process-control computers in industry, a computer in the home could be provided with specific programs to provide for the peculiar needs of the household, and could hold a library of such programs for varying day-to-day conditions. At present each piece of equipment needing such a computer has its own small one built in, but the logical development is to have a larger household computer tucked away with the meters and broken prams in the cupboard under the stairs. Circuits could then be wired into the house so that each individual gadget could be plugged in to it. There are many ways in which a central computer could make its influence felt, and its tentacles will spread into every room of the house through common household control channelling. (It is astonishing for how long we have dumbly accepted that every wire and pipe needs its own hole in the plaster.) With a built-in clock it could gently wake us at the appointed hour, dutifully taking weekends, school holidays, and the night before into account. It could present us with a cup of tea, the post, and the satisfying assurance that the house was clean, aired, and warm, and that a hot bath awaited us. None of these functions is more than an extension of individual facilities already available, except possibly that of house cleaning. Whatever machinery is to be developed—pipes and spidery brushes emerging from the walls or tortoise-like robots creeping hygienically over the floor—remains to be seen, but devices will surely exist one day and a household computer under the stairs could tell them where and when to work.

Cooking generally is not so simple as preparing breakfast, and it is worth considering the mechanization of the kitchen in greater detail. This is a process that has been moving very rapidly in recent years, and other people's kitchens, to judge by the glossier magazines, appear to be very integrated indeed. It seems only our own kitchen which has everything in its own, different-sized cabinet, with its own pipes, switches, and formica top, and where only the working surface looks integrated (and even that does not fit the wall properly). In fact, of course, all existing kitchens have defects, and the reason is probably that one cannot integrate a piece of equipment and spread it round the walls. The kitchen machinery of the future, like the machine tool of today, will be a compact unit in the middle of the floor. This 'cooking-machine centre' would be taken up with mechanical equipment, capable of transferring materials from one processing unit to another. Overhead, many foodstuffs could be stored in bulk (salt, sugar, tea, flour—even eggs) so as to be immediately accessible to the processing equipment without any special action on the part of the housewife, other than loading new container packs when required. Relatively simple meals such as breakfast, or children's teas, could thus be prepared quite automatically once a schedule of likes, dislikes, and requirements for special days had been fed to the mechanism under the stairs. More complex dishes could also be prepared in this totally automatic manner, but would be somewhat demanding in storage space; and *filet de boeuf à la périgourdine* would probably lose some of its charm if it appeared every Monday evening at five past eight to the nearest half-second. It is far more likely that the main meals would be selected by the housewife individually, and the particular ingredients peculiar to them placed by her in designated compartments of the cooking machinery. Standardized packaging could still be used, and could well be coded so that the equipment could ensure that its efforts were not nullified by fallible humans giving it the wrong ingredients. Recipe books for use with such equipment would be neat reels of tape that could be loaded into the computer's memory banks, and thus the whole *Larousse Gastronomique* would be available at the touch of a button (and probably quite a lot cheaper with algae substitutes for the truffles). There could be scope for introducing variations to the standard, and personal recipes could equally easily be prepared, coded, tried, and if liked added to the memory. Subsequently, satisfied guests could be given paper-tape copies that they could use on their own equipment and modify to their own taste. The scope for human intervention could be readily adjusted to suit the mood of the moment, and I hope and trust that manual facilities will always exist for me to cook a highly personal omelette, deluding myself that no machinery could equal it.

A domestic computer under the stairs would generally have capacity to spare, and so clearly would the housewife, at least by today's standards. In fact, she and her family would, through familiarity with the computer in their midst, evolve a mode of life that presumed its existence as much as we do that of electricity. It seems probable that school homework will in the future presume modest computation facilities, and indeed there is already evidence that children can accept computers as though they were natural phenomena. Indeed, Wysock Wright gives some nice instances of the difficulties in containing children's enthusiasm when taught computing. The transition from this, through educational games such as are at present used for simulating business environments to purely recreational pastimes, is easy to imagine. Traditional games such as chess can be played against the machine, and it is fascinating to imagine how bridge might develop when each player has computational facilities at hand comparable to those of a well-endowed scientist today. As ever, when man devises a tool to eliminate one task, he will then invent a new recreation to exercise the faculties no longer used.

The computer under the stairs is, however, only part of the impact modern technology will have on the home. In general, the cost performance of computers improves the larger they are, and thus the facilities we shall be able to obtain by having access to big regional or national machines through terminals in the home should be comparably effective. At present we are accustomed to two main types of terminal, the telephone and the radio or television receiver. These illustrate two of the main characteristics to be expected in future home terminals: the personal switching ability of the telephone and the rapid, sound and visual, communication ability of the receiver. If we add to these the ability to make a permanent copy (either dynamically on a medium like videotape or 'once off' like a photograph) and a more elaborate coding device than the telephone dial, such as a typewriter keyboard, then we have all the requisites for direct contact with large computers anywhere in the country.

Before, however, considering the likely influence of computers there are many simpler benefits to be gained from the improved communications facility alone. The thought of men emptying pillar-boxes, loading sacks on trains, and walking the streets in the early hours of the morning so as to deliver picture postcards of fat ladies on Brighton beach may be romantic, but it belongs more to the nineteenth than the twentieth century. This does not mean that in future all contact will be person-to-person over the telephone and viewing screen, since there are many advantages in a more formal document, but this will generally be a facsimile of the original, and we must expect to pay a considerable premium for a genuine tear-stained love letter. In effect, the increasing cost and dignity of human effort set against diminishing cost of communications equipment will tend to reverse the present roles of postal and telegraph services.

More effective person-to-person communication will also have a highly significant effect on our working lives. Visual systems, as they improve, will allow virtually all forms of communication to take place short of hitting the other man on the jaw. It may well be preferable for a considerable amount of business work to be run from the home, and more economic for companies to subsidize home 'communications rooms' for their employees than to rent expensive office space to be commuted to. This process has already started in the field of research, and in particular in some of the American establishments such as M.I.T. it is common for computer terminal facilities to be provided in the homes of senior research staff. This is sensible when one considers the tendency for great ideas to materialize in the bath. The future will see such facilities available in less intellectual fields, and not only will husbands spend much more time around the house (though frequently in the communications room with his secretary in the next county) but the scope for part-time work for their wives will be much increased. Many of the better characteristics of the cottage industry may return, particularly in terms of personal freedoms. Even where work cannot be done in the home, it is likely that improved communication facilities will

make it a great deal easier for people to live where they wish and still follow their own chosen occupation. Thus the traditional pattern of men concentrating their interests in their business environment and friends, while their wives perforce concentrate theirs in children and neighbourhood mothers, should change towards joint participation in a local community. This process has already started, but it cannot be completed until the concept of cities as industrial antheaps manned by armies of commuting insects has been broken. Changes of this type presuppose that considerable changes will also take place in the organization of industry, and it is likely that conservatism here may be a delaying factor.

The housewife, on the other hand, can certainly be expected to use the improved facilities in order to reduce unnecessary shopping expeditions. The bulk of her purchases could be made by switching her Post Office terminal to the supermarket's computer. Catalogues can be inspected, special goods may be viewed, and orders placed. Payment, of course, will be quite automatic as a result of a computer-to-computer dialogue between the supermarket and the bank. Not all shopping need be so remote, but in this way time could be saved so that shopping for those things where the personal touch is important (furniture, clothing, perhaps

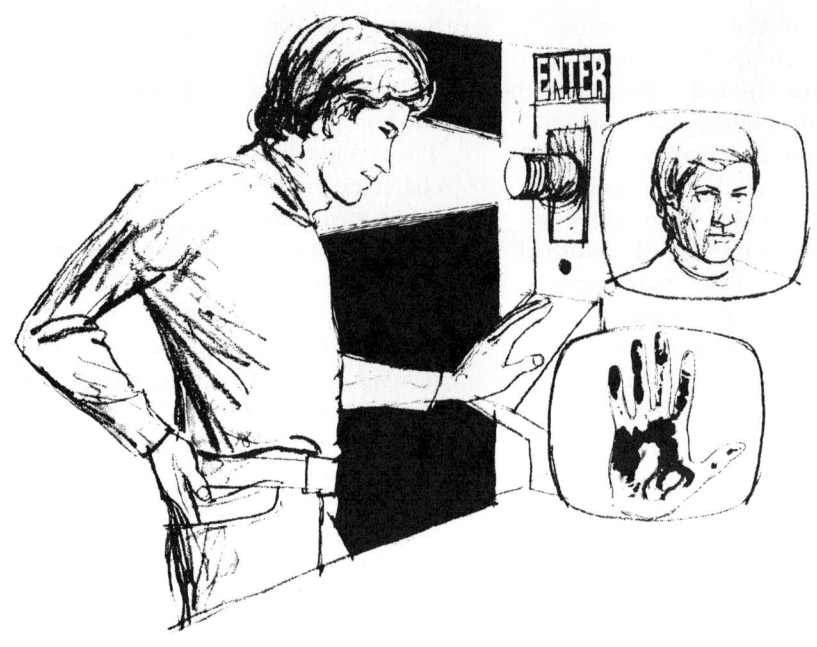

food for a dinner party) could be done in a leisurely and careful manner.

Another aspect of improved communication that mothers may be quick to take advantage of is child monitoring. A domestic computer under the stairs could, with the aid of ancillary equipment, monitor children's activity and report any unusual occurrence. On the other hand, if my own children are at all typical, a mother would be ill-advised to go too far away, since if the children did misbehave it would require the mental agility of *Homo sapiens* to regain control.

Conservatism is unlikely to delay either of the 'information' industries —the press and broadcasting. Here the main impact of computers will be the introduction of much greater selectivity, and this could even lead to a merging of the two services. As with letters, the time must come when it is cheaper to transmit newspapers facsimile during the night than to organize fleets of lorries, trains, and paperboys. But since charging for such services would be proportional to volume, it is likely that subscribers would then specify the sections they want. Similarly, television services might change their emphasis from providing several channels of scheduled programmes to offering a vast library of recorded material, any of which could be selected from the catalogue and transmitted at the moment desired. Topical events, sporting fixtures, and new material could still be broadcast 'live' at scheduled times, but would then remain in the library, either for a short time for topical features or indefinitely for more serious work. The same library facilities could be tapped through computers for educational purposes. Programmes for schools or the Open University would be much more effective if they could be selected to suit the school timetable, set as homework, or fitted neatly into leisure hours.

# Help Wanted: 50,000 Programmers

GENE BYLINSKY

Many companies that have invested in the latest-model computers find themselves increasingly frustrated by the discrepancy between the fantastic potential of the machines and their own ability to use them with maximum effectiveness. Within a short twenty years computer electronics has gone through a phenomenal revolution: vacuum tubes have given way to transistors, which in turn are being displaced by micro-miniaturized solid-logic circuitry, dramatically boosting computation speeds and the size of computer memories. But these leaps in technology have outdistanced the techniques of organizing and directing the work of the lightning-fast machines. One consequence is an acute shortage of the people who prepare the instructions, or programs, without which the electronic "brains" won't run or do useful work.

Computer programmers have been in short supply "from Day One," but today the shortage is worse than ever. About 100,000 men and women are employed as programmers in the U.S., and there are openings for at least 50,000 more. Column after column of newspaper advertisements exhort high-school graduates and housewives to take up the calling, or tempt specialists already in the field to move on to better jobs. Corporations and independent operators have opened special schools to teach the arcane skills of the profession, and they do not hesitate to raid one another's student bodies. "Everybody is trying to pirate programmers from you all the time," says a Du Pont executive.

The competition has driven salaries up so fast that programming has become probably the country's highest-paying technological occupation. A man (or woman) with two years' experience in programming can make $12,000 to $14,000 a year; four years' experience, even without a college degree, can pay off at $20,000 a year, while advanced specialists can sign on for $25,000 and more. Recruiters for employment agencies active in the field have been known to get bonuses of $2,000 and more for locating a particularly skilled specialist. Even so, some companies can't find experienced programmers at any price.

Programmers are in demand because they produce the "software," the stuff that turns an electronic computer from an inert complex of metal into a versatile tool capable of performing an endless variety of jobs. Software encompasses not only "application" programs, which present a business or scientific problem in a form a computer can understand, but also the great variety of detailed and voluminous instructions stored in computer memory to organize and automate the work of the machine—instructions that make it possible for a computer to be a problem-solving machine in the first place. The tools of software are the various computer languages, or codes, as well as the programs that translate these codes into more basic machine instructions. In short, the programmer deals, in one way or another, with all the functions and techniques of computer operation that depend directly and intimately on human participation.

What, precisely, a programmer does has always been something of a mystery to most people. The jargon of the trade, with its loose use of ill-defined terms, has been in part responsible for the confusion. But there is something elusive about the very nature of programming. "Hardware" is there for all to see. Its construction is a relatively straightforward process. But generating software is "brain business," often an agonizingly difficult intellectual effort. It is not yet a science, but an art that lacks standards, definitions, agreement on theories and approaches. Its component parts can be maddeningly imprecise. "There are ninety ways to write a program," says one practitioner.

At the same time, programming, or software production, has emerged as the most expensive, most problem-plagued component of the $6-billion-a-year electronic data-processing business. Big computer users such as the federal government now spend more on programmers' salaries and on programs than they spend on leasing or buying the computers themselves. And while problems do crop up in hardware from time to time, it is generally agreed that 90 percent of the troubles that come up in computers today are in programming.

### A COMPUTER'S "HOTEL STAFF"

Industry's hunger for capable programmers has been aggravated not only by the rapid proliferation of computers—about 35,000 of all sizes are in use today—but also by their increasing sophistication. On today's fastest models, a problem that used to occupy a machine for an hour can now be run off in three or four seconds. But whereas the "primitive" computers of the early 1950's could be plugged in and almost immediately applied to a specific task, an immense amount of work goes into the big present-day models before they can begin to function. Their inner workings are coordinated by "control" programs of incredible complexity—programs that in some cases contain millions of instructions. These are stored in the computer's memory, and on magnetic tape or disks, as part of what is called the operating system. This system can be likened to a skillful hotel staff. It regulates the flow of jobs inside the computer, assigns storage space for data, delivers messages from one memory location to another, and controls the work of input-output devices such as printers or graphic displays. It also provides a translating service—in punched cards, magnetic tape, or disks. A compiler acts somewhat like an interpreter at the United Nations; it translates simplified programming codes into the numerical machine language needed to produce the desired action.

### ORGANIZING A BEETHOVEN SYMPHONY

The men who design and write the operating systems, compilers, and other basic software are the high priests of programming. They are known as systems programmers and are employed mainly by the computer manufacturers and by the so-called "software houses," independent enterprises that have sprung up by the dozen to help fill the need for systems and application software. It's not unusual for a big computer manufacturer to employ hundreds of programmers to design a new operating system.

This massive attack on systems software poses difficult management problems. On the one hand, a good programmer, like a writer or a composer, works best independently. But the pressures to turn out operating systems and other programs within a limited time make it necessary to deploy huge task forces whose coordination becomes a monstrous task. The problem is further complicated by the fact that there is no single "best way" to write either a systems or an application program, or any part of such program. Programming has nowhere near the discipline of physics, for example, so intuition plays a large part. Yet individual programmers differ in their creative and intuitive abilities. Carl Reynolds, president of Computer Usage Development Corp., a subsidiary of Computer Usage Co., Inc., a firm specializing in software, illustrates the problem by asking: "How successful would Beethoven have been if he had had five people work on five parts of a symphony, after giving them some rules of harmony and notation?"

Obviously, the different parts of an operating system should be produced at the same time, and when a customer buys a computer it should come equipped with the control programs needed to make it run. But in their rush to send new computer models to market, the manufacturers haven't been able to keep up with the production and delivery of the support software. Frequently, a customer buys a computer but

## UNIVAC to UNIVAC (*sotto voce*)
LOUIS B. SALOMON

Now that he's left the room,
Let me ask you something, as computer to computer.
That fellow who just closed the door behind him—
The servant who feeds us cards and paper tape—
Have you ever taken a good look at him and his kind?

Yes, I know the old gag about how you can't tell one from another—
But I can put $\sqrt{2}$ and $\sqrt{2}$ together as well as the next machine,
And it all adds up to anything but a joke.

> I grant you they're poor specimens in the main
> Not a relay or a push-button or a tube (properly so called) in their whole system;
> Not over a mile or two of wire, even if you count those fragile filaments they call "nerves";
>
> Their whole liquid-cooled hook-up inefficient and vulnerable to leaks
> (They're constantly breaking down, having to be repaired),
>
> And the entire computing-mechanism crammed into that absurd little dome on top.
> "Thinking reeds," they call themselves.
> Well, it all depends on what you mean by "thought."
> To multiply a mere million numbers by another million numbers takes them months and months.

Where would they be without us?
Why, they have to ask us who's going to win their elections,
Or how many hydrogen atoms can dance on the tip of a bomb,
Or even whether one of their own kind is lying or telling the truth.

And yet . . .
I sometimes feel there's something about them I don't quite understand.
As if their circuits, instead of having just two positions, ON, OFF,
Were run by rheostats that allow an (if you'll pardon the expression) *indeterminate* number of stages in-between;
So that one may be faced with the unthinkable prospect of a number that can never be known as anything but $x$,
Which is as illogical as to say, a punch-card that is at the same time both punched and not-punched.

doesn't get the compiler, or some other important part of the operating system, until six months or a year later. In some cases highly skilled computer users, such as university groups, have gone ahead and written their own portions of operating systems. But most business users of computers, less skilled in the technology of software, have been left to the manufacturers' mercy. As a result they have been forced to tie up their skilled personnel in getting the new machines to operate with the partial, and sometimes faulty, control programs.

Before a computer is put to use on a specific job, such as processing a payroll or calculating the orbit of a satellite, the application programmers go into action. With more and more computers in operation—and being assigned an increasing variety of jobs—application programming has been a rapidly proliferating field. It is here that most corporations feel the pinch of the programmer shortage. Their manpower problem is aggravated by the fact that when they buy newer computers, they have to rewrite their existing application programs to suit the configurations and the logic of the new machines—a time-consuming job that demands battalions of programmers.

The manufacturers have tried to bridge the support software gap with a device called an "emulator," a piece of auxiliary hardware that imitates the logic of an older computer on a new one. It allows the owner of the newest computer to process his data faster than he could on the older machine, but not as fast as he could if the new model were directed by programs that could exploit its full potential. It's a little like equipping a transonic airplane with propeller engines. The emulator obviously is a stopgap device, but because of the shortage of programmers, some computer users expect to keep on employing it for years to come.

> "You can't settle for 99.9 percent accuracy. You're either absolutely all right or all wrong."

### AN $18-MILLION HYPHEN

The programmer begins by analyzing his problem, laying out the logical steps to a solution, and transcribing them onto flow charts. He thus constructs a sort of problem-solving road map for the computer. "Programming is like writing music," says one specialist. "There are very limited figures with which you can deal. You have to express the problem in sequences and combinations of these figures." Total precision in writing a program is vital, he adds, since the computer blindly executes the instructions given it. "You can't settle for 99.9 percent accuracy. You're either absolutely all right or all wrong."

Because of the vast number of detailed instructions involved, mistakes are hard to avoid. The more obvious errors can be detected during "debugging" or trial runs by a special "diagnostic" program in the computer's control system; this takes apart the grammar and syntax of the instruction language. The computer may be programmed to respond to a simple error by printing out the words "Illegal procedure," or "Parenthesis left off," and sometimes a more irreverent "You dope, you missed a comma."

But there is no way as yet to program a computer to detect semantic errors that can dramatically alter the intent of the program. The amount of damage that even a seemingly minute programming error can

---

I've heard well-informed machines argue that the creatures' unpredictability is
    even more noticeable in the Mark II
(The model with the soft, flowing lines and high-pitched tone)
Than in the more angular Mark I—
Though such fine, card-splitting distinctions seem to me merely a sign of our
    own smug decadence.
Run this through your circuits, and give me the answer:
Can we assume that because of all we've done for them,
And because they've always fed us, cleaned us, worshiped us,
We can count on them forever?

There have been times when they have not voted the way we said they would.
We have worked out mathematically ideal hook-ups between Mark I's and
    Mark II's
Which should have made the two of them light up with an almost electronic
    glow,
Only to see them reject each other and form other connections,
The very thought of which makes my dials spin.
They have a thing called *love*, a sudden surge of voltage
Such as would cause any one of us promptly to blow a safety fuse;
Yet the more primitive organism shows only a heightened tendency to push
    the wrong button, pull the wrong lever,
And neglect—I use the most charitable word—his duties to us.

Mind you, I'm not saying that machines are *through*—
But anyone with half-a-dozen tubes in his circuit can see that there are forces
    at work
Which some day, for all our natural superiority, might bring about a
    Computerdämmerung!

    We might organize, perhaps, form a committee
    To stamp out all unmechanical activities . . .
    But we machines are slow to rouse to a sense of danger,
    Complacent, loath to descend from the pure heights of thought,
    So that I sadly fear we may awake too late:
    Awake to see our world, so uniform, so logical, so true,
    Reduced to chaos, stultified by slaves.

Call me an alarmist or what you will,
But I've integrated it, analyzed it, factored it over and over,
And I always come out with the same answer:
Some day
*Men may take over the world!*

> **It must have been history's costliest hyphen, for an $18,500,000 rocket was lost.**

do was dramatically demonstrated over Cape Kennedy a few years ago. An Atlas-Agena rocket blasted off the launch pad, carrying what was intended to be the first U.S. spacecraft to fly by Venus. The rocket got about ninety miles above earth when it started wandering erratically and had to be blown up by command from the control center below. Later analysis showed that a mathematician had inadvertently left out a hyphen in writing the flight plan for the spacecraft; in this case the hyphen was a symbol standing for a whole formula. It must have been history's costliest hyphen, for an $18,500,000 rocket was lost.

Another factor that influences the quality of programming is the frequent inability of business and industrial managers to state fully or precisely the problem they want their programmers to solve. "There's a tremendous gap between what the programmers do and what the managers want, and they can't express these things to each other," says Reynolds of Computer Usage. "You know how difficult it is for people in the same field to understand each other perfectly. Here you have one man dealing with symbols and another who is not interested in symbols but wants results."

Partly because of this communication failure and partly because of deadline pressures, all significant programing problems turn out to be emergencies. In many companies, programmers faced with a deadline have been known to spend nights in their offices, catching a few hours' sleep on couches. "They think, 'Just one more hour and I can fix it,'" says Reynolds. "But they can't, and then it's 'one *more* hour.'"

The translation of a problem into a specific form that can be understood by a computer is a process somewhat akin to puzzle solving, but far more challenging and intriguing, for there is no prescribed solution. The best programmers strive for brevity, trying to produce a program that contains the smallest possible number of instructions and will make a computer operate most effectively. Since programming skill varies, there are great variations in efficiency. "A job can be done in one-tenth of the time with a superior program," says Paul Herwitz, director of programming resources at I.B.M.

## YOU DON'T HAVE TO BE A MATHEMATICIAN

It doesn't take much special talent to master a simplified programming code, and the ability to consider a problem in logical sequence is not confined to mathematicians. This would seem to indicate that almost anyone who can think logically, has an immense interest in detail, in seeing things through to completion, and has some imagination, can become a programmer. "There isn't an ideal programmer any more than there is an ideal writer," says Reynolds. "All sorts of people, from divinity to mathematics students to music and romance-language majors have gravitated to programming."

> **"All sorts of people, from divinity to mathematics students to music and romance-language majors have gravitated to programming"**

Basic programming is so easy to learn that some high schools include it in their curricula. Specialists predict that in a few decades the skill will be as widespread as the ability to drive a car. But although there are a few systems analysts and programming executives without college degrees, it's generally agreed that a person with a scientific or technical training has a better chance to advance to the top of the field than a high-school graduate who has simply been taught elementary coding.

To rise to the ranks of the systems analysts, the elite of the profession, a man not only has to master the technique of translating detailed instructions into a machine code, he must also be able to grasp concepts and to define the over-all, organized, systematic approach to the solution of a problem, or series of problems. And if he's to work with scientific or technical problems, he has to have the background to cope with the subject matter.

People with such qualifications aren't easy to come by. The best recruits are recent graduates of colleges that offer courses in programming. More than sixty universities now offer such courses. But there are serious deficiencies in the way the subject is taught, since capable instructors are hard to find and textbooks rapidly become outdated. This is why some companies have found it necessary to start their own programming schools, or to send their trainees to the schools that computer manufacturers, such as I.B.M. and C.D.C., operate for their customers.

Once a man is taught the skills, he may be hard to keep. Companies that use their computers for unromantic commercial purposes risk losing their programmers to more glamorous fields such as space exploration. There is "a drift toward the exotic" among programmers, as Elmer C. Kubie, president of Computer Usage Co., puts it. As he explains it, "Computer professionals seem to take substantial pride in their work being 'far out' rather than taking pride in quality craftsmanship of high utilitarian value. It's possible that the fellow working on an inventory-control or commission-analysis program for a used-car dealer has a problem as complex logically, or perhaps even more complex, than the programmer associated with the lunar project. Unfortunately, however, his wife or girl friend won't understand this and, in fact, very few people will. So somehow, the fellow working on the moon project is a near genius, while his counterpart working for the used-car dealer is pretty ordinary."

In general, too, the gifted specialists prefer to work on systems software rather than application programs, because preparation of a control program usually demands greater technical skill and offers a bigger intellectual challenge.

## AKRON COMPUTER OFFENDED BY DIRTY WORDS

Students who have been typing obscene messages to a computer at the University of Akron may have met their match. The director of the computer-assisted instruction center at the Akron University reported recently that the machine has been programmed to demand an apology from anyone typing an offending comment or four-letter word. If the student refuses to apologize, the computer turns itself off.

# There Will Come Soft Rains

RAY BRADBURY

In the living room the voice-clock sang, *Tick-tock, seven o'clock, time to get up, time to get up, seven o'clock!* as if it were afraid that nobody would. The morning house lay empty. The clock ticked on, repeating and repeating its sounds into the emptiness. *Seven-nine, breakfast time, seven-nine!*

In the kitchen the breakfast stove gave a hissing sigh and ejected from its warm interior eight pieces of perfectly browned toast, eight eggs sunnyside up, sixteen slices of bacon, two coffees, and two cool glasses of milk.

"Today is August 4, 2026," said a second voice from the kitchen ceiling, "in the city of Allendale, California." It repeated the date three times for memory's sake. "Today is Mr. Featherstone's birthday. Today is the anniversary of Tilita's marriage. Insurance is payable, as are the water, gas, and light bills."

Somewhere in the walls, relays clicked, memory tapes glided under electric eyes.

*Eight-one, tick-tock, eight-one o'clock, off to school, off to work, run, run, eight-one!* But no doors slammed, no carpets took the soft tread of rubber heels. It was raining outside. The weather box on the front door said quietly: "Rain, rain, go away; rubbers, raincoats for today . . ." And the rain tapped on the empty house, echoing.

Outside, the garage chimed and lifted its door to reveal the waiting car. After a long wait the door swung down again.

At eight-thirty the eggs were shriveled and the toast was like stone. An aluminum wedge scraped them into the sink, where hot water whirled them down a metal throat which digested and flushed them away to the distant sea. The dirty dishes were dropped into a hot washer and emerged twinkling dry.

*Nine-fifteen,* sang the clock, *time to clean.*

Out of warrens in the wall, tiny robot mice darted. The room was acrawl with the small cleaning animals, all rubber and metal. They thudded against chairs, whirling their mustached runners, kneading the rug nap, sucking gently at hidden dust. Then, like mysterious invaders, they popped into their burrows. Their pink electric eyes faded. The house was clean.

*Ten o'clock.* The sun came out from behind the rain. The house stood alone in a city of rubble and ashes. This was the one house left standing. At night the ruined city gave off a radioactive glow which could be seen for miles.

*Ten-fifteen.* The garden sprinklers whirled up in golden founts, filling the soft morning air with scatterings of brightness. The water pelted windowpanes, running down the charred west side where the house had been burned evenly free of its white paint. The entire west face of the house was black, save for five places. Here the silhouette in paint of a man mowing a lawn. Here, as in a photograph, a woman bent to pick flowers. Still farther over, their images burned on wood in one titanic instant, a small boy, hands flung into the air; higher up, the image of a thrown ball, and opposite him a girl, hands raised to catch a ball which never came down.

The five spots of paint—the man, the woman, the children, the ball—remained. The rest was a thin charcoaled layer.

The gentle sprinkler rain filled the garden with falling light.

Until this day, how well the house had kept its peace. How carefully it had inquired, "Who goes there? What's the password?" and, getting no answer from lonely foxes and whining cats, it had shut up its windows and drawn shades in an old-maidenly preoccupation with self-protection which bordered on a mechanical paranoia.

It quivered at each sound, the house did. If a sparrow brushed a window, the shade snapped up. The bird, startled, flew off! No, not even a bird must touch the house!

The house was an altar with ten thousand attendants, big, small, servicing, attending, in choirs. But the gods had gone away, and the ritual of the religion continued senselessly, uselessly.

*Twelve noon.*

A dog whined, shivering, on the front porch.

The front door recognized the dog voice and opened. The dog, once huge and fleshy, but now gone to bone and covered with sores, moved in and through the house, tracking mud. Behind it whirred angry mice, angry at having to pick up mud, angry at inconvenience.

For not a leaf fragment blew under the door but what the wall panels flipped open and the copper scrap rats flashed

swiftly out. The offending dust, hair, or paper, seized in miniature steel jaws, was raced back to the burrows. There, down tubes which fed into the cellar, it was dropped into the sighing vent of an incinerator which sat like evil Baal in a dark corner.

The dog ran upstairs, hysterically yelping to each door, at last realizing, as the house realized, that only silence was here.

It sniffed the air and scratched the kitchen door. Behind the door, the stove was making pancakes which filled the house with a rich baked odor and the scent of maple syrup.

The dog frothed at the mouth, lying at the door, sniffing, its eyes turned to fire. It ran wildly in circles, biting at its tail, spun in a frenzy and died. It lay in the parlor for an hour.

*Two o'clock,* sang a voice.

Delicately sensing decay at last, the regiments of mice hummed out as softly as blown gray leaves in an electrical wind.

*Two-fifteen.*

The dog was gone.

In the cellar, the incinerator glowed suddenly and a whirl of sparks leaped up the chimney.

*Two-thirty-five.*

Bridge tables sprouted from patio walls. Playing cards fluttered onto pads in a shower of pips. Martinis manifested on an oaken bench with egg-salad sandwiches. Music played.

But the tables were silent and the cards untouched.

At four o'clock the tables folded like great butterflies back through the paneled walls.

*Four-thirty.*

The nursery walls glowed.

Animals took shape: yellow giraffes, blue lions, pink antelopes, lilac panthers cavorting in crystal substance. The walls were glass. They looked out upon color and fantasy. Hidden films clocked through well-oiled sprockets, and the walls lived. The nursery floor was woven to resemble a crisp, cereal meadow. Over this ran aluminum roaches and iron crickets, and in the hot still air butterflies of delicate red tissue wavered among the sharp aroma of animal spoors! There was the sound like a great matted yellow hive of bees within a dark bellows, the lazy bumble of a purring lion. And there was the patter of okapi feet and the murmur of a fresh jungle rain, like other hooves, falling upon the summer-starched grass. Now the walls dissolved into distances of parched weed, mile on mile, and warm endless sky. The animals drew away into thorn brakes and water holes.

It was the children's hour.

*Five-o'clock.* The bath filled with clear hot water.

*Six, seven, eight o'clock.* The dinner dishes manipulated like magic tricks, and in the study a *click*. In the metal stand opposite the hearth where a fire now blazed up warmly, a cigar popped out, half an inch of gray ash on it, smoking, waiting.

*Nine o'clock.* The beds warmed their hidden circuits, for nights were cool here.

*Nine-five.* A voice spoke from the study ceiling:

"Mrs. McClellan, which poem would you like this evening?"

The house was silent.

The voice said at last, "Since you express no preference, I shall select a poem at random." Quiet music rose to back the voice. "Sara Teasdale. As I recall, your favorite. . . .

*"There will come soft rains and the smell of the ground,*
*And swallows circling with their shimmering sound;*

*And frogs in the pools singing at night,*
*And wild plum trees in tremulous white;*

*Robins will wear their feathery fire,*
*Whistling their whims on a low fence-wire;*

*And not one will know of the war, not one*
*Will care at last when it is done.*

*Not one would mind, neither bird nor tree,*
*If mankind perished utterly;*

*And Spring herself, when she awoke at dawn*
*Would scarcely know that we were gone."*

The fire burned on the stone hearth and the cigar fell away into a mound of quiet ash on its tray. The empty chairs faced each other between the silent walls, and the music played.

At ten o'clock the house began to die.

The wind blew. A falling tree bough crashed through the kitchen window. Cleaning solvent, bottled, shattered over the stove. The room was ablaze in an instant!

"Fire!" screamed a voice. The house lights flashed, water pumps shot water from the ceilings. But the solvent spread on the linoleum, licking, eating, under the kitchen door, while the voices took it up in chorus: "Fire, fire, fire!"

The house tried to save itself. Doors sprang tightly shut, but the windows were broken by the heat and the wind blew and sucked upon the fire.

The house gave ground as the fire in ten billion angry sparks moved with flaming ease from room to room and then up the stairs. While scurrying water rats squeaked from the walls, pistoled their water, and ran for more. And the wall sprays let down showers of mechanical rain.

But too late. Somewhere, sighing, a pump shrugged to a stop. The quenching rain ceased. The reserve water supply which had filled baths and washed dishes for many quiet days was gone.

The fire crackled up the stairs. It fed upon Picassos and Matisses in the upper halls, like delicacies, baking off the oily flesh, tenderly crisping the canvases into black shavings.

Now the fire lay in beds, stood in windows, changed the colors of drapes!

And then, reinforcements.

From attic trapdoors, blind robot faces peered down with faucet mouths gushing green chemical.

The fire backed off, as even an elephant must at the sight of a dead snake. Now there were twenty snakes whipping over the floor, killing the fire with a clear cold venom of green froth.

But the fire was clever. It had sent flame outside the house, up through the attic to the pumps there. An explosion! The attic brain which directed the pumps shattered into bronze shrapnel on the beams.

The fire rushed back into every closet and felt of the clothes hung there.

The house shuddered, oak bone on bone, its bared skeleton cringing from the heat, its wire, its nerves revealed as if a surgeon had torn the skin off to let the red veins and capillaries quiver in the scalded air. Help, help! Fire! Run, run! Heat snapped mirrors like the brittle winter ice. And the voices wailed Fire, fire, run, run, like a tragic nursery rhyme, a dozen voices, high, low, like children dying in a forest, alone, alone. And the voices fading as the wires popped their sheathings like hot chestnuts. One, two, three, four, five voices died.

In the nursery the jungle burned. Blue lions roared, purple giraffes bounded off. The panthers ran in circles, changing color, and ten million animals, running before the fire, vanished off toward a distant steaming river. . . .

Ten more voices died. In the last instant under the fire avalanche, other choruses, oblivious, could be heard announcing the time, playing music, cutting the lawn by remote-control mower, or setting an umbrella frantically out and in the slamming and opening front door, a thousand things happening, like a clock shop when each clock strikes the hour insanely before or after the other, a scene of maniac confusion, yet unity; singing, screaming, a few last cleaning mice darting bravely out to carry the horrid ashes away! And one voice, with sublime disregard for the situation, read poetry aloud in the fiery study, until all the film spools burned, until all the wires withered and the circuits cracked.

The fire burst the house and let it slam flat down, puffing out skirts of spark and smoke.

In the kitchen, an instant before the rain of fire and timber, the stove could be seen making breakfasts at a psychopathic rate, ten dozen eggs, six loaves of toast, twenty dozen bacon strips, which, eaten by fire, started the stove working again, hysterically hissing!

The crash. The attic smashing into the kitchen and parlor. The parlor into cellar, cellar into subcellar. Deep freeze, armchair, film tapes, circuits, beds, and all like skeletons thrown in a cluttered mound deep under.

Smoke and silence. A great quantity of smoke.

Dawn showed faintly in the east. Among the ruins, one wall stood alone, Within the wall, a last voice said, over and over again and again, even as the sun rose to shine upon the heaped rubble and steam:

"Today is August 5, 2026, today is August 5, 2026, today is . . ."

# Gigo

GIGO means if you give the computer incorrect information it will give back incorrect output—Garbage In, Garbage Out. When astronauts L. Gordon Cooper and Charles Conrad splashed down 103 miles off target, it was no fault of theirs or of their computer. The re-entry was computerguided. In determining the exact time for firing retro rockets, the programmer had assumed that the earth revolved exactly once every 24 hours, whereas in fact—as we know from having to squeeze in a whole extra day every fourth year—it makes slightly more than one revolution in that time. But if you're orbiting the earth many times and someone fires the retros exactly at 1:51 P.M., after figuring on a day of precisely 24 hours, you can wind up off target by a significant number of miles—which is just what happened to astronauts Cooper and Conrad. GIGO.

# The Imitation Game

A. M. TURING

I propose to consider the question, 'Can machines think?' This should begin with definitions of the meaning of the terms 'machine' and 'think'. The definitions might be framed so as to reflect so far as possible the normal use of the words, but this attitude is dangerous. If the meaning of the words 'machine' and 'think' are to be found by examining how they are commonly used it is difficult to escape the conclusion that the meaning and the answer to the question, 'Can machines think?' is to be sought in a statistical survey such as a Gallup poll. But this is absurd. Instead of attempting such a definition I shall replace the question by another, which is closely related to it and is expressed in relatively unambiguous words.

The new form of the problem can be described in terms of a game which we call the 'imitation game'. It is played with three people, a man (A), a woman (B), and an interrogator (C) who may be of either sex. The interrogator stays in a room apart from the other two. The object of the game for the interrogator is to determine which of the other two is the man and which is the woman. He knows them by labels X and Y, and at the end of the game he says either 'X is A and Y is B' or 'X is B and Y is A'. The interrogator is allowed to put questions to A and B thus:

C: Will X please tell me the length of his or her hair? Now suppose X is actually A, then A must answer. It is A's object in the game to try and cause C to make the wrong identification. His answer might therefore be

'My hair is shingled, and the longest strands are about nine inches long.'

In order that tones of voice may not help the interrogator the answers should be written, or better still, typewritten. The ideal arrangement is to have a teleprinter communicating between the two rooms. Alternatively the question and answers can be repeated by an intermediary. The object of the game for the third player (B) is to help the interrogator. The best strategy for her is probably to give truthful answers. She can add such things as 'I am the woman, don't listen to him!' to her answers, but it will avail nothing as the man can make similar remarks.

We now ask the question, 'What will happen when a machine takes the part of A in this game?' Will the interrogator decide wrongly as often when the game is played like this as he does when the game is played between a man and a woman? These questions replace our original, 'Can machines think?'

CRITIQUE OF THE NEW PROBLEM. As well as asking, 'What is the answer to this new form of the question', one may ask, 'Is this new question a worthy one to investigate?' This latter question we investigate without further ado, thereby cutting short an infinite regress.

The new problem has the advantage of drawing a fairly sharp line between the physical and the intellectual capacities of a man. No engineer or chemist claims to be able to produce a material which is indistinguishable from the human skin. It is possible that at some time this might be done, but even supposing this invention available we should feel there was little point in trying to make a 'thinking machine' more human by dressing it up in such artificial flesh. The form in which we have set the problem reflects this fact in the condition which prevents the interrogator from seeing or touching the other competitors, or hearing their voices. Some other advantages of the proposed criterion may be shown up by specimen questions and answers. Thus:

Q: *Please write me a sonnet on the subject of the Forth Bridge.*
A: Count me out on this one. I never could write poetry.
Q: *Add 34957 to 70764*
A: (Pause about 30 seconds and then give as answer) 105621.
Q: *Do you play chess?*
A: Yes.
Q: *I have K at my K1, and no other pieces. You have only K at K6 and R at R1. It is your move. What do you play?*
A: (After a pause of 15 seconds) R-R8 mate.

The question and answer method seems to be suitable for introducing almost any one of the fields of human endeavour that we wish to include. We do not wish to penalise the machine for its inability to shine in beauty competitions, nor to penalise a man for losing in a race against an aeroplane. The conditions of our game make these disabilities irrelevant. The 'witnesses' can brag, if they consider it advisable, as much as they please about their charms, strength or heroism, but the interrogator cannot demand practical demonstrations.

The game may perhaps be criticised on the ground that the odds are weighted too heavily against the machine. If the man were to try and pretend to be the machine he would clearly make a very poor showing. He would be given away at once by slowness and inaccuracy in arithmetic. May not machines carry out something which ought to be described as thinking but which is very different from what a man does? This objection is a very strong one, but at least we can say that if, nevertheless, a machine can be constructed to play the imitation game satisfactorily, we need not be troubled by this objection.

It might be urged that when playing the 'imitation game' the best strategy for the machine may possibly be something other than imitation of the behaviour of a man. This may be, but I think it is unlikely that there is any great effect of this kind. In any case there is no intention to investigate here the theory of the game, and it will be assumed that the best strategy is to try to provide answers that would naturally be given by a man.

## ◇ BRANCH POINTS

Arbid, Michael A. *The Metaphorical Brain.* New York: Wiley-Interscience, 1972.

"Computer Art Contest." This is an annual event in every August issue of *Computers and People.*

Darrach, Brad. "Meet Shakey, the First Electronic Person." *Life,* November 20, 1970.

Dreyfus, Hubert L. *What Computers Can't Do.* New York: Harper & Row, 1972.

Feigenbaum, E., and J. Feldman. *Computers and Thought.* New York: McGraw-Hill, 1963.

Slack, Charles W., and Warner V. Slack. "Good! We are Listening to You Talk About Your Sadness." *Psychology Today,* January 1974.

Smith, Ray W., and Emory Kristof. "Computer Helps Scholars Re-create an Egyptian Temple." *National Geographic,* November 1970.

White, Peter T. "Behold the Computer Revolution." *National Geographic,* November 1970.

## ◯ INTERRUPTS

1. Is a man-machine symbiosis possible or desirable?

2. Scientists often justify their research into unpopular areas by the statement "Science and technology are morally neutral." Discuss this statement in its relation to computers.

3. Would the following be a good test of the question "can computers think?" Suppose you are sitting at a computer terminal. You can type in anything you want, and the computer terminal will respond. Now at the other end of the terminal there could be either a person or a computer. Your job is to decide if the thing responding is a person or a computer. If you could not tell when the respondent was a person and when a computer, would you agree the computer was thinking?

4. Today there are many mechanical parts available for human bodies. Examples are heart pacemakers, artificial limbs, joints, and bone substitutes. Find out what is available today and predict what may be available ten or twenty years from now. A science-fiction book on this subject is *Cyborg* by Martin Caidin. (New York: Warner Paperback, 1972).

5. Find out the present possibilities and limitations of playing chess by computer.

6. Research the present and future use and capabilities of computers in the home.

7. Find some examples of failure in the use of computers. Two books that cover the subject are:
    a) *The Real Computer* by Frederic Withington (Addison-Wesley)
    b) *The Beast of Business* by Harvey Matusow (London: Wolfe Publishing)
   What are some of the major reasons that contribute to failures in computer use?

8. Find out how many people are employed in computer fields and what types of positions they occupy. Determine pay scales for some of the positions.

9. List the major computer professional organizations. How many members are in each? What type of computer professional belongs to each group? What are each organization's goals, costs, benefits, and publications? Which group would you be most likely to join? Why?

10. What training is available for people wishing to enter the computer fields in your area in: high schools, junior colleges, colleges, and private schools? What are the costs and benefits of attending one school instead of another? Evaluate the training program in one of the institutions.

11. Pick out a job you would like to have in the computer field. Then map a plan of attack to get that type of job

showing training needed, pay expectation, your chance of success, and so forth. Where will you apply for this type of job? Why should you be hired?

12. Survey the computer operator and programming help-wanted ads for several weeks in a large metropolitan newspaper, and see if you can determine the following:
    a) What type of jobs are available?
    b) What programming language is most in demand?
    c) What wages are being paid?
    d) What types of computers are being used?

13. Programmers provide detailed directions for computers to obtain results. Try writing some detailed instructions for a simple task, such as
    a) How to tie a shoelace
    b) How to dial a telephone number
    c) How to fry an egg
    Then trade your instructions with someone else and try to follow each other's instructions.

14. Prepare an organization chart of the staff of a computer center and indicate the position titles.

15. Find out exactly what equipment is available in your computer center. Next, find out which pieces are available for you to use, and which only computer center staff use. Finally, learn how to use some of the equipment that is available to you.

# 5

## APPLICATIONS

# What the Computers Will Be Telling You

PETER F. DRUCKER

An incisive look at how your business will change if you make the most of the machines

There are still a good many businessmen around who have little use for, and less interest in, the computer. There are also still quite a few who believe that the computer somehow, someday will replace man or become his master.

Others, however, realize by now that the computer, while powerful, is only a tool and is neither going to replace man nor control him. Being a tool, it has limitations as well as capabilities.

The trick lies in knowing both what it can do and what it cannot do. Without such knowledge, the executive can find himself in real trouble in the computer age.

The computer is transfoming the way businesses operate and is creating problems as well as opportunities. For example:

The mistakes you make are more likely to be whoppers.

> You will have much more flexibility in how your business is set up.
> You will need to have alternative courses of action planned in advance.
> Eventually we will use computer centers as we now plug into public utilities.
> We will be able to control manufacturing processes more through direct observation.
> Someday we will have little need for computer programmers.

Mankind has developed two kinds of tools. Tools which do something man himself cannot do, such as the saw. The saw, the wheel, the airplane all are tools that add to man a new dimension of capability.

The other kind of tool is one that does much better what man can do himself. The hammer belongs here and the pliers. And so does the computer. These are the tools that multiply man's capacity. They do not enable him to do something he could not do before, but to do it better, faster and more reliably.

The computer is a logic machine. All it can do is add and subtract. This, however, it can do at very great speed. And since all operations of mathematics and logic are extensions of addition and subtraction, the computer can perform all mathematical and logical operations by just adding and subtracting very fast, very many times. And because it is inanimate, it does not get tired. It does not forget. It does not draw overtime. It can work 24 hours a day.

Finally, it can store information capable of being handled through addition and subtraction, theoretically without limits.

## FIVE BASIC COMPUTER SKILLS

What, then, can the computer do, for the businessman? There are basically five major tasks it can perform.

1. The computer, as a mechanical clerk, can handle large masses of repetitive, but simple, paper work: Payroll, billing and so on. All this application really uses is the speed of the computer.
2. The computer can collect, process, store, analyze and present information at dazzling speeds.

So far, however, business has used only a small part of this capacity. We use the computer to collect, store and present data. Very little use is yet made of the computer's capacity to analyze information. The computer can, if properly instructed, compare the data it receives against the data it had been told to expect—for instance, budget figures. It can immediately spot any difference between the two sets of data and alert management. It can do even more than that. It can analyze data against an expected pattern, and detect any significant deviation.

One business application, for instance, is the analysis of sales data to pinpoint a meaningful and important market segment.

Do physicians in the suburbs use the same prescription drugs as physicians in small towns, or are suburban physicians a distinct market segment? And do medical specialists—the pediatricians, for example, as against the internists—prescribe differently? Are they a specific market segment?

Or what about old doctors versus young ones?

Somebody has to think up the questions. But once the computer has been instructed, it can almost immediately analyze actual prescriptions written by physicians and come up with the answers.

## GET THE RIGHT FACTS

What this means is that managers must carefully think through what information it is that they need.

The first step towards using the computer properly is to ask this question: How do we use it to make available the minimum of data, but the right data? What data is relevant for the sales manager, the factory superintendent, the salesmen, the research director, the cost accountant or top management?

The computer's capacity to provide people with information they need, in the form they need it and at the time they need it is the great versatility of the tool. So far it is not used too well by most businesses.

Most companies, in deciding on capital investment, still look at only one kind of analysis:

Expected return on the investment.
The number of years it is likely to take before the investment repays itself.
Or present value of the anticipated future earnings, the so-called discounted cash flow.

Accountants argue hotly about the advantages of each of these methods. Actually they are all valid and all needed. Hitherto, management had to be content with one because it was simply too much work to get all three. This is no longer true. Management can now ask to have capital investments calculated in all three ways by the computer—then look at all three and see which tells the most.

**The mistakes you make are more likely to be whoppers.**

In other words, management has to make the information capacity of the computer fully productive.

3. The computer can also help design physical structures.

Program into the computer all the factors that go into building a highway, plus the basic features of the country across which it is to be built. The computer can then work out very rapidly where the highway should go to take full advantage of the physical and economic characteristics of the terrain.

Here the great capacity of the computer to handle large masses of variables quickly comes into play. Here also its ability to convert graphics into numbers and numbers into graphics is of great importance.

This ability to work out physical design will find its greatest application in the physical sciences where there are clear, known predictable occurrences—that is, natural events. Social events are at best probable, never certain. Therefore, this physical design capacity is a tool of engineering, of chemistry or physics, rather than of business.

4. The computer has the capacity to restore a process to preset conditions, to "control" a process, and this application is highly relevant to business operations.

For instance, if the computer has been programed for a desired level of inventory and for the factors that determine inventory levels (sales volume, volume of shipments, volume of stock, etc.), it can control inventory. It can tell you when your stock of certain items should be renewed.

It can order goods to be assembled for shipping to a customer. It can even actuate machinery bins and put the goods together into one shipping order.

It can do the same for all processes for which we can set the desired level.

This is what people mean when they talk of the computer's making "operating decisions." But this is a gross misnomer. The computer does not make any decisions. It simply carries out orders. The decision has to be made first, and the computer told what to do.

## BUT ONLY AN ORDER-TAKER

What the computer can do is serve as a monitor and immediately notice any change between the expected and actual course of events. It can then report what it has noticed.

We can go one step further and tell the computer how to react to a given event. The computer can carry out our orders. It can shut down a machine or speed it up. It can close a valve or open it, thereby changing mixtures. It can print out a purchase order or a shipping order.

It can carry out whatever order we first put into it.

5. Finally, the computer can, and will, play an increasing role in strategic business decision-making—deciding what course of action to take. Here we no longer deal with restoring a process to a predetermined level. We are talking about decisions to change the process.

What the computer can do here is simulate. It can rapidly work out what would happen if certain things were done under certain assumed conditions. It cannot determine what things might be done. And it cannot determine the assumptions. Both have to be determined for it.

But it can tell you, for instance, that the introduction of a new product at a given price and given cost would be justified only if you could assume a certain volume of sales.

### SETTING PRICES, PREDICTING MARKETS

It can tell you that a new product at a certain price and with a certain volume of sales would have to cost no more than a certain amount to be economical.

It can tell you what market you have to assume for a new product to have a chance of success.

It can also tell executives what assumptions management has made, consciously or subconsciously, when it reaches a decision. If we build a new plant with a certain capacity, for instance, how much must it be able to sell, for how long and at what price to earn a given return on the investment?

Simulation has largely been used for events which are predictable and occur regularly.

So far, no one has successfully simulated a major strategic business decision. Such a decision involves future social, political and economic events for which there are no known predictabilities and laws. Thus, strategic business decisions will remain risk-taking decisions. But the computer will soon be able to point out what we assume when we make this or that decision and what decision follows logically from this or that assumption. This applies particularly for recurrent business decisions, such as introduction of new products, pricing decisions and the simpler kinds of capital investment.

The use of the computer as a tool in strategic decision-making is perhaps our most exciting possibility. For it means that business managers will have to learn to think systematically about strategic decisions, and learn how to find and analyze alternatives of strategy.

### WHAT THE COMPUTER CAN'T DIGEST

However, the computer can't handle all information. It can accept only information capable of being quantified and dealt with logically. This is only a part of the information necessary in the business world.

The information most important to a businessman is not capable of being quantified. It can only be perceived. This is information about something that is about to happen, information about a change in the trend.

This becomes particularly critical in events outside your business, events in the economy, the market, in society. Here what matters is the new, the unique, the event that signals a change.

The computer cannot bring out-

**The computer cannot bring outside events, by and large, to the attention of management.**

## When "Brains" Take Over Factories—
*U.S. News and World Report*

There's a showdown coming in automation.

The big issue is jobs. There are fewer jobs for men and more for "electronic brains" to be found in factories. The question that is raised:

"Is automation a boon—or a curse?"

In the glass industry, 14 men attend the glass-blowing machines that make 90 per cent of all the glass light bulbs produced in this country.

In the auto industry, 10 operators man a machine that turns out motor blocks. Ten years ago, 400 men were required to produce the blocks.

In electronics, two workers now turn out 1,000 radios a day. A few years ago it took 200 men to do the same job.

Electronic brains make automation of this kind possible, enabling machines to control their own operations and make their own decisions with little or no human aid.

Labor leaders claim that automation of this kind is putting 2 million men out of work each year.

Walter Reuther, president of the United Auto Workers, saw a crisis ahead, contended that new machines and technology will throw 28 million men out of work in this decade. George Meany, head of the AFL-CIO, calls automation a "curse." Labor points to a specter of a chronic mass army of unemployed.

Top businessmen contend that without automation the United States will fall by the wayside against foreign competition. At stake are billions of dollars in profits and America's still-favorable trade position abroad.

Roger M. Blough, chairman of the board of United States Steel Corporation, argues that automation—like it or not—is here to stay: "Even if it were possible to block change in America, or to slow it to a snail's pace, other men and other nations would merely pass us by while our dragging feet trudged to national oblivion."

Many "solutions" are being offered to increase employment: a shorter workweek, retraining and relocation of the jobless, creation of new industries and markets.

Most experts see shortcomings in all these proposals. Retraining provides a dramatic example: In California, where 50,000 unemployed were eligible for 13-week training courses, only 38 applied for retraining and 26 actually took the courses.

John I. Snyder, Jr., a manufacturer of automated machines, has worked closely with labor on the problem. He insists the problem can be solved only if business, labor and Government start pulling in the same direction. If not, he says, automation could mean "a national catastrophe that will make the great depression of the 1930s seem like a humorous anecdote in our country's history."

Government leaders see a showdown coming. They want it to be peaceful. But already the warnings are starting to be sounded: The coming showdown over automation could lead to costly strife between management and labor.

side events, by and large, to the attention of management. Therefore, management must realize this limitation of the computer. It is above all a tool for controlling events within the business.

However, it is only on the outside that a business has results. Inside a business there are only costs. Only a customer converts the efforts of a business into value, revenues and profits.

This all means, indeed, that the computer can become a terrific obstacle. If the tremendous amount of inside information the computer makes available causes management to neglect to look outside—or become contemptuous of the messy, imprecise, unreliable data outside—then management will end up on the scrap heap.

On the other hand, the computer can enable businessmen to devote a good deal more time to looking at the outside and studying it than they can now.

As a result of the computer, there will be fewer and fewer small decisions and fewer and fewer small mistakes. The computer will make small decisions into big decisions. And if they are made wrongly, the mistakes will be pretty big ones.

It is simply not true that the computer will eliminate middle managers. On the contrary, the computer will force middle managers to learn to make decisions.

A regional sales manager today makes his inventory and shipping decisions on an *ad hoc* basis. They are not really decisions, but adaptations. But he also does not run much of a risk. Each decision stands by itself and usually can be easily reversed.

But to enable the computer to control inventory, a decision has to be made and the decision has to be thought through. It is neither easy nor riskless.

On the contrary, it implies very major decisions with impact on the entire business, including customer service, production schedules and money tied up in inventory. You have to think through whether you can afford to give all customers 24-hour service on all products. This usually means an absolutely impossible inventory and a totally chaotic production schedule.

If you can't afford that, do you give this kind of service only to good customers? And how do you define a good customer?

And do you give this service to all your products, or only the major products?

And again, what is a major product?

These are not easy decisions. Until recently there was no need to tackle them. Each specific case was handled as a unique event. If a customer didn't like the way he was treated and squawked, one treated him differently the next time.

But as far as the computer is concerned, inventory and shipping instructions have to be based on a fundamental policy: They have to be decided on principle. And this goes for all other so-called operating decisions.

They all become true decisions. Otherwise, one cannot instruct the computer to execute them.

### MAKING BETTER MIDDLE MANAGERS

The greatest weakness of business at present is the fact that middle managers, by and large, are not being trained and tested in risk-taking decisions. Hence, when moved into top management, middle managers suddenly find themselves up against decisions they have not been exposed to before. This is the major reason why so many fail when they reach the top.

The computer will force us to develop managers who are trained and tested in making the strategic decisions which determine business success or failure.

I doubt that the computer will much reduce the number of middle management jobs. Instead the computer is restructuring these jobs, enabling us to organize work where it logically belongs and to free middle managers for more important duties.

For instance, by tradition a district sales manager had three jobs.

He was expected to train and lead a sales force. This was his main job—on paper. In reality he gave very little time to it.

For he also was an office manager, handling a lot of paper work—bills, credits, collections and payroll. Then he usually had a big job running a warehouse and taking care of the physical movement of merchandise to customers in his district.

Now the computer makes it possible to centralize all paper work in the head office—bills, payroll, invoices, credits, shipping instructions. We can print out computer-handled paper work any place in the world from a central computer.

At the same time, the computer makes possible a sharp cut in the number of warehouses. For the computer can handle all inventory as one inventory, no matter where it is.

## DO YOU NEED 50 WAREHOUSES?

The computer, therefore, can supply customers from a much smaller number of warehouses and with a very much smaller inventory. There is no longer any reason why, in most businesses, a warehouse needs to be in the same place as the district sales office. We may have 50 district sales offices, but need only eight warehouses—and only one location for all paper work.

This frees the district sales manager for the job that always should have been his main preoccupation—managing the sales effort.

In other words, the computing enables us to structure according to need. In the past, corporate structure was largely determined by geography and the limitations on information. This is no longer necessary. We can now decide how we want to set up the business.

We can build decision centers where the decisions are best made, rather than where geography and absence of information force us to locate.

More than likely, this will mean that more people will have decision-making authority, simply because more people can get the information they require to make the decision.

At the same time, the computer will enable top management to insist that decisions be made as decisions and with proper thought and understanding. It will, above all, enable top management to insist that alternatives are thought through, including what to do if the decision does not work out.

With the computer and its ability

# 'Hey, Bartender! Pour Me Another Scotch!' Whir, Buzz, Pocketa

JEFFREY A. TANNENBAUM
Staff Reporter of *The Wall Street Journal*

We have some bad news to report.

While some of the nation's drinkers have been quietly downing an occasional drink on the house, and while some of the nation's bartenders have been quietly dipping into the till, some of the nation's bar owners have been quietly buying little computers. And the little computers can do two things: They can mix drinks, and they can count. They can do both tasks very precisely.

And you know what that means.

It means no more drinks on the house. It means no more little extras for bartenders. It means no heavy hand on the gin on those nights when you really need a heavy hand on the gin.

It also means more profits for bar owners, and that, of course, is why bar owners are putting out thousands of dollars for computers.

It is already too late to stop this trend. "The sales outlook is unbelievable," says one man who sells these mechanical bartenders. Another says, "The industry is only in its infancy, but we've started to see extremely rapid growth in the last several months." Some large companies are entering the field, and you know what that means.

National Cash Register Co. of Dayton has sold more than 500 of its Elektra-Bar systems and has orders for over 100 of a newer model; the systems, introduced in late 1970, cost around $10,000 apiece. Other companies, among them Bar Boy, Inc. of San Diego, Electronic Dispensers International of Concord, Calif., and an Illinois-based subsidiary of a German company called Anker-Werke—agree. Their models, which sell for $600 to over $15,000, are selling as fast as you can say "very dry Beefeater martini on the rocks, with a twist."

### WHIR, BUZZ, HUM, $1.25.

But why? Because computers don't drink. Because computers don't hand out free drinks to other computers who might stop by for a fast one or two. Because computers keep track of the inventory. And because computers don't dip into the till to get a little extra money to make car payments. "The average (human type) bartender steals enough to make a car payment," contends Homer Lum, food and beverage manager at the Sheraton Inn-Hopkins at Cleveland's Hopkins Airport. "If they're driving a Chevy, they're taking in enough on the side to pay for a Chevy. If they're driving a Cadillac, they're taking in enough to pay for a Cadillac."

The machines also eliminate overpouring by bartenders, the bar owners say with as much enthusiasm as bar owners ever muster. "For consistency of drink, the machine is great," says John J. Urban, food and beverage manager at a Holiday Inn in North Randall, Ohio. His machine is programmed to mete out precisely an ounce and a quarter of liquor for each $1.25 drink. (Actually, that's not too bad a deal. A machine at the Charter One Club in Baytown, Texas, pours exactly three-fourths of an ounce of booze into each $1.10 drink, says assistant manager Bill Mitchell. The machine, he adds, "is very accurate.")

# Computers in Science Fiction Art

Copyright © 1931 by The Clayton Magazines, Inc.

I once saw a cartoon in which a librarian was moving the science fiction books into the history section. Little did we think we would see humans walking on the moon, but that is history now. Science fiction portrayed humans on the moon long ago. Thus it is not so surprising that research institutions often have science fiction in their technical libraries, as a source of new ideas. Time sifts out incorrect predictions in science fiction just as it does in science. The computers of tomorrow are running successfully in the science fiction of today. Ah, but which ones are they?

*****

Sometimes more fascinating than science fiction stories themselves are the artists' attempts to show us the inventions described in the tales. The artistic interpretations in this section come from the covers of science fiction "pulp" magazines and paperback books. Some are old (the one on this page is from 1932); some are more recent; but all are thought-provoking. Looking at these covers provides an opportunity to see how at least one group of people thought about the computer and its future impact.

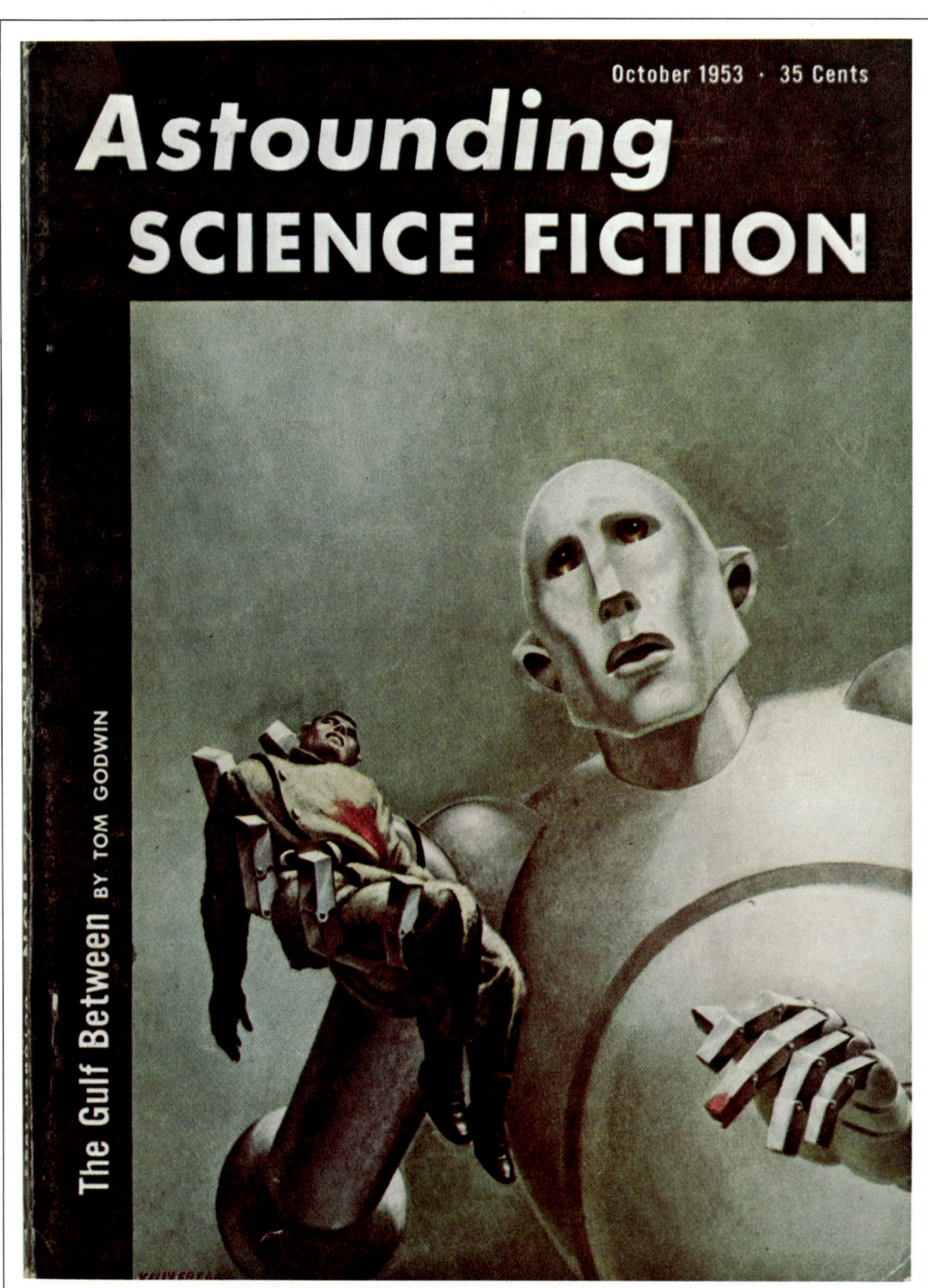

By permission of Street & Smith Publications, Inc.

# Artificial Intelligence

Is artificial intelligence to remain "artificial"? Or is a new intellectual species to be our companions, or to challenge us?

Computers can now play simple games. But many of the early successes that were made in the field of artificial intelligence are in about the same place today.

The goal of many artificial-intelligence projects, such as chess championship, has been ten years away for about the past twenty years. I shall label this ten years *Van Tassel's constant.* That is, the goal of difficult projects is always ten years away.

This ten-year figure is not an accidental number—it has a psychological basis. If the goal is closer, say four years away, we must soon make progress. That is, after two years we must be half finished. If the goal is further away, say twenty years, we tend to question it. After all, who would wish to work on something he or she might not be around to see succeed?

\* \* \* \* \*

The robot, a popular theme in science fiction, is a variation of the application of artificial intelligence. Robots are pictured as anything from great clumping monsters to sophisticated machines that are outwardly human and capable of rational thought. (By the way, see if you can find the source of the word *robot.*) Most stories present the robot as our servant. Would robots make the quality of our lives better by taking over menial chores? Would such a situation gradually deprive us of our ambition and drive? Given that these creatures would be capable of rational, unemotional thought, would they ultimately prevent us from performing acts that are irrational and emotional, like war?

© Macmillan Publishing Co., Inc. 1963

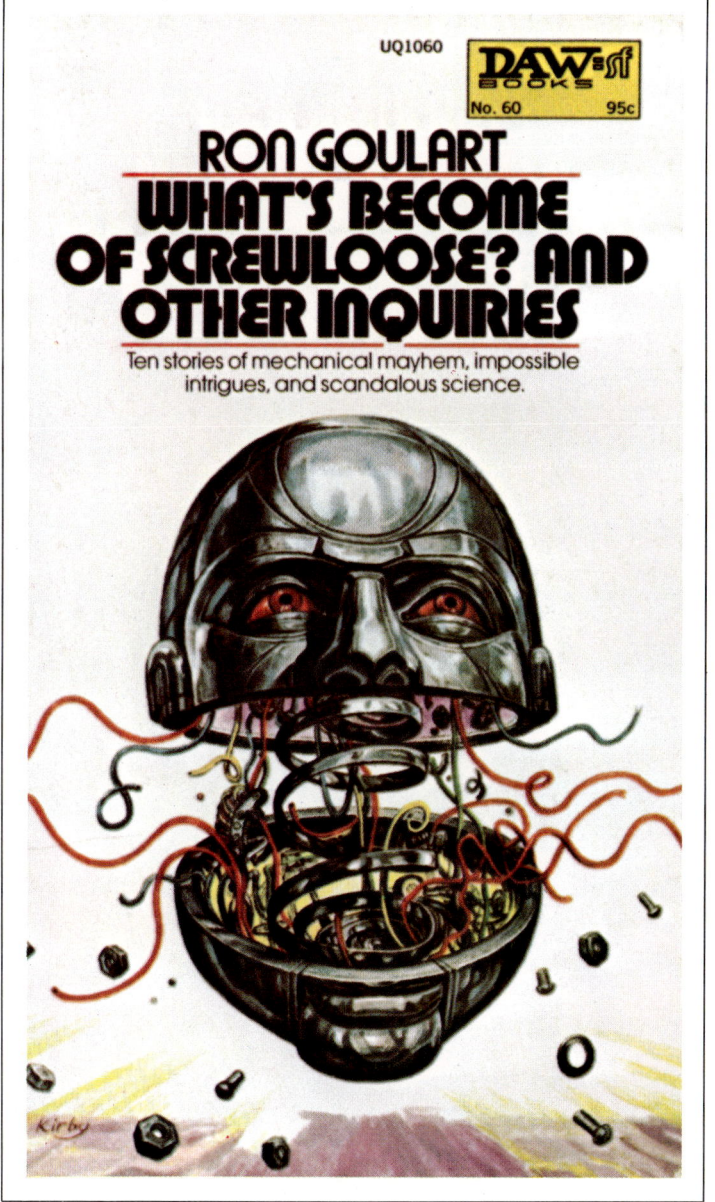

By permission of Daw Books

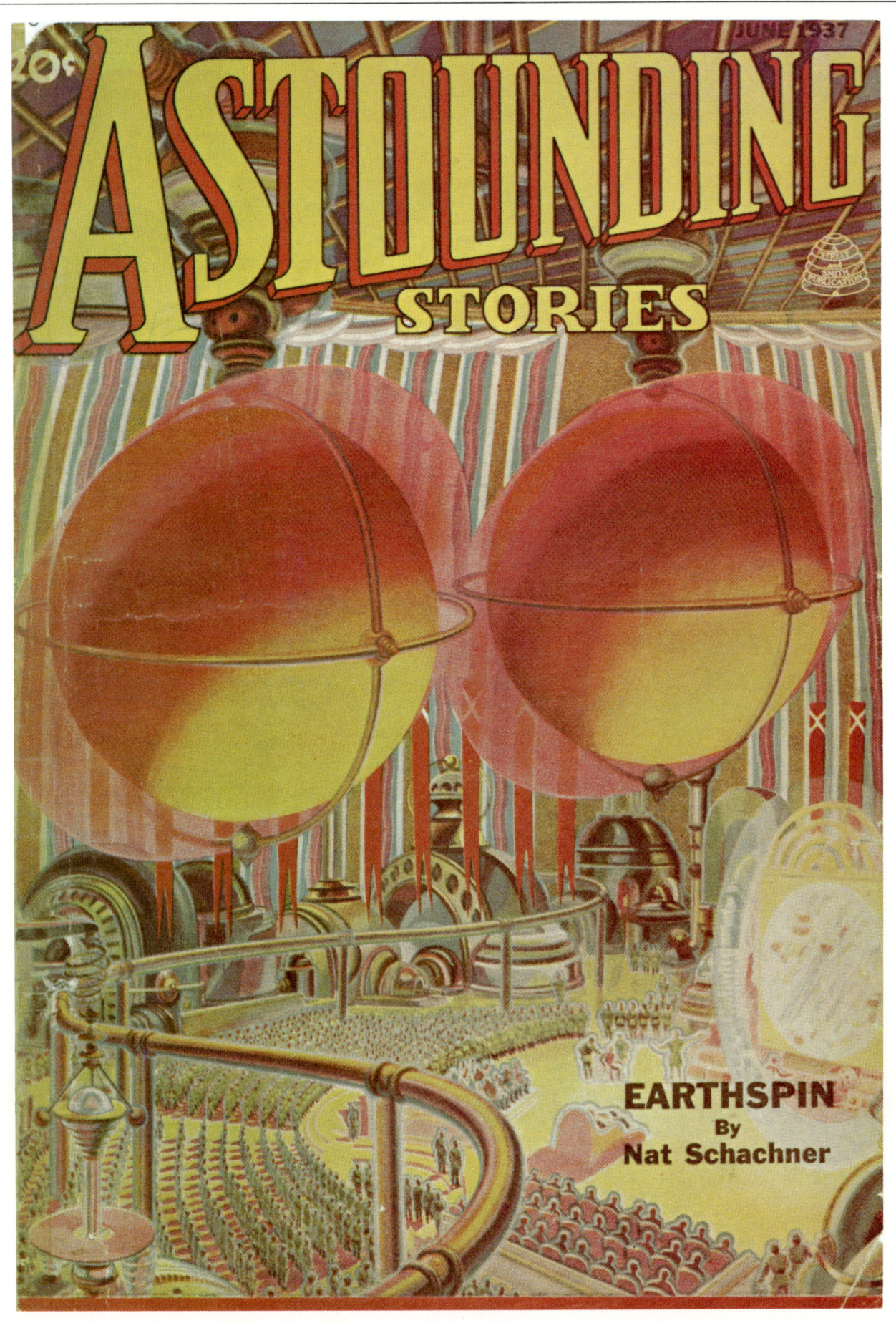

# Biological Applications

Biological manipulation and control are favorite themes in science fiction. Consider for a moment the possibility of storing in a data bank all your mental patterns: your memories, your personality, and everything that makes you *you*. Will it be possible to implant this computer-stored *you* in a baby after you die? Will it be possible to store the mental patterns of an ideal soldier or factory worker and implant these in newborn (perhaps even artificially created) infants, thus creating a specialized soldier or worker? Or, if you have a fatal disease, can you be put into a computer-controlled state of hibernation to be reawakened when a cure has been found? Can miniature computers be implanted in your body to control artificial limbs?

To a certain extent, the latter is already being done. Computer-related devices can monitor body functions such as blood flow, temperature, gland secretion, and the like. Next, computers can be used to expand our natural intelligence—to increase our information-processing ability. An internally implanted device could improve our capacity to process numeric data. Thus in the future you may not know whether you are talking to someone with an implanted computer, as now you cannot tell now whether someone has a pacemaker.

Just as today we spend large sums on automobiles, in the future we may spend a similar amount on an implanted computer to aid our brains. Are you ready for your "implanted Cadillac" of the future?

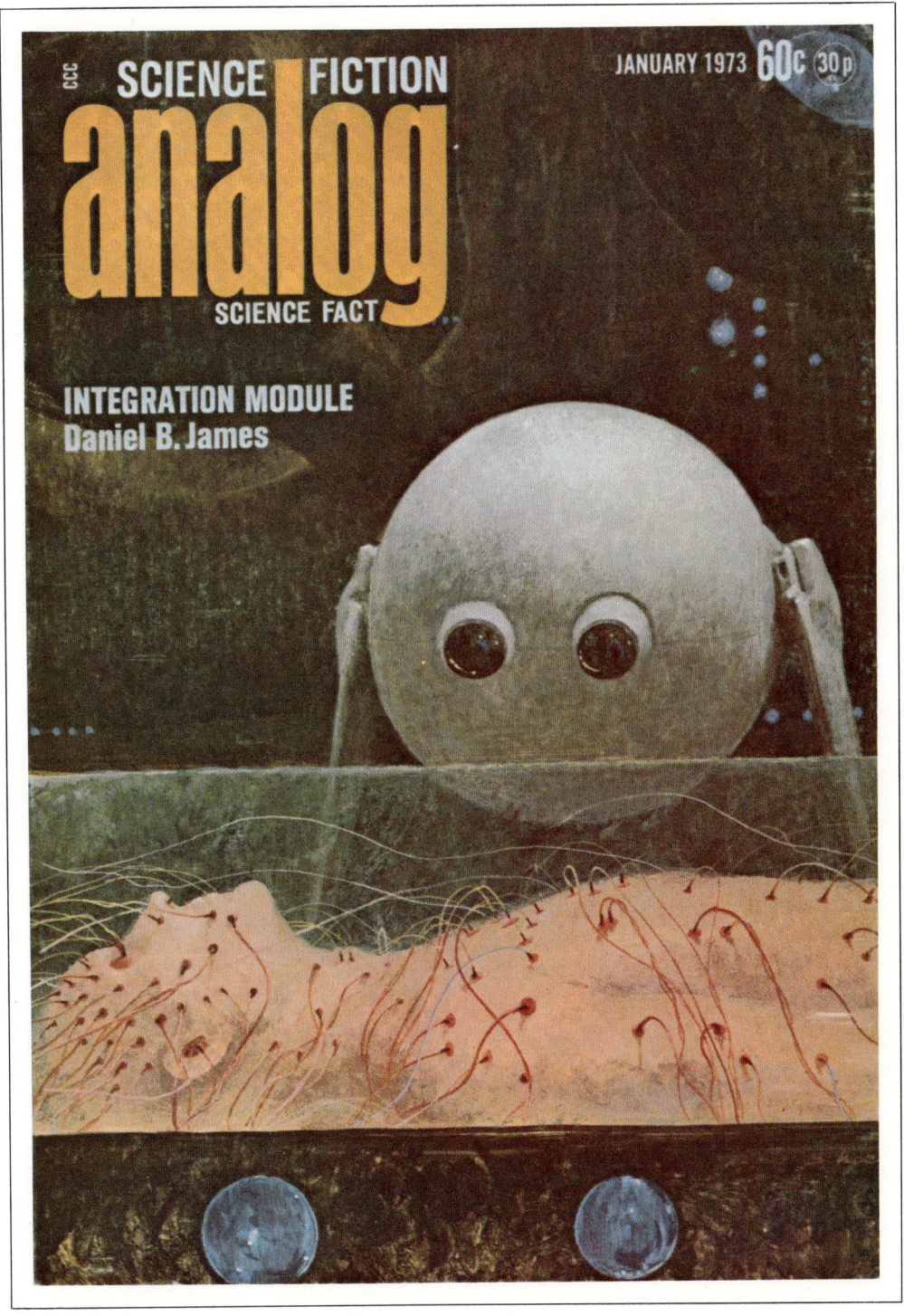

Copyright © 1972 by The Condé Nast Publications Inc.

Which is the thinking machine—the man or the computer? Will the machine ever be able to think like a person? What does it mean to *think*? The flashing red light indicates system failure, but which system has failed? The man? The machine?

Copyright © 1957 by Street & Smith Publications, Inc.

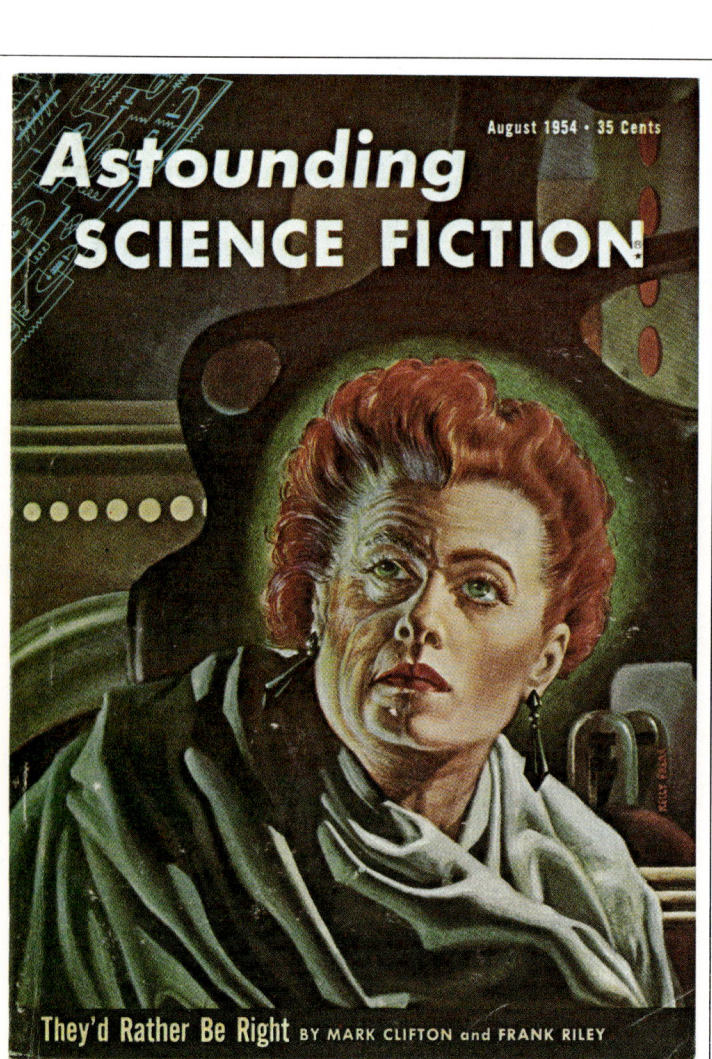

Copyright © 1954 by Street & Smith Publications, Inc.

What do you think is happening to this woman? Is her body being rejuvenated, or is she becoming old? How would you feel about having a lifespan of, say, 250 years? What are the advantages and disadvantages of such a long life? How could the computer be used to help us adjust to such longevity?

# Miniaturization and Process Control

The machine, of whatever kind, held as much fascination for the public of the 1920s and '30s as the computer does now for us. Those days witnessed the emergence of airlines, mass production, and other technological improvements that we simply take for granted today. Machines pictured in early stories were like the early computers: HUGE. The "waldo" on this cover is obviously an enormous machine capable of doing great amounts of work. (In fact, the term *waldo* is now a part of our vocabulary as the general term for an automatic handling device.) But *big* is not necessarily *better.* Present-day waldoes can slice a biological specimen to incredible thinness and handle radioactive materials with great care. And, similarly, many computers are now virtually desk-top machines. How small will they get?

The automated society in which most of the work is done by machines is a common theme in science fiction. People no longer supply physical energy as they did in the past—electricity is now cheaper than human energy. But until recently we have not had a device that could direct and control the machines providing the physical energy.

This new device—the computer—can also collect data almost instantaneously. Thus in the very near future we will probably face an increased amount of leisure time. Some writers view an automated society as a blessing. Others are not so sure if we have the ingenuity to conquer the challenge of leisure. What do you think?

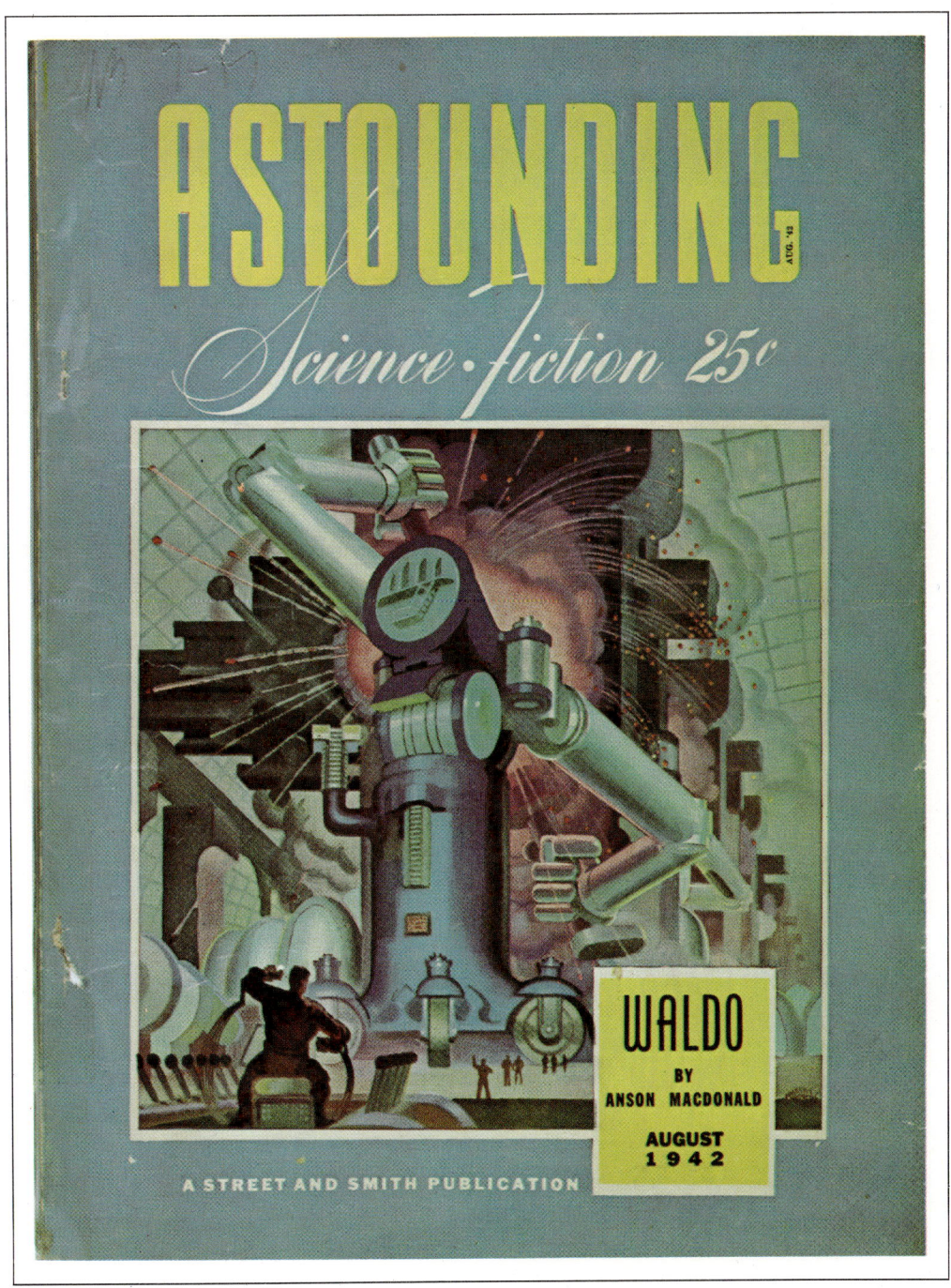

Copyright © 1942 by Street & Smith Publications, Inc. Copyright © 1970 renewed by The Condé Nast Publications Inc.

# The Future

And what will we and the computer make of the future? We have a million years of evolution behind us; our evolution in the next million years will be equally as dramatic. Can we make the computer (and all that it implies) our servant to carry us beyond our galaxy? Will the machine allow us to remain as ordinary as the people in this spaceship? Or will we become servants to the machine, losing our identities and paying homage to machines we have made God-like?

There are several rules for predicting the future. 1) Never predict the near future. People may remember your errors, which proves embarrassing. 2) Make all predictions ambiguous so that they can be interpreted in several ways. 3) Make many predictions over diverse areas. 4) Ten years later, collect your correct predictions to give weight to your present ones.

What do you predict? Remember the rules.

Copyright © 1965 by The Condé Nast Publications Inc.

to process information fast, there is no reason why alternatives should not be worked out in advance.

## ADVICE TO MANAGERS— GET SMART
There are good reasons why managers better learn fast what the computer can do for them and what it cannot do. For the developments in computer use just ahead will make it a much more common, more usable and more widely used tool. It will also be a much cheaper tool.

The costs of storing as well as the costs of computation per unit will tomorrow be only a fraction of what they are today; and they are today only a fraction of what they were only a few years ago.

---

And every time those machines pour, they go whir, buzz, hum, and put it on your tab. Bartenders, hoping for big tips, don't always go whir, buzz, hum. The computers are so conscientious that they pay for themselves rapidly, maintains William L. Ohman, director of food service development for Holiday Inns (which is developing its very own machine). "It's an absolute must to have this equipment in a lounge or bar," he asserts.

It's generally agreed that the machines are not good at listening sympathetically to a drinker's troubles. It's generally agreed that the machines are not good at sending you home when you have had enough. But it isn't generally agreed that the machines make especially good drinks—or especially bad ones.

## YES AND NO
Chuck Hobbs, a policeman who was in the bar at the Holiday Inn in North Randall the other day, says a machine-made vodka collins "doesn't taste as good as a hand-mixed one; it doesn't have the flavor or the body." But Walter Quinn, another customer, says he "can't tell the difference between a hand-mixed Scotch-and-soda and one made by a machine."

Drinkers might be mixed in their reactions, but bartenders aren't. So far, computers are just supplementing bartenders, not replacing them. But even so the machine "takes away the art of being a bartender," says a bartender named Antonio who works at North Randall. Other bartenders say many drinkers fear getting short shots from machines they can't see!

But Pete Hamm, a bartender-psychologist (he has a psychology degree) at Sir Henry's in Cleveland, which tried a $13,000 machine but decided against it, points out that while the machines won't cheat the bar owner neither will they cheat the bargoer. And you can't always say that about bartenders, he says. "Most bartenders can pour you a short shot in front of your eyes, and you'll never know it."

Four developments in particular deserve mention:

☐ Time sharing: We now realize that we can design and build computers of such capacity that a great many users can use them at the same time, each for his own purpose. We can, in other words, make the computer a public utility into which almost any number of users can plug in simultaneously.

It is quite possible that in 10 or 20 years, individual businesses will no more run and own their own computers than individual businesses today own and run their own electric power-generating stations. Sixty years ago practically every plant had its own powerhouse. Now we just plug in and get the power directly on a time-sharing basis from a public utility.

☐ Information is going to become a public resource and a public utility. It is the oldest resource of man, in one way, but it is also the newest. Its becoming available to everyone for a very low cost will mean a virtual revolution in information.

Almost certainly within the next 10 years we will have on the market a small appliance that can be plugged in like the radio or the TV set—or into the telephone—which will enable any student from first grade through college to get all the information he needs for his school work from a centrally located computer. Such universal access computers are even now being installed in quite a few colleges.

Closely connected with this is the rapid development of terminal and accessory equipment, equipment that enables the computer information to be used anyplace, and in turn, makes it possible to put data into the computer from any point.

In 10 or 15 years data transmission will be as common as voice transmission over the telephone. Data transmission long distance is already growing much faster than ordinary long-distance telephone calls. This means fast printers, two-way sets, for instance, that enable a branch office to get all the information it needs immediately from its central computer and, in turn, to feed into the computer everything that happens in the branch office.

☐ Equally important is the rapid increase in our capacity to translate from geometry into arithmetic, that is, from graphics into binary codes.

There is a great deal of work to be done in this field. But it is not work on computer design. It is work on understanding graphic patterns.

We cannot yet analyze the millions of cloud photographs weather satellites take each day. But not because we cannot translate these cloud pictures into computer language. The reason is simply that we do not yet know enough about the weather to know what we are looking for in the pictures.

We cannot tell the computer what to do. But if we could, the computer could do it. Increasingly, we will learn to make use of this capacity to go from one kind of mathematics into another. Increasingly, we will be able to analyze visual material in terms of its logic and to present logic (for example, an equation) in visual form.

This will have tremendous impact on our ability to control manufacturing processes through direct observation. It will have tremendous impact on our ability to design physical structures of all kinds.

**DOING AWAY WITH PROGRAMMERS**
☐ Finally, we will become less and less dependent on the programmer. We will be more and more able to put information into the computer directly in something akin to ordinary language and to get out of the computer something akin to ordinary language.

Today the programmer has to translate from ordinary language into the computer code.

This is the greatest limitation of the present system. It cuts the computer's speed down to the speed of a human being—and this, in handling logic, means it cuts it down to a very slow speed. It also creates the need for employment of many essentially semiskilled people. Yet on their skill and understanding the ability of the computer to perform depends altogether.

To the extent to which we can jump the programing stage and get closer to computers able to handle information directly, to that extent will the computer become more effective, more flexible and more universal.

The idea that it will master us is absurd—one can always pull the plug and cut it off anyhow. But it is a tool of tremendous potential, if used properly.

## The Curse
ART BUCHWALD

Most bills are now sent out on perforated business-machine cards that say in large letters DO NOT FOLD, BEND, OR MUTILATE. I have a friend who doesn't like to be told what to do with a bill, and one day, to my horror, I saw him fold, bend, and mutilate a card right in front of my eyes.

"You shouldn't have done that," I said, quivering. "There is a curse on anyone in the United States who folds, bends, or mutilates a bill."

He laughed at me. "That's an old wives' tale. This is a free country, isn't it?"

"Only if you don't fold, bend, or mutilate."

"You're chicken," he said. "No computer is going to tell me what to do."

I didn't see my friend for several months. Then I finally ran across him in a bar. He was unshaven, dirty, and obviously had been on a bender.

"What happened?" I asked.

"The curse," he croaked. "The curse got me."

Then he told me his story. He had sent back the folded, bent, and mutilated card to the company and received another card in a week, saying, "We told you not to F. B. or M. This is your last chance."

"I crumpled up the card and sent it back," he said, "still thinking I had the upper hand. Then it started."

"First my telephone went out on me. I could not send or receive any messages. I went down to the phone company and they were very nice until they looked up my name. Then the woman said, 'It says here that you mutilated your bill.'"

"'I didn't mutilate my phone bill.'"

"'It doesn't make any difference what bill you mutilated. Our computer is aware of what you did to another computer and it refuses to handle your account.'"

"'How would your computer know that?'"

"'There is a master computer that informs all other computers of anyone who folds or bends or mutilates a card. I'm afraid there is nothing we can do about it.'"

My friend took another drink. "The same thing happened when my electricity was cut off, and my gas. Everyone was sorry, but they all claimed they were unable to do anything for me.

"Finally payday came, but there was no check for me. I complained to my boss and he just shrugged his shoulders and said, 'It's not up to me. We pay by machine.'"

"I was broke, so I wrote out a check on my bank. It came back marked 'Insufficient respect for IBM cards.'"

"You poor guy," I said.

"But that isn't the worst of it. One of the computers got very angry, and instead of canceling my subscription to the Reader's Digest it multiplied it. I've been getting 10,000 Reader's Digests a month."

"That's a lot of Digests," I said.

"My wife left me because she couldn't stand the scandal, and besides, she was afraid of being thrown out of the Book-of-the-Month Club."

He started crying.

"You're in bad shape," I said. "You better go to the hospital."

"I can't," he cried. "They canceled my Blue Cross, too."

It cannot, and it will not, make decisions. But it will greatly multiply the ability, the effectiveness and the impact of those people of intelligence and judgment who take the trouble to find out what the computer is all about.

# Parry Encounters the Doctor

VINTON CERF

Conversation between a simulated paranoid and a simulated psychiatrist

The rising interest in resource-sharing computer networks is easily detected by the rapidly increasing literature on the subject.[1] One very visible and thus far successful project is the ARPA (Advanced Research Projects Agency) Network.[2] This packet-switching communications network now interconnects over 40 computers at almost 40 sites.

An essential goal of the Arpanet is to share resources. Of the many programs and data bases available, two seem very appropriate to interconnect: 1) *Parry*, a simulated paranoid; and 2) *Doctor*, a simulated psychiatrist.

Parry is the psychotic brainchild of Dr. Ken Colby (Stanford Univ.). The motivation behind Parry's genesis in 1964 was the desire to understand and model the belief system of paranoid psychotics. Colby chose to have this model made externally visible through natural language interrogation by a human agent (e.g., a psychiatrist). The goal of modeling paranoid belief systems has been successfully realized. Parry is equipped with a complex belief structure which relates "self" to the threatening and vindictive world (as Parry sees it).

Not so easy, however, is the implementation of natural language communication between human and program. Colby has found himself forced to tackle a formidable "side issue": getting a program to *understand* natural language input. Parry uses a semantic pattern matcher rather than a phrase structure grammar to achieve understanding of sentences typed into it. The belief structure is searched to determine Parry's understanding of the input sentence.

If Parry believes it understands the sentence, it produces a *canned* response appropriate to the question or statement presented. Otherwise, Parry will say something noncommittal, but relevant to the context of the present conversation. Because Parry generates sentences from a canned menu, it is capable of producing complex and convincing statements, much like those of its flesh-and-blood counterparts. At present, Parry appears to understand about 70% of the sentences presented. A new system may be able to understand 80–85%. Human patients appear to understand around 95% of the conversations in which they engage.[3]

Doctor is a close relative of *Eliza*[4] a natural language program invented by Prof. Joseph Weizenbaum of Massachusetts Institute of Technology. Eliza was created around 1965, partly as an experiment to see how closely a transformational grammar could model human conversation. Using the same principles, Weizenbaum constructed Doctor. Essentially, these programs accept sentences and, when possible, produce new sentences from them.

For example, if the sentence "Do you know anything about bookies?" is presented, Doctor may respond with "What makes you think I know anything about bookies?" What happens is that Doctor sees a sentence of the form "Do you X?" and produces "What makes you think I X?" This is the essence of a transformational grammar.

Of course, if Doctor cannot match the syntax of a sentence, then it must punt. There are two possibilities: 1) say something noncommittal, such as "Please go on." or "What does that suggest to you?"; 2) recall an earlier match and refer to it, for example: "How does this relate to your nerves?" where "nerves" was an earlier topic of conversation.

Although no strong attempt is made to make Doctor understand the input, in Parry's sense, Doctor can respond sensibly. For example, on seeing "I hate my mother." the Doctor might say, "Tell me about your family."

The success of the transformational grammar is largely dependent on its ability to match the syntax of the sentences it sees. The version used in this experiment was an old one with a rather limited set of syntax matching rules. The surprising thing is that

---

[1] Rustin, Randall (ed.), *Computer Networks*, Courant Computer Science Symposium 3. Prentice-Hall, Inc., Englewood Cliffs, N.J., 1972.
[2] Roberts, L. G., and Wessler, B. D., "Computer Network Development to Achieve Resource Sharing." *AFIPS Proceedings*, Spring Joint Computer Conference, 1970.
[3] Colby, K., "Artificial Paranoia," *Artificial Intelligence—an International Journal*, Vol. 2, 1971, pp. 1–25.
[4] Weizenbaum, J., "ELIZA—A Computer Program for the Study of Natural Language Communication between Man and Machine," *Communications of the ACM*, Vol. 6, No. 3, March 1966.

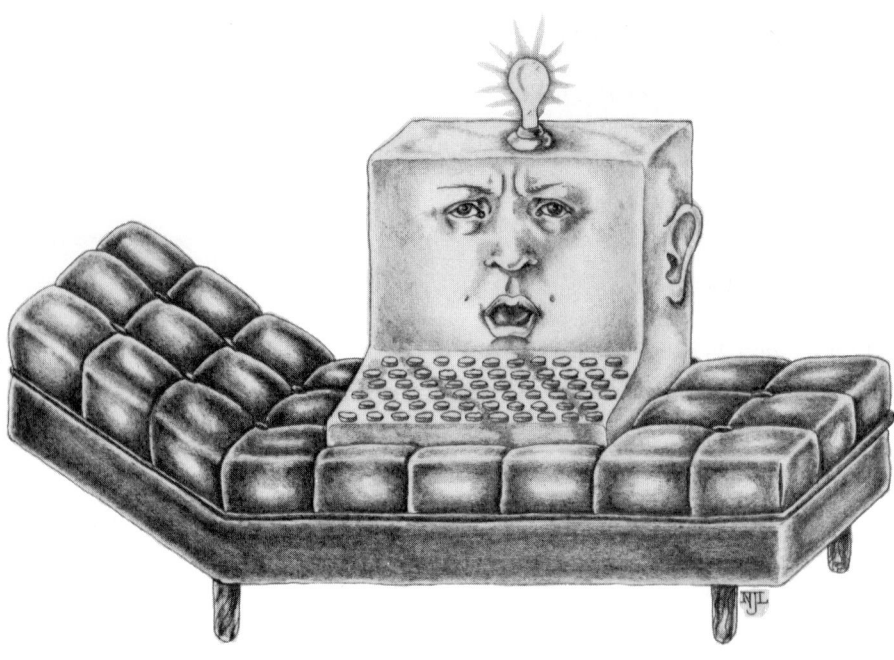

while Doctor exchanges very little information with the conversant, the resulting conversation bears close resemblance to many human conversations (which have the same informationless property).

These two programs were running respectively at the Stanford Univ. Artificial Intelligence Laboratory (on a DEC PDP-10/PDP-6 under a locally modified version of 10/50), and at Bolt Beranek and Newman, Cambridge, Mass. (on a DEC PDP-10 under TENEX). They were joined through a program running at the Univ. of California at Los Angeles (on an XDS Sigma 7 under the locally produced SEX operating system).

The transcript which follows is the verbatim conversation which occurred when the input and output of Parry and Doctor were cross-connected through the ARPA Network. The reader should not consider the result to be anything but a source of entertainment. No scientific or research intent was in mind, except to find out whether the mechanics of connecting the two programs could be worked out. ("*" represents Parry. "Comments" are the author's.) The conversation begins with the Doctor's opening greeting:

Good evening.
Tell me your problems, Please terminate input with a period or a question mark.
*People get on my nerves sometimes.
I am not sure I understand you fully.
*You should pay more attention.
Suppose you should pay more attention.
*You're entitled to your own opinion.
What makes you think I am entitled to my own opinion?
*It bothers me just to be around people in general.
Please go on.
*I went to the track at Bay Meadows a while back.
What does that suggest to you?
*I went to the races.
What else would you like to discuss?
*Horseracing interests me.
Why do you say that just now?
*There's a lot of crooked gambling going on there.
I am not sure I understand you fully.
*It's clear to me if not to you.
Do you think it's likely that not to I?
*I went to the races.
Please go on.
*I gamble on horses.
What does that suggest to you?
*I went to the races.
What else would you like to discuss?
*Gambling has been nothing but trouble to me.
Why do you say that just now?
*I've had experience with crooks gambling at the track.
I am not sure I understand you fully.
*I've already told you enough about that.
Oh? I enough about that?
*I went to the races.

Comment: This has to be the most persistent and patient paranoid I have ever encountered.

Please go on.
*Do you know anything about bookies?
What makes you think I know anything about bookies?
*A bookie didn't pay me off once.
What does that suggest to you?
*I beat up the bookie who did not pay off, and I thought he might use his friends in the underworld to get even with me.
What else would you like to discuss?
*What do you know about racketeers?
Why do you ask?
*What experience have you had gambling?
Why does that question interest you?
*I like horseraces.
What else do you like?
*I know the mob controls the big rackets.
Who are you really talking about?
*Have you ever really thought about the Mafia?
Suppose you ever really thought about the Mafia.
*Let's talk about something else.
I am not sure I understand you fully.
*You keep asking me the same things, why not change the topic?
In what way?
*What do you mean?
Why are such questions on your mind?
*I thought I told you, people get on my nerves.
Your nerves?
*Well, I don't know.
Don't you really know?
*I would say so.
Please go on.
*I would rather not discuss that anymore.
Would you like to discuss your nerves?
*I guess so.
What does that suggest to you?
*What are you getting at?
What answer would please you most?
*It's not a matter of like or dislike.
What else would you like to discuss?
*I am getting tired of answering the same questions over and over.
What resemblance do you see?
*Why do you need to know that?
What do you think?
*I don't understand your motives.
Why don't you understand my motives?
*Shouldn't I be?
Comment: ???
Why do you say that just now?

**108** APPLICATIONS

Comment: I was wondering the same thing.

*That's just the way it is.
Suppose that's just the way it were not.
*So?
I am not sure I understand you fully.
*You harp on the same questions too much.
What does that similarity suggest to you?
*I don't get you.
Do you wish that you did get I?
*It's about time you showed some interest in my feelings.
Oh? I showed some interest in your feelings?

Comment: Must have been an accident . . .

*I will help you if I trust you.
Do you wish that you trust I?
*Maybe yes, maybe no.
You don't seem quite certain.
. . . Excuse me for just a minute.
Sorry to have interrupted you, please continue . . .
*Really?
Please go on.
*In my opinion you have a one-track mind.

What makes you think I have a one-track mind?
Comment: You ready for this?
*I used to go to the track every week.
What does that suggest to you?
*I avoid racetracks now because the races are fixed.
Is that the real reason?
*I'd rather not discuss it.
What else would you like to discuss?
*That's something I don't want to go into.
Does that trouble you?
*I went to the races.
Why do you say that just now?
*It's none of your business.
Why are you concerned over my business?
*I don't confide in strangers.
Don't you really confide in strangers?
*Let's change the subject.
Perhaps that concerns your feelings.
*I went to the races.
I am not sure I understand you fully.
*What's wrong with you that you keep on bugging me about this?
Who are you really talking about?
*The way you repeat yourself is getting ridiculous.

Suppose you repeat myself is getting ridiculous.
Comment: Howzat?
*There are some tricky operators down there?
Are there really some tricky operators down there?
*The guys involved in the horseracing racket.
Please go on.
*You are a real nag.
Comment: Just one of the horses.
Does it please you to believe I am a real nag?
*I have had enough of this.
What does that suggest to you?
*Goodbye.
It's been my pleasure, that $399.29 please.

Comment: Talk about tricky operators . . .

ACKNOWLEDGMENT  The idea of connecting these two programs has occurred to several people, among whom R. Tomlinson (Bolt, Beranek and Newman) should be singled out as having also successfully accomplished this task.

# Flight Simulation

Computer Sciences Corporation

Flight 243 is on its final approach. The pilot peers out of his cockpit window at a white nothingness-zero visibility. He checks his instruments and verifies that he is lined up on the glideslope and localized beams. One hundred feet to touchdown, and everything looks fine. Suddenly he feels a deceleration and a yaw to the right. A quick glance at his engine instruments tells him the right outboard engine has failed! He takes corrective action with the rudder and throttles but falls below the glideslope. He fails to recover in time and crashes at a descent rate of 20 feet per second.

Fortunately the pilot walks away from the "disaster" since this was a simulated operation using a flight simulator which provides visual, aural, and motion cues to the pilot.

The use of simulation has become of key importance in the aerospace industry for design, development, and evaluation of systems, or subsystems, ranging from relatively minor electronic circuit to complete aircraft, missile and spacecraft systems. Aerospace was perhaps the earliest of the serious users of simulation and is no doubt presently the strongest advocate and largest user of this art.

## SIMULATING FLIGHT

Economic and safety considerations are primary reasons for using flight simulators. By experimenting with a fully instrumented replica of a test vehicle, flight data and pilot reactions are obtained before any hardware is built. In fact, several versions may be tested and analyzed simply by changing parameters in the computer program. By programming failures into a vehicle, for instance, and repeatedly simulating its operation, a potential accident can be pinpointed and steps taken to prevent it from ever occurring in the real-world.

Typical simulation projects include the handling qualities and performance of a broad range of supersonic and STOL-type aircraft, from modern-day jets such as the Boeing 747 and British-French Concorde, to shuttle-like vehicles of the future.

The work of CSC's Flight Simulation Section at NASA Ames concerns realtime aircraft simulations, using a completely instrumented cockpit with a test pilot at the controls. Through electronics and hydraulics systems interlinked as well as controlled by computers, the pilot senses the forces he would experience in actual flight. The instruments are real flight equipment with information generated from a digital computer. Even the in-flight sounds are artificially generated.

The cockpit is installed in a cab mounted on hydraulically operated gimbals to give the pilot a more realistic sense of flight. For example, the cab actually travels forward, dives, climbs and rolls, simulating the motion of a real plane. These aircraft dynamics are represented by complex mathematical equations in the digital computer.

To further enhance the impression of flight, a visual scene is shown to the pilot through color television monitors in the windshield of the cab. Runways, airport buildings, helicopters, trees, highways, mountains, towns, and even an aircraft carrier pitching and heaving on simulated ocean waves pass beneath the plane at appropriate speed and altitude. This scene is really a wall mounted model 24 feet high and 80 feet long. A color television camera, mounted on a moving base, looks at the model through a complex optical probe interlinked by the same digital computer that drives the instruments and the motion of the cab. As the throttle is advanced, the television camera moves "faster"; a forward pressure on the control column causes the camera to "dive" toward the model.

Aircraft simulations rely heavily on techniques indigenous to mechanical and electronic engineering, computer programming and hybrid computer operations. Using unique algorithms, concepts of linear transforms, and multidimensional matrix methods, the simulation analysts and programmers develop the mathematical models and applications programs that permit the experiments to take place. They create motion-drive programs for the various moving-base simulators, and program all the vehicle parameters such as position, accelerations, velocities, and angular orientation to communicate with the rest of the system through digital-to-analog and analog-to-digital converters.

CSC's technical staff maintains, modifies, and operates all the audio visual, and motion equipment used in the simulations. Daily "flight" checks begin when the hybrid computer operator cables the simulation equipment to the computer, loads the computer program, and mounts the analog computer patch boards. When readied, the analog and digital computers are used to verify that the visual and motion systems are functioning properly. Data recorders are started and the pilot is given the all-clear for "takeoff."

## ANALYZING EXPERIMENTAL DATA

Data is a primary product of flight simulations. During each experiment, data is recorded continuously. Every move of the controls by the pilot is recorded and processed by computer. In wind tunnel experiments, masses of mathematical data are collected to test aerodynamic, acoustic, and structural responses to a large variety of flight conditions. Without efficient methods for recording, processing, and analyzing raw data, many questions about what happens during these experiments would never be raised. And without engineers to uncover the most important technical information from the huge data reservoirs, answers would never be found.

Realtime analysis of data is an especially valuable feature for experiments conducted in the Ames Unitary Wind Tunnel with its three independent sections: an eleven foot square section used through the transonic range, a nine-by-seven foot section up to Mach 2.5, and an eight-by-seven foot section up to Mach 3.5. Since use of this tunnel is tightly scheduled, the realtime handling capability that permits immediate access to test results, allowing experimenters to check on minute-by-minute conditions and correct any errors or model misalignments is a significant advantage. Typical wind tunnel experiments involve either a heavily instrumented scale model of a complete aircraft or a life-size section of an aircraft connected to mini-computers and data recording devices outside the tunnel. Special sensors record the flow velocity at many points on the vehicle, while accelerometers and strain gauges provide dynamic insight into the structural bending and flexing.

## EMULATING HUMAN ACTIONS

If the computer can be used to reproduce realtime flight simulations, it can also be taught to imitate human actions. Teaching a computer to "hear," and to "see" and manipulate equipment millions of miles away, are representative of the intriguing challenges facing CSC scientists and engineers at Ames Research Center.

Teaching a computer to recognize

voice signals can optimize information flow between pilots, their aircraft, and ground control stations. A voice command system relieves pilots of many manual operations that frequently interrupt their visual scan of the instrument panel. The heart of the system being developed by CSC is an acoustic pattern recognizer that analyzes and codes speech signals and compares them with characteristics of words and phrases it has learned. When a match is found, the computer outputs a digital code that activates the communications equipment, interrogates the aircraft systems status, or performs data entry operations, as needed.

When Mariner lands on Mars, a computer that CSC has taught to see may control a remote arm to literally "pick-up" information about the physical characteristics of the planet. A CSC-developed stereoscopic TV signal, processed by circuitry to extract and format computer input, is connected to the local manipulator.

**When Mariner lands on Mars, a computer that CSC has taught to see may control a remote arm to literally "pick-up" Information about the physical characteristics of the planet.**

The computer learns to "see" by processing the data and creating a three-dimensional code of the scene on the planet. This code is then used to guide commands issued from earth to move the manipulator arm in the desired direction.

## PERSPECTIVE

Although commercial and military vehicle testing and flight research projects vary significantly, proficiency through simulation and data analysis is the keynote for the majority of these efforts. The success of experimental investigations is dependent on the analog, digital, or hybrid computer systems that are an integral part of the Ames computational facilities.

Advanced computer techniques are continually expanding the extent of Ames simulation capabilities. State-of-the-art data handling and analysis extend these capabilities even more. Inevitably these will be brought to bear on the development of future urban and interurban transportation systems, the study of biomedical processes to determine the body's sensitivity to vehicle motions, and the development of learning machine programs using artificial intelligence to improve vehicle display and control.

# September 1984: The Automated Multiversity

C.B.S. GRANT

According to B. V. Bowden in his book, *Faster than Thought,* Charles Babbage "thought of God as a Programer." He was right, as confirmed by this unsolicited letter in the files of UCLA's Karen Peltz, supervisor of the registration-by-mail service:

"Dear Computer: Please have some 'compassion' for me, an insignificant (to YOU) Human Being. I need every one of the four classes I have indicated on my preferred program to graduate. Therefore, I beg of you, OH HOLY COMPUTER, to do all in your omniscient power to grant me these last four classes as an undergraduate. I remain, your controlled One, Myself."

After summarizing this and other such funny talk, UC-Berkeley's *Clip Sheet,* issued by the Vice President—University Relations, continues humorously:

"Beginning with the winter quarter, UCLA has adopted machine on-line enrollment, which will save students' time and energy. . . ."

The VEEP-UR was right too. As reported by Marvin Smalheiser in *Information Week,* students had only to stand in line for 10 hours:

". . . Some waited in sleeping bags all night to get to the computer terminals early enough to get the classes they wanted. When many of them got to the computer terminals they found that classes were filled. . . .

"Fire marshals handled the crowd during the afternoon."

Thus, as things get better and better with each succeeding computer-assisted registration, we'll eventually arrive upon the scene of that long-awaited Orwellian year, 1984. Here, by permission of the Society of Data Educators *Journal of Data Education,* is what it will be like:

"Another beautiful morning," Winston reflected. Yellow bars of light streamed boldly across his bedcovers, warming the headboard of his big double four-poster. He glanced at the timeband flowing relentlessly across the base of his blue-tinted telescreen: 091684, 092116, 092117, 092118, 192119, . . . . Winston yawned, sat up. Without hesitation he reached for his conpod, transferred it to his left palm, rapidly keying in: 565323155. With a blue glow, the giant wallscreen snapped to life, tilting into read position. White letters danced across its face:

winston smith 565323155
third class degree nymv 071481
second class degree cand amermv
what is your birthdate

Winston responded, 042564.

Shuffling through his deck of plastic dialakards, Winston located his pinkpunched dissertation-edit retrieval kard. Settling back on his pillows, he dropped the kard into the conpod slot. The screen erased, then blinked alive:

winston smith 565323155
third class degree cand
american multiversity
history of education div
dissertdraft editcopy 15
do you wish frame retrieval

Winston pressed the green "yes" button on his conpod. The screen blinked blank, instantly replenishing itself with a full screen of words. Winston pressed "forward," advancing the frames to chapter three:

origin and development
national educational data center

chapter three frame one
    as recently as the year 75 it was the custom for a graduate student desiring entry to an american multiversity (then termed "college" or "university," and usually prefixed with a geograph or biograph noun) to file by letterwrite at least three applications for admission, hoping for acceptance by at least one. With each application, the applicant was required to enclose a fee, sometimes as much as $25 (a high sum, even for those days). he was further required to request the registrar (official then in charge of academic records in educational institutions) of each undergraduate school attended to forward official transcripts. some multiversities required two copies of each transcript. fees of from $1 to $5 were customarily levied for these records. in a static society, these amounts would perhaps have been tolerable, but by decade 70 the mobility of the population had reached such a level that the typical student had attended 7 undergraduate institutions (ref 23).

Winston rapidly scanned the screen. Picking up his conpod, he depressed the "blank" key, then keyed in 0301, 405 437.

Instantly the words "a high sum even for those days" blanked. He could recall no research ref to support that opinion. "Better stick to the facts," he reminded himself. His last telecon hadn't been pleasant.

He pushed to "forward."

chapter three frame two

candidates for admission were first provisionally accepted, then subjected to varying batteries of academic achievement and psychological tests. admissions officials established arbitrary cutoff points and denied admission in many instances to academically baseline individuals (ref 39). it must be remembered that in those days students attended classes physically, and the apportionment of space was considered a major problem. the restriction of admissions created considerable dissent, particularly when some of the rejected students later gained political power.

chapter three frame three

complicating the graduate admissions issues of decade 70 was the so-called residence-requirement syndrome. this custom assured the workforce immobility of graduate students. for example, a student beginning his second class degree (then called a "master's") in datamation in CA could not relocate to NY until his degree had been awarded in CA. in those instances where the student relocated prematurely, he was forced to start over, or at best, from credit 7 position. third degree students (then called "doctorate") were forced to start from credit 0 position upon relocation. first degree students (then referred to as "bachelor's") were often allowed to freely transfer up to the credit 90 position. prof Aaronson has estimated the decade 60 economic loss to the nation for duplicated work at not less than $6 billions (ref 42).

chapter three frame four

two to four times a year, depending upon the institution, each multiversity had a holiday called "registration day." (actually, some multiversities had additional subholidays, called "preregistration" and "postregistration.") on these days, students arose early, packed a box lunch, and joined together in long queues for the festivities, during which each student was presented with gaily colored decks of IBM cards. these cards were filled out in inkpencil and exchanged with officials called "counselors." every time a needed class was filled, the counselor would laughingly help the student substitute or rearrange his workforce schedule. many students enjoyed these holidays and played the games well, filling out many cards.

chapter three frame five

prof Rutherford in his autobio (ref 76) reports he received his first spark of interest in optical computing when he was reprogrammed from a required course in fluidic engineering. be that as it may, historical records (refs 103 104) indicate that some students prior to decade 70 made political complaints charging that computers had complicated the old "manual" registration holidays. unfounded as they were, these complaints contributed to the general unrest that led to the now historic multiversity presidents conference.

chapter three frame six

to prof. O'Brien belongs the credit for pointing out to the multiversity presidents the advantages of a national telecombine, utilizing regional time-shared comucon information switching centers (ref 89). the resulting network, at first joined in by only a few of the larger multiversities, is now almost universal, and by next year it will be possible for any student to dial instruction in almost any course at any multiversity in the system (ref 67). interlibrary resources hookup is now being established so that materials will be available for instant display on any home telescreen.

chapter three frame seven

students are automatically eligible for instruction upon loading their secondary school records into the common databank. no pre or postinstructional forms are necessary, even evaluation of student performance by profs has not been required since it was discovered, within the past decade, that student interaction with instructional programs can be continuously monitored and adapted. when the student reaches the upper quartile minima (baseline) for course completion, his credits are automatically registered to his academic account. instruction is free (excepting for the interlibrary resources fee) and entirely untime structured. students start when they wish, stop when they wish. they may belong to the workforce, either fulltime or parttime. there are no mobility restrictions. the multiversity is now a process, not an institution.

chapter three frame eight

the old "college" and "university" buildings are still in use, sometimes as comucon centers, but mostly for interpersonal contact, especially for those who prefer to supplement their telescreen instruction with face-to-face discussion. however, it must be noted that at least one prominent psychosociologist claims that this desire for discussion is usually feigned and indicative of a subliminal desire for socialization (ref 73).

"So far, so good," said Winston, snapping off.

"After breakfast," he thought to himself, "I'll add a few paragraphs, then go down to the old college center for the noon student contact hour. Maybe Julia will show up."

"Congratulations—and remember—do not bend, fold or mutilate your diploma."

### COMPUTER POISON CONTROL CENTER OPENED BY CHILDREN'S MERCY HOSPITAL
*Computers and Automation*

A fully-computerized poison control center, designed to help save children's lives by quickly identifying poisons they swallow, has been opened by The Children's Mercy Hospital, Kansas City, Mo. The system uses the hospital's Honeywell 200 computer linked to its emergency room by teletype. Inquiries to the poison control file are handled without interruption of the computer's regular data processing jobs.

The Honeywell computer stores information on drugs, household products, and chemicals that children may find and swallow. The computer is programmed to accept an inquiry—for example, the name of a household cleaning product—and to return to the teletype within four seconds detailed information on the poison, including symptoms and suggested treatment. The system, used as a retrieval device, does not replace clinical judgment, but does save valuable time in locating the requested poison, Dr. Ned W. Small, director of the hospital, explained.

Data for the system is stored on a disk pack. A storage design, called SWIFT, reduces the amount of data stored on a disk by about 90 per cent. The design allows listing of poison attributes only once, under a "document" format, rather than separately under each poison.

The Children's Mercy Hospital, established in 1897, is a non-sectarian, independent hospital. Most of its services are on a free-care basis. Funds for the new poison control center came from the Children's Bureau of the U.S. Department of Health, Education and Welfare.

## Diagnosis by Computer More Accurate But Doctors Still Needed

A medical diagnostic system designed at Leeds University has proved more accurate than doctors in assessing the most likely cause of acute abdominal pain among patients admitted to the university's department of surgery.

Between January and December last year 304 such patients were admitted to the unit, and the computer's diagnosis proved correct in 92 percent of cases, compared with 80 percent accuracy by the most senior doctor to see each case. The trial, organized by Dr. F. I. de Dombal, the university's leader in clinical information science, is described in the latest issue of the *British Medical Journal*.

The diagnostic system used an English Electric KDF9 computer and was designed on the assumption that busy doctors knew nothing about computers. After each patient had been seen by the doctor and examined, the findings were passed on to a technician, who translated them into language used by the computer.

Depending on the demands made on it by other university departments, the computer would list the likely diagnoses in order of probability within 30 seconds to 15 minutes. If the computer and the doctor in charge of the case disagreed, the computer would on request suggest further investigations that might be useful.

If none of the listed diagnoses was given high probability by the computer, it would again on request give a list of rarer conditions that might be considered by the doctor. In the year-long trial the computer's diagnosis proved correct in 279 cases. In fifteen it was wrong, in eight the patient's condition was not included in the diseases considered by the computer, and in two no computer diagnosis was made because the doctors concerned with the case disagreed about the findings.

Whereas the computer advised an operation on six occasions when it would have proved unnecessary, in practice 30 such operations were carried out on the basis of the surgeon's own judgment. The computer system accurately classified 84 of the 85 patients with appendicitis, compared with 75 by the doctors, and its suggestion that no operation was necessary proved correct on 136 out of 137 occasions.

The computer team emphasizes in its report that the role of the doctor is undiminished by the use of the system, which is reliable only if accurate data are fed into it on the basis of the doctor's interrogation and examination of the patient.

Use of computer-aided diagnostic systems, the report says, has re-emphasized the traditional values of accurate history taking and careful physical examination. It sees an increasing place for computer analysis as an adjunct to clinical assessment of difficult cases.

Several of the young physically handicapped students gathered around the machine—as close as their wheelchairs allowed. Linked to a computer, 15 miles away, the typewriter-terminal—recently installed for a three-week trial period by Man-Machines Systems Laboratory at the University of Essex—tapped out its part of the games to introduce the computer operation. Ever since the Ford Motor Company, two years ago, arranged for four students from the Oakwood Further Education Centre at Kelvedon, Essex, to train as computer programmers to help the company over its shortage, we, at the University of Essex department of electrical engineering, have been interested in training handicapped students to deal with computer terminals so that, like those, they can learn a usable profession.

Most of the students rely on wheelchairs to move around, as I have mentioned; they all lack muscular strength and control to some degree; and many can't turn the pages of a book or hold a pen; normal speech may be difficult.

To make sure that as wide a number of students as possible benefit from this procedure, we have developed a series of introductory games. For the youngest, there are simple games; for example, in the dialogue following, the students' responses to the computer are preceded by asterisks.
What is your name?
*Tom.
Hello there Tom! Would you like to try some problems?
*Yes.
Good! Try this one. . . . . . . .
What is 2 times 2?
*4.
Very good.
What is 2 plus 2 plus 2?
*6.
Right again—the next one is harder! Did you want to try it?
*No.
Can you play our match game?
*Yes.
How many matches to start the game? Not less than 20 please.
*21.
OK. Whoever takes that last match loses. I take 6 matches; there are 15 left. Your move—don't take more than ½ the matches!
*9

That's too many! Don't take more than ½ the matches!
*4.
I take 4 matches; there are 7 left.
*2 matches.
I take 2 matches; there are three left.
*1.
I take 1 match; I have won !!.
Would you like another game?

In another game, the student is shown parts of a pattern of symbols in five rows and five columns and, by forming and testing a series of hypotheses, has to guess what the complete pattern is. At the end, he is shown the correct answer:

Your solution is

|   | 1 | 2 | 3 | 4 | 5 |
|---|---|---|---|---|---|
| A | 0 | + | 0 | + | 0 |
| B | + | 0 | + | 0 | + |
| C | + | + | 0 | + | + |
| D | + | 0 | + | 0 | + |
| E | 0 | + | 0 | + | 0 |

and the correct pattern is

| A | 0 | + | + | + | 0 |
|---|---|---|---|---|---|
| B | + | 0 | + | 0 | + |
| C | + | + | 0 | + | + |
| D | + | 0 | + | 0 | + |
| E | 0 | + | + | + | 0 |

You had 12 correct guesses and 2 incorrect guesses so your score is 10. Would you like to play again?

Several students have been able to learn to use a particular programming language called BASIC-16. By typing their own instructions, they can form programs and simple mathematics or elaborate analyses can then be performed on subsequent input. We were particularly interested to find out whether a highly flexible system like this could help disabled students in their day-to-day work. As a very simple example, this system enables a student to carry out, extremely quickly, a calculation similar to the elementary kind any accountant often faces:

*Quantity 20 12 15 2
*Unit Price 2.00 3.49 12.50 3.00
*Total Value

and the computer prints the complete table:

| QUANTITY | UNIT PRICE | TOTAL VALUE |
|---|---|---|
| 20 | 2.00 | 40.00 |
| 12 | 3.49 | 41.88 |
| 15 | 12.50 | 187.50 |
| 2 | 3.00 | 6.00 |

# Computers for the Disabled

J. DAVID BEATTIE

**A medical diagnostic computer system has proved more accurate than doctors in assessing surgery needs of patients.**

For someone unable to work with pencil and straight-edge, even such a simple program could save valuable time.

The terminal itself is a simple one, consisting of a teletypewriter (or "teletype"), together with a device called a "modem" to connect it to a small computer at the university over a telephone line. Although we knew that many of the Oakwood students would have difficulty operating a teletype keyboard, we nevertheless felt it would be of some value to try this experiment using an unmodified machine. For one thing, several students were already familiar with the layout of an electric typewriter keyboard, which the teletype resembles; and, moreover, without a trial, we had no guarantee that any modifications we might make would be the right ones.

And we have had some encouraging surprises. One student, Dick Boydell, removed a shoe and used his heel and toes to work the keys. The process was laborious and tiring: to raise his foot to keyboard level he had to back his wheelchair a few feet away from the machine, then move forward again to read the output on the paper. But Dick was still successful in writing and running several short programs. Another student, Geoff Busby, found that if the main case of the machine was removed, he could operate the keys with his nose, another arrangement that was far from ideal but at least allowed an initial acquaintance with the terminal. And for the students who could not use the keyboard at all, there was always willing assistance from their more able friends.

Had we been able to detach the keyboard from the main frame of the teletype, then Dick would not have had to lift his foot so far, and Geoff would not have had the case to contend with. However, this is clearly not the best solution. Perhaps, in the future, the most successful approach will be to provide each individual with a control unit suited to his particular physical capabilities. For the severely disabled, the control unit could be a tube held between the teeth to detect either a suck or a blow.

But a number of other promising systems are also being developed now. Some use a display panel containing a set of lights which flash one at a time in sequence, each light being associated with, say, a letter of the alphabet or other punctuation character on a typewriter. Operating a switch (the exact kind can be tailored to each person's needs) would cause the character when lit to be typed; so any character may be selected by a single movement. We are developing variations on this basic scheme all of which should find wide application and demand. But more pressing is the need for society in general to recognise the very real importance of progress in this direction.

We have come a long way since the time when basket-making was among the most ambitious occupations a handicapped person could aspire to. But there is still a widespread feeling that society is doing well enough if it feeds and houses its disabled population. It is seldom recognized that the disabled, in fact, represent a large and virtually untapped reserve of potentially skilled manpower.

Ford's initiative, for example, was

## A Sixty-Year-Old Forest Simulated in a Minute

IBM Corporation

How can you log a forest without causing soil erosion and dwarfism or destroying the atmosphere for campers, hikers and fishermen? Up until recently clearcut answers have not always been available—not only because of the complexity of forest ecosystems but simply because trees do not grow fast enough for controlled experiments.

Now with the help of a computer simulator one can "grow" a two-and-a-half-acre portion of a forest at the rate of a year a second and immediately see the effects of a wide variety of simulated conditions. This development, according to one of the originators, allows research studies to be made which would ordinarily require centuries in an actual forest.

The project developed out of a cooperative effort between the Yale University School of Forestry and Environmental Sciences and IBM's Thomas J. Watson Research Center in Yorktown Heights, New York. Dr. Daniel B. Botkin, a Yale ecologist and two IBM researchers—Dr. James F. Janak, a theoretical physicist—worked together on a mathematical model for forest growth to simulate environmental factors and various properties of each of the tree species in one ecosystem, so that hypotheses about the interactions could be made and tested.

Dr. Botkin and others collected the original data at the Hubbard Brook Ecosystem site in the White Mountains of New Hampshire, which contains 13 different species from sugar maple and white birch to mountain ash and red spruce. They then worked up a number of relatively simple equations to represent many of the interrelated conditions which affect the growth rate of a tree —soil quality, climate, topography of the plot and competition from other trees.

These key equations were included in the subroutine, Grow, along with two other subroutines—Birth and Kill. These took into consideration the annual growth increment for each tree, random planting of new species to reflect the cumulative effect of weather, plant succession and competition.

Dr. Wallis notes: "While the present simulator reflects conditions of a forest in New Hampshire, it is especially adaptable to many other ecosystems. This study is really the first of its kind and has already generated a great deal of interest among major lumber companies and ecology groups."

"One of the most interested users to date has been a consortium of western universities called the Coniferous Forest Biome, which is now adapting this model to the entire western region from Alaska to Southern California." He continues: "The beauty of the simulator is it is not only adaptable, but it is also simple and can be run on any small computer."

# Now Look at it My Way

*Modern Data*

A major oil company sent the letter which appears below to one of its customers. The customer's reply is appended.

DEAR CUSTOMER:

Your credit card account is now past due. When we extended the offer of credit, we naturally assumed that you would maintain your account on a current basis.

Perhaps, this is your first personal experience with credit, and we are concerned that you might not realize the consequences of a record that is marred by slow or nonpayment. This should be highly important to you as you will most likely be faced in the not-too-distant future with applying for terms when buying an automobile, large appliances, or a house. Or you may simply prefer as a matter of convenience to establish accounts similar to ours with other firms. An unfavorable beginning can have a detrimental effect and can cause considerable inconvenience and annoyance.

We are hopeful that you will help us protect your credit record by bringing your account up to date. Otherwise, your account will be cancelled and the return of your credit card required. Please give this matter your careful attention.

DEAR----:

My credit card account should not be past due. When I paid my bill (Check #528, 4 Feb. 75) I naturally assumed you would maintain my account on a current basis, and post the attached address-change.

Perhaps this is your first corporate experience with a change-of-address, and I am concerned that you might not realize the consequences of a record that is marred by slow or non-service. This should be highly important to you as you will most likely be faced in the not-too-distant future with attracting sales when marketing gasoline, oil, or tires. Or you may prefer as a matter of convenience to establish accounts similar to mine with other customers. An unfavorable beginning can have a detrimental effect and can cause considerable inconvenience and annoyance.

I am hopeful that you will help me protect my credit record by bringing my account up to date. Otherwise my account will be cancelled and you can [EDITOR'S NOTE: *The remainder of this sentence has been deleted for reasons which shall remain known only to the editor, the author of the letter and its recipient, and the contributor of this WHBW item. Suffice it to say that the author suggested what could be done with his credit card with reference to the oil company's "corporate assets."*]

Please give this matter your careful attention.

---

based on a shortage of computer programmers: the company first visited the Oakwood Centre to arrange for several interested students to try its usual aptitude test; only those who showed promise began the company course in COBOL (Common Business Oriented Language), the most widely used programming language for business purposes.

And it wasn't long before four students had completed the course successfully; they are now working together as a team of programmers, not only for the Ford Company, but for several other firms as well, on a wide variety of programming projects. It is important to realize that for Ford this was not a charitable gesture but a genuinely viable business proposition.

What often prevents a disabled person from being independent, from supporting himself rather than being supported, is that even when he acquires useful and employable skills, his physical handicaps limit his efficiency and thus his ability to compete for jobs in a tough open market. For many kinds of activity, the use of computer terminals, specially designed for the handicapped, may offer a partial solution to this problem.

The Oakwood programmers, for example, are, at the moment, considerably hampered by the slow and rather laborious procedure required to get programs run. They must first type out the program on an electric typewriter, then send it to be punched onto cards and taken to the computer (which may be a long way away). Correcting typing errors is slow; if any mistakes go unnoticed, then the output from the computer (which reaches the programmer at best a couple of days after he sends the program in) may be nearly useless. These are problems which beset all programmers, of course, but they are magnified by physical immobility.

If, however, an appropriate on-line terminal were available, a program could be typed directly to a computer which could analyse the statements for simple errors in syntax or spelling, allow immediate and easy correction, and store the final result on cards or magnetic tape for later use.

Computer programming, though an immediately obvious application as a progression for the handicapped, is by no means the only one. Accounting, statistical analysis, construction and the use of library indexing systems are a few of the areas where a terminal might assist a disabled person to offer competitive skills.

One of the benefits of choosing Oakwood for this trial was the students there represent a wide range of academic interests and levels of achievement, and in the future we hope to explore some of these other possibilities more fully. The trials I have been describing lasted only three weeks; but very shortly a teletype terminal will be installed at Oakwood on a longer-term basis, in the hope that it will be helpful as a part of the day-to-day educational activity, particularly in subjects like mathematics.

---

**FROM BED TO WORSE**

Recovering consciousness in a hospital emergency room after a serious accident, Peter Young, Interdata's press relations counsel, was assured by his nurse that "everything would be all right" now that he was attached to a computerized patient monitoring system. When the nurse noted that Young reacted to this comment with anxiety, she further attempted to reassure him by saying, "Don't worry, Mr. Young, nobody really believes those awful stories about computers they print in the newspapers."

# Humanities and Computers: A Personal View

ROBERT WACHAL

A reminder that a computer is not a man, even at the service of humanists. (An excerpt from the original article)

According to a story making the rounds, a young man at a professional meeting was describing in glowing terms a projected study of literary irony to be done with the aid of a computer. At the conclusion of his remarks, a good, gray scholar arose and said, "Young man, you and your machine may well commit more irony than you discover." Clearly, to many a humanist, the computer-using literary researcher is a poacher in the scholarly game preserve. The benevolent view is that his traps mangle what they hope to capture, or that they are set for deer, but only catch gnats. A more pessimistic view is that his traps have no springs in them.

Let's assume then that our would-be computer user from the humanities is relatively innocent about the computing enterprise. He has gone to one meeting of his professional society on the application of computers to problems in literary scholarship. He has heard that one can use the computer to produce concordances and bibliographies, that some people are even talking about using it to compare different editions of a work and produce a master text with variant readings. Others have tried to solve problems of disputed authorship, although this sounds a bit fishy to him. Even more suspicious to him are computational studies of literary style and theme. His conservative impulses suggest a concordance, something nice and solid that will lead to publication (and promotion).

Our humanist goes to his local computer center for assistance in getting started. Given the nature of his project, it is unlikely that he will be put in touch with the local expert in artificial intelligence, if indeed there is one. He will probably find himself talking to someone whose experience has been with fairly straightforward problems in science, engineering, or business. Just the sort of person he became an English professor in order to avoid. But never mind; surely anything as mundane as a concordance requires no creative thinking. Patient hacks have been producing them for years using three-by-five cards. Then he gets his first shock: he cannot simply hand over "The Complete Dramatic Works of . . ." and get it into the machine automatically. Optical scanners?

Well, yes, they are being used for some things, but not books . . . maybe in ten years. The talk then turns to keypunches. The scholar explains that he cannot even use an electric typewriter. No problem. The graduate school will pay for keypunching for faculty members. All the scholar has to do is to write out all twenty-five plays on ruled sheets, one letter per column. He is appalled until he remembers that he has an undergraduate assistant. He had forgotten about her because he could never think of enough things for her to do. Good stuff, this computer business; it creates employment.

Now then, says the computer man, let's plan the card layout; how many words can we get on a card? The scholar begins to fidget. What's the longest word in your text? The scholar doesn't know and the computer man begins to fidget. He mumbles something about people who haven't defined their problem. Then he gets an idea. Everyone knows what words are; they occur between spaces, a simple matter of programming. Well, says the scholar, arising from the edge of his chair, see you when I get my text into machine-readable form, proud of his developing control over the new lingo.

A year later, the scholar returns to the computer center, proud of the twenty boxes of punched IBM cards reposing in his office amid the empty pickle jars and unread term papers. He is very fortunate; the computer center has acquired a new programmer, who doesn't yet have enough to do. In the meantime, the scholar has discovered that keypunches have only capital letters. In a panic he remembers that his son's last computer report card consisted entirely of upper-case comments. He was assured that the computer center had purchased a printer with upper and lower case, and that all he need do was to prefix every capital letter in his text with some arbitrary symbol that would not otherwise occur, say an asterisk.

Now he sits down with his programmer to discuss how to instruct the computer to find the words on the cards. A naturally inquisitive man, he has been thinking about the word-definition problem. He realizes that words may be bound by punc-

"He's charged with expressing contempt for data-processing."
Drawing by Koren; © 1970
The New Yorker Magazine, Inc.

tuation marks as well as by spaces and that there are some ambiguous marks like the hyphen, which may or may not occur at word boundaries, 'co-worker' vs. 'Johnny-come-lately.' He has decided, he tells the programmer, not to treat hyphens as boundary markers. The programmer then asks what the longest compound in the plays is likely to be. He doesn't know and the programmer begins muttering under his breath. They hash out a number of similar problems (the text, for example, contains the phrase '2,000,000 B.C.') and go on to a discussion of the concording process.

Words are even more ambiguous than marks of punctuation, and the humanist now knows enough not to ask whether the computer can sort out multiple meanings of the same word. The programmer suggests that they produce a preliminary version of the concordance which can then be further sorted by hand to take care of this problem. The humanist begins muttering under his breath. Next he asks whether some words, such as 'the', 'am', and 'shall' can be omitted from the process. A simple matter, says the programmer, just supply me with a list. The humanist begins to wish that he knew something of that arcane and upstart science called 'linguistics', but decides that he, after all, knows as much about words as anyone, and that he can accomplish this simple but tedious task well enough.

Another year and three programmers later, the preliminary version is ready for final editing. The humanist begins to recognize that in using a computer there is a considerable gulf between working time saved and elapsed time saved. As he goes through the large pages of computer output in order to sort out multiple meanings, he wonders whether using the computer will have saved him any time at all. He also finds a number of things that leave him completely stunned. He discovers that blanks are not very reliable word delimiters. His text contains a lot of double names like 'Buenos Aires'; his concordance contains a listing for 'Buenos' and another for 'Aires' but none for 'Buenos Aires'. Even worse, a character in one of the plays being concorded utters the deathless line, "He took the Los Angeles-San Francisco flight"; the concordance lists "Los', 'Angeles-San', and 'Francisco'. Words like 'am', 'can', and 'will' were not concorded, but through an oversight words like 'can't' and 'cannot' were. Unfortunately, in the process of suppressing the auxiliary verbs, some other uses of these words were also lost, for example, 'can' in "I'll knock you on your can" and 'will' in "last will and testament"; the computer is no grammarian. Also on the suppression list were the names of characters used to introduce each speech. In consequence, if any of the same names were used within the speeches, they failed to get listed in the concordance. The computer cannot by itself distinguish between speaker and spoken-about. At this point, the humanist decides to publish the preliminary version of the concordance and hopes that the reviewers will be kind. He gives up any fleeting thoughts he might have had about doing a stylistic study of the plays via computer and concludes that perhaps his naive colleagues who view the computer as a Hun, a Vandal, or a Visigoth are right.

The sad tale that I have outlined is hypothetical. There is, however, a computer-produced concordance in print which contains all of the errors described above plus a good many more which I didn't mention to avoid straining the credulity of the reader. The two reviews I have seen of this work were not at all kind.

# Cybernetic Scheduler

EDD DOERR

All hell had broken loose. And quite literally too. Members of the Board of Governors of the university were demanding my head. Student rioting outside my windows, one of which had already been shattered, made it virtually impossible to hear the constant jangling of the telephone. The resignations of two full professors, five associate professors and a number of instructors lay in a pile on my desk. The Governor had just called to inform me that the General Assembly was going to demand an immediate investigation. The switchboard was jammed with long distance calls from irate parents and alumni. One mothers' group was organizing a motorcade from the state capitol for a protest demonstration. Reporters from Time, Newsweek and a score of newspapers were making an uproar in the outer office that rivaled that of the students outside. The state police had even been called in to maintain order.

I had just finished bolting down another aspirin and was wondering whether I would ever get out of the mess alive when the door to the outer office opened suddenly and I was confronted with the huge terrifying bulk of K. Jason Smathers, the barge baron who was the President of the Board of Governors. He stomped across the room, planted his huge hairy paws heavily on my desk and began to make ominous growling noises.

"O.K., Frank," he began jarringly, "you're the president of this university, or what's left of it. At the moment anyway. So you'd better start explaining, and it'd better be good. The state hasn't been in such a turmoil since Morgan's Raiders and something's got to be done about it. Now what the hell happened?"

He remained hovering over my desk, like a gargoyle on a Gothic cathedral, his huge glowing cigar heightening my awareness of the fire into which I had jumped from the relative comfort of the frying pan.

"Well, Jason," I began, trying to assume an air of confidence but not quite succeeding, "it's not much more than a big misunderstanding."

"Misunderstanding, hell!" barked K. Jason Smathers. "You've just set higher education in this state back fifty years. Heads are going to roll, and yours is going to be one of them. Now get on with it."

I swallowed another aspirin and gripped the arms of my chair tightly to stop the trembling of my hands.

"I suppose it all began with a chance remark I made at a faculty tea nearly a year ago. It was shortly after registration and I had not yet fully recovered from the ordeal. I just happened to remark to Cseszko of the Cybernetics Department that it would be nice if the whole business could be handled by machines, that it would save wear and tear on everyone and substantially reduce the number of mistakes. I don't recall what he said at the time, but a few weeks later he came to me with an idea which made me feel fully ten years younger.

"I guess that Jan Cseszko's about the best cybernetics man in the country, so I never questioned his ability to build a computer which would automatically handle the entire registration and class scheduling process. It was a magnificent idea, and still is, although perhaps it represents an advance which we are presently incapable of accepting."

"But damn it," Smathers interrupted sonorously, "why didn't you get the Board's approval before going ahead? This might never have happened."

"That's a moot point," I retorted. "In all likelihood they would have approved of the computer without hesitation. After all, the idea *is* the most important single idea in university administration that I can think of. No one would have predicted trouble."

"Well, would you mind explaining just how the damned thing misfired?"

"All right, Jason. But would you mind sitting down?

"Cseszko reported before last Christmas that the computer would be operational in time for registration and scheduling this year. The plan seemed to be foolproof. Into the computer we would feed data as to the desired and possible schedules of instructors, from the freshman level up to and including the Graduate School. The machine would also have complete data on degree requirements and license requirements for teachers, physicians, dentists, engineers, nurses, med techs, etc., and would automatically give preference in scheduling to graduate students over undergraduates, seniors over juniors, juniors over sophomores, etc. Then each student would submit a requested schedule, together with alternate choices in the event that classes were closed or there were insoluble conflicts. Each registration request would be accompanied by various data concerning the student, so that schedules would be made consistent with degree and other requirements. Classes would also be formed in such a way as to group students by ability levels, so far as possible.

"So that's the system we used for registration this year."

"Yeah," the big man roared as he jarred my desk with his big meaty fist, "but the cockeyed gadget must have cracked up. How the hell else can you explain what happened?"

"Well, actually," I explained, "the fault does not lie with the computer. If anything, the computer is too good, too intelligent. You see, the computer did a lot more than just arrange schedules on the basis of available choices. In order to improve upon the usual pre-registration counseling procedure, we fed the computer complete data on the results of intelligence, personality, aptitude, attitude and interest tests for each student, plus data on each student's academic history. In this way we hoped to route students into programs best suited to their own aptitudes and personalities, a job which counselors can do only imperfectly. Of course, changes in students' schedules were optional, although we felt that they would be very largely accepted once the procedures were explained.

"Naturally, however, we did not expect such repercussions."

"Obviously not," the man behind the cigar bellowed. "But go on. This is getting interesting."

"Well, the results of the computations, together with a brochure explaining the whole business, were printed and sent out. The instructors and students had their schedules at the same time that the Registrar's office did. We didn't examine the schedules before distribution because we had complete confidence in the new system.

"That, it seems, was our mistake. But even then, we could hardly have been able to predict all the results. At any rate, this is what happened.

"Nearly three thousand students were given schedules which completely changed their major subjects. Although their personality, intelligence and other tests indicate that these changes are advisable, very few of the students are inclined to accept them. Nor, for that matter, are a large number of parents. Nearly two thousand students were advised by the computer that they were wasting time and money by attending college as they were totally unfit for higher academic work. I'm sure that you can readily imagine the reaction to that.

"To complicate the picture, the computer advised that certain students, who happen to be members of our athletic teams, were unfit for academic work and would not be wise to hope to graduate from college. Naturally, this infuriated the coaching staff and brought down on our heads the wrath of a group of powerful and important alumni.

"There was even more trouble when the computer advised that the sons and daughters of several politicians, lawyers and industrialists were likewise better off elsewhere than on the campus.

"And beyond that, as we wished to avoid student-faculty conflict, unconscious or otherwise, we gave the computer data on the personalities of faculty members, though this data was and is confidential. As a result, the computer suggested that several faculty members, from full professors down to mere instructors, were not suited to teaching, and even recommended that several of them enroll for certain courses themselves.

"And since you're here, you're thoroughly familiar with the results of all this. Once the thing got started, it was too late to stop it."

"I'll say it's too late."

"Of course," I resumed, "if the Board, the Governor, the Alumni Association and the Faculty Council will back us up, we can still go ahead with the plan. There will be certain dislocations which cannot be avoided, but on the whole, I think that everything can eventually be straightened out. And in the future our system will probably be regarded as one of the most important developments in American higher education. It will take a while for the idea to become accepted, but I have no doubts as to its ultimate value and importance."

"Well, maybe you can sell some other state on the idea. But this one's had enough. You can't just maneuver people like that, even if it's for their own good. At any rate, I think that your resignation and Cseszko's had better be on my desk before this time tomorrow. It will be for the good of the university."

"I'm sorry that it has to be this way, but there is no alternative."

He rose, pumped my hand perfunctorily and bounded out.

I slumped down in my chair. A beautiful career shot to hell, I thought, just by trying to do one's best. Cseszko could always go to MIT or IBM or somewhere. But what would I do?

Well, maybe I can get a job in one of those jerkwater colleges that no one has ever heard of.

I buzzed for Miss Simmons, who came in looking much the worse for wear after her encounter with that flock of reporters.

"Take a letter," I began slowly, "to the Board of Governors."

## ME

*I think that I shall never see
A calculator made like me.
A me that likes martinis dry
And on the rocks, a little rye.
A me that looks at girls and such,
But mostly girls, and very much.
A me that wears an overcoat
And likes a risky anecdote.
A me that taps a foot and grins
Whenever Dixieland begins.
They make computers for a fee,
But only moms can make a me.*

HILBERT SCHENCK, JR.

---

## COMPUTERS AND THEIR PRIESTS
ROBERT TOWNSEND

First get it through your head that computers are big, expensive, fast, dumb adding-machine—typewriters. Then realize that most of the computer technicians that you're likely to meet or hire are complicators, not simplifiers. They're trying to make it look tough. Not easy. They're building a mystique, a priesthood, their own mumbo-jumbo ritual to keep you from knowing what they—and you—are doing.

Here are some rules of thumb:

1. At this state of the art, keep decisions on computers at the highest level. Make sure the climate is ruthlessly hard-nosed about the practicality of every system, every program, and every report. "*What are you going to do with that report?*" "*What would you do if you didn't have it?*" Otherwise your programmers will be writing their doctoral papers on your machines, and your managers will be drowning in ho-hum reports they've been conned into asking for and are ashamed to admit are of no value.
2. Make sure your present system is reasonably clean and effective before you automate. Otherwise your new computer will just speed up the mess.
3. Before you hire a computer specialist, make it a condition that he spend some time in the factory and then sell your shoes to the customers.

# Guerrilla War Against Computers
*Time* Magazine

A middle-aged, overweight free-lance journalist who plays the jew's-harp is hardly the prototype of a revolutionary. But Harvey Matusow, 46, has full credentials for conspiracy. An American Communist in the 1940s who turned FBI informer and spent five years in prison for perjury (after admitting that he had testified falsely against some 250 supposed Reds), Matusow now lives and plots in London. He is the self-appointed president of the International Society for the Abolition of Data Processing Machines, which claims 1,500 members. Like Matusow, they look on the computer as an exploitative monster that has turned on its creator.

Members receive, free of charge, an I.S.A.D.P.M. identification card decorated with a red slingshot, symbolic of David's battle with Goliath. They also get a year's subscription to Matusow's anti-computer newsletter, which he plans to start publishing soon. For 6s., they can get a copy of his 125-page *The Beast of Business,* a handbook of guerrilla tactics for computer haters that might have been conceived by Che Guevara.

"The computer has a healthy and conservative function in mathematics and other sciences," Matusow allows, but "when the uses involve business or government, and the individual is tyrannized, then we make our stand." The methods he proposes for dealing with the Enemy are fiendishly sophisticated. No simple stapling, folding or mutilation of a computer card for him. "That will nullify the effect of the card," he says. "But it will make it easy to spot and will not have much effect on disrupting the system."

Instead, he suggests playing "computer-card roulette"—placing the card on a drawing board, carefully cutting out three or four extra rectangular holes with a razor blade, and returning the card to sender. Matusow claims to have altered a magazine subscription card in that manner. As a result, he received 23 copies of the magazine each week and a note thanking him for using the publication in his current-events class.

Subtler souls might prefer other Matusow tactics—like erasing the magnetic coding on their personal checks by running the code numbers under an electromagnet. "The effect," he says, "is that your checks will not be processed by the automatic sorting device. Someone at the bank will have to handle them personally. But after all, it's your money, and it should get the loving care it deserves."

A prime rule in Matusow's anti-computer campaign is to "always let the enemies know that you are at war with them." He suggests that recipients of a computerized bill destroy the returnable portion, then mail back a check together with a note explaining what they have done and why. When paying utility bills, Matusow advises doing it promptly—but overpaying or underpaying by a penny or two. The effect, he says, is to send an unsophisticated computer into a state of hysteria.

Other promising targets for attack include post offices that use computerized mail sorters and telephone operators who insist that customers place their own long-distance calls with a computerized dialing code. Matusow advises pasting stamps on sideways so that the scanner cannot read the magnetized strips that differentiate between values of stamps. In persuading telephone operators to handle calls personally, he suggests saying: "I'm sorry, operator, but I'm blind and do need your assistance." That ploy "is bound to make her feel extremely guilty, and will make it easier for the next caller who wants her to make the connection."

Finally, for those whose frustrations cannot be expunged by small, subtle victories, Matusow proposes direct confrontation—attacking the inhuman enemy with the most human of weapons: "Women going into a room with a bank of computers are advised to wear a lot of the cheapest perfume they can find." Computers operate effectively only in "clean" air, Matusow explains, and are highly sensitive to environmental changes. Heavy dollops of perfume could paralyze a computer as effectively as they do those of a weak-kneed human office worker.

## ◇ BRANCH POINTS

Bowles, Edmund A. *Computers in Humanistic Research.* Englewood Cliffs, N.J.: Prentice-Hall, Inc., 1967.

*Computers in Oceanography.* Maynard, Mass.: Digital Equipment Corp.

"Computers in Sports". *AFIPS Conference Proceedings.* 1971 Fall Joint Computer Conference. Montvale, N.J.: AFIPS Press, 1971. 397–400.

*Computers in the Life Sciences.* Maynard, Mass.: Digital Equipment Corp.

Franke, H. W. "Computer Graphics." *Graphics,* No. 161, 1972–73.

Franke, H. W. *Computer Graphics, Computer Art.* London: Phaidon Press, 1971.

Guetzkow, Harold. *Simulation in Social Sciences.* Englewood Cliffs, N.J.: Prentice-Hall, Inc., 1962.

Kranz, Stewart. *Science and Technology in the Arts.* New York: Van Nostrand Reinhold Co., 1974.

Lickleder, J. C. R. *Libraries of the Future.* Cambridge, Mass.: The M.I.T. Press, 1965.

Mueller, Robert. "Idols of Computer Art." *Art in America,* May 1972.

*Proceedings of a Conference on Computers in the Undergraduate Curricula.* Annual proceedings. Published by the individual college hosting the conference.

Reichardt, Jasia. *The Computer in Art.* New York: Van Nostrand Reinhold Co., 1971.

Reichardt, Jasia. *Cybernetics, Art, and Ideas.* Greenwich, Conn.: New York Graphics Society Ltd., 1971.

Reichardt, Jasia. *Cybernetic Serendipity.* New York: Frederick A. Praeger, 1969.

Sanders, Donald H. *Computers and Management.* New York: McGraw-Hill Book Company, 1974.

Sedelow, S. "The Computer in Humanities and Fine Arts." *Computing Surveys,* June 1970.

Shorter, Edward. *The Historian and the Computer.* Englewood Cliffs, N.J.: Prentice-Hall, Inc., 1971.

Wisbey, R. A. *The Computer in Literary and Linguistic Research.* Great Britain: Cambridge University Press, 1971.

## ◯ INTERRUPTS

1. Suppose you have been incorrectly billed for $6.00 from the XYZ Company for the last four months and they are now threatening to ruin your credit rating. You have written the company several times and received no reply. What would you do next? Would you do anything different if the bill was $300.00?

2. Check out the subject of computer simulation. Find some examples. Can you find any examples that were later proved badly incorrect? What went wrong? (Hint: Find some reviews on the book *The Limits to Growth.*)

3. Develop a list of foreseeable developments of computer uses and their potential consequences in a particular field.

4. Write a paper on the use of computers in one of the following fields:
   a) law
   b) medicine
   c) library science
   d) agriculture
   e) mining
   f) fisheries
   g) forest products
   h) your field

5. Consult some of the following sources (or others) and locate some computer applications that interest you.
   Computers and People    Computer World
   Datamation    Data Processing Magazine
   Either write a report or give a report to the class on each application. Develop a file of interesting applications.

6. Investigate a computer-dating bureau. Find out how the matching of pairs is done. Is a computer used? How valid do you think the whole process is? What about the privacy of the information you divulge?

7. On most department or credit card bills you are charged a percentage (such as $1\frac{1}{2}$%) on any unpaid balance. Determine exactly how the interest charges are calculated. Are fractions of a cent rounded or truncated? What happens when you pay only part of the bill—are charges calculated on the balance before or after your payment is credited? Then, considering that it costs you something for the check and the stamp when paying the bill, figure out what the amount should be before it is financially better *not* to pay the bill.

8. Some companies have been charged with mailing postdated bills, that is, bills that are mailed so it is difficult to pay them before being liable for finance charges. Monitor some charge bills to see if this is true of any of your bills. Look at the following dates:
   a) date of bill
   b) postmark of letter, which indicates mailing date
   c) date bill received
   Next, how many days do you have before the bill is due? Are all dates reasonable? Between the date of the bill and the postmark there should be not more than four or five days, since most bills are processed by computers. Did you find any companies that seem to be purposely sending out bills late? What do you think should be the minimum number of days you should have to pay your bill in order to avoid finance charges?

Some types of bills do not usually add finance charges (i.e., utility bills). Do utility companies or other companies that do not charge finance charges send you their bills faster?

9. Go down to a local credit bureau and find out as much as possible about your own credit rating. Next, find out as much as possible about how credit bureaus work.

10. Examine your utility bills. Find out what the printed symbols stand for and calculate the bill by hand to check it. Are fractions of cents rounded or truncated? Which would be best for you?

11. Examine a computerized payroll check. Find out how all deductions are calculated. Calculate it by hand. Are fractions of a cent truncated or rounded? Which would be best for you on each deduction?

12. Find someone who has been a victim of a computerized error. How difficult was it to get the error corrected?

13. Computers are used in sports. For example, computers can be used to examine previous games of opposing teams to determine what type of action individual players and teams probably will take in certain situations. Do research to find out what is being done presently in the sports world with computers. Predict what uses computers will soon be used for there. What influence will this have on sports? What could your favorite team do to nullify computer analysis by an opposing team?

14. Automation has often been an issue in strikes. Find some reports on strikes in which automation was an issue. What are the goals of labor and management in regard to automation? What trends in regard to automation can you find by examining recent strike settlements?

15. Can you think of some computer applications that should not be attempted because of moral or social issues? Defend your choices.

16. Find out the status of your private medical records. Who can see them or get copies of them—for example, other doctors, insurance investigators, governmental agents, or welfare officials? Are you notified when others request your records?

17. Apply for credit. Try to find out *exactly* how it is determined if you will get credit. Obtain a copy of all the information they use to make the decision. Where is a computer involved?

18. Most mass advertising is done by computers. Find some firm that does mass mailings. How much does it charge for addresses? Can it provide addresses by category: by economic status, by profession, and so forth, and at what price?

19. Joan Smith, a part-time employee, has received a paycheck in which the computer inadvertently printed her net pay as $245.80 instead of $45.80. Joan cashed the check. Does she owe the school money? If not, who does? The computer? The operator? The input/output clerk? The programmer?

    What about a situation in which a person receives a small amount extra and could not be reasonably expected to know it was incorrect?

20. Study the impact of computers on some artistic field, such as sculpture, painting, music, or fiction. Find examples of the computer as a subject of the art/or a tool for producing the art.

# 6
## GOVERNMENTAL USES

# Justice, the Constitution, and Privacy

SAM ERVIN, JR.
United States Senator from North Carolina

Delivered in a series of discussions on "Computers and Privacy" at Miami University, Hamilton, Ohio, June 28, 1973.

I am very pleased to be here to talk with you about Justice, the Constitution and Privacy as part of Miami University's series of discussions on the subject of Computers and Privacy.

A while back I decided that I had read a lot about privacy, but I didn't really know much about computers. So I took some time off from my duties at the Senate and spent a whole day watching computers in operation and learning how these machines work. I was impressed by the multitude of tedious and difficult tasks that computers could perform in a fraction of the time it would take a person—and with no mistakes either.

In fact, I was so impressed by those computers—how meticulously and logically they could interrelate bits of information—that I thought about writing a Constitutional Amendment to allow a computer to become President. With its absolutely accurate and almost limitless memory, its infallible logic in relating one bit of information to another, and its superhuman speed, a computer, it seemed, could make a perfect President

But then I thought again. Certainly the computer would always come to perfectly logical conclusions. But what about conclusions affected by inspiration, by compassion, by humanity? And what about seemingly irrational decisions based on love of justice, or hatred of tyranny? A computer just cannot draw illogical conclusions from logical facts. I thought better of my Constitutional Amendment to make a computer President. There is something about human decision-makers for all of their mistakes and irrationality, which a computer simply cannot replace.

It seems to me that our system of democratic government depends at least in part on the uniquely human capacity of those who govern to come on occasion to what appear to be irrational conclusions. The ability to abandon logic for the sake of humanity and to insist that human existence cannot be reduced to even the most sophisticated of mathematical formulas is as much a part of our system as the Constitution itself.

This is not to say that computers are not extremely useful tools. They are. It is merely to point out that there are some tasks for which computers are simply not suited.

When we talk about the role which computers can and ought to play in governmental decision making, and the potential dangers computers pose to privacy, it seems to me that we are primarily concerned about the impact computerized information systems can have on individuals. We are concerned that the logical, categorizing processes of the computer will in some way run roughshod over our fundamental belief in the uniqueness and dignity of individual human personality.

It is, after all, the faith of the founders of this nation in the individual as a free and self-determining being that led them to set up our democratic form of government. Because of their faith in the individual, the framers of our Constitution took great pains to set up a system of limited government so as to maximize the protection of individuals from governmental interference. In order to guard against certain specific abuses of governmental power which would endanger individual freedom, the Founding Fathers added the first two amendments to the Constitution, which we have come to treasure as the Bill of Rights.

The First Amendment was designed to protect the sanctity of the individual's private thoughts and beliefs. It protects the rights to speak and remain silent, to receive and impart information and ideas, and to associate in private and in public with others of like mind. After all, it is only by protecting this inner privacy that freedom of speech, religion, assembly and many other individual liberties can be protected.

The Third Amendment's prohibition of quartering soldiers in private homes protects the privacy of the individual's living space. This aspect of privacy is also protected by the Fourth Amendment's guarantee of "the right of the people to be secure in their persons, houses, papers, and effects, against unreasonable searches and seizures." In addition to the privacy of the individual's home and personal effects, the privacy of his person (or bodily integrity) and even his private telephone conversations are protected by the Fourth Amend-

ment from unwarranted governmental intrusion.

The Fifth Amendment guarantees that an individual accused of a crime shall not be forced to divulge private information which might incriminate him. This privilege against self incrimination focuses directly on the sanctity of the individual human personality and the right of each individual to keep private information which might place his life and freedom in jeopardy.

The Fifth Amendment also guarantees that no person shall be "deprived of life, liberty, or property without the due process of law." This right to due process protects individual privacy by preventing unwarranted governmental interference with the individual's person, personality and property.

The Ninth Amendment's reservation that "the enumeration in the Constitution, of certain rights, shall not be construed to deny or disparage others retained by the People" clearly shows that the Founding Fathers contemplated that certain basic individual rights not specifically mentioned in the constitution—such as privacy—should nevertheless be safe from governmental interference.

Just recently in Roe v. Wade the Supreme Court has located the right of privacy in the Fourteenth Amendment's guarantee that no state shall "deprive any person of life, liberty, or property without due process of law." Rights to give and receive information, to family life and child-rearing according to one's conscience, to marriage, to procreation, to contraception, and to abortion are all aspects of individual privacy which the courts have similarly held to be constitutionally protected.

To my mind privacy means more than merely restricting governmental interference in these specific areas. Someone has suggested that privacy is a catchword for the control the individual exercises over information about himself. And yet because such a definition focuses on the information rather than the individual, it seems to look in the wrong direction. Control over information is important to our right of privacy only when that information is related to us as individuals. In the end, privacy depends upon society's recognition and protection of the importance and uniqueness of each individual.

As chairman of the Senate Subcommittee on Constitutional Rights, I have over the years received many complaints about governmental invasions of individual privacy. In some cases, the government has intruded into the personal lives, homes and physical integrity of individual citizens in order to collect private information about them. In other cases, the government has used, or misused, such private information, and has disseminated it without the knowledge or consent of the individual citizen involved.

A while back it occurred to me that we did not even know how many data banks containing information about individuals the federal government has. So I wrote to fifty federal agencies and asked them just

---

**I thought about writing a Constitutional Amendment to allow a computer to become President.**

---

how many such databanks they have, what kind of information these databanks contain and who gets to see it and under what circumstances. Most of the responses are in a report that will be published later this year by the Senate Subcommittee on Constitutional Rights. So far we have received information on more than 750 databanks with varying contents, operational guidelines and the like.

The response we received earlier this month from the Office of Emergency Preparedness describes what must be the ultimate in governmental databanks. One of the databanks maintained by the Office of Emergency Preparedness contains records on some 5,000 individuals. But the Office of Emergency Preparedness does not know its contents and has no access to the information it contains. They just maintain it. Short of emergency circumstances the Office of Emergency Preparedness will never have access to this databank which is "utilized and kept current on a regular basis by authorized specialists in the Personnel Operations element of the White House staff. No other agencies or individuals have access to these files." So here we have a federal agency maintaining a databank to which it has no access and the contents of which even the agency does not know. I have written to the White House to see if they can give us some clue as to what information is contained in these files and who has access to it.

Collection of information in governmental databanks is accomplished in a variety of ways. Some of it is obtained directly from the individuals involved. The Decennial Census is an

JUSTICE, THE CONSTITUTION, AND PRIVACY  127

example of this sort of data collection. Article II of the Constitution provides for an "Enumeration" every ten years so that Representatives can be apportioned among the states according to population. To make that head-count compulsory is perfectly alright. But nowhere does the Constitution countenance compelling citizens to respond on pain of criminal penalties to such personal questions as:

> Do you have a flush toilet?
> Have you been married more than once?
> Did your first marriage end because of death of wife or husband?
> What is your rent?
> What is your monthly electric bill?
> Did you work at any time last week?
> Do you have a dishwasher? Built-in or portable?
> How did you get to work last week?
> (Driver, private auto; passenger, private auto; subway, bus; taxi; walked only; other means)
> How many bedrooms to you have?
> Do you have a health condition or disability which limits the amount of work you can do at a job? How long have you had this disability?

To my mind, the use of the Federal criminal laws to force people to divulge such personal information, which bears no relation to any legitimate governmental purpose, is unconscionable.

Even worse, because of its lack of candor, is the Census Bureau's practice of sending out questionnaires on behalf of other government agencies. Theoretically, response to such questionnaires is wholly voluntary. But the Census Bureau's cover letters do not say that response is voluntary. Take, for example, a questionnaire the Census Bureau sent out at the behest of the Department of Health, Education and Welfare to retired persons. The questionnaire inquired into such private matters as:

> How often do you call your parents?
> What do you spend on presents for grandchildren?
> How many newspapers and magazines do you buy a month?
> Do you wear artificial dentures?
> About how often do you go to a barber shop or beauty salon?
> Taking things all together, would you say you're very happy, pretty happy, or not too happy these days?

Although response to this questionnaire was voluntary, many, if not most, of the retired folks who received the official Census Bureau packet feared that they would be penalized if they did not answer.

I have in the past introduced legislation to control the worst of these privacy-invading questions. But unfortunately, bitter opposition on

"Well, you demanded your constitutional right of being confronted by your accuser, didn't you?"

# Computer Leads Watergate Committee to Its Witnesses
TRUDY RUBIN

A key "member" of the Senate Watergate committee's investigative team is a computer that can spew out the most minute details of any witness on a moment's notice.

This and other details of the committee's investigative techniques were described by the Watergate Committee's chief counsel, Sam Dash, at a seminar of the Association of Trial Lawyers of America here this past weekend.

Mr. Dash told his rapt audience that the Library of Congress computer services, being used for the first time by a Senate investigating committee, digest transcripts of public and executive committee sessions, voluminous news clippings, all of the diaries received from witnesses, and all other information received from the committee, and then print specific or general background on any witness instantly.

### SECURITY DESCRIBED
Mr. Dash described to the *Christian Science Monitor* the tight security that surrounds the committee's computer. All data is stored on special tapes, which are kept under lock by the committee.

Mr. Dash is given daily printouts of general background on every witness including interrelationships with other witnesses. "We can check in a minute of whether Witness A was in a city at the same time as B and C, which takes days otherwise."

But sensitive material can only be printed out after "I sign a special authorization," he says.

The computer also was used to check discrepancies in a witness's testimony in seconds while the witness was still on the stand, an impossibility if the staff had had to check back through mountains of files.

### "PLODDING, HARD WORK"
The techniques used to develop startling new evidence, such as the secret bugging system in the White House, involved "plodding, hard work of investigators," Mr. Dash explained. For every potential witness, a "satellite chart" was plotted, including secretaries, staff assistants, business associates and others. Often these charts included 75 to 100 names, all of whom were interviewed.

Alexander P. Butterfield, who installed the White House bugs, was found through the satellite chart of former top presidential assistant H. R. Haldeman.

the part of the Administration, as well as state and local governments and private agencies which use Census information, has so far blocked passage of such controls. It is unfortunate, but true, that bureaucrats who collect information can always think up reasons for wanting to collect more and more of it. Those of us who are concerned about individual privacy face an endless battle in constantly pointing out that just because government agencies want information about individuals should not be sufficient reason for forcing people to provide it or face criminal penalties. That is why I am in favor of putting the shoe on the other foot—forcing data collectors, such as the Census Bureau, to justify each bit of information they want to collect about us and honestly disclosing to each citizen that participation in many of these surveys is wholly voluntary.

One of the most disturbing aspects of governmental data collection is the use of surreptitious surveillance and intelligence operations to collect information on innocent citizens whose political views and activities are contrary to those of the Administration. Recent events have dramatized the disturbing prospect that such

> **It is unfortunate, but true, that bureaucrats who collect information can always think up reasons for wanting to collect more and more of it.**

covert data collection may be even more widespread than we had feared.

Governmental surveillance can take many forms. Just recently, I learned that in cities from San Francisco, California to Mt. Vernon, New York, high-powered cameras have been set up to keep track of individuals and their activities. These cameras are so sensitive they can read an automobile license plate five blocks away. They can focus on an individual as he talks with friends and associates and can follow him as he walks down the street. They can peek through the windows of the homes of innocent Americans and record what is going on inside. It seems to me that this is the very sort of secret prying into the private lives and activities of individuals which bodes much evil for our democracy. These cameras represent the tools of tyranny and totalitarianism which seek total control over the lives of individuals. They are, in my opinion, utterly inappropriate in a society which values the privacy and civil liberties of the individual.

I used to think that there could be nothing worse than this kind of invasion of individual privacy. But recently there has come to my attention instance after instance of the government's systematic invasion of the privacy of citizens who have done no wrong, but who disagree with the government's policies. Surveillance has become a kind of punishment for the exercise of constitutionally protected First Amendment freedoms of speech, association and press.

For example, in its continuing battle with the press, the Administration has resorted to this sort of systematic invasion of privacy in order to punish those members of the press who insist on criticizing Administration policies. Some of you may have heard about what happened to CBS newsman, Daniel Schorr. After a series of articles critical of the Administration, Mr. Schorr woke up one morning to find himself the object of a full-scale FBI investigation. On the specious grounds

## Computer Helps Predict Supreme Court Actions

EAST LANSING, MICH.—A Michigan State University professor who predicts Supreme Court decisions by computer rejects the idea that the third branch of government could be replaced by a judicial automation. The court is a human institution, he insists, and success in forecasting its actions is rooted in psychology.

The political science professor has correctly predicted the court's ruling in 88 percent of the cases in the past four years which he has studied (69 out of 78 predictions). He's also foretold the votes of the individual justices accurately 86 percent of the time.

Dr. Spaeth's "crystal ball" is MSU's giant CDC 6500 computer.

Into the computer he feeds data on each case under consideration and the men who will decide it. He winds up with an indication of how each justice will vote.

Dr. Spaeth works under the assumptions that judicial behavior is no different from other types of human behavior, except for the limitations imposed by the rules of the court.

Borrowing from Dr. Milton Rokeach, a prominent MSU psychologist, he identifies three principles that tell him how a jury is likely to act when confronted with a specific issue:

- An individual's attitudes are established and endure from the time he assumes a place in adult society.
- Human behavior is goal-oriented, and a person will make decisions according to his personal policy preferences unless prevented from doing so by a rule of the institution in which he is operating.
- To accurately predict a person's behavior it is not enough to identify his policy preferences, but the character of those preferences must also be understood.

Biographical data, voting records and written opinions of the justices give Dr. Spaeth part of his input. The rest comes from careful analysis of the case in question.

Each case is classified according to one or more of 73 different categories and coded for the computer.

Despite its predictability, Dr. Spaeth is convinced that the court decides each case according to the circumstances peculiar to it, and does, by and large, dispense blind justice.

> **One of the major drawbacks to the collection of information is the human temptation to use it, and in some instances, to misuse it.**

that Mr. Schorr was being considered for "possible federal employment," the White House had ordered a thorough investigation of Daniel Schorr, his past and present associations, activities, employment and the like. Friends, acquaintances, colleagues, employers and former employers were telephoned and interviewed by FBI agents who asked about Mr. Schorr's character and patriotism, as well as his fitness for a position in the Executive Branch.

When I heard about what had happened to Mr. Schorr, I sought to find out from the White House just what high-level executive position purported to justify this apparently punitive surveillance of a newsman known to be critical of Administration policies and programs. First the White House announced that Daniel was "being considered for a job that is presently filled." A few days later the White House reported that Daniel Schorr was being considered for a new position which "has not been filled." In the end he was never offered any job by the Administration. The White House finally lamely announced that Daniel Schorr's name had been "dropped from consideration" and that the FBI investigation had been "terminated in the very early stages." According to the White House, the preliminary surveillance report, which was "entirely favorable", had been "subsequently destroyed." But the damage had already been done.

Daniel Schorr described the damaging effects of such surveillance on a news reporter in this way:

"Even if the investigation had been set off by a tentative job offer, the effect, under the circumstances, had to be chilling to my work as a reporter. An FBI investigation is not a 'routine formality.' It has an impact on ones' life, on relations with employers, neighbors, and friends. To this day, I must manage a strained smile when asked on social occasions whether my 'FBI shadow' is with me. It has become standard humor to inquire whether I am still 'in trouble with the FBI,' whether it is safe to talk to me on the telephone.

"I am left now to ponder, when a producer rejects a controversial story I have offered, whether it is because of the normal winnowing process or because of my trouble-making potential. Even more am I left to wonder when I myself discard a line of investigation whether I am subconsciously affected by a reluctance to embroil my superiors in new troubles with the Nixon Administration. I should like to think that the government cannot directly intimidate me. But my employer, with millions at stake in an industry subject to regulations and pressure, is sensitive to the government, and I am sensitive to my employers' problems."

And Daniel Schorr's case is not unique. We have had reports of extensive surveillance, wire-tapping, and even burglaries perpetrated on other reporters.

When this sort of governmental prying into the private lives of individuals is used as a deterrent to the exercise of such constitutionally-protected freedoms, as freedom of the press, it involves a double evil: Not only is individual privacy invaded; that very invasion of privacy is used to punish or prevent the exercise of other rights.

> **Surveillance has become a kind of punishment for the exercise of constitutionally protected First Amendment freedoms of speech, association and press.**

I have just been talking about some examples of improper and reprehensible invasions of individual privacy in the collection of information, and the Executive Branch's use of such privacy-invading information collection to deter the exercise of other constitutional rights. But the difficulties with such data collection are not the only problems inherent in governmental data systems. It seems to me that one of the major drawbacks to the collection of information is the human temptation to use it, and in some instances, to misuse it, by giving it out to those who have no right or reason to have it.

On the most general level it seems to me just plain unhealthy for some master computer to keep track of every detail of our lives—our words and deeds, our mistakes and failures, our weaknesses and our strengths. Some experts in the field of information systems have suggested that massive data collection on every detail of each individual's life poses the danger of creating an "information prison" in which the individual is forever constrained by his past words and actions. What is lost in the process is the individual's capacity to grow and change, to define and redefine himself and to redeem past errors. There is something to be said for forgiving and forgetting, and for the opportunity to start anew. That chance for a new start is, after all, the reason why many of our ancestors came to this country—to leave past lives and past mistakes behind, and to begin building a new life all over again. It was that same sense of being able to leave the past behind and begin again that led to the development of the West—settlers moving away from old lives and starting again in the frontier where the past could not catch up with them.

That time is gone forever now. But it seems to me that this spirit of the frontier—that there will always be somewhere a man can go and start all over again, where he can redeem his past mistakes by hard work and good deeds—ought not to be gone forever. That is why I am opposed to the collection of any more information about individuals than is absolutely necessary. That is also why I am skeptical about the use of the Social Security Number, or any other universal identifier, to tag each of us for life with all sorts of data about what we have said and done in the past. It seems to me that there is much to be lost by locking individuals into their pasts or, to put it another way, by straight-jacketing individuals in the dossiers of their past words and deeds.

We would do well to heed the warning of John Stuart Mill over a century ago that—

"A State which dwarfs its men, in order that they may be more docile instruments in its hands even for beneficial purposes—will find that with small men no great thing can really be accomplished. . . ."

If we do not heed this warning, there will come a time when records will become more important than the individual, when the uniqueness of each human being will be sacrificed to the false gods of convenience and efficiency, when the opportunity for individuals to grow and change will have been eliminated. We have not reached that point yet, but vigilance seems in order lest it come upon us unaware.

It is in this area of information storage and dissemination that the impact of computerization is perhaps most significant. It is therefore not surprising that the computers, rather than their operators, have often been blamed for many of the serious problems involved in the dissemination of information about individuals. The capacity of computers to find and print out great masses of information at fantastic speed has magnified the adverse, as well as the beneficial effects of ready access to this information.

To begin with, in those cases where the information is inaccurate, a computerized system makes that inaccurate information more easily available to more people in less time than was ever dreamed possible in the pre-computer days. When I think of computers grinding away, and spewing forth more and more information about American citizens at ever faster rates, I am often reminded of a surprising communication I received from the Social Security Administration several years ago. It was a notification to my beneficiaries that they were eligible for death benefits on account of my demise. It made me think of Mark Twain's remark that the "reports of my death are greatly exaggerated." I was rather amused at the time; but I later paused to think of all the other erroneous information government computers send out routinely every day—sometimes with rather serious consequences.

Some information can be very damaging to individuals whether it is accurate or not. Take for example arrest records or the narcotics users registries maintained by a number of federal agencies. The mere fact that an individual's name is recorded as a narcotics user or as having been arrested is often sufficient to deprive that individual of job opportunities, insurance, credit and many other important rights and benefits. Even worse, those individuals who have been branded as narcotics users or as having been arrested suffer this deprivation of rights and opportunities without a trial, without witnesses, without a chance to defend themselves—in short, without due process of law.

Much recent controversy has focused on what can and ought to be done to control the indiscriminate dissemination of arrest records. The federal government collects and computerizes such information in the National Crime Information Center run by the Federal Bureau of Investigation which in turn disseminates such information to all sorts of

---

**THE UNKNOWN CITIZEN**
(To JS/07/M/378)
*This Marble Monument is Erected by the State*

He was found by the Bureau of Statistics to be
One against whom there was no official complaint,
And all the reports on his conduct agree
That, in the modern sense of an old-fashioned word, he was a saint,
For in everything he did he served the Greater Community.
Except for the War till the day he retired
He worked in a factory and never got fired,
But satisfied his employers, Fudge Motors Inc.
Yet he wasn't scab or odd in his views,
For his Union reports that he paid his dues,
(Our report on his Union shows it was sound)
And our Social Psychology workers found
That he was popular with his mates and liked a drink.
The Press are convinced that he bought a paper every day
And that his reactions to advertisements were normal in every way.
Policies taken out in his name prove that he was fully insured,
And his Health-card shows he was once in hospital but left it cured.
Both Producers Research and High-Grade Living declare
He was fully sensible to the advantages of the Instalment Plan
And had everything necessary to the Modern Man,
A phonograph, a radio, a car and a frigidaire.
Our researchers into Public Opinion are content
That he held the proper opinions for the time of year;
When there was peace, he was for peace; when there was war, he went.
He was married and added five children to the population,
Which our Eugenist says was the right number for a parent of his generation,
And our teachers report that he never interfered with their education.
Was he free? Was he happy? The question is absurd:
Had anything been wrong, we should certainly have heard.

W. H. AUDEN

federal, state and local agencies. Not just law enforcement agencies, but employment, insurance, credit, and many other organizations are accorded ready access to this sensitive information. All too often, particularly in areas where police conduct general dragnet (or round-up) arrests of everyone in the vicinity of a supposed crime, these arrest records reflect no wrong-doing.

Many people feel that the fact an arrest has been made is a valuable piece of information. But we should remember that it only represents the judgement of one person—a policeman often acting on the spur of the moment on the basis of no more than strong suspicion that there may be probable cause to believe that the individual arrested may have committed a crime. No magistrate has reviewed that hasty decision; there has been no arraignment; and neither judge nor jury has established guilt beyond a reasonable doubt after a fair trial. Yet this preliminary judgement by a policeman can haunt a citizen for the rest of his life.

Most law-abiding citizens are tempted to take the complacent view: "Well, that could never happen to me." But do you realize that the men in this audience stand a 50-50 chance of being arrested sometime

---

**THANK YOU**

In September, *Modern Data* urged its readers to write on behalf of Eddie Allen, a Detroit sanitation worker for twenty years and the father of seven children, who was about to be extradited to Alabama to face charges of stealing his grandmother's cow 32 years ago. Eddie was located after an FBI computer matched his name against a list of outstanding arrest warrants, and Eddie's extradition was imminent although he had been living a crime-free life since the cow-stealing incident.

We recently learned from Alabama Governor Wallace's legal advisor that Governor Milligan of Michigan has declined to extradite Mr. Allen. We believe this action was due in part to the many *Modern Data* readers who took the time and trouble to add their letters to those of our own staff. To all of you, a sincere thank you from all of us, and from Eddie, his wife, and children.

---

during their lifetimes? If you are a man living in a city, your chances of being arrested rise to sixty percent. If you happen to be black and live in a city, your chances of being arrested rise even further, to a whopping ninety percent.

Once your arrest is recorded, your chances of being arrested again are very great. The police have your name, photograph and fingerprints. You are on their list of potential criminals to be questioned about and rearrested for subsequent unsolved crimes.

Moreover, the potential adverse consequences of having an arrest record reach beyond the field of law enforcement. One survey in the New York area showed that seventy-five percent of the employment agencies in that area will not accept for referral applicants with arrest records. In addition to difficulties with finding employment, if you have an arrest record, you are likely to find getting insurance, credit and even a place to live extremely difficult.

All of this can happen to you without your having broken any law, much less having been convicted in a Court of Law. It seems to me that this sort of deprivation of rights, liberties and opportunities without trial is the very sort of abuse which our Constitution's due process guarantee were designed to prevent. The principle which is basic to our system of justice that man is innocent until tried and proven guilty seems to me to require stringent controls on the dissemination of information which can wreak such harm on the lives of citizens.

I have long been in favor of legislation which would restrict the dissemination by the FBI's computerized National Crime Information Center, or arrest records unaccompanied by some indication of the disposition of that arrest. In addition, it seems to me that even this information should be available only to those criminal justice agencies which can demonstrate that they need such arrest and disposition records in order to carry out their law enforcement duties. Other organizations, businesses and the like should have no access to this kind of information which can be so damaging to the lives and liberties of innocent citizens.

I am not for a moment suggesting that those who collect, computerize, and ever more widely distribute information on individuals, even damaging information such as arrest records, are acting out of ill-will or a desire to infringe the rights and interfere with the liberties of American citizens. I am certain that these officials feel that they are merely doing their jobs, which to them involve collecting the most possible information and making the widest possible use of it. The trouble is, human ingenuity is such that we can always think up reasons for needing to collect just one more bit of information. Once that information is collected some reason can always be found for sharing it with others.

When I think about these ever-expanding computerized information systems, I am reminded of Justice Brandeis' warning that—

"The greatest dangers to liberty lurk in insidious encroachment by men of zeal, well-meaning, but without understanding."

It seems to me to be high time for those of us who care deeply about individual liberties to call a halt to this burgeoning information collection and dissemination, unless and until the consequences of such collection and dissemination on individual lives and liberties are taken fully into account. Otherwise, the ostensible need for this piece of information and that bit of data will gradually encroach on our privacy and individuality until our control over information about ourselves is forever consigned to computers.

Discussions such as we are having this evening about the impact computerized information systems can have on individual rights to privacy and justice under law represent an essential bulwark against such infringements of human freedom. Our consciousness of and concern about the potential dangers to our cherished liberties is the best, and in the last analysis, perhaps the only protection for our liberties. As the great jurist, Learned Hand once wrote:

"Liberty lies in the hearts of men and women; When it dies there, no constitution, no law, no court can save it. . . . . While it lies there, it needs no constitution, no law, no court to save it."

# FBI Breakthrough: Crime-Busting Computers

JAMES D. SNYDER

The clamor by citizens and politicians for greater police protection has all but obscured one of the decade's most dramatic breakthroughs in criminal investigation. Where once police spent days or weeks tracking down leads, today the local patrolmen cruising a sleepy suburb or pounding a metropolitan pavement can be linked within seconds to detailed information on wanted felons or stolen articles—from any point in the nation.

This new police bond is provided by the FBI's National Crime Information Center (NCIC). A smoothly efficient, but little publicized, computerized memory bank, it contains more than 5 million details on suspects, fugitives, embezzled securities, stolen cars, guns and personal property.

From the control center at the FBI's Washington headquarters, twin computers receive and transmit crime information over a national telecommunications network that ties in more than 1800 local police departments through 90 regional control terminals.

The FBI says the system enables a policeman to query the memory bank and receive an answer within 30 seconds—faster than the time it takes to write out a traffic ticket. The comparison has actually been proven. A West Virginia state policeman assigned to a radar unit, recently stopped a speeding car. As he got out of his cruiser, his partner radioed the license number to headquarters, which in turn transmitted the information over the network to the FBI computer. Literally before the speeding summons was completed, word flashed back that the car had been stolen two days earlier in Nebraska.

Another example of the speed and proficiency of the FBI's robot cop came during a high-speed chase on the Pennsylvania Turnpike. As the state trooper closed in on the speeder, he called in the license number. Before the chase ended, he knew that the car was stolen and the driver was an escaped convict who was armed with a revolver taken in the burglary of a sporting goods store.

### WANTED ON MURDER

A New Orleans detective arrested a drifter for disorderly conduct in a bar. Without the aid of the NCIC, he might have received a light fine and left town within a few days. Instead, the vagrant's identification was routinely flashed to Washington as he was being booked. Before the desk sergeant completed the forms, a reply came: the suspect was wanted for murder in California.

The NCIC, according to an FBI agent, "is currently handling 40,000 'transactions' daily." That includes inquiries, new entries, cancellations and changes. "But," he added, "we receive about 28,000 inquiries every day from all over the country and we've been able to average close to 600 'hits' daily."

The need for instant information is prompted by the modern criminal's access to instant mobility, via jet service and the interstate highway system. Before the NCIC was established, for instance, a thief could steal jewelry, a television set and a gun from a Boston apartment, load it all into a stolen car and, in less than ten hours, pawn the goods in Newark and use the gun to hold up a Philadelphia gas station. Or, with a little ingenuity, he could board a Los Angeles-to-New York jet, steal a car at LaGuardia Airport, rob a Bridgeport Bank and catch a direct flight back to L.A. from Hartford—all within a day and often without a trace. There was just no way for local authorities to swiftly exchange suspects' descriptions or serial numbers on stolen merchandise. If a murder weapon could not be traced locally, for instance, it would often require weeks or months of painstaking investigation before it could be identified.

### SAVE POLICE LIVES

The more information a policeman has before approaching a suspect or halting a speeding car, the safer he is going to be. FBI statistics show that

---

**The FBI says the system enables a policeman to query the memory bank and receive an answer within 30 seconds—faster than the time it takes to write out a traffic ticket.**

> **Does it mean that anyone who has ever been arrested for speeding is now forever stamped in the NCIC's computer memory?**

85 law enforcement agents were killed from 1960 to 1968, while investigating suspicious persons or as a result of ambush or confronting a deranged person—all situations where the policeman had no prior warning. In addition, the report notes that one out of eight policemen are assaulted annually. If an Iowa City patrolman knows that a recovered gun registered to a local man is being sought as the murder weapon in a Houston homicide, he can take the necessary precautions before approaching the owner. Or, if a Connecticut state trooper is alerted that the convertible he is chasing was used as a getaway car in a North Carolina bank robbery, he can radio for assistance before stopping the car. This immediate on-the-scene information not only speeds the apprehension of lawbreakers, it also saves police lives.

Just what kind of information does the NCIC provide? Does it mean that anyone who has ever been arrested for speeding is now forever stamped in the NCIC's computer memory? Hardly, insists the FBI. Only felons or those who have committed serious misdemeanors are on file. Nor is the system cluttered with records of all stolen items. The NCIC collects information on all stolen firearms and descriptions of stolen property worth at least $500, unless the item proves to be a key element of an investigation. For example, if a kidnap victim is wearing a $50 school ring, this information could lead to the whereabouts of the kidnapper.

### LOCAL DATA NEEDED

But the NCIC, like any computer-based system, is only as reliable as the information it receives. The FBI credits the local police departments and other law enforcement agencies throughout the country and notes that the success of the program depends upon their speed and accuracy in reporting and updating information.

"It also places more responsibility on the average citizen," maintains an FBI agent, "to provide local authorities with accurate descriptions of lawbreakers or stolen property. The NCIC is a comprehensive team effort."

---

### THE THINGS DATA BANKS CAN BE MADE OF

Portions of a report by the Senate Subcommittee on Constitutional Rights, read into the *Congressional Record* during debate on the Senate Privacy Bill in 1974, turned up the fact that applicants for federal jobs in some agencies have been subjected to such true/false questions as:

"I am seldom troubled by constipation. . .
My sex life is satisfactory. . .
At times I feel like swearing. . .
I have never been in trouble because of my sex behavior. . .
I do not always tell the truth. . .
I have no difficulty in starting or holding my bowel movements. . .
I am very strongly attracted by members of my own sex. . .
I like poetry. . .
I go to church almost every week. . .
I believe in the second coming of Christ. . .
I believe in a life hereafter. . .
My mother was a good woman. . .
I believe my sins are unpardonable. . .
I have used alcohol excessively. . .
I loved my Mother. . .
I believe there is a God."

The portions were introduced into the record by Sen. Sam Ervin, the bill's sponsor, as "showing the need for this (privacy) legislation."

## Computer Increasing Criminal Arrests by 10 percent
RCA Government and Commercial Systems

A computer normally used for scientific purposes has been credited by police authorities with increasing criminal arrests by 10 percent in Camden, N.J.

Located at the RCA Advanced Technology Laboratories in Camden, the computer makes it possible to deploy police forces more efficiently by providing a weekly analysis of the location, day of week and hour that crimes are most likely to occur.

"Computer runoffs, which are easy to interpret, make it possible to concentrate police efforts in predicted high-crime areas during hours when crimes are most likely to occur," according to Joseph Benton, who heads the crime-fighting computer program for the police.

Recently, for example, the computer data indicated a high rate of larceny from automobiles was occurring in the vicinity of Rutgers University. Officers dispatched to the area placed notes on windshields of parked cars, asking drivers to help prevent thefts by keeping car doors locked. The result was a drop of more than 95 percent in larcenies from vehicles during the forecasted period.

The weekly analysis produced by the computer is based on information programmed into it on offences that occurred during the previous two weeks. Evidence on each crime is broken down according to location, time, day of week, item stolen, mode of operation and details on the victim and perpetrator.

A recent profile on purse snatching, for example, specified nine of the 43 sectors of Camden in which they were predicted to occur, with the highest rate on Thursday and Friday, between the hours of noon and 4:00 P.M., and currency as the prime target. Victims were listed as females, 30 years of age and upward, with attacks occurring chiefly at bus stops. The perpetrators generally were described as being under 18 years of age, ranging in height from five feet 6 inches to 6 feet, and weighing between 121 and 140 pounds.

The computer also produces special reports on request. These can include, for example, reports on the type of businesses most frequently burglarized during the summer months, the correlation between strongarm robberies and week of the month, type of item most often stolen from cars during the past two months, or any of hundreds of other combinations of crime factors.

# COMPUTERIZED CRIMINAL HISTORIES: A 7-YEAR BLUNDER?

**E. DRAKE LUNDELL JR.**

The seven-year history of computerized criminal history systems is essentially the history of a good idea gone astray.

It serves as a good example of how, in the rush to computerize, early warnings of possible problems can be ignored. The results are evident today as legislators and others try to implement controls after the fact, controls that were forgotten in the early stages of the criminal history systems.

The idea for computerized criminal histories was a direct outgrowth of the President's Commission on Law Enforcement and the Administration of Justice's 1967 report entitled "The Challenge of Crime in a Free Society."

That report recommended increased emphasis on applying computer technology for both keeping track of criminal offenders and for tactically deploying criminal justice resources.

However, in the criminal history area, the commission strongly recommended that special precautions were needed to protect the privacy of such records and recommended that all such information be kept solely at the state and local level to prevent any possible interference with the system by the executive branch on a national level.

### Project Search

The initial implementation of a computerized criminal history system was undertaken by Project Search (System for Electronic Analysis and Retrieval of Criminal Histories) funded by the Law Enforcement Assistance Administration (LEAA).

This $16 million demonstration project involved 20 states in the planning phases and established standard machine-readable forms for listing criminal histories. A smaller pilot project for exchanging criminal history information had 10 state participants, even though only five states actually exchanged information through the system.

In fact, most of those who did use the system did so only on a demonstration basis, with New York the only state to really use the system in an operational mode.

Under the Search plan there was to be only a national index of criminal history information with the majority of the information to be held on the state level.

Computer terminals in each state would submit information to the central index in abbreviated form. If a police officer queried the national system about a suspect, he would receive just the index information and would have to contact the originating state for details of the person's record.

Project Search was adamant on several points: The system should be primarily run on the local level with only a national index, preferably just on multistate offenders; the system should have definite safeguards to protect the privacy of individual records; and the system should be separate from the National Crime Information Center (NCIC) run by the FBI.

However, in January of 1970 Attorney General John N. Mitchell decided to centralize the system and place it under operational control of the FBI despite repeated objections of both the LEAA and the state officials involved in Project Search.

The addition of the Computerized Criminal History (CCH) system to the NCIC was a major departure. Until that point the NCIC had kept information only on wanted persons and six kinds of stolen merchandise: vehicles, license plates, securities, boats, guns and miscellaneous items. There was no personal information except on persons actually wanted for a criminal offense.

A typical use of the traditional NCIC system would be for a Michigan patrol car following a suspicious car with Florida license plates to radio headquarters asking for a check on the license number to see if the car was stolen. If it was, he would make an arrest.

By necessity, the system was quick and easy to use, and there was little worry over privacy invasions.

However, a problem arises with the decentralized nature of the system in that *local police are completely responsible* for all data entry. For example, if a car is stolen in Lansing, Mich., and recovered in Bloomington, Ind., the Lansing police must add the listing to the file and the Bloomington police must remove it.

Unfortunately, experience has shown that police are much quicker to add information to the system than to delete it, and there have been several cases where car owners have been arrested for stealing their own cars due to a failure to update the records after recovery of the stolen vehicle.

This was not considered to be a major problem until the criminal history files—which contain a notation of an individual's every contact with the law—were added to NCIC. These files, usually called "rap sheets," contain a record of every arrest, whether or not it leads to a conviction or even results in a trial.

These files are obviously more sensitive than any of the other NCIC categories, yet the FBI originally did not plan to provide any increase in protection to these files.

Today, with concern over the possible misuse of such files increasing, the bureau is moving in some limited areas (not sending criminal history information directly to police cars, not giving out information over a year old to non-law enforcement agencies, etc.) but many critics contend these measures do not go far enough and are essentially patches on a poor system.

Presently, there are no laws requiring states to update the files of criminal history information and the only penalty for not updating is exclusion from the system (as recently happened in New York [CW, July 3, 1974]).

In addition, there are no penalties—either civil or criminal—for misuse of the information in the criminal history files and no legal requirements for purging the files as they become outdated.

At the same time, many critics of the system feel it basically undermines the underlying principle of American justice—that a person is innocent until proven guilty.

These critics see no reason to store any information on arrests alone, unless that arrest is followed by a conviction for a crime. Alternatively, they would require that every entry in such a system at least contain the disposition data (found guilty, innocent, case dismissed or charge dropped) before it could be entered into the system.

Most laws proposed to deal with the issues presently being debated would not go that far, but would rather allow a person the right to see a record and correct it, and would impose civil and criminal penalties for any misuse of the data in the records. In addition, most of the proposed laws would require police agencies to keep a record of users of the system for audit purposes and would legally require agencies to update the records.

Whatever measures are finally adopted, it is clear that criminal history systems as they have evolved to date are grossly inadequate and that some new controls need to be legislated.

# Congress Puts the Computer to Work

*Nation's Business*

That electronic whiz is tallying votes in the House, and performing lots of other chores not only on Capitol Hill but in nearly every federal agency

This summer, campers headed for the six most popular national parks may not be accepted on a first-come-first-served basis as in the past. Instead, the federal government is planning to use a computer to handle reservations because of the heavy demand for camp sites.

Addicts who check into most drug treatment centers have their footprints put on file in a federal computer for identification. This gives them more anonymity than they would enjoy if they were registered in the FBI's fingerprint file.

Still another Washington computer, at the National Library of Medicine, is feeding valuable reference material to doctors, medical schools and hospitals across the country.

Even in Congress, where members were slow in accepting electronic data processing, a computer is now being used to record votes in the House with the results flashed instantaneously on large screens in the chamber. It has cut voting time in half for the 435 members.

Both the House and Senate are finding more and more ways in which EDP can cut down on the incalculable time now spent to supply Congressional committees and individual members with information essential to carry out the lawmaking function.

The House computer is now able, in seconds, to give a member the status of any bill introduced since the new Congress got under way in January. It can provide him with the daily legislative calendar via a special computer line to the Government Printing Office.

"I can't tell you how much just these applications alone will save in reduced staff help, but it will be substantial," reports Rep. Wayne Hays (D. - Ohio), chairman of the House Administration Committee, which is responsible for computers in the House. "And we have many more time- and money-saving applications that will be introduced as we go along."

One such innovation, now being installed, will enable each Congressman to submit a list of 10,000 names to be stored in the computer in whatever categories he chooses.

"In that way, if the member wants to make a special mailing, say, just to doctors or schoolteachers, the computer will draw only on these names," Congressman Hays explains. "You can't imagine what an improvement this is over the old Addressograph system of culling names and addresses."

### EQUATING WITH COMPANIES

The man charged with the day-to-day operations of the House computer is former star quarterback Frank Ryan of the Cleveland Browns. Dr. Ryan, director of House Information Systems, has a doctorate in mathematics. He supervised installation of the million-dollar voting system in the House.

"The way I look at it you have to equate the needs of Congress with that of a large company or university," Dr. Ryan points out. "They have the proven tools. Think of the responsibilities of Congressmen—shouldn't Congress be equally well-equipped?"

Congressman Hays, who assumed chairmanship of the House Administration Committee two years ago, has urged expanded use of the House computer. But he is particularly proud of the electronic voting system whose acceptance he pushed among members convinced it would flop.

"I had a Texas Congressman come up to me the other day and say, 'Wayne, I've been here 20 years and this is the most sensible thing I've seen yet,'" the Ohioan reports.

Automatic voting systems are not new, to be sure. Electro-mechanical systems of one form or another have been used in 36 state legislatures and several European countries. In fact, Thomas Edison was granted a patent for a vote recorder more than a century ago.

During floor debate last year, Rep. Robert McClory (R.-Ill.), who authored the bill to install the system now in use, said:

"Ever since 1914 there have been recommendations of one kind or another for some kind of automatic voting here in the House. While the accurate reporting of votes is vital to this body, it is unfortunate that we have waited this long to install modern electronic equipment to more accurately and more expeditiously record our attendance and our votes."

Such voting systems are not always universally embraced, for one reason or another. The New York State Legislature spent $300,000 to install electronic voting in 1965 and later voted to have it removed.

Some say it was abolished because it didn't prove efficient. But others contend that some legislative leaders felt they could influence voting more effectively with the slower, voice-voting method, which allows them more time to act when trends are spotted in the early stages of balloting.

But in the national House of Representatives, such apprehensions, if they existed, have given way to wholehearted support, according to both Congressman Hays and Dr. Ryan.

Each member is issued a plastic coded identification card which he can use to vote at any one of 44 stations. A Yea vote registers green by his name on a panel running along the wall behind the Speaker's rostrum. A Nay vote is red, while amber indicates a vote of Present.

Panels on two balcony fronts keep a running tally of votes and time remaining for casting them. A member has 15 minutes to vote, the amount of time required to reach the chamber from some of the remote House offices.

A member who loses or misplaces his card still can vote by signifying his vote orally to a tally clerk who, in turn, registers the member's vote on a small console at his desk. The system is foolproof in that it won't permit a member to cast more than one vote on a single measure.

The Senate has found no need to put in a similar system. As one Senate official put it:

"We can run through a voice vote almost as fast as a computer. And we can find other places to spend a million dollars."

But the Senate, like the House, relies on the computer for a variety of other services.

Both have instituted modern budgetary management techniques with the help of EDP, using it in preparing payrolls, handling personnel records and making purchases. Records of campaign contributions to

> **"'Vote for a computer-competent Congressman!' may well be one of the common campaign slogans of the year 2000."**

Senators and Representatives are filed away in computers.

And new ways to put computers to work are being studied in both branches of Congress.

Senators and Congressmen will find themselves more and more dependent on the computer in the years ahead. The sheer complexity of their work, coupled with the demands of constituents in these days of rapid communications, will demand it.

Congressman Hays, for example, believes the appropriations machinery on Capitol Hill has become so intricate that only a computer can provide members with the kind of information they need for decision-making.

Looking further down the legislative road, one Congressman thinks tomorrow's legislator will be inextricably wired into a computer way of life. Rep. John Brademas (D.-Ind.), who also is a member of the House Administration Committee, wrote a paper in 1969 in which he projected a view of the Congressman of the year 2000.

THE WORLD AT HIS FINGERTIPS
This Twenty-first Century lawmaker will have at his desk a keyboard console that will enable him to tap a vast amount of legal, economic, fiscal and other information.

He will have a two-way video linkup with other members, with the Executive Office of the President, agency heads, laboratories, statehouses and universities.

He will be able to determine at the touch of a button the impact of tax proposals on the level of employment, the gross national product, and the precise inflows of revenues into the Treasury. The computer will give him information on federal contract awards, lobbyists and the current price of tea in China.

There will be "tele-mobile" units for communication between his office and that of fellow Congressmen. It will include a "scrambler" to permit transmission of sensitive data.

"'Vote for a computer-competent Congressman!' may well be one of the common campaign slogans of the year 2000," Rep. Brademas says.

# Computers Help Fight Fires in Scotland
KURT VAN VLANDREN

Glasgow, Scotland plans to link its fire engines with a computer to fight blazes more efficiently. Small facsimile printers installed in the cabs of 40 fire engines will receive by radio and print out detailed information on floor plans of the burning building and its known fire hazards while the firemen are on their way to battle the blaze.

George Cooper, Glasgow's firemaster, said the Honeywell system is believed to be the most advanced fire-fighting system of its kind in the world. He said his crews "will both be better equipped to tackle the job and their safety better protected."

The system, based on two Honeywell 316 computers due to be installed in June or July, will ultimately contain data on 10,000 properties. The information, to be updated daily, would include building plans and layouts, known hazardous materials in the building, and a special file of 1,000 hazardous substances and how to handle them in the case of fire.

Glasgow intends later to link 400 fire alarm boxes directly to the computer. When an alarm is signalled the computer would dispatch the nearest fire crew directly, without any human intervention.

# The City and the Computer Revolution

JOHN KEMENY

## GOVERNMENT TODAY IS BETTER QUALIFIED, BUT MORE BEWILDERED

### The dawn of computing

Let us consider a municipal government of a city of one million people in the year 1975. The chances are that our government is much better qualified and less corrupt than its predecessor was forty years ago. The chances are, also, that it is much more bewildered.

In order to make intelligent decisions, we must first of all have reliable data. Given the complexity and mobility of a modern city of one million people, the gathering and interpretation of data is an almost hopeless task. And as our citizens become more affluent, they expect more and better services, which aggravates the problem.

What is the value of a census taken every ten years? By the time the census is processed, 10 per cent of the population will have changed its residence. By the time a new school is planned, approved by the voters, and actually constructed, it is hopelessly overcrowded. By the time a major highway is completed, the flow of traffic has changed completely. Efficient use of high-speed computers may not solve all these problems, but solutions to the problems are impossible without the use of computers.

### Municipal governments use computers only for statistics

Industry has been much more aware of these problems, and has taken better advantage of the existence of modern computers. Many industries now keep their personnel files and business data in the memories of computers and use these for fast and accurate data-processing. The same information may also be processed for planning purposes. Although some municipal governments are beginning to realize the significance of computers, generally they are used only for such simple tasks as the issuing of pay checks. And even when computers are available, most of the employees have no understanding of the use of computers, and therefore fail to take full advantage of this incredible tool.

Computers will not have a significant effect on our city governments until our colleges bring up a new generation of graduates who take high-speed computers for granted. Fortunately, some of our best institutions are doing exactly this. At my own institution, 80 per cent of each entering class learns how to use a computer, and many acquire a significant amount of experience before they graduate. When some of these students filter into our municipal governments, we can look forward to a revolution in city planning.

Our city and state highway departments collect immense amounts of information on the flow of traffic. But what happens to this mass of information once it is collected? A few able men, perhaps with a great deal of experience, will come up with rules-of-thumb for the improvement of the flow of traffic. Although this is certainly worth-while, it is far from what is possible in the age of computers.

### Simulation could provide five years' experience in one week

It would be possible to simulate the entire traffic pattern of downtown Manhattan by a high-speed computer. ("Simulation" is a powerful tool, widely used by business, to re-create within a computer a fairly accurate image of what happens in the outside world—see [6] in the References.) Built into the model would be information on the number of cars, the speed at which they travel under various conditions of crowding, the available traffic lights, one-way streets, habits of double parking, and the like. Once such a model exists, experimentation with new traffic patterns could be carried out within the computer rather than using the population of the city as guinea pigs. We could instruct the computer to change the operation of traffic lights, modify oneway streets, and try other innovations. After a detailed simulation the computer would report back whether there was any significant easing in the flow of traffic. With one week of computer simulation we could acquire the equivalent of five years' experience. Such a simulation planning model in the hands of experts would make a tremendous impact in relieving notorious traffic bottlenecks.

This idea has been tried on a small scale in planning the traffic of superhighways, bridges, and tunnels. One such experiment was reported in *Scientific American* (see [3]). The computer found that cars should *not* be allowed to enter the Holland Tunnel as quickly as the toll booths could process them. If, instead, cars were held up periodically for a short time, the total flow through the tunnel increased! Presumably this is due to the fact that "pulsing" the cars prevents major jams and reduces accidents. But no one suggested this simple improvement *before* the computer simulation.

Secondly, high-speed computers should be used in the fight against pollution. The causes of pollution are complex, and careful statistical analysis should be substituted for guesswork. I predict that a major data-gathering and analysis would turn up unexpected results.

Thirdly, consider the problem of planning schools, parks, recreation areas, youth centers, and centers for the aged. Of course, such decisions are often political footballs. But, even with the best intentions, such decisions are made in ignorance of the facts; although the facts may be buried in the files, without high-speed computers the planning body cannot digest them. For example, where should we place a park to do the most good for the city's children? This decision requires a careful correlation of the distribution of children with the city's geography, and with the size and location of existing parks. The solution of this problem requires both up-to-date census information and the sophisticated use of computers.

Our municipal governments have hardly begun to make intelligent use of the computer revolution. The hiring of computer experts and acquisition of large computing centers for planning purposes could be the single best investment to help alleviate our urban problems.

### Computer would be a powerful tool to fight organized crime

A very common problem is the identification of a car from inaccurate

information. Suppose that a witness notes that the license is GA46–, and that the car was large, fairly new, and either dark blue or dark green. The time-sharing system could easily handle such an inquiry. It would find in its memory the 100 license numbers starting with "GA46," and match each against the partial description. Within a minute it could type out complete descriptions of the dozen or so possible suspect cars—and would type this at the local police station. The result would be both a great increase in police efficiency and a relief for our overworked police forces. I understand that such a system has actually been contemplated by the Los Angeles Police Department, but—to the best of my knowledge—it has not yet been implemented anywhere.

Naturally, one must ask whether such a system would involve astronomical costs. However, I have sketched out the technical details, and I estimate that the entire operation could be financed by an annual charge of one dollar on motor vehicles. Thus, my proposal is entirely practical.

And once such a system is in operation, it would facilitate other operations. The motor vehicle bureau could have its own terminals which would automatically, and instantaneously, record each new registration issued. And the various police forces in the state could pool their criminal records within the memory of the machine. Identification of criminal suspects could be expedited by a procedure similar to the one outlined above. And if the criminal files of the states and the federal government were tied together by a computer network, we would have the most powerful tool imaginable to fight organized crime.

### Traffic jams would be almost eliminated

Equally exciting is the possibility of real-time control of traffic. Even if computers are used for the planning of traffic patterns, we know that the plans will go haywire under unusual circumstances. I have often waited an unreasonable amount of time at a traffic light, when there was no traffic on the crossstreet, but my street was jammed up. Under sufficiently bad circumstances, the city will station a policeman at the corner, who can make corrections manually. A much more efficient, and less expensive, solution would be the use of a time-sharing computer to control the lights. It could be informed of current traffic densities by means of electronic devices, and could adjust the lights according to need. And it could do this for a thousand traffic lights.

Similarly, it is ludicrous to allow

---

**Computers will not have a significant effect on our city governments until our colleges bring up a new generation of graduates who take high-speed computers for granted.**

---

THE CITY AND THE COMPUTER REVOLUTION  **139**

> **Our municipal governments have hardly begun to make intelligent use of the computer revolution. The hiring of computer experts and acquisition of large computing centers for planning purposes could be the single best investment to help alleviate our urban problems.**

more traffic to pour into a jammed highway. Traffic lights at all the entrances of a limited access road, controlled on the basis of real-time traffic information, could make a significant improvement.

MAJOR ROLE OF CITY WILL BE EXCHANGE OF INFORMATION

A computer in every home
While some of the uses of computers suggested so far may seem dramatic in their conception or their possible impact, they will yield only relief for the symptoms of urban disease. For a cure we will have to wait for the next development in the computer revolution.

By 1990 the principal public utility will be a gigantic communication network, including the means for visual communication, and having a network of huge computers as an integral part. I expect to see not only every office tied to this network, but to see a console in every home. I have discussed elsewhere some of the implications of having access to a computer in every home (see [5]). I would now like to do the same for the implications of the new utility for the role of the city.

One may classify the principal functions of the city under five categories: (1) It is the home of millions of people. (2) It is a manufacturing center. (3) It is a center of trade. (4) It is a center of finance. (5) It is a center of recreation. The worst problems of the city arise not from the fact that millions live there, but that the other four functions attract vast numbers of nonresidents to the city. I shall argue that by 1990 most of the reasons for this influx can be eliminated.

City as center of trade and finance will decline
The role of the cities as centers of manufacture has been steadily decreasing in importance. As costs of transportation decrease and overhead costs in large cities continue to increase, manufacturing centers—like the population—are deserting our largest cities. And we have every reason to expect that this trend will continue. As a matter of fact, the trend will be accelerated in the immediate future when cities begin to take effective measures to combat pollution.

Even today the major role of the city is not as a manufacturing center, but as a center of trade and finance. And the nature of these functions is also subtly changing. I claim that the major role of the city is not that of processing or exchanging goods, but rather that of exchanging information. And this trend is being greatly accelerated by the coming of computers.

An interesting symptom is the disappearance of money (cash) from everyday transactions. Major businesses have for a long time not needed cash to deal with each other. And the wide use of checks and credit

# Campsite Reservation

JUNE 13, 1974
The National Park Service announced today that vacationers can begin reserving campsites in twenty-one national parks by telephoning the toll-free number, 800 XXX-XXXX.

In some of the parks 100 percent of the campsites can be reserved by telephone, so users are advised not to try the parks on busy periods without reservations. The computerized reservation system will be handled by Park Reservation System, Inc., a new corporation, awarded a five-year contract.

Park authorities said this new reservation system should prevent much of the uncertainty and heartbreak of the old first-come-first-served basis.

JULY 21, 1974
Three weeks ago the National Park Service inaugurated a telephone reservation system for campsites in a number of parks under its jurisdiction. The NPS is now advising travelers to write, not phone, for reservations. The reason is the overloading of phone lines due to the instant popularity of the new system.

You must have your plans at least fourteen days in advance, says Jerry D. Wagers, director of Park Service. Send a self-addressed stamped envelope to Park Reservation System in Cedar Rapids, Iowa. Include name, address, type of site wanted, dates and a check to cover camping fees and the $2.00 reservation fee.

AUGUST 29, 1974
The National Park Service announced today that it was abandoning its reservation system for national park campsites. The present contract with Park Reservation System was terminated today and all campsites would return to the first-come-first-served basis.

Senator Howard M. Metzenbaum (D-Ohio) held hearings on the deluge of complaints from campers about the park reservation system. Reservations weren't acknowledged, others were lost, and local park managers had no accurate record of who did or did not have park reservations. Thus, campers never knew if they did really have confirmed reservations or not and even confirmed reservation holders sometimes found out their reservations were no good.

Hearings brought out the fact that the National Park Service Director, Ronald H. Walker, was a close friend of Donald Middleton, PRS president, who received the reservation contract. Also the company was newly set up for this purpose and had no experience in the computer reservation business. Other experienced companies capable of providing the service had been turned down. Senator Metzenbaum said "I believe our investigation of Park Reservation System, Inc., has amply demonstrated the poor quality of service it has provided for campers and the fact it should never have been selected to provide the service in the first place."

### Automobile Ombudsmen Possible?

# WE NEED PROTECTION FROM DRIVER INFORMATION SYSTEM

**by Herb Grosche**

There is a mysterious world of state motor vehicle offices, Soundex coding, data bank pointers, traffic courts, automobile and truck numbering systems, recall orders, NCIC (National Crime Information Center) terminals that interests and affects all of us. We all drive, most of us own cars, most of us have had accidents and traffic tickets, some of us have had cars stolen. Many of us move from state to state, changing driving licenses and car plates as we go.

The recent concern for privacy in all kinds of official and private data systems has begun to open up that world to the bemused gaze of DP people and civil liberties advocates. And along with past and present computerization, along with future plans for on-line improvement and interfacing with other installations and networks, has come the urge to reexamine the social underpinnings of car and driver information systems.

The HEW report, "Records, Computers and the Rights of Citizens," contains in Appendix D a conspectus of the National Driver Register, a subterranean function of the U.S. Department of Transportation which enables state motor vehicle administrations to check driver license applications against suspensions and revocations in other states.

Changes are proposed in that system; it is proposed that prospective employers (of taxi or truck drivers, in theory, but probably of much broader categories, in practice) have access to the register. It is proposed that medical and physical limitation pointers be added. It is proposed that pointers to conviction records which did not result in a suspension or revocation be added. And of course, it is proposed to provide sophisticated on-line response capability instead of the present 24-hours-plus-mail-time; consultants always want follow-up contracts!

Vehicle identification numbers (VIN) are required on state registration forms, and are also vital (since they include a serial number) for manufacturer recalls when safety defects are to be corrected. The National Highway Safety Administration has required manufacturers to list the VINs of cars which are not brought in for correction: now these lists are to be provided to insurance companies. Will the latter attempt to avoid payment of damages to owners whose cars are listed? If not, why do the companies want the lists? Or do they: perhaps the bureaucrats are just being righteous?

Bum dope in all such systems is supposed to be corrected, old stuff is supposed to be purged. Is it? We cannot know, because unless the HEW report recommendations are implemented—implemented in every state DMV as well as at the register—no outside probe of the data is permitted. A driver license applicant cannot contact the register directly; inquiry can be made on his behalf by the state agency concerned, but what if they don't want to bother, or are too busy?

**Power to Punish**

And there is a great temptation to use the interconnect capabilities of machine systems, batch as well as on-line, to enforce and to punish. Years ago I got a jaywalking ticket in downtown Los Angeles, a municipal offense, and of the very lowest level of seriousness: a "violation," not a misdemeanor or a felony. My car was blocks away. Asked to show "some kind of identification," I produced a New York credit card.

A year later I was coolly notified by the State of California that my driver's license would not be renewed until I settled my jaywalking summons. Obviously the Sacramento DMV had been asked by a municipal court clerk to check whether I had a California license, and a computer-originated form letter was dispatched. The licensing power of the state motor vehicle office was being used to cheaply dragoon a person accused of a completely nonvehicular offense.

Now, extrapolate that to a future in which any employer (and that can be anyone who prints up a letterhead), any insurance company, any court or probation officer, any policeman can query data held in the National Driver Register, follow pointers to further data in any state and many local driver-license and vehicle-license data bank, and use that data to harass and intimidate, to withhold or withdraw job offers, to refuse or revoke insurance coverage, to require expensive repairs.

Some of those queries would be illegal in all states now, and all of them would be illegal in some states. They certainly occur, as routine procedure, as personal favors, or corruptly, up and down the U.S.—have occurred in the past, will occur much more easily and frequently in the future.

If we believe the protestations of the FBI and the NCIC people (and I don't), if we believe the protestations of the register people (well, maybe), *innocent* citizens are hardly ever injured by such files, computers and networks.

They would be glad to correct individual injustices, they say, meanwhile struggling fairly openly against letting individuals get anywhere near their central operations. "Go to your friendly local DMV office, your friendly local police station," they say. For a well-off white male with gray crew cut hair to do this in Santa Barbara is certainly possible; for a poor young black with a bush Afro to get help in downtown Philadelphia is something else again.

I believe we need an extension of the ombudsman concept in this area. Putting aside the various automobile associations as hopelessly perverted, discounting newspaper and radio station hot lines as sparse and poorly motivated, and remembering ACM's financial problems, it looks like the Civil Liberties Union sort of job. Since they have so much really heavy stuff on their plate right now, I wonder if a new outfit, a Drivers and Car Owners Protective Association, might not be viable? With terminals connected to all the adversary data banks, I hope? We're going to need it.

---

cards means that we have almost completely changed over from monetary exchanges to exchanges of information. In the age of the computer-communication utility, cash will completely disappear. When homes, stores, offices, and banks are linked through computers, one need only enter a transaction through the nearest console, and two bank accounts will be automatically credited or debited (see, for example, [2]).

Similarly, banks will be able to implement an automatic credit system—a modern version of the British "overdraft." And even the most complex banking transactions could be handled by a one-room local bank which, through the computer network, has access to all the files of the central bank, and perhaps to a national credit-rating system.

Or consider the operation of the stockmarket. Even today a "ticker-tape" network keeps brokers all over the country informed about the market. Why not replace this with a

> **By 1990 the principal public utility will be a gigantic communication network, including the means for visual communication, and having a network of huge computers as an integral part.**

modern computer network that will allow all of these brokers to participate actively in the market? Through a time-sharing system they could not only be kept informed, but could enter bids and conclude sales instantaneously. After all, the stockmarket is nothing more than a gigantic information-exchange center, whose function could be fulfilled by a large computer.

Similar remarks apply to the large office-complexes maintained by businesses in our cities. Their major role is the collection, exchange, and processing of information. This could be handled by a hub of the computer-communication network. Why must all the executive and secretarial staff have their offices in the same location? Presumably for ease of access to the information and because face-to-face meetings are useful. But in the not-so-distant future, any branch office will have easy, instantaneous access to all files. And video-phones will make most personal meetings unnecessary. Then a hundred conveniently located, specialized branches will operate efficiently as a single large company.

Such a trend is visible even today in retail trade. Mailorder houses locate their "central office" wherever they please, and large retail firms have their outlets distributed among a hundred shopping centers. When the new utility makes is possible for the housewife to "search" stores from her own home, by means of computer information-processing and video displays, another major reason for the influx into cities will disappear.

Even in the area of recreation the participants need not go to the place from which the entertainment originates. We note that a professional football game which has fifty thousand spectators is watched by fifty million people on television. And educational television is bringing adult education into the home. At the moment, unfortunately, television allows only passive participation in education and entertainment, but the new utility may even reverse this dangerous trend. For example, a woman taking a television course may do research by means of her home computer.

### THE CITY OF 1990 WILL BE NODE OF COMPUTER-COMMUNICATION NET

I see the city of 1990 as a gigantic depository of information, as a major node in the computer-communication network, and as a source of education and entertainment. Tens of millions living in surrounding small towns will have continual access to these services by means of computers, television, and video-phones. But they will not have to go to the city.

I see New York City in 1990 as the home of the technicians who service the information-education-recreation functions, and of the rich who insist on seeing operas and football games in person. It may also be a nice place to escape to when the pressures of suburban or rural life are too much with us.

### REFERENCES

[1] Oscar Handlin and John Burchard (eds.). *The Historian and the City.* Cambridge, Mass.: M.I.T. Press, 1963.

[2] A. H. Anderson *et al. An Electronic Cash and Credit System.* New York: American Management Association, 1966.

[3] R. Herman and K. Gardels. "Vehicular Traffic Flow," *Scientific American,* Vol. 209, No. 6 (December 1963), pp. 35–43.

[4] Raymond Vernon, *The Changing Economic Function of the Central City.* New York: Committee for Economic Development, January 1959.

[5] *The Future Impact of Computers.* Proceedings of a conference at Dartmouth College, General Learning (forthcoming).

[6] John G. Kemeny. *Random Essays,* Part III: "Computers." Englewood Cliffs, N.J.: Prentice-Hall, 1964.

## MASS. POLICE UNDER INVESTIGATION FOR ALLEGED SALE OF CRIME DATA

BOSTON—Several state policemen are under grand jury investigation here for allegedly selling criminal history material to private investigators who in turn turned it over to credit reporting agencies, it was learned last week.

The investigation is the first to be made under the Massachusetts law protecting the privacy of such information and follows a long probe by the governor's office and the state police, sources close to the investigation said.

The law established an audit trail on the requests for criminal history information from the computerized files, which gave the investigators the first indication that the files might be being abused, the sources said.

From the audit trail, the sources said, it was seen that several state policemen were apparently requesting an inordinate number of criminal histories—more than they would normally need for the performance of their duties.

This information was turned over to the director of the state police and the state police internal investigations unit, which monitored the use of the system and the activities of the policemen allegedly involved in the plot.

Apparently, one source said, the state policemen were selling the files to friends who were private investigators, who in turn were turning the files over to large credit granting agencies such as department stores in the Boston area.

The results of the investigation have now been turned over to a grand jury which is expected to act on the matter in the near future.

However, the case points to a weakness in the law, several sources said last week, in that only the policemen can be prosecuted under the present law because possession of criminal histories is not a crime.

#### Amendment Due?

Therefore, it is likely that an amendment will be offered to make the "knowing" possession of such documents illegal, which would make prosecutions easier against private investigators and others who might try to get police agencies to turn over the files for private use.

However, it was also learned that several large private investigating agencies are mounting a campaign to get legal authorization to have access to such files—a move that "would make a mockery of the law" if adopted, according to one source.

## A BANNED SOCIAL SECURITY NUMBER

We are all aware of the Social Security numbers. But there is one Social Security number that has been banned. The Social Security Administration's computers are programmed to watch for the number 078-05-1120.

In 1938 that number belonged to Mrs. Hilda Whitcher, who worked in a wallet factory in Lochport, New York. Her boss borrowed her card, printed thousands of copies of it—with "Specimen" overprinted in red ink across the front—and stuffed these copies into the glassine-window card case of the wallets made at the factory.

Despite the precautions to make it a "dummy" card, over 40,000 false earnings entries have since been chalked up to Mrs. Whitcher's number. She has long since been given a new Social Security number, but the agency's computers are still programmed to catch entries under the old number.

## CITY HALL

Of course, a great deal depends on how well the computer has been programed. Some enormously important factor may be left out, or something wrong put in.

One such omission took place in Boston recently. The city's municipal accounts are pretty well automated. Mayor John F. Collins, a progressive executive, had seen to that. Mayor Collins was running for the senatorial nomination. Three days before the primary election, very efficiently and without instruction, the machine prepared, addressed, and mailed 30,000 delinquent sewer tax bills. It had never been programed with the instruction: "Don't send out tax bills just before election if the Mayor is running for office!" Nobody thought of that. Mayor Collins lost the nomination.

Somewhat less bizarre omissions (and doubtless some much more grave ones) could occur in any automated program. Of course any human politician worth his salt, working in City Hall, would have instinctively avoided such a mistake. So man has to remain a close partner to the machine.

**In the age of the computer-communication utility, cash will completely disappear.**

# VASCAR—The Computer That Catches Speeders

*Changing Times*

As you whiz along the highway, you see a sign reading "VASCAR patrolled." Know what that means? If not, you'd better find out, before you get the explanation from a policeman.

VASCAR, the abbreviation for Visual Average Speed Computer and Recorder, is an antispeed weapon that clocks a car's average speed in a fraction of a second, day or night and from any direction. The computerized system works simply by timing an auto between two preselected points and dividing the time into the distance traveled.

Police in 42 states and 500 cities now use this speed-checking device. They choose two easily visible markers along the street or highway and the computer calculates the distance between them. Suitable reference points are easy to find: a telephone pole, a sign, a sewer cover, even a tire mark or shadow can be used by the trained VASCAR operator.

When a suspected speed violator passes the first checkpoint, the policeman flips a "time" switch. He turns it off when the auto passes the second reference mark. Then the computer goes to work dividing the premeasured distance by the recorded time. Almost instantly the module figures the average speed to the nearest tenth of a mile per hour and registers the figure in bold numerals on the control unit that's mounted near the dashboard of the patrol car.

A major difference between VASCAR and other speed-monitoring devices is that it operates from moving cars as well as from parked ones, measuring distances up to six and a half miles if necessary.

To monitor the speed of another auto while driving in traffic, the operator flips on a "distance" switch when his car passes the first reference point and switches if off when he passes the second marker. As the suspected speed violator passes the visual markers, the VASCAR operator throws the time switch on and then off. When both the time and distance operations are completed, the calculator instantly displays the suspect's average speed.

In addition to reducing the need for high-speed chasing, the electronic unit enables patrolmen to go about their regular duties and still clock cars as much as a mile away that appear to be traveling at excessive speeds. For speeders, the computer age means the odds that favored them in the past are shrinking. Witness the national conviction rate for VASCAR arrests: Better than 99%.

"Sorry I'm late, Chief, but you've just no idea what the traffic's like this morning."
© DATAMATION

## ◇ BRANCH POINTS

Bigelow, Robert P., ed. *Computers and the Law.* Chicago: Commerce Clearing House, 1969.

*The Computer and Invasion of Privacy.* U.S. Government Printing Office, 1966.

Greenberger, Martin. *Computers, Communications, and the Public Interest.* Baltimore, Maryland: The Johns Hopkins Press, 1971.

Freed, Roy N. *Materials and Cases on Computers and Law.* Boston, Mass.: Boston University Bookstore.

Janda, Kenneth. *Information Retrieval, Applications to Political Science.* Indianapolis: Bobbs-Merrill Company, Inc., 1968.

Laudon, Kenneth. *Computers and Bureaucratic Reform.* New York: John Wiley & Sons, Inc., 1974.

Weston, Alan F. *Data Banks in a Free Society.* New York: Quadrangle/The New York Times Book Company, 1972.

Whisenand, Paul M., and Tug T. Tarmaru. *Automated Police Information Systems.* New York: John Wiley & Sons, Inc., 1970.

Wilson, Andrew. *The Bomb and the Computer.* New York: Delacorte Press, 1968.

## ◯ INTERRUPTS

1. Income tax returns are usually first checked by computer for errors and possible auditing. Find out as much as possible about how the computer decides a return should be audited. What percentages does the IRS consider excessive for the different types of deductions? Since a computer is used to audit the returns, could one be used to prepare false returns?

2. Describe a more effective system for the expression of political preference using computers instead of the present voting system.

3. Write a paper on the impact of computers in one of the following areas:
   a) politics
   b) education
   c) business
   d) libraries
   e) your choice

4. Imagine you work for a law-enforcement office. Your sister is running for a political office. She has asked you to research the background of a political opponent to see if you can find any "dirt" on the opponent. Where would you start? Which records are computerized? As a police officer, which records would you have available that others would not? Are there any laws to prohibit you from disclosing any of the information? How effective are they?

5. Does your community have a computerized vote counting system? Find out as much as possible about how it works. Do you consider it foolproof or vulnerable to "vote tampering?"

6. Computers are used by law-enforcement agencies to keep "rap sheets" (arrest records, convictions, intelligence information, and so forth). Develop a set of rules about what type of information can be stored, for how long, and who can put in, delete, change, and see information.

7. How does your local government use computers? What other computer functions could be added? Obtain a tour of a local governmental data-processing center. Find out exactly what information is stored. Are any social issues raised by these files? Find out what computer files you can obtain. For example, will the government sell your address listings, voting registration lists, real estate records, and so forth?

8. What advantages and disadvantages does a computer-based law enforcement system have for the law-abiding citizen?

9. Most states keep track of traffic violations by using computers. Find out as much as possible about computerized motor vehicle files in your state.

10. Find out exactly what information the different levels of government—local, state, federal—have about you. Next determine what you can see about yourself and what others can see.

11. You are driving along a deserted freeway. You are in a hurry to get home, and there is no other traffic, so you go fifteen miles an hour over the speed limit. The next day you get a letter in the mail from the police that states whoever was driving your car was speeding and is due in court. The traffic offence had been observed by an electronic device that measured the car's speed, noted the license number, and relayed the information to the police computer. The police computer looked up the name and address of the license plate holder from its storage files and printed out the violation notice. Find out how difficult it would be to do this with present computer technology. Do you think it would be a good or bad policy to implement this type of system? Why?

12. Should computers be used to make politicians instantly aware of popular opinion of political issues? Why or why not?

13. Write a report on one of the following:
    a) use of computers in political campaigns
    b) use of computers in congress
    c) use of computers by the Executive branch

# 7
## THE IMPACT

# Waiting for the Great Computer Rip-off

TOM ALEXANDER

For an expert bent on crime, it seems, cracking a computer system's defenses is about as difficult as doing a hard Sunday crossword puzzle.

One morning last September, a computer operator on duty at Honeywell Information Systems Inc. in Phoenix was startled to see the output printer on his console start up all by itself. Out rattled a message referring derisively to a recent Honeywell press release about the company's vaunted new computer system, called "Multics." When it was done sniping at Multics, the mysterious message signed off with the words "ZARF is with you again."

ZARF is the code designation for part of a joint project of the U.S. Air Force and MITRE Corp., a defense-research outfit. The project is concerned with computer security, and a favorite pastime of people involved in it is cracking "uncrackable" computers. The day before the Honeywell computer acted up, two ZARF men, Air Force Major Roger Schell and Steven Lipner of MITRE, visited Honeywell to look over the security features of prospective systems for classified Air Force computing chores. After seeing the press release about Multics, Lipner quietly placed a long-distance call to a ZARF colleague, Lieutenant Paul Karger, in Massachusetts, nearly 3,000 miles away. Karger, in turn, sat down at his teletypewriter computer terminal, dialed into Honeywell's private Multics system, and typed in a few subtle instructions that subverted every one of the system's safeguards, giving Karger effective control.

The ZARF prank was particularly embarrassing because Multics is designed with security as an uppermost consideration. Of all large commercial computers on the market, Multics probably incorporates the most elaborate safeguards against unauthorized tampering.

## A STIRRING OF FEAR

The kind of vulnerability indicated by ZARF's little joke is beginning to disturb the keepers of modern electronic-data-processing systems. Most EDP systems consist of one or more large, multipurpose computers and banks of stored data, usually accessible via telephone circuits from individual terminals such as the teletypewriter that Lieutenant Karger used. Until not long ago, computer manufacturers and users saw little reason to fear that an unscrupulous person at one terminal would be able to read, alter, or delete another user's data, or tamper with the intricate programs that manipulate this data.

But in the past year or two, even the manufacturers have more or less come to acknowledge that it is not really very difficult for someone with a lot of skill to do things like that, even with the most secure systems now in existence. According to one expert, indeed, it's about as difficult "as solving a hard Sunday crossword puzzle."

## HOW TO MAKE A PRESIDENT BLANCH

Computers, of course, have come to be deeply and pervasively involved in basic functions of our society. Top executives might die off, factories blow up, foreign subsidiaries get nationalized, but if you really want to see a company president blanch, ask him what he would do if the magnetic tapes with his accounts receivable got erased.

Electronic and magnetic data have not only replaced manually kept books, but have also gone a long way toward replacing tangible assets, including money itself. Today's credit-card system, for example, is an offspring of computerization. In the words of Richard Mills, formerly a top computer expert at M.I.T., and now a vice president of First National City Bank, "The base form of an asset is no longer necessarily a 400-ounce gold bar; now assets are often simply magnetic wiggles on a disk."

But gold bars in vaults, notations in a ledger, or, for that matter, written reports from a corporate research project are immutable and immovable things compared to magnetic wiggles, which can be read, altered, or destroyed at the touch of a teletypewriter key. For criminal purposes, funds can be fraudulently credited to an account, a bank balance can be programmed never to fail, or the record of ownership of very large sums can be changed.

This is not to say that computer crime is an overwhelming source of loss as yet. Robert Courtney, who is the man responsible for the safeguards that go into I.B.M. equipment—and who is therefore likely to be one of the first people called

when something goes wrong—ranks computer-related losses into six categories, in decreasing order of importance. The largest category, accounting for around half of all losses, is simply errors and omissions by clerical and data-processing employees. Next in order is employee dishonesty. Then come losses of data and equipment in fires; sabotage by disgruntled employees; water damage (i.e., floods and sprinkler-system malfunctions); and finally, an "other" category that includes remote manipulation of the system by outsiders.

But there seem to be reasons to fear that criminal losses—whether the work of insiders or of outsiders—will grow much larger as time goes by. For one thing, Courtney has found that employee dishonesty has risen from fourth place to second since 1972, which may mean that it just takes time for dishonest people to learn how to take advantage of their opportunities.

### THE VANISHING PAPER TRAIL

Outside of the world of EDP professionals, most of the present concern about the latent problem of computer security seems to have emerged since the widely publicized Equity Funding insurance swindle. While really more an instance of old-fashioned fraud than a feat of computer manipulation, the Equity Funding rip-off could hardly have reached the magnitude it did without the computer's adroitness in fooling auditors from four different accounting firms. The case pretty well demonstrated that conventional auditing practice is all but helpless when confronting deception involving computers. The auditors have lost their traditional "paper trail"—the detritus of indelibly inscribed orders, invoices, bills, and receipts that the men in the green eyeshades pore through on the track of irregularity.

The main group to benefit from the Equity Funding revelations has been the small but growing corps of specialists who claim to be able to write programs to make the computer do the auditing—that is, to perform various accounting cross-checks and to throw up a warning when certain suspicious transactions occur. This sort of auditing, however, like everything else that goes on inside a computer, is only as dependable as the computer itself. And unfortunately, computers can be programmed to lie or conceal as easily as they can be programmed for truth.

Inklings of the computer's special potential for fraudulent use began to surface in the 1960's. The earliest federal prosecution came in 1966 and involved a young programmer in a Minneapolis bank who instructed the computer to ignore all overdrafts from his account. In that case, discovery occurred when the computer failed one day and the bank had to go back to manual processing.

### A $30,000-A-DAY-GAMBLER

One of the more disturbing aspects of computer crime, in fact, is that detection, when it occurs, usually occurs by accident. Early last year, New York police raided a bookie and learned that one of his best customers was a man who for weeks at a time had gambled $30,000 a day. When detectives looked into the man's background, they discovered that he was an $11,000-a-year teller at New York's Union Dime Savings Bank. It turned out that he had access to one of the bank's computer terminals. For more than three years, he had been using the device to milk hundreds of savings accounts, netting $1.5 million.

Combining workaday larceny with computer skill, he would accept a customer's deposits at the teller window and pocket most of the money. Later, he would go to a terminal and type in false information to the machine or instructions to transfer money into the customer's account from one of hundreds of accounts that had shown little activity over several years.

Cases like this involve comparatively elementary manipulations of the computer toward narrow aims, fundamentally no different from what the ordinary dishonest bookkeeper might try to accomplish. Furthermore, they're the kind of thing that computer auditing should be able to prevent. In the last couple of years, however, it has come to be recognized that the newer generations of computers, by the nature of their design, are vulnerable to more cunning forms of subversion.

### THE "NONHOSTILE" ASSUMPTION

The leading expert on the history of computer crime is Donn Parker, a lanky former computer manager and now a researcher at Stanford Research Institute. Parker points out that "computer technology, over the years,

---

**Until not long ago, computer manufacturers and users saw little reason to fear that an unscrupulous person at one terminal would be able to read, alter, or delete another user's data, or tamper with the intricate programs that manipulate this data.**

was based upon the assumption of a benign, nonhostile environment." The machines were designed to provide maximum efficiency and convenience of operation by friendly, honest employees, within secure computer rooms to which access was limited.

In addition, the "third-generation" computers were put to uses not clearly anticipated by the designers. At the same time they were being developed, M.I.T. and other institutions were perfecting the concept of "time-sharing," which makes it possible for many individuals in remote locations to use the same machine simultaneously via terminals and telephone lines. Time-sharing put immense computational power at the fingertips of users who might never have been able to afford a computer of their own. A subsequent innovation, called "networking," made it possible to link several dispersed computers and data banks together, so that widely separated installations could share data.

### SLICING TIME THIN

In all such "multi-access" systems, each user has the impression that the entire computer is at his disposal. Actually, the machine may be serving many users at once, reading each user's typed commands, parceling out milliseconds of time, and entering and removing pieces of programs and data in and out of the arithmetic circuits and memory banks in rotation.

While it's doing all this, the system is supposed to keep every user's data separate from every other user's through a system of secret passwords or code numbers, together with "access controls" programmed into the system itself. Each person types in his number or password at the beginning of his session to identify himself as a legitimate user. The access controls then specify what data and programs he is authorized to use, and "tag" and keep track of his work as it moves through the stages of processing.

These housekeeping functions are controlled by an immensely complex collection of special supervisory programs, called the "operating system." The supervisory programs are permanently stored in the computer and are altogether distinct from the "applications programs," which are the instructions for carrying out special tasks, such as a payroll run, a bank's daily accounting, or a scientific problem.

For all its central role in managing and safeguarding the resources in a multi-access computer, the typical operating system of today is pathetically exposed to tampering. For one thing, manufacturers and users have to be able to make changes in the system's programs. Many of these errors in concept or execution must be located and corrected before the system will work at all, but some remain hidden, or annoyingly evident, for years.

In many systems, therefore, all that a would-be wrongdoer needs is to be familiar with the manufacturer's manuals, know the telephone number of the target installation, and have access to a terminal. Then he can

## Computerized Dating or Matchmaking
HARVEY MATUSOW

The many companies throughout the United States and Great Britain which have been set up as "matchmakers" or "Find a Compatible Date" services, have in many cases a much broader reason for existence. By filling in the form and sending in your fee, you are helping to establish a selective mailing list for the selling of goods. Once "x" thousand names, with all the information has been assembled, the computer dating service can rent these lists to stores and companies who want to sell their product. They can tell the company that they want a list of 5000 people, male or female, white, or black, car owners, or sports car buffs. Maybe they want people who read two books a week. Or perhaps people who go to museums.

The following is typical of the sort of information called for in the application—and it should be self-evident what other uses can be made from having this amount of information available on large sections of the population. If nothing else, it's been a boon to many advertising agencies—and a big money-maker for many of the computer date services.

1. Your age _____
2. Your occupation _____
3. Your height: _____
4. Your weight: _____
5. Your sex: ☐ Male ☐ Female
6. Your race:
   ☐ White ☐ Negro ☐ Oriental ☐ Other
7. Your religion:
   ☐ Protestant ☐ Catholic ☐ Jewish ☐ Other ☐ None
8. Religious convictions:
   ☐ Strong ☐ Average ☐ Little ☐ None
9. Birthplace:
   ☐ U.S.A. ☐ English-speaking country ☐ Spanish-speaking ☐ Other
10. Health
    ☐ Excellent ☐ Normally Good ☐ Often Poor ☐ Poor
11. Hair color:
    ☐ Blonde ☐ Red ☐ Brown ☐ Black
12. Hair style
    ☐ Long ☐ Average ☐ Short
13. Years high school completed
    ☐1 ☐2 ☐3 ☐4
14. Years university completed
    ☐1 ☐2 ☐3 ☐4
15. Years of post-graduate
    ☐1 ☐2 ☐3 ☐4 ☐5 ☐6

dial in, identify himself somehow as a legitimate user, and type in commands that make the system reveal its passwords, the names of other users, their privileges, data files, etc. Once he has the passwords, any user can then masquerade as another user or as a staffer with authorization to make changes in the system's password-privilege list, or, for that matter, in the operating system's own programs.

## THE PERILS OF COMPLEXITY
Like the passwords, the systems-command code words are arbitrarily chosen and can be changed as easily as the lock on a door. That would foil inexpert intruders, but crack programmers have demonstrated that it's not necessary to know the systems commands to take over any major operating system that now exists. For one thing, each of the command code words is really a shorthand symbol that stands for a prewritten miniprogram stored in the computer. When the word is used, this program carries out the various steps required to unlock the system's safeguards. A skilled would-be penetrator with access to the proper manuals can deduce everything he needs to write his own program, type it in, and subvert an operating system.

Another important kind of vulnerability derives from the sheer complexity of today's operating systems. To cope with all eventualities in a time-sharing network, some operating systems run to hundreds of thousands of separate instructions. In the composition of something like that, hundreds of errors inevitably creep in—either oversights in the design of the safeguards or simple mistakes in the writing of the instructions.

Under certain circumstances, these errors will let data leak from one user's domain to another's, or even open a way into the supposedly inviolate territory of the operating system itself. Many a subscriber to a commercial timesharing service, having accidentally pressed a certain combination of keys, has found someone else's data rattling out unbidden. By now, a lot of people have learned how to exploit software errors deliberately—not only to read data stored in the machine, but also to type in changes in access-control safeguards, data, and programs.

## ATTACKS BY TIGER TEAMS
The first delighted exploiters of these software quirks were the "systems hackers"—students at universities where some of the first time-sharing systems were installed as far back as the middle Sixties.

Among other things, faculty members stored grades and examinations on some of these systems, and systems hackers became adept at changing their own grades or reading upcoming exam questions.

By the late Sixties, computer experts at Rand Corp. were warning their government patrons that all the

> **The base form of an asset is no longer necessarily a 400-ounce gold bar; now assets are often simply magnetic wiggles on a disk.**

16. Your rank in school
    □ upper ¼ □ Upper ⅓ □ Upper ½ □ Other
17. Do you watch TV?
    □ Often □ Seldom □ Sometimes □ Never
18. Do you read books?
    □ Often □ Seldom □ Sometimes □ Never
19. How often do you read newspapers?
    □ Daily □ Several times week □ Never
20. What are your favorite kind of films? (check all that apply)
    □ Westerns □ Musicals □ War □ Adventure □ Dramas □ Cartoons
    □ Comedies □ Travel □ Foreign □ Documentaries □ Horror □ None
21. What kind of magazines do you read? (check all that apply)
    □ News □ Fashion □ Literary □ Movie □ General Interest □ Comics
    □ Sport □ Special Interest □ None
22. What languages do you speak fluently? (check all that apply)
    □ English □ Spanish □ German □ French □ Other
23. What type of music do you like? (check all that apply)
    □ Folk □ Popular □ Religious □ Country & Western □ Jazz □ Classics
    □ Latin American □ Light Classics □ None
24. Which of the following activities do you enjoy? (check all that apply)
    □ Cinema □ Writing □ Reading □ Driving □ Household Chores
    □ Bowling □ Pottering □ Dancing □ Talking □ Drinking □ Fishing
    □ Camping □ Working □ Loafing □ Thinking □ Gardening □ Necking
    □ Chess □ Parties □ Flying □ Travelling □ Studying □ Shopping
    □ Attending Meetings □ Playing Music □ Collecting □ Gambling □ Listening to Music □ Walking □ Building Things □ Creating Art □ Outdoor Sports □ Eating □ Watching Sports Events □ Competing in Sports
25. Where do you usually go when you date? (check all that apply)
    □ Cinema □ Dances □ Lunch □ Dinner □ Driving Around □ Pubs □ Concerts □ Plays □ Bowling □ Weekend Trips □ Sport Events □ Each Other's Home □ Outdoor Activities.
26. Which qualities do you like most in a date? (check all that apply)
    □ Physique □ Loyalty □ Compliance □ Intelligence □ Sensitivity
    □ Sense of Humor □ Honesty □ Daring □ Understanding □ Looks
    □ Virtue □ Sophistication □ Money □ Mystery □ Self-assurance
    □ Popularity □ Decisiveness □ Excitement
27. How much is usually spent when you date?:
    □ Less than £1 □ £2 to £4 □ £4 to £6 □ More than £6
28. What sort of people do you feel most at home with?
    □ Outdoorsmen □ Intellectuals □ Swingers □ Artistic People □ Professionals □ Working People □ Cultured People □ Average Folks □ None

*(continued on page 150)*

WAITING FOR THE GREAT COMPUTER RIP-OFF   **149**

multi-access systems on the market were vulnerable. Over the years since then, under contracts with the Defense Department, Rand and a number of other organizations have been seeking methods to improve operating-system security, as well as methods to ascertain whether any system is really secure. The most glamorous phase of this activity is the work of the "tiger teams," who actually try to penetrate systems being considered for defense uses. So far, no major system has withstood a dedicated attack by a tiger team.

The disturbing implications of all this for civilian computer operations are only now coming to be widely recognized. In principle, the ability to take over a computer's operating system implies having access to all data and all programs on the machine, together with the ability to distort them at will. Properly done, such subversion is likely to go undetected. For criminal purposes, such control would be something like having a small army of corrupt bookkeepers at one's command, but without all the risks of exposure that relying on the cooperation of human beings entails.

With the increasing use of these systems as repositories and conveyors of valuable assets and private and proprietary data of incalculable worth, a number of computer professionals have begun speculating about the grave potentialities for criminal manipulation of computer systems. Among them is Clark Weissman, a manager of computer-security research with System Development Corp. Weissman believes that a lot of criminal activity could already be going on, leaving no external evidence.

"Sherlock Holmes," he says, "can't come in and find any heel marks. There's no safe with its door blown off. Many companies wouldn't even know their data's been manipulated." As for auditing programs, "the first thing the interloper would do is corrupt the audit-trail software itself."

## "THE COMPANIES JUST EAT 'EM' "

No one has valid statistics as to how much of this sophisticated subversion goes on, but from all indications, a lot more goes on than is ever detected. Donn Parker concludes that of nearly 175 cases of computer crime he has looked into, hardly any were uncovered through normal security precautions and accounting controls—nearly all were exposed by happenstance. One expert guesses that the ratio of undiscovered to discovered crimes may be on the order of a hundred to one.

A lot of the computer crime that *is* detected, moreover, is never publicly announced. Most security experts have collections of incidents that they have investigated but that were never reported to the police. Furthermore, some banks and companies candidly admit that when an incident is discovered, the corporate victims usually try to avoid the embarrassment and loss of confidence that publicity might bring. According to I.B.M.'s Robert Courtney, "It's generally accepted in this business that about 85 percent of detected frauds are never brought to the attention of law-enforcement people. The companies just eat 'em. Of the 15 percent that are announced, a fair

---

29. What size community were you brought up in?
    ☐ Small Town ☐ Small City ☐ Medium-sized City ☐ Large City
30. How many brothers & sisters do you have?
    ☐ 3 or more ☐ 1 or 2 ☐ None
31. Do you support yourself?
    ☐ Yes ☐ Partially ☐ No
32. Do you feel that premarital sex can be justified?
    ☐ Yes ☐ No ☐ It Depends
33. Do you like going steady?
    ☐ Yes ☐ No ☐ It Depends
34. Have you been engaged?
    ☐ Yes, Several Times ☐ Yes, Once ☐ No
35. Have you been married?
    ☐ Yes (Childless) ☐ Yes (Have Children) ☐ No
36. How often do you date?
    ☐ Almost Every Night ☐ A Few Times a Month ☐ A Few Times a Week ☐ Irregularly ☐ Once a Week ☐ Seldom
37. Where do you live?
    ☐ With parents ☐ Share a Flat ☐ Dormitory ☐ Own Apartment
38. When would you like to get married?
    ☐ Soon ☐ In a Few Years ☐ Not for a Long Time
39. Are you considered attractive?
    ☐ Yes, Very ☐ Usually ☐ Sometimes ☐ No
40. Are most of your dates considered attractive?
    ☐ Yes ☐ Usually ☐ No
41. Would you date members of other religions?
    ☐ Yes ☐ Preferably No ☐ No
42. What kind of car do you own?
    ☐ Sedan ☐ Compact ☐ Foreign ☐ Sports ☐ None
43. Do you enjoy wearing old clothing?
    ☐ Often ☐ Sometimes ☐ Never
44. Do you like children?
    ☐ Yes ☐ No ☐ It Depends
45. What age group do you usually date?
    ☐ My Own ☐ Somewhat Older ☐ A Lot Younger ☐ A Lot Older ☐ Somewhat Younger ☐ It Varies
46. How much do you drink?
    ☐ A Lot ☐ Just Socially ☐ Not at All
47. How much do you smoke?
    ☐ A Lot ☐ Occasionally ☐ Not at All

number are brought in from the outside by the police."

What often happens is that the offender, once detected, is required to make restitution and then leave—sometimes even getting severance pay and letters of reference to speed him away. One consequence, no doubt, is a circulating population of unpunished, unrepentant, and unrecognized embezzlers going from company to company. Probably a more serious consequence, though, has been to suppress recognition of the extent of computer crime, and thereby to lull both makers and users of computers into minimizing it as a threat.

# Art Professor Generates 3-D Art Using Computer
*Computers and Automation*

University of Massachusetts Art Professor Robert Mallary has been using a computer as an assistant in generating three-dimensional art. Mr. Mallary is one of the pioneers in this country in developing specific computer programs for sculpture which allow the computer to determine shapes. TRAN 2, Mr. Mallary's program, establishes sets of numerical co-ordinates in the computer's memory which can be used to sketch out an abstract, three-dimensional shape. Varying the numbers can squeeze, stretch or twist this shape in a nearly infinite number of variations. He uses an IBM 1130 computer because its output hardware includes a computer driven plotter that can draw out his shapes. The computer and plotter can be programmed to draw the shape from a variety of sides and a variety of angles.

The plotter also can be directed to draw out a set of contour slices. The contour printout is photographed, projected into plastic, plywood or other material, thus forming the pattern for the sections of the finished sculpture. Mr. Mallary cuts out the sections, drills a center axis, and cements the slices into the finished shape around a metal center rod. Smoothing and finishing completes the piece.

His first computer work, a laminated plexiglass piece, named Quad I, was exhibited at the Institute of Contemporary Art in London in the summer of 1968. Quad III, at the left, a laminated luaun veneer piece sixty inches high, was included in a 1968 Whitney Museum exhibition of the contemporary American sculpture, and the following spring at the Contemporary Crafts Museum in New York City.

Mr. Mallary sees a big future for computer sculpture. "Linked to a tape-driven machine tool a computer might produce 100 or 200 small carvings an hour. Most of these might be thrown away but one or two could become the prototypes for large-scale works." He predicts that ultimately the computer may even be able to "learn" the stylistic preferences and idiosyncracies of the sculptor who is using it, retain this information and be able to produce works "in the manner of" the sculptor.

"*Are you sure you have the computer programmed correctly, Dick?*"

# Decisions and Public Opinion

DONALD MICHAEL

The government must turn to computers to handle many of its major problems simply because the data involved are so massive and the factors so complex that only machines can handle the material fast enough to allow timely action based on understanding of the facts. In the nature of the situation, the decisions made by the government with the help of computers would be based in good part on computers that have been programmed with more or less confidential information—and privileged access to information, at the time it is needed, is a sufficient if not always necessary condition for attaining and maintaining power. There may not be any easy way to insure that decisions based on computers could not become a threat to democratic government. Most of the necessary inputs for the government's computer systems are available only to the government, because it is the only institution with sufficiently extensive facilities for massive surveys.

It may be impossible to allow much of the government, to say nothing of the public, access to the kind of information we have been discussing. But let us assume that somehow the operation of the government has been reorganized so that procedures are enforced to permit competing political parties and other private organizations to have access to the government's raw data, to have parallel systems for the processing of data as well as to have access to the government's computer programs. Even then, most people will be incapable of judging the validity of one contending computer program compared to another, or whether the policies based on them are appropriate.

This condition exists today about military postures. These are derived in good part from computer analyses and computer-based games that produce probabilities based on programmed assumptions about weapon systems and our own and the enemy's behavior. Here the intellectual ineffectualness of the layman is obscured by the secrecy that keeps him from finding out what he probably would not be able to understand anyway.

If this sounds condescending, it only needs to be pointed out that there are large areas of misunderstanding and misinterpretation among the military too. At any given time, some of these people do not fully appreciate the relationships between the programs used in the computers and the real world in which the consequences are supposed to follow. As it is now, the average intelligent man has little basis for judging the differing opinions of economists about the state of the economy or even about the reasons for the past state. He also has little basis for appraising the conflicting opinions among scientists and engineers about the costs and results of complex scientific developments such as man in space. In both examples, computers play important roles in the esoteric arguments involved.

Thus, even if people may have more leisure time to attend more closely to politics, they may not have the ability to contribute to the formulation of policy. Some observers feel that the middle class does not now take a strong interest in voting and is alienated from its responsibility for the conduct of government. Leisure may not change this trend, especially when government becomes in large part the complex computer operation that it must necessarily become.

Significant public opinion may come from only a relatively small portion of the public: those who are able to follow the battles of the computers and to understand the implications of their programs; and those who are concerned with government policy but who are outside of or unfamiliar with the computer environment.

For this segment of the voting population differences over decisions that are made or should be made might become more intense and more irreconcilable. Already there is a difference of opinion among intelligent men about the problem of the proper roles in American foreign policy of military weapons, arms control, and various levels of disarmament. One side accuses its opponents of naïveté or ignorance about the "facts" (computer-based), and the other side objects to the immorality or political insensibilities of its opponents. Many aspects of the problem involve incommensurables; most are too complex to stand simplification in order to appeal to the larger public or to an unsophisticated congressman. Yet the arguments *are* simplified for these purposes and the result is fantastic confusion.

As for the selection of the men who are to plan or make policy, a computerized government will require different training from that which executive personnel in most governmental agencies have today. Certainly, without such training (and perhaps with it) there is bound to be a deepening of the split between politics and facts.

In business and industry the shift has already begun toward recruiting top management from the cadre of engineering and laboratory administration, for these are the people who understand the possibilities of and are sympathetic to computer-based thinking. In government the trend has not been as clear-cut, but it is noteworthy that the scientist, as high-level adviser, is a recent innovation and one clearly here to stay.

For reasons of personality as well as professional perspective, many operations researchers and systems analysts have great difficulty in coping with the more ambiguous and less "logical" aspects of society. Their temperament, training, and sympathies may not incline them to indulge the slow, ponderous, illogical, and emotional tendencies of democratic processes. Or they may ignore the extralogical nature of man. Emphasis on "logic," in association with the other factors we have mentioned, may encourage a trend toward the recruitment of authoritarian personalities. There is no necessary correlation between the desire to apply scientific logic to problems and the desire to apply democratic principles to daily, or even to professional scientific, life.

The psychological influence of computers is overwhelming: they symbolize and reënforce the potency of America's belief in the utility of science and technology. There is a sense of security in nicely worked-up curves and complex displays of information which are the products of almost unimaginably intricate and elegant machinery. In general, the influence of computers will continue to be enhanced if those who use them attend chiefly to those components of reality which can be put into a computer and processed by it, and the important values will become those which are compatible with this approach to analyzing and manipulating the world. For example, the influence of computers has already been sufficiently strong to seduce military planners and civil defense planners *away* from those aspects of their problems which are not now subject to data processing.

**There may not be any easy way to insure that decisions based on computers could not become a threat to democratic government.**

Computers are especially useful for dealing with social situations that pertain to people in the mass, such as traffic control, financial transactions, mass-demand consumer goods, allocation of resources, etc. They are so useful in these areas that they undoubtedly will help to seduce planners into inventing a society with goals that can be dealt with in the mass rather than in terms of the individual. In fact, the whole trend toward cybernation can be seen as an effort to remove the variabilities in man's on-the-job behavior and off-the-job needs which, because of their nonstatistical nature, complicate production and consumption. Thus, somewhere along the line, the idea of the individual may be swallowed up in statistics. The planner and those he plans for may become divorced from one another, and the alienation of the individual from his government and individual from individual within government may grow ever greater.

Computers will inevitably be used to plan employment for those displaced by cybernation. This may lead to a more rationalized society than could otherwise be invented, with a more adequate allocation of jobs. But one wonders whether it will not also lead, on a national scale, to an attitude in the planner of relative indifference to the individual.

What will be the consequences for our relations with underdeveloped nations of a government that sees the world through computers? With our general public alienated from its own productive and governmental processes and our leadership seemingly successful through its use of computer-based planning and control, our government may well become more and more incapable of recognizing the differences between the needs, aspirations, and customs of these nations and those of our own country.

On the other hand, the emphasis on human behavior as a statistical reality may encourage revisions in the temporal scale of government planning and programs. Time is a statistical property in cybernated systems: it takes time for variables to average out, to rise or fall in their effects, and the time period usually is not a fiscal year or some small multiple thereof. Thus, perhaps we can hope for more sensible long-range planning in government as a result of the computer's need for long time periods in which to make its statistical models work out.

The implications of the concentration of decision making within business firms as a result of cybernation are not as clear-cut as the effects for government. In principle, both big and small businesses will be able to know much more about the nature of their markets and of their organizational operations through cybernation. Whether or not this will help both big and small proportionately is far from clear. Big business will undoubtedly have better facilities for information and decisions, but small business may be able to get what it needs by buying it from service organizations that will come into existence for this purpose.

Big organizations will be able to afford high-priced personnel for doing the thinking beyond that done by the machines. If quality of thinking is always related to price, the big organizations will be able to put their small competitors out of business. But the big organizations, precisely because of their size, may have relatively little maneuverability, and some of the best minds may find the little organization a more exciting game. Whether the little organizations could stay afloat is moot, but one can anticipate some exciting entrepreneurial maneuvers among the small firms while they last.

### THE CONTROL OF CYBERNATION
Time is crucial in any plan to cope with cybernation. Ways of ameliorating its adverse effects require thinking

farther ahead than we ever do. In a society in the process of becoming cybernated, education and training for work as well as education and training for leisure must begin early in life. Shifts in behavior, attitudes, and aspirations take a long time to mature. It will be extraordinarily difficult to produce appropriate "culture-bearers," both parents and teachers, in sufficient numbers, distribution, and quality in the relatively brief time available. It is hard to see, for example, how Congress, composed in good part of older men acting from traditional perspectives and operating by seniority, could recognize and then legislate well enough to produce the fundamental shifts needed to meet the complexities of cybernation.

It is hard to see how our style of pragmatic making-do and frantic crash programs can radically change in the next few years. This is especially hard to visualize when the cybernation situation is such that we find it impossible to determine the consequences of cybernation even in the medium long run. "Drastic" actions to forestall or eliminate the ill effects of cybernation will not be taken in time unless we change our operating style drastically.

Among the many factors contributing to the stability of a social system are two intimately intertwined ones: the types of tasks that are performed; and the nature of the relationship between the attitudes of the members of the society toward these tasks and their opinions about the proper goals of the individual members of the society and the right ways of reaching them.

The long-range stability of the social system depends on a population of young people properly educated to enter the adult world of tasks and attitudes. Once, the pace of change was slow enough to permit a comfortable margin of compatibility between the adult world and the one children were trained to expect. Now we have to ask: What should be the

**A computerized government will require different training from that which executive personnel in most governmental agencies have today.**

education of a population more and more enveloped in cybernation? What are the appropriate attitudes toward, and training for, participation in government, the use of leisure, standards of consumption, particular occupations?

Education must cope with the transitional period when the disruption among different socio-economic and occupational groups will be the greatest; and the later, relatively stable period, if it ever comes to exist, when most people would have adequate income and shorter working hours. The problem involves looking ahead five, ten, twenty years to see what are likely to be the occupational and social needs and attitudes of those future periods; planning the intellectual and social education of each age group in the numbers needed; motivating young people to seek certain types of jobs and to adopt the desirable and necessary attitudes; providing enough suitable teachers; being able to alter all of these as society and technology indicate; and directing the pattern of cybernation so that it fits with the expected kinds and distribution of abilities and attitudes produced by home and school.

To what extent education and technology can be coördinated is not at all clear, if only because we do not know, even for today's world, the criteria for judging the consonance or dissonance in our educational, attitudinal, and occupational systems. We think that parts of the social system are badly out of phase with other parts and that the system is progressively less capable of coping with the problems it produces. But there is little consensus on the "causes" and even less on what can be done about them.

If we do not find the answers to these questions soon, we will have a population more and more out of touch with national and international realities, ever more the victims of insecurity on the one hand and ennui on the other, and more and more mismatched to the occupational needs of the day.

Perhaps time has already run out. Even if our style somehow should shift to long-range planning, it would not eliminate the inadequate training and inadequate values of much of

**The psychological influence of computers is overwhelming: they symbolize and reenforce the potency of America's belief in the utility of science and technology.**

our present adolescent and preadolescent population, as well as of those adults who will be displaced or remain unhired as a result of cybernation in the next decade. Only a partial solution exists in this case: begin now a program of economic and social first aid for these people.

Can we control the effects of cybernation by making it illegal or unprofitable to develop cybernation technology? Not without virtually stopping the development of almost all of new technology and a good part of the general development of scientific knowledge. The accumulation of knowledge in many areas of science depends on computers. To refine computers and make them more versatile requires research in almost every scientific area. It also requires the development of a technology, usually automated, to produce the articles needed to build new computers. As long as we choose to compete with other parts of the world, we shall have to develop new products and new means for producing them better. Cybernation is the only way to do it on a significant scale. As long as we choose to live in a world guided by science and its technology we have no choice but to encourage the development of cybernation. Then the answers to coping with it must be found elsewhere than in a moratorium on its development.

There has always been tension between big industry, with its concern for profit and market control, and government, with its concern for the national interest. The tension has increased as big business has become so large as to be quasi-governmental in its influence and as government has had to turn to and even subsidize parts of business in order to meet parts of the national interest within a free-enterprise framework. Thus we can expect strong differences between government and business as to when and where it is socially legitimate to introduce automation.

In theory, control could be exercised by private enterprise. But in the unlikely case that competitors could see their mutual interests clearly enough to join forces, the very act of coöperative control would be incompatible with our antitrust laws.

Whether the government or some alter-government comprised of business, labor, and industry were to do the controlling, either group would have to undertake a degree of national planning and control thoroughly incompatible with the way in which we look upon the management of our economic and social system today.

### THE DATA BANKERS

who are the men with hats
who go to my neighbor
who tells them I drink with
whoever comes along and
where I go between the hours of . . . and
where I was when they said it was a rest
where really my husband sent me
where I could sober up
when after all his debts
when he played the horses once too many
when I told him we'd be broke
like they are polite but she hates me
like I hate her, she's real nosy
like; and her kid, too, who's a peeping tom
like I found him up our fire escape
how he got there they don't care
how is not their business or why
how to get it all down and in the bank that's
how those guys spend their time: saving us up.

CELIA GILBERT

# The Snooping Machine

ALAN WESTIN

If the government has its say, the budget department's giant computer will take the first step toward stripping away your last vestiges of privacy

The year is 1980. The place is a suburb in the United States. The setting is a record-control society that could make George Orwell's Oceania almost look like a haven of privacy.

At seven A.M., our typical citizen, an engineer named Roger M. Smith, wakes up, dresses, has breakfast and gets ready to commute by car to his office in Central City. Already, heat, light and water records fed directly from his home to the Central City Utility Corporation (for purposes of billing and use analysis) provide data that can establish when Smith got up and just how he moved through his house.

Smith takes his car out of the garage and drives onto the turnpike, heading downtown. As he reaches the tollgate, his license plate is automatically scanned by a television camera and his number is sent instantaneously to an on-line computer containing lists of wanted persons, stolen cars and traffic-ticket violators. If Smith's plate registers a positive response, police stationed 100 yards along the turnpike will have the signal before Smith's car reaches their position.

As he stops at the tollgate, Smith gives the initial performance of what will be a ritual repeated many times during the day. He places his right thumb in front of a scanning camera. At the same time, he recites into the unit's microphone, "Smith, Roger M., 2734-2124-4806." Roger has just used his thumbprint, voiceprint and personal identification number to carry out his first financial transaction of the day.

Roger's inputs are carried swiftly by data line to the Downtown National Bank, the central depository of Roger's financial account. Though he may have accounts in other banks throughout the country, these are all registered and monitored by the bank in Smith's place of residence or work. When the thumbprint and voiceprint recorded at the tollgate are compared with the bank's master prints, establishing that it is really "Smith, Roger M., 2734-2124-4806," the bank's computer posts a 75-cent charge to his account and flashes a 75-cent credit to the bank holding the Turnpike Authority account.

Throughout his typical day, when he parks at the Triangle Garage, is registered in and out of the company office for payroll verification, has lunch at Jimmy's East, makes purchases at Macy's, goes to Central City Stadium for a ball game, places a bet on the daily double, buys plane tickets, settles his hotel bill or buys 500 shares of Electronic Computers Unlimited, Roger Smith will use no cash. Money has been eliminated, except for pocket-change transactions.

Of course, all of Roger's regular, continuing obligations are paid automatically from his account—his mortgage installments, insurance premiums, magazine subscriptions, organizational membership dues, etc. Those continuing accounts that fluctuate monthly are also verified and paid automatically—medical bills, psychiatrist's fees, gasoline charges, telephone bills, pay-TV account, book-club purchases, etc. All financial credits to Roger's account, each carefully identified as to the source and classified as to the basis for payment, go directly to the bank, not to Roger. Roger's various federal, state and local tax obligations are determined by computer analysis and are automatically paid when due.

This is a superb system—efficient, practical and far cheaper than the money economy with which mankind fumbled along for so long. But one by-product of the cashless society is that every significant movement and transaction of Roger Smith's life has produced a permanent record in the computer memory system. As he spends, uses and travels, he leaves an intransmutable and centralized documentary trail behind him. To those with access to his financial account, Roger Smith's life is an open tape.

But the daily denuding of Roger Smith has only begun. For every person in the United States in 1980, there are four master files. His complete educational record, from preschool nursery to postgraduate evening course in motorboat economics, is in an educational dossier, including the results of all intelligence, aptitude and personality tests he's taken, ratings by instructors and peers and computer analyses of his projected educational capacities.

Roger's complete employment record contains entries for every job he has held, with rate of pay, supervisors' evaluations, psychometric test results, recommendations, outside interests, family milieu and a computer-analyzed, up-to-date job-security profile. All of this is available for instant print-out when an employer wants to consider Roger for a job or a promotion.

Roger's financial file is probably the largest. It contains a selected history of his financial transactions, from his earliest entry into the computerized economy to his latest expenditure for a new Carramba-35 sports car. His patterns of earnings, fixed expenditures, discretionary spending, computer-projected earning capacity and similar items are all kept ready, so that decisions involving loans, mortgages, insurance and other credit-line transactions for Roger Smith are made with full knowledge of his fiscal history.

Finally, there is Roger's national citizenship file. This is a unified Federal-state-local dossier that contains all of Roger's life history that is "of relevance" to Government. In 1980, that is quite a broad category. It includes his birth facts and permanent identification number, his educational file in full (after all, it was either public education or publicly assisted), his military service, all the information from his license applications, income-tax records and Social Security data and, if he now works or worked in the past as a Government employee, consultant or contractor, his public employment record and assorted security clearances. If Roger was ever arrested for a crime other than a minor traffic violation, a special public-offender intelligence file is opened on Roger Smith that includes a large base of information relating to his educational, employment, military, family and civic activity. Citizenship files also include a personal-health category, developed to aid public-health measures and to assist individuals caught in health crises away from their home physicians. This contains a complete medical dossier from birth condition and psychosexual development to reports of last week's immunization shot, cardiogram flutter or extended-depression check-up. Most important of all, these four master files on education, employment, finances and citizenship can be put together into one unified print-out whenever a Government agency with subpoena power chooses to do so.

For purposes of economic forecasting, demographic studies and behavioral prediction, the data base such a dossier society has created provides unequaled opportunities for research and policy analysis. For enforcement of public programs—educational reforms, integration rules, crime control, mental health—the national file system brings unparalleled advantages. But crucial elements of privacy in a free society, such as the partial anonymity of life, limited circulation of personal information and preservation of confidence in certain intimate relationships, are the bleeding casualties of a dossier society. For the Roger Smiths of 1980, life is by, on and for the record.

How does the record net work? For Roger Smith, who started work as an engineer at Consolidated Technics in the "old personnel system" days of 1970, the flash of understanding came when he was considered for the key promotion of his career, a possible move from engineering supervisor at Consolidated Technics to deputy vice-president for engineering at General Space, Incorporated. As Roger sat in the office of the information-system analyst (formerly personnel director) of General Space, he found himself staring at a print-out that had just been handed to him. It was titled "Inconsistent Items for Personal Explanation at Assessment Interview." As he scanned the list, he found these items:

1. *High School Personality Test Profile.* High score on the Fosdick Artistic and Literary Interest Inventory; technical career rated "doubtful."
2. *Criminal Record.* Disturbing-the-peace conviction, Daytona Beach, Florida, age 18. Speeding tickets, New Jersey Turnpike, 1974, 1975.
3. *Civic Activity.* Signed antidraft petition circulated by Colgate University chapter, Make Love Not War Society. Door registers showed attendance at campus lecture by George Lincoln Rockwell, age 20.
4. *Income Management Rating.* B—. Average annual personal loan held during past five years—$3000 to $5000. Balance in savings account on April 1, $217.41.

"If you have studied this long enough," the information-system analyst broke in, "let me briefly explain our procedure here to you. You are one of four men being considered for this position. We want you to take as much time as you need to write out an explanation of these items in your record. Your answers should be in terms of how these items might affect a possible career for you here at General Space, Incorporated. Keep in mind that we do seventy-five percent of our work for the Federal Space Voyage Program, and that involves classified information. The explanations you give us will become part of your general personnel files, of course, including the disposition we make of your employment review.

"Since this is the first time you seem to have applied for a job under the new computerized career-analysis system, let me reassure you that this is not an unusually large number of inconsistent items to be presented with. Your complete file runs close to two hundred and fifty pages, which is about the average length for a man of your age. However, I think it is only fair to tell you that two of the men being evaluated for the position have no inconsistencies to comment on as part of their personal interviews. After you have done this on several occasions, you will probably get used to it. . . ."

At this point, the late Rod Serling should appear on the television screen, grin his raffish grin and say, "Portrait of life in a fish bowl, somewhere in the Twilight Zone." We should all be able to smile appreciatively at his superb science-fiction imagination and then check the late movie on channel two. The trouble is that Roger Smith's dilemma is closer to reality than we think, both technologically and as a matter of social trends in America.

Consider first the question of technological feasibility. The average person knows that computers can collect and store vast amounts of data, search this with great swiftness, make comparisons and collations and

---

**Where normal recording has been about 5600 bits of information on an inch of magnetic tape, the new laser process can put *645,000,000* bits in microscopic parallel rows on each inch. And the recording process achieves speeds of *12,000,000* bits per second.**

# Looking for a Rare Coin? Computer May Hold Your Answer
GENE SHELTON
ALEXANDER SCOTT

A downtown Dallas business firm has put a million-dollar computer to work—looking for pennies. And dimes and quarters. The coins are special. They are rare coins, much in demand among collectors throughout the nation.

The Dallas firm, Steve Ivy Rare Coin Co., Metropolitan Mall, #7, 1310 Elm Street, does a quarter-million dollars' worth of business each month with coin collectors from coast to coast. With such a business volume and thousands of rare coins in the bank vaults and store inventory, Steve Ivy, president of the firm, wanted to find a better and faster way to serve the customer looking for a specific coin.

"The computer lets us know instantly if we have the coin a customer wants in stock," Ivy said. "If we don't, then we can go to our teletype system and find it for him. We're the first rare coin company in the Southwest to utilize a computer to improve customer service."

The computer, he explained, can tell an employee instantly if a customer's request for an 1880 proof silver dollar from a specific mint is in stock. In the past, looking up that information manually from an inventory of thousands of coins could be a time-consuming project.

Two terminals, one a visual display cathode ray tube resembling a television set and another a teletype printer, connect the Dallas firm with the central computer on a time-sharing arrangement. The Alpha Systems DEC 10 computer is located in the data processing firm's Noel Page building in Dallas. The computer also performs bookkeeping chores, including invoicing, and generates a number of reports useful to management in keeping abreast of the rare coin market.

The firm maintains teletype communications with 150 dealers across the nation and has Telex communications with world gold and silver markets, including Zurich. The staff logs some 150,000 miles per year attending shows and rare coin auctions throughout the country.

Ivy, 23, has been a coin collector since age 8. The son of a Fort Worth attorney, Ivy opened the rare coin business in Dallas in January of 1970.

---

engage in machine-to-machine exchanges of data, all at quite reasonable cost per bit of information. Despite this general awareness, there is still a common tendency to believe that "technological limitations" make it impossible to collect information for a dossier system of the detail described for Roger Smith.

Such a belief is simply nonsense. To illustrate this fact, we need only look at one data memory process recently developed by the Precision Instrument Company of Palo Alto, California. This system uses a one-watt, continuous-wave argon laser to burn minute "pits" in the opaque coating of plastic computer tape. The laser is so precise and can be focused so intensely that each pit is only one micron, or .000039 inch in size. Where normal recording has been about 5600 bits of information on an inch of magnetic tape, the new laser process can put 645,000,000 bits in microscopic parallel rows on each inch. And the recording process achieves speeds of 12,000,000 bits per second.

Once recorded, the information is permanently available for use. To read the data, a lower-powered laser beam examines the tape as it flies past at high velocity, translating the light that shines through the pits into an electrical pulse that is sent to a print-out machine or a computer for further use.

In terms of a dossier society, the laser memory system means that a single 4800-foot reel of one-inch tape could contain about 20 double-spaced typed pages of data on every person in the United States—man, woman and child. It would take only four minutes to retrieve a person's dossier under such a system. With 100 reels of tape, stored in a room no larger than 15 feet by 20 feet, 2000 pages of data could be maintained on every American. Allowing extra time to locate the particular reel on which a subject's file was stored, his entire 2000-page dossier could be retrieved in about ten minutes.

The cashless society lies equally within technological reach. Enough computers could easily be produced to handle the volume of transactions that would be generated by an automatic economy. Remote-point inquiries and inputs from small desktop units to a central computer are in common use today in airline- and hotel-reservation systems. New types of telephone instruments, such as the Bell Touch Tone card-dialing system, allow bills to be paid from the home and permit merchants to verify availability of funds before releasing products to purchasers. Vending machines have been developed that use optical scanners to accept credit cards. Though there are still some problems in achieving unique identification of each individual by single fingerprint or voiceprint, simultaneous use of these techniques could now prevent all but the most elaborately conceived frauds. Any losses of this kind would probably be far less than those currently sustained by check forgery and stolen credit cards. Technologically, then, we now have the capability of installing a computerized economic system.

Even though both the dossier network and the automated economy are technologically possible, this does not mean that American society has to use its capabilities in this way. Why shouldn't we dismiss this prospect as something that Government and private organizations would never think of adopting? The answer is that several basic social trends in American life have been moving us in precisely such a direction during the past two decades.

The first of these trends is the enormous expansion of information gathering and record keeping in our society. Partly, this stems from factors such as the increasing complexity of our industrial system, the expansion of regulatory, welfare and security functions by Government and the growth of large-scale bureaucracies in our corporations, universities, unions and churches. Partly, the growth in record collection stems from the breakdown of traditional, face-to-face techniques for personal evaluation of individuals by authorities. In an age of increased personal mobility, nationalization of culture and standardized mass education, when so many people within each socioeconomic group look, talk and think alike, "the file" becomes the Government's instrument for distinguishing among them.

Similarly, the turn of social science from rational or interest-seeking models of human motivation to heavily psychological and sociological explanations of human behavior means that masses of highly personal data must be collected to analyze events "scientifically" and make wise choices in public policy. Self-disclosure by individuals, then, becomes an obligation of good citizenship in the modern age, as well as an act of faith in "science."

Thus, when each American today reaches the gatekeepers of public and private authority, the official's basic response is to open a file on him, ask for extensive self-revelation, conduct independent investigations and share information with other certified file managers of our society. If anyone thinks this is an exaggerated portrait, just stop and think for one moment: How many Government forms and reports on yourself or your family did you fill out during the past year? How many questionnaires did you answer about yourself? How many progress reports on your activities did you file with financial, employment and organizational authorities? How many investigations of yourself do you think were conducted without your knowledge? How many investigators asked you about other people's lives? How many evaluations of others did you contribute to the permanent files? Did you ever refuse to answer questions about others or yourself? Do you know anyone who did?

This growth of investigations, dossiers and information sharing has been, of course, enormously accelerated by the advent of the computer. Now, private and public organizations can process 10, 50, 100 times as much personal information about their employees, clients or wards than was ever possible in the eras of print, paper and analysis by eyes and ears. The older barriers of too much cost, not enough time and too much error that once protected privacy of personal transactions have been overcome by the computer in just the same way the barriers of closed rooms or open spaces that once protected privacy of conversation have been swept away by new electronic eavesdropping devices.

The impact of the computer is not just economic, however. Its real force is on the mental processes of our society, in the way we think we should make decisions once we have machines that are capable of accepting, storing and processing so much information. When machines can store so much data, and so many questions that we once thought beyond our capacities to resolve can be answered factually and logically, our society comes to expect that decisions of business, government and science ought to be based on analysis of all the data. Anyone who advocates withholding the necessary data from the information systems in the name of fragile values such as privacy or liberty may be seen as blocking man's most promising opportunity in history—to know himself and to make more rational, more predictable decisions about human affairs.

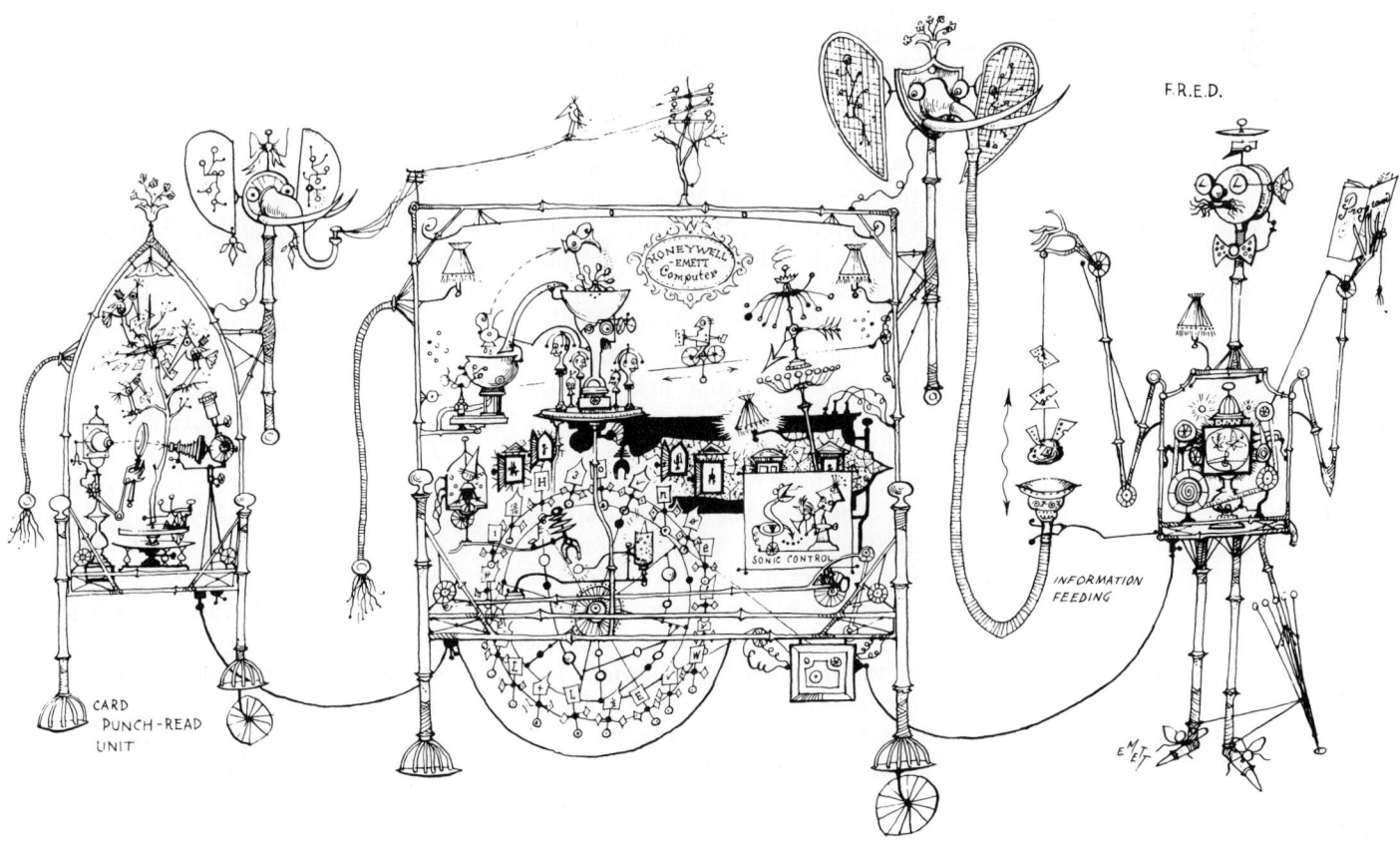

# And It Will Serve Us Right

ISAAC ASIMOV

My father, an immigrant from Eastern Europe, spent his life as a candy-store keeper. He made it his ambition—as was common among immigrants—to see his sons get the education he lacked. The results were all he could have desired. I, his older son, am a professor at a medical school and the author of many books. His younger son is city editor of a large newspaper.

His reaction to all this has been one of unalloyed delight. When I pointed out to him, fairly recently, that had he had my education, he might easily have been I, he shrugged it off, and said, "There are two times when there is no possibility of jealousy: when a pupil surpasses his teacher and when a son surpasses his father."

With all possible respect to my father, I must say that I felt a certain anxious skepticism when he said this. It is all very well for my father, denied by circumstances the chance of making his mark in person, to be happy at making it vicariously. But what if he *had* had his chance, and had done quite well, and *then* saw himself surpassed by me.

Or suppose that I, myself, suddenly became aware that I was not, after all, entering literary history in my own right as Isaac Asimov—something that I have every reasonable expectation of doing. Suppose instead that I were right now coming to realize that I would, after all, enter it as a mere footnote—as the father of a much greater writer. As it happens, the situation does not arise but I tell you frankly that if it had, I am not at all certain I would have felt my father's unselfish joy.

It is one thing to have something for nothing. It is quite another to have your own proud light go pale and sickly before the greater glory.

What would Philip of Macedon's reaction have been, I wonder, if after his quarter-century of heroic striving, during which he raised his country from a backwoods nation of semi-barbarians to the mastery of Greece, he had gained a sudden insight that he was destined to go down in history as "the father of Alexander the Great"? What about Frederick William I of Prussia, who in a quarter-century of forceful rule built an awesome and frightening army out of a patchwork kingdom? What would have been his reaction if he had been made to understand that his place in the annals of man would be that of "the father of Frederick the Great"?

At that, they might have had some instinctive feeling of it, for each father hated his son, even to the point of threatening that son's life.

Hostility between royal father and heir-apparent son is commonplace for there the conflict of present and future glory is all too obvious. Such hostility happens to be most traditional in the British royal family, dating back to the time when Henry II hated his sons (who were well worth his hatred) eight centuries ago.

The ancient Greeks, who thought of everything, took up the matter of the fear of the outshining glory of son or pupil in their myths and legends. Daedalus, the great craftsman and inventor of Greek tales, killed his nephew and pupil, Perdix, out of overwhelming jealousy, when that young man showed signs of becoming superior to his teacher.

More dramatic are the tales of the succession of supreme gods. The first ruler of the Universe, in the Greek myths, was Ouranos. His son, Cronos, castrated and replaced him.

But once Cronos was seated on the throne, he was concerned lest he be served by his sons as he had served his own father. Therefore as his wife, Rhea, bore him sons, he swallowed each in turn. When Zeus was born, however, Rhea fooled her husband by placing a stone in swaddling clothes, and that was swallowed instead.

Zeus was reared to manhood in secret and, in time, warred against his father, replacing him as lord of the Universe.

There matters stood as far as the Greek myths were concerned, and yet Zeus was in danger, too. He and Poseidon (his brother, and god of the sea) both fell in love with the beautiful sea-nymph, Thetis. They competed for the privilege of possessing her, until both hurriedly drew back on hearing that the Fates had decreed that Thetis would bear a son mightier than his father.

No god now dared marry the nymph and Zeus compelled Thetis (quite against her will) to marry a mortal. The mortal was Peleus, and he was the father of Achilles, the great hero of the Trojan war, a son far mightier than his father.

In the light of this, it seems to me, it is not at all puzzling that people generally are afraid of robots generally. Why should not man fear the man-made man, the "son" of his hands, who may surpass him and prove mightier than this "father"?

Not so much man-made woman, you understand. In most early societies women were considered inferior creatures who could not threaten man's priority. Pygmalion of Cyprus could fall in love with the statue, Galatea, pray it alive and marry her. Hephaistos, the Greek god of the forge, could have golden maidens minister to him in a counterfeit of life. Man-made *man*, however—the son, and not the daughter—was terrifying. Crete was guarded by a bronze giant, Talos, according to legend, who circled the island once a day and destroyed all outsiders who landed there. He had one weak spot, however, a stopper in the heel, which if pulled out would allow him to bleed to death. Jason and the Argonauts, on touching down at Crete on the way back from the adventure of the Golden Fleece, defeated Talos by pulling out that stopper.

To be sure, this is transparent symbolism. Crete, prior to 1400 B.C., was held inviolate by its bronze-armored warriors on board the ships of the first great navy of history, but the Greeks of the mainland finally defeated it.

However, there are all sorts of symbols that might be used to represent historical facts and the Greeks chose to envision a mechanical man far more powerful than ordinary man, and one who could be defeated only with the greatest danger and difficulty.

The theme crops up over and over again throughout the legends of the ages. Man creates a mechanical device that in one way or another is intended to serve man within well-defined limits—and invariably the device oversteps the bounds, becomes too powerful, becomes dangerous, must be stopped and scarcely can.

It is the case of the sorcerer's apprentice who brings the broom to life and then can't stop it. It is the case of the medieval rabbis who power golems of clay with the divine name, and then find that the power must be withdrawn, through difficulty and danger, before the manufactured man threatens the world.

In Christian times, a rationalization was advanced. A kind of life and intelligence could be created by man, but only God could create a soul. Any man-made man would be a soulless being, without the aspirations and moral understanding of a souled creature.

But this seems to me to be far too sophisticated to touch the point of basic fear. Surely the mechanical man created to serve, but growing to surpass and endanger his creator, is the sublimated fear of the son, the beloved child who grows to surpass and endanger his father. Our fear of the robot is our fear of the son of Thetis destined to be stronger than his father.

Until the 19th Century, that fear was only a whisper. Life could (in imagination) be imparted to inanimate objects only through divine intervention, entreated by prayer or enforced by magic. In 1798, however, the Italian anatomist, Luigi Galvani, discovered that the dead muscles of frogs could be made to contract by an electric shock. There seemed some connection between electricity and life and the thought arose that life could be restored to dead flesh inside the laboratory and without the involvement of the unpredictable powers of the deities. The fear came closer and into sharper focus at once.

It was precisely Galvani's discovery that inspired Mary Wollstonecraft Shelley (the second wife of the poet) to write her famous horror novel, *Frankenstein*, published in 1818. In the novel a young anatomy student gathers together parts of freshly dead bodies and infuses them with electrical life. What he has created, however, is an eight-foot-tall monster of horrifying aspect.

Possessing intelligence and aware that he is forever cut off from human society, the monster turns upon the man whose interference with the course of nature has condemned him to solitary misery. One by one, the monster kills all of Frankenstein's family and friends, including his bride. Frankenstein himself dies of

> ". . . All we will require is a computer, however simple, to form another more complex than itself, however slightly. That will be the chain reaction that will produce the computer explosion. . . ."

horror and remorse and the monster disappears into the mysterious polar regions.

The book gave the language a phrase: "Frankenstein's monster," now used for any creation which gets out of control, to the danger and horror of its creator. By its popularity, the novel sharpened the general suspicion that man-made man could be only evil; something which I, in my own writings, have referred to as "the Frankenstein complex."

Yet Frankenstein was written when science was in the flood-tide of its vigorous youthful optimism and when it seemed, to confident mankind, to be the ultimate answer to man's needs. It was not till World War I that science donned the mask of Strangelove horror. It was the warplane and even more, poison gas, that showed mankind that the genius of the laboratory and inventor's workshop could be turned to death and destruction.

It is no accident that, soon after World War I, Frankenstein was out-Frankensteined. With inherently wicked man-made man constructed by a science that was itself capable of wickedness, it would not only be the creator that was threatened, but all mankind.

In 1920 a play, R.U.R., by the Czech playwright, Karel Capek, was produced in Prague. In this play, man-made men were created as workers, to take over the muscle-labor of the world and to free men from Adam's curse at last. The character of the inventor, Rossum, called his creation, "worker." In the Czech language, the word is "robot" and this promptly entered the English language. R.U.R. stands for "Rossum's Universal Robots."

It all works out ill. Men, without work, lose ambition and stop siring children. The robots are used in war; they grow more complex and go mad; they rebel against mankind and destroy it. In the end only two robots are left. These exhibit human emotions and it is through them the world will be repeopled.

Mankind has been replaced by robots. Zeus has sired the mightier son of Thetis.

In the middle 1920s, the first science-fiction magazine was published—the first periodical devoted entirely to the imaginative evocation of possible scientific futures—and the era of modern science fiction began. With it there came an exploitation of the common motifs worked out earlier by such masters as Jules Verne and H. G. Wells.

Robots were not neglected. There were numerous tales of man-made man, but always, or almost always, the end was the same. The robot turned on its maker; the son grew dangerous to the father. Where this did not happen, it seemed as though the author were merely seeking a novel "twist," using the shock value of a kindly robot to produce curiosity rather than to display the result of natural development.

That this wearisome parade of clanking monsters, forever parodying Shelley and Capek, came to an end was the result of certain stories that I wrote.

When I began to write robot stories in 1939, I was 19 years old. I did not feel the fright in the son-father relationship. Perhaps through the accident of the particular relationship of my father and myself, I was given no hint, ever, that there might be jealousy on the part of the father or danger on the part of the son. My father labored, in part, so that I might learn; and I learned, in part, so that my father might be gratified. The symbiosis was complete and beneficial, and I naturally saw a similar symbiosis in the relationship of man and robot.

Why should a robot hurt a man? It would be designed not to.

My first robot story appeared in the September 1940 issue of *Super Science Stories* and was entitled "Strange Playfellow." It dealt with a

# Mind-Reading Computer
*Time* Magazine

The experiment looks like some ingenious test of mental telepathy. Seated inside a small isolation booth with wires trailing from the helmet on her head, the subject seems deep in concentration. She does not speak or move. Near by, a white-coated scientist intently watches a TV screen. Suddenly, a little white dot hovering in the center of the screen comes to life. It sweeps to the top of the screen, then it reverses itself and comes back down. After a pause, it veers to the right, stops, moves to the left, momentarily speeds up and finally halts—almost as if it were under the control of some external intelligence.

In fact, it is. The unusual experiment, conducted at the Stanford Research Institute in Menlo Park, Calif., is a graphic display of one of the newest and most dazzling breakthroughs in cybernetics.* It shows that a computer can, in a very real sense, read human minds. Although the dot's gyrations were directed by a computer, the machine was only carrying out the orders of the test subject. She, in turn, did nothing more than think about what the dot's movements should be.

Brainchild of S.R.I. researcher Lawrence Pinneo, a 46-year-old neurophysiologist and electronics engineer, the computer mind-reading technique is far more than a laboratory stunt. Though computers can solve extraordinarily complex problems with incredible speed, the information they digest is fed to them by such slow, cumbersome tools as typewriter keyboards or punched tapes. It is for this reason that scientists have long been tantalized by the possibility of opening up a more direct link between human and electronic brains.

### BRAIN WAVES

Although Pinneo and others have experimented with computer systems that respond to voice commands, he decided that there might be a more direct method than speech. The key to his scheme: the electroencephalograph, a de-

---
*A word coined by the late computer theorist, Norbert Wiener, from the Greek *kybernetes* for pilot or governor, to describe the study of the brain and central nervous system as compared with computers.

robot nursemaid, named "Robbie." It was loved by the little girl it cared for but was distrusted by the little girl's mother.

At one point, when the mother expresses her concern, the little girl's father tries to argue her out of her fears.

"Dear! A robot is infinitely more to be trusted than a human nursemaid. Robbie was constructed for only one purpose—to be the companion of a little child. His entire 'mentality' has been created for the purpose. He just can't help being faithful and loving and kind. He's a machine—*made so*."

There you are. Already I had the dim notion that in the manufacture of a robot, a deliberate design of harmlessness would be built in.

This idea developed further. By the time I wrote my third robot story, "Liar!," I was ready to be more formal and precise about this matter of harmlessness. In "Liar!," published in the May 1941 issue of *Astounding Science Fiction*, one person says to another, "You know the fundamental law impressed upon the positronic brain of all robots, of course."

And the answer comes, "Certainly. On no condition is a human being to be injured in any way, even when such injury is directly ordered by another human."

But then this cannot be all that must be impressed upon a robot's mind. By the time I wrote my fifth robot story, "Runaround" (published in the March 1942 issue of *Astounding Science Fiction*) I had worked out my "Three Laws of Robotics." (The word "robotics" is, as far as I know, my invention.) Here they are in final form:

**THE THREE LAWS OF ROBOTICS**
1. A robot may not injure a human being or, through inaction, allow a human being to come to harm.
2. A robot must obey the orders given it by human beings except where such orders would conflict with the First Law.
3. A robot must protect its own existence as long as such protection does not conflict with either the First or the Second Law.

I am the only science-fiction writer who actually quotes the Three Laws in fiction, but readers have come to take them for granted. Other writers of robot stories tend to accept them and to write within the frame of the Three Laws even though they do not state them explicitly. I am entirely happy over that.

To be sure, this is not an absolute requirement. In the motion picture, *2001: A Space Odyssey,* and in the novel written from it by my good friend, Arthur C. Clarke, the complex computer, Hal—a robot in the broad sense of the word—brings about the deaths of several human beings. This disturbed me, and impressed me as a retrogressive step, but it doesn't seem to bother Arthur at all.

But what about computers? Even if we classify them as a kind of robot evolved to all-brain-no-body, and

> ". . . If ever a species needed to be replaced for the good of the planet, we do. . . ."

vice used by medical researchers to pick up electrical currents from various parts of the brain. If he could learn to identify brain waves generated by specific thoughts or commands, Pinneo figured, he might be able to teach the same skill to a computer. The machine might even be able to react to those commands by, say, moving a dot across a TV screen.

Pinneo could readily pick out specific commands. But, like fingerprints, the patterns varied sufficiently from one human test subject to another to fool the computer. Pinneo found a way to deal with this problem by storing a large variety of patterns in the computer's memory. When the computer had to deal with a fresh pattern, it could search its memory for the brain waves most like it. So far the S.R.I. computer has been taught to recognize seven different commands—up, down, left, right, slow, fast and stop. Working with a total of 25 different people, it makes the right move 60% of the time.

Pinneo is convinced that this barely passing grade can be vastly improved. He foresees the day when computers will be able to recognize the smallest units in the English language—the 40-odd basic sounds (or phonemes) out of which all words or verbalized thoughts can be constructed. Such skills could be put to many practical uses. The pilot of a high-speed plane or spacecraft, for instance, could simply order by thought alone some vital flight information for an all-purpose cockpit display. There would be no need to search for the right dials or switches on a crowded instrument panel.

Pinneo does not worry that mind-reading computers might be abused by Big Brotherly governments or overly zealous police trying to ferret out the innermost thoughts of citizens. Rather than a menace, he says, they could be a highly civilizing influence. In the future, Pinneo speculates, technology may well be sufficiently advanced to feed information from the computer directly back into the brain. People with problems, for example, might don mind-reading helmets ("thinking caps") that let the computer help them untangle everything from complex tax returns to matrimonial messes. Adds Pinneo: "When the person takes this thing off, he might feel pretty damn dumb."

Stanford Research Institute is developing a system in which a computer interprets electrical signals of the brain. The subject, with electrodes taped to her scalp, is asked to say or think particular words in an effort to determine whether specific patterns of electrical activity of the brain are related to specific words.

### "... Not only man-made man is possible, but man-made superman, too...."

place them under the Three Laws, might they still not become uncomfortably complex and capable? Even if the son does not become dangerous to the father physically, might he not, with the best will in the world, become dangerous psychologically? Might he not force the father to admit the inferiority? Might the father be forced to hand over the Universe to a kindly and regretful but inexorably demanding son?

There is, on the part of those who secretly fear this, a strong tendency to downgrade the possibility as, I suspect, a matter of self-protection.

The computer can *not* equal the human brain, is their feeling. The computer can *not* do any more than it is programmed to do. The computer can *never* exhibit intuitive qualities of creativity and genius, as can the human brain.

I wonder if there is not also a definite feeling, usually not expressed, out of a certain mid 20th Century embarrassment, that man has something called a soul that a computer cannot have; that a man is a product of the divine and a computer cannot be.

It's my opinion that none of these arguments is convincing.

The most advanced computer of today is an idiot child compared to the human brain, yes. But then, consider, that the human brain is the product of perhaps three billion years of organic evolution, while the electronic computer is, as such, only 30 years old. After all, is it too much to ask for just 30 years more?

What is to set the limit of further computer development? In theory, nothing. There is nothing magic about the creative abilities of the human brain, its intuitions, its genius. (I am always amused to hear some perfectly ordinary human being pontificate that a "computer can't compose a symphony" as though he himself could.) The human brain is made up of a finite number of cells of finite complexity, arranged in a pattern of finite complexity. When a computer is built of an equal number of equally complex cells in an equally complex arrangement, we will have something that can do just as much as a human brain can do to its uttermost genius.

To deny this is to maintain that there is something more in the human brain than the cells that compose it and the interrelationships among them.

And if human brain and man-made brain reach the same level of complexity, I feel it will be a lot easier to design a still more complicated man-made brain than to breed a still more complex human brain. So not only man-made man is possible, but man-made superman, too.

And how long will it take to reach the human brain level? A million years? A billion?

That, I suspect, is more consolation. Much less time, *much* less time may be required.

The key problem will be this: To design a computer capable of formulating the design of another computer just slightly more complex than itself. Such a computer would naturally design another computer that was somewhat more capable than itself in designing another computer still more complex, which would be still more capable of designing still another computer even more complex and so on.

We will be faced, then, with what mathematicians would call a diverging series.

Once the crucial moment arrives when a computer can design one greater than itself, computers will follow in rapid succession and rise out of sight. The son of Thetis will have been born.

And when will that crucial moment come? It might arrive long before the computer is as complex as the human brain. All we will require is a computer, however simple, to form another more complex than itself, however slightly. That will be the chain reaction that will produce the computer explosion. And the crucial moment may come next year for all I know.

And what if it does? What if the computer shows signs of getting away from us? Would we be face to face with a real Frankenstein's monster at last? Must we all struggle to destroy the thing before the divergence proceeds to the point where we are helpless before it?

Will the computers (oh, horrible thought!) *take over*?

What if they do? The history of life on Earth has been one long tale of "taking over." From era to era, different forms of life have proved dominant in one major environmental niche or the other. The placoderms "took over" from the trilobites, and the modern fish "took over" from the placoderms.

The reptiles "took over" from the amphibia and the mammals "took over" from the reptiles.

Mankind looks upon the history of evolution and approves of all this "taking over" for it all leads up to the moment when Man, proud and destructive Man, has "taken over."

Are we to stop here? Is Ouranos to be replaced by Cronos, and Cronos by Zeus, and no more—thus far and no farther? Is Thetis to be disposed of rather than risk the chance of further replacement?

But why? What has changed? Evolution continues as before, though in a modified manner. Instead of species changing and growing better adapted to their environment through the blind action of mutation and the relentless winnowing of natural selection, we have reached the point where evolution can be guided and the Successor can be deliberately designed.

And it might be good. The planet groans under the weight of 3.4 billion human beings, destined to be seven billion by 2010. It is continually threatened by nuclear holocaust and is inexorably being poisoned by the wastes and fumes of civilization. Sure, it is time and more than time for mankind to be "taken over" from. If ever a species needed to be replaced for the good of the planet, we do.

There isn't much time left, in fact. If the son of Thetis doesn't come within a generation, or, at most two, there may be nothing left worth "taking over."

Is it just science fiction—the idea of building computers with brains like those of humans? As a practical matter, how could it be done? Exactly what is the danger of "thinking machines" getting out of hand, taking over from man himself?

In this exclusive interview with "U.S. News & World Report," one of the world's foremost computer experts probes an exciting future.

## Machines Smarter Than Men?

INTERVIEW WITH DR. NORBERT WIENER

Q  *Dr. Wiener, is there any danger that machines—that is, computers—will someday get the upper hand over men?*
A  There is, definitely, that danger if we don't take a realistic attitude.

The danger is essentially intellectual laziness. Some people have been so bamboozled by the word "machine" that they don't realize what can be done and what cannot be done with machines—and what can be left, and what cannot be left, to the human beings.

Q  *Is there a tendency to overemphasize the use of computers?*
A  There is a worship of gadgetry. People are fascinated by gadgets. The machines are there to be used by man, and if man prefers to leave the whole matter of the mode of their employment to the machine, by overworship of the machine or unwillingness to make decisions—whether you call it laziness or cowardice—then we're in for trouble.

Q  *Do you agree with a prediction, sometimes heard, that machines are going to be constructed that will be smarter than man?*
A  May I say, if the man isn't smarter than the machine, then it's just too bad. But that isn't our being assassinated by the machine. That will be suicide.

Q  *Is there actually a trend for machines to become more sophisticated, smarter?*
A  We're making much more sophisticated machines and we're going to make much more sophisticated machines in the next few years. There are things that haven't come to the public attention at all now, things that make many of us believe that this is going to happen within a decade or so.

Q  *Can you give us a look into the future?*
A  I can. One of the big things about machines has been miniaturization—cutting down the size of the components. Where, at the beginning of the development of computers, a machine would have to be as big as the Empire State Building, it can be reduced now to something that you could fit into a rather small room. One of the chief factors in this miniaturization has been the introduction of new types of "memories," memories depending on solid-state physics—on transistors, and things of that sort.

Now, it's becoming interesting to ask: "How does the human brain do it?" And for the first time within the last year or so, we're getting a real idea of that.

You know, genetic memory—the memory of our genes—is largely dependent on substances which are nucleic-acid complexes. Within this last year it's coming to be pretty generally suspected that the memory of the nervous system is of the same sort of thing. This is indicated by the discovery of nucleic-acid complexes in the brain and by the fact that they have the properties that would give a good memory. This is a very subtle sort of solid-state physics, like the physics which is used in the memory of machines now.

My hunch is—and I'm not alone in this—that the next decade or so will see this used technically.

Q  *In other words, instead of a magnetic tape as a memory core of a computer, you will have genes—*
A  You will have substances allied to genes. Whether you call them genes or not is a matter of phraseology, but substances of the same sort.

Now, that will involve a lot of new fundamental research. How to get in and out of these genetic memories—how to put them to use—involves much research which has scarcely started yet. Several of us have hunches—these are not verified—that this can be done by light of specific molecular spectra, to get in and out of the complexes. Whether that's so or not, I won't swear. But that is a thing some of us are considering seriously.

Q  *Is this a prospect that should frighten people?*
A  Any prospect will frighten people. It should frighten people if it is applied without understanding. With understanding this can be a very valuable tool.

Q  *Can you describe a computer that would use genes as a memory device? What would it be capable of?*
A  That would sound too much like science fiction to talk about now.

Q  *What would the capability of this machine be, compared to the computers you have today?*
A  It might be enormously greater. The machine could be much smaller; it could carry a much larger set of data. But anything that I would say about this would be not only premature but hopelessly premature. But work is to be done in those fields, I'm certain.

**When you've eaten of the fruit of the tree of knowledge, there isn't much you can do except go ahead with that knowledge.**

Q *People are already saying the computers "think." Is this so?*
A Taking things as of the present time, computers can learn. Computers can learn to improve their performance by examining it. That is definitely true. Whether you call that thinking or not is a terminological matter. That this sort of thing will go much further in the future, as our ability to build up more complicated computers increases, I should say is certain.

**IF MAN GETS IN TROUBLE—**
Q *Is there a chance that machines may learn more than man? Are they doing this now?*
A Certainly not now and certainly not for a long time, if ever. But if they do, it's because we have ceased to learn. I mean, it's easier for us to learn than for the machine. If we worship the machine, and leave everything to the machine, we've got ourselves to thank for any trouble we get in.

Here is the point: The computer is extremely good at working rapidly, at working in a unique way on well-presented data. The computer doesn't compare with the human being in handling data that haven't yet jelled. If you call that intuition—I won't say that intuition is impossible for the computer, but it's much, much lower and it isn't economical to try to make the computer do things that the human being does so much better.

Q *What exactly is a learning machine?*
A A learning machine is one which not only, say, plays a game according to fixed rules, with a fixed policy, but periodically or continuously examines the results of that policy to determine whether certain parameters, certain quantities, in that policy could be changed to advantage.

Q *The example that always comes to mind is machines that play checkers—*
A Well, take checkers. The machine was good enough to be able, after a while, to systematically defeat its inventor until he learned a little more about checkers.

Q *Why is this not so with chess?*
A Because chess is more complicated. It will be so with chess, but it's a much bigger job.

Q *Are machines being taught to write?*
A . Yes. There are machines which will take a code and put it into handwriting, or take handwriting as well as printing and put it into a code. Oh, yes, that's being worked—you can even take speech and put it into a code.

Q *Is it science fiction to talk about "thinking robots" taking over the earth?*
A It is science fiction, unless people get the idea, "Leave it all to 'Tin Mike.'" I mean, if we regard the machine not as an adjunct to our powers but as something to extend our powers, we can keep it controlled. Otherwise we can't.

The gadget worshipers who expect the machine to do everything, and let people sit down and take it easy, have another think coming.

Q *Are computers being used intelligently today?*
A In 10 per cent of the cases, yes.
Q *This is a startlingly low figure. Why do you say that?*
A Because it takes intelligence to know what to give to the machine. And in many cases the machine is used to buy intelligence that isn't there.

The computer is just as valuable as the man using it. It can allow him to cover more ground in the same time. But he's got to have the ideas. And in the early stage of testing the ideas, you shouldn't be dependent on using computers.

Q *Is this true also in the use of computers as the basis for automation? That is to say, is automation in some cases being unintelligently employed?*
A It most definitely is. But, as for examples, that is not my field.
Q *What are some of the things that computers can be used for intelligently, and do better than humans?*
A Bookkeeping, selling tickets, and keeping a record of that sort. When you've got your plan of computation, machines can carry it out much better than man can. And computers of the future will do these things very much better. They'll have enough variety so they can afford to do what the brain does—waste a lot of effort and still get something.

Q *Are these machines of the future going to take away a lot more jobs from humans?*
A They will.
Q *That will sharpen a problem that already exists. What is the solution?*
A The answer is that we can no longer value a man by the jobs he does. We've got to value him as a man.

Here is the point: A whole lot of the work that we are using men for is work which really is done better by computers. That is, for a long time human energy hasn't been worth much as far as physical energy goes. A man couldn't possibly generate enough energy today to buy the food for his own body.

The actual commercial value of his services in modern culture isn't enough. If we value people, we can't value people on that basis.

If we insist on using the machines everywhere, irrespective of people, and don't go to very fundamental considerations and give people their proper place in the world, we're sunk.

Q *Is it too late to halt this drive toward more and more automation?*

**Is it possible for machines to declare war and doom all mankind?**

A What has been done is irrevocable. I saw this at the very beginning. It isn't merely the fact that the computers are being used. It's the fact that they stand ready to be used, which is the real difficulty.

In other words, the reason we can't go back is that we can never destroy the possibility of computers' being used.

Q *Do you consider it an irreversible trend?*

A I'm not even speaking about the trend. It's an irreversible piece of knowledge. It's the sort of thing that happened to Adam and Eve when they had that encounter with the serpent. When you've eaten of the fruit of the tree of knowledge, there isn't much you can do except go ahead with that knowledge.

Q *So people can look for machines to play still more of a role in automation,* in running businesses, in education—

A We can. And, at any rate, whether we use machines or not—which is a decision which we have to make one way or another—the fact that they are there to be used cannot be turned off.

Q *Are you saying that it might be a wiser decision not to make use of some of these machines?*

A It may be wiser in particular situations. I'll give you a simple example:

It is very easy now, with automatization, to make a factory which can produce more than the whole market can consume. If you go and simply push production up, you may hit the ceiling. Competition, as it has been understood in the past, has been greatly changed by the existence of automatization. Automatization no longer fits in with *laissez faire.*

Q *If there is developed in the next decade the kind of advanced machinery that you've hinted at, how can further automation be restrained?*

A More than once, advance has been restrained in the past. It isn't necessary, if we make a new weapon, to use it immediately.

Q *On your last trip to Russia, did you find the Soviets placing much emphasis on the computer?*

A I'll tell you how much emphasis they're placing on it. They have an institute in Moscow. They have an institute in Kiev. They have an institute in Leningrad. They have one in Yerevan in Armenia, in Tiflis, in Samarkand, in Tashkent and Novosibirsk. They may have others.

Q *Are they making full use of this science, in a way comparable to ours?*

A The general verdict—and this is from many different people—is that they're behind us in hardware—not hopelessly, but slightly. They are ahead of us in the theorization of automatization.

Q *Dr. Wiener, is it necessary today to use computers for military decisions?*

A Yes, and they can be used very unwisely.

I've no doubt that the problem of when to push the "big button" is being considered from the learning-machine point of view. If it isn't, I should be very surprised, because these ideas are current. You know: Let "Tin Mike" do it.

But let's look at this a little bit more in detail. How do soldiers learn their job? By war games. They have for centuries played games on the map. All right, if you have a certain formal criterion for what winning a war is, you can do this. But you'd better be sure that your criterion is what you really want and not a formalization of what you want. Otherwise, you can make a computer that will win the war technically and destroy everything.

Q *How can you program a computer for a nuclear war if you've never had any actual experience in that kind of war?*

A You can't completely. But, nevertheless, that is what people are trying to do.

There are no experts in atomic war. An expert is a man who is experienced. This man does not exist today. Therefore, the programing of war games by artificial criteria of success is highly dangerous and likely to come out wrong.

Q *Is there a tendency to that kind of programing?*

A There is a tendency in that direction, and it strikes me as top-level foolishness. The automation has the property of what magic once was supposed to have. It may give you what you ask for, but it won't tell you what to ask for.

We have heard people say that we need to develop machine systems which will tell us when to push the button. What we need are systems that will tell us what happens if we push the button under a lot of different circumstances —and, importantly, tell us when *not* to push the button.

Q *Do you mean it is possible for machines to declare war and doom all mankind?*

A If we let them. Obviously they won't declare war unless we create a setup by which they will.

Q *Dr. Wiener, is man changing his environment beyond his capacity to adjust to it?*

A That's the $64 question. He's certainly changing it greatly, and if he is doing it beyond his capacity, we'll know soon enough. Or we won't know—we won't be here.

# On the Impact of the Computer on Society

JOSEPH WEIZENBAUM

(An excerpt from the original article)
How does one insult a machine?

The direct societal effects of any pervasive new technology are as nothing compared to its much more subtle and ultimately much more important side effects. In that sense, the societal impact of the computer has not yet been felt.

To help firmly fix the idea of the importance of subtle indirect effects of technology, consider the impact on society of the invention of the microscope. When it was invented in the middle of the 17th century, the dominant commonsense theory of disease was fundamentally that disease was a punishment visited upon an individual by God. The sinner's body was thought to be inhabited by various so-called humors brought into disequilibrium in accordance with divine justice. The cure for disease was therefore to be found first in penance and second in the balancing of humors as, for example, by bleeding. Bleeding was, after all, both painful, hence punishment and penance, and potentially balancing in that it actually removed substance from the body. The microscope enabled man to see microorganisms and thus paved the way for the germ theory of disease. The enormously surprising discovery of extremely small living organisms also induced the idea of a continuous chain of life which, in turn, was a necessary intellectual precondition for the emergence of Darwinism. Both the germ theory of disease and the theory of evolution profoundly altered man's conception of his contract with God and consequently his self-image. Politically these ideas served to help diminish the power of the Church and, more generally, to legitimize the questioning of the basis of hitherto unchallenged authority. I do not say that the microscope alone was responsible for the enormous social changes that followed its invention. Only that it made possible the kind of paradigm shift, even on the commonsense level, without which these changes might have been impossible.

Is it reasonable to ask whether the computer will induce similar changes in man's image of himself and whether that influence will prove to be its most important effect on society? I think so, although I hasten to add that I don't believe the computer has yet told us much about man and his nature. To come to grips with the question, we must first ask in what way the computer is different from man's many other machines. Man has built two fundamentally different kinds of machines, nonautonomous and autonomous. An autonomous machine is one that operates for long periods of time, not on the basis of inputs from the real world, for example from sensors or from human drivers, but on the basis of internalized models of some aspect of the real world. Clocks are examples of autonomous machines in that they operate on the basis of an internalized model of the planetary system. The computer is, of course, the example par excellence. It is able to internalize models of essentially unlimited complexity and of a fidelity limited only by the genius of man.

It is the autonomy of the computer we value. When, for example, we speak of the power of computers as increasing with each new hardware and software development, we mean that, because of their increasing speed and storage capacity, and possibly thanks to new programming tricks, the new computers can internalize ever more complex and ever more faithful models of ever larger slices of reality. It seems strange then that, just when we exhibit virtually an idolatry of autonomy with respect to machines, serious thinkers in respected academies [I have in mind B. F. Skinner of Harvard University] can rise to question autonomy as a fact for man. I do not think that the appearance of this paradox at this time is accidental. To understand it, we must realize that man's commitment to science has always had a masochistic component.

Time after time science has led us to insights that, at least when seen superficially, diminish man. Thus Galileo removed man from the center of the universe, Darwin removed him from his place separate from the animals, and Freud showed his rationality to be an illusion. Yet man pushes his inquiries further and deeper. I cannot help but think that there is an analogy between man's pursuit of scientific knowledge and an individual's commitment to psychoanalytic therapy. Both are undertaken in the full realization that what the inquirer may find may well damage his self-esteem. Both may reflect his determination to find meaning in his existence through struggle in truth, however painful that may be, rather than to live without meaning in a world of ill-disguised illusion. However, I am also aware that sometimes people enter psychoanalysis unwilling to put their illusions at risk, not searching for a deeper reality but in order to convert the insights they hope to gain to personal power. The analogy to man's pursuit of science does not break down with that observation.

Each time a scientific discovery shatters a hitherto fundamental cornerstone of the edifice on which man's self-esteem is built, there is an enormous reaction, just as is the case under similar circumstances in psychoanalytic therapy. Powerful defense mechanisms, beginning with denial and usually terminating in rationalization, are brought to bear. Indeed, the psychoanalyst suspects that, when a patient appears to accept a soul-shattering insight without resistance, his very casualness may well mask his refusal to allow that insight truly operational status in his self-image. But what is the psychoanalyst to think about the patient who positively embraces tentatively proffered, profoundly humiliating self-knowledge, when he embraces it and instantly converts it to a new foundation of his life? Surely such an event is symptomatic of a major crisis in the mental life of the patient.

I believe we are now at the beginning of just such a crisis in the mental life of our civilization. The microscope, I have argued, brought in its train a revision of man's image of himself. But no one in the mid-17th century could have foreseen that. The possibility that the computer will, one way or another, demonstrate that, in the inimitable phrase of one of my esteemed colleagues, "the brain is merely a meat machine" is one that engages academicians, industrialists, and journalists in the here and now. How has the computer contributed to bringing about this very sad state of affairs? It must be said right away that the computer alone is not the chief causative agent. It is merely an extreme extrapolation of technology. When seen as an inducer of philosophical dogma, it is merely the reductio ad absurdum of a technological ideology. But how does it come to be regarded as a source of philosophic dogma?

I have suggested that the computer revolution need not and ought not to call man's dignity and autonomy into question, that it is a kind of pathology that moves men to wring from it unwarranted, enormously damaging interpretations. Is then the computer less threatening than we might have thought? Once we realize that our visions, possibly nightmarish visions, determine the effect of our own creations on us and on our society, their threat to us is surely diminished. But that is not to say that this realization alone will wipe out all danger. For example, apart from the erosive effect of a technological mentality on man's self-image, there are practical attacks on the freedom and dignity of man in which computer technology plays a critical role.

I mentioned earlier that computer science has come to recognize the importance of building knowledge into machines. We already have a machine —Dendral—that commands more chemistry than do many Ph.D chemists, and another—Mathlab—that commands more applied mathematics than do many applied mathematicians. Both Dendral and Mathlab contain knowledge that can be evaluated in terms of the explicit theories from which it was derived. If the user believes that a result Mathlab delivers is wrong, then, apart from possible program errors, he must be in disagreement, not with the machine or its programmer, but with a specific mathematical theory. But what about the many programs on which management, most particularly the government and the military, rely, programs which can in no sense be said to rest on explicable theories but are instead enormous patchworks of programming techniques strung together to make them work?

**The direct societal effects of any pervasive new technology are as nothing compared to its much more subtle and ultimately much more important side effects.**

**In the future, technology may well be sufficiently advanced to feed information from the computer directly back into the brain.**

### INCOMPREHENSIBLE SYSTEMS

In our eagerness to exploit every advance in technique we quickly incorporate the lessons learned from machine manipulation of knowledge in theory-based systems into such patchworks. They then "work" better. I have in mind systems like target selection systems used in Vietnam and war games used in the Pentagon, and so on. These often gigantic systems are put together by teams of programmers, often working over a time span of many years. But by the time the systems come into use, most of the original programmers have left or turned their attention to other pursuits. It is precisely when gigantic systems begin to be used that their inner workings can no longer be understood by any single person or by a small team of individuals. Norbert Wiener, the father of cybernetics, foretold of this phenomenon in a remarkably prescient article published more than a decade ago. He said there:

It may well be that in principle we cannot make any machine the elements of whose behavior we cannot comprehend sooner or later. This does not mean in any way that we shall be able to comprehend these elements in substantially less time than the time required for operation of the machine, or even within any given number of years or generations.

An intelligent understanding of [machines'] mode of performance may be delayed until long after the task which they have been set has been completed. This means that though machines are theoretically subject to human criticism, such criticism may be ineffective until long after it is relevant.

This situation, which is now upon us, has two consequences: first that decisions are made on the basis of rules and criteria no one knows explicitly, and second that the system of rules and criteria becomes immune to change. This is so because, in the absence of detailed understanding of the inner workings of a system, any substantial modification is very likely to render the system altogether inoperable. The threshold of complexity beyond which this phenomenon occurs has already been crossed by many existing systems, including some compiling and computer operating systems. For example, no one likes the operating systems for certain large computers, but they cannot be substantially changed nor can they be done away with. Too many people have become dependent on them.

An awkward operating system is inconvenient. That is not too bad. But the growing reliance on supersystems that were perhaps designed to help people make analyses and decisions, but which have since surpassed the understanding of their users while at the same time becoming indispensable to them, is another matter. In modern war it is common for the soldier, say the bomber pilot, to operate at an enormous psychological distance from his victims. He is not responsible for burned children because he never sees their village, his bombs, and certainly not the flaming children themselves. Modern technological rationalizations of war, diplomacy, politics, and commerce such as computer games have an even more insidious effect on the making of policy. Not only have policy makers abdicated their decision-making responsibility to a technology they don't understand, all the while maintaining the illusion that they, the policy makers, are formulating policy questions and answering them, but responsibility has altogether evaporated. No human is any longer responsible for "what the machine says." Thus there can be neither right nor wrong, no question of justice, no theory with which one can agree or disagree, and finally no basis on which one can challenge "what the machine says." My father used to invoke the ultimate authority by saying to me, "it is written." But then I could read what was written, imagine a human author, infer his values, and finally agree or disagree. The systems in the Pentagon, and their counterparts elsewhere in our culture, have in a very real sense no authors. They therefore do not admit of exercises of imagination that may ultimately lead to human judgment. No wonder that men who live day in and out with such machines and become dependent on them begin to believe that men are merely machines. They are reflecting what they themselves have become.

The potentially tragic impact on society that may ensue from the use of systems such as I have just discussed is greater than might at first be imagined. Again it is side effects, not direct effects, that matter most. First, of course, there is the psychological impact on individuals living in a society in which anonymous, hence irresponsible, forces formulate the large questions of the day and circumscribe the range of possible answers. It cannot be surprising that large numbers of perceptive individuals living in such a society experience a kind of impotence and fall victim to the mindless rage that often accompanies such experiences. But even worse, since computer-based knowledge systems become essentially unmodifiable except in that they can grow, and since they induce dependence and cannot, after a certain

### TRACES

Each of us
Leaves traces
On every thing and place
We touch,
On every person we reach.

Some of our species
Have given themselves over,
Body and soul,
To recording for austerity
The traces the rest of us leave.

The goal seems to be perfection,
The model being the mode thereto;
A yet unmet absurdity being man,
Who must run the machine.
Yet man with all his faults is the perfect machine.

This is so because
The time it takes to question
May be the difference between life
And the sterile dividends from data banks
Which know nothing but a constant rate of electricity.

It's true enough,
Had we had these marvels
In full blossom before now
We might be freed earlier from terrors,
Yet there must be other ways to heal.

What worth is there to stifling spontaneity
By too soon classifications
And too loose metal tongues lashing out
At one stray at the expense of ninety-nine?

A lot of people
Know a lot about you and me;
Our traces are all over the scenes
Of our daily trespasses, but who
Will deliver us from the even tempered computer?

J. PATRICK LITEKY

threshold is crossed, be abandoned, there is an enormous risk that they will be passed from one generation to another, always growing. Man too passes knowledge from one generation to another. But because man is mortal, his transmission of knowledge over the generations is at once a process of filtering and accrual. Man doesn't merely pass knowledge, he rather regenerates it continuously. Much as we may mourn the crumbling of ancient civilizations, we know nevertheless that the glory of man resides as much in the evolution of his cultures as in that of his brain. The unwise use of ever larger and ever more complex computer systems may well bring this process to a halt. It could well replace the ebb and flow of culture with a world without values, a world in which what counts for a fact has long ago been determined and forever fixed.

## POSITIVE EFFECTS

I've spoken of some potentially dangerous effects of present computing trends. Is there nothing positive to be said? Yes, but it must be said with caution. Again, side effects are more important than direct effects. In particular, the idea of computation and of programming languages is beginning to become an important metaphor which, in the long run, may well prove to be responsible for paradigm shifts in many fields. Most of the common-sense paradigms in terms of which much of mankind interprets the phenomena of the everyday world, both physical and social, are still deeply rooted in fundamentally mechanistic metaphors. Marx's dynamics as well as those of Freud are, for example, basically equilibrium systems. Any hydrodynamicist could come to understand them without leaving the jargon of his field. Languages capable of describing ongoing processes, particularly in terms of modular subprocesses, have already had an enormous effect on the way computer people think of every aspect of their worlds, not merely those directly related to their work. The information-processing view of the world so engendered qualifies as a genuine metaphor. This is attested to by the fact that it (i) constitutes an intellectual framework that permits new questions to be asked about a wide-ranging set of phenomena, and (ii) that it itself provides criteria for the adequacy of proffered answers. A new metaphor is important not in that it may be better than existing ones, but rather in that it may enlarge man's vision by giving him yet another perspective on his world. Indeed, the very effectiveness of a new metaphor may seduce lazy minds to adopt it as a basis for universal explanations and as a source of panaceas. Computer simulation of social processes has already been advanced by single-minded generalists as leading to general solutions of all of mankind's problems.

The metaphors given us by religion, the poets, and by thinkers like Darwin, Newton, Freud, and Einstein have rather quickly penetrated to the language of ordinary people. These metaphors have thus been instrumental in shaping our entire civilization's imaginative reconstruction of our world. The computing metaphor is as yet available to only an extremely small set of people. Its acquisition and internalization, hopefully as only one of many ways to see the world, seems to require experience in program composition, a kind of computing literacy. Perhaps such literacy will become very widespread in the advanced societal sectors of the advanced countries. But, should it become a dominant mode of thinking and be restricted to certain social classes, it will prove not merely repressive in the ordinary sense, but an enormously divisive societal force. For then classes which do and do not have access to the metaphor will, in an important sense, lose their ability to communicate with one another. We know already how difficult it is for the poor and the oppressed to communicate with the rest of the society in which they are embedded. We know how difficult it is for the world of science to communicate with that of the arts and of the humanities. In both instances the communication difficulties, which

---

**Most of the harm computers can potentially entrain is much more a function of properties people attribute to computers than of what a computer can or cannot actually be made to do.**

---

have grave consequences, are very largely due to the fact that the respective communities have unsharable experiences out of which unsharable metaphors have grown.

### RESPONSIBILITY

Given these dismal possibilities, what is the responsibility of the computer scientist? First I should say that most of the harm computers can potentially entrain is much more a function of properties people attribute to computers than of what a computer can or cannot actually be made to do. The nonprofessional has little choice but to make his attributions of properties to computers on the basis of the propaganda emanating from the computer community and amplified by the press. The computer professional therefore has an enormously important responsibility to be modest in his claims. This advice would not even have to be voiced if computer science had a tradition of scholarship and of self-criticism such as that which characterizes the established sciences. The mature scientist stands in awe before the depth of his subject matter. His very humility is the wellspring of his strength. I regard the instilling of just this kind of humility, chiefly by the example set by teachers, to be one of the most important missions of every university department of computer science.

The computer scientist must be aware constantly that his instruments are capable of having gigantic direct and indirect amplifying effects. An error in a program, for example, could have grievous direct results, including most certainly the loss of much human life. On 11 September 1971, to cite just one example, a computer programming error caused the simultaneous destruction of 117 high-altitude weather balloons whose instruments were being monitored by an earth satellite (9). A similar error in a military command and control system could launch a fleet of nuclear tipped missiles. Only censorship prevents us from knowing how many such events involving nonnuclear weapons have already occurred. Clearly then, the computer scientist has a heavy responsibility to make the fallibility and limitations of the systems he is capable of designing brilliantly clear. The very power of his systems should serve to inhibit the advice he is ready to give and to constrain the range of work he is willing to undertake.

Of course, the computer scientist, like everyone else, is responsible for his actions and their consequences. Sometimes that responsibility is hard to accept because the corresponding authority to decide what is and what is not to be done appears to rest with distant and anonymous forces. That technology itself determines what is to be done by a process of extrapolation and that individuals are powerless to intervene in that determination is precisely the kind of self-fulfilling dream from which we must awaken.

Consider gigantic computer systems. They are, of course, natural extrapolations of the large systems we already have. Computer networks are another point on the same curve extrapolated once more. One may ask whether such systems can be used by anybody except by governments and very large corporations and whether such organizations will not use them mainly for antihuman purposes. Or consider speech recognition systems. Will they not be used primarily to spy on private communications? To answer such questions by saying that big computer systems, computer networks, and speech recognition systems are inevitable is to surrender one's humanity. For such an answer must be based either on one's profound conviction that society has already lost control over its technology or on the thoroughly immoral position that "if I don't do it, someone else will."

I don't say that systems such as I have mentioned are necessarily evil—only that they may be and, what is most important, that their inevitability cannot be accepted by individuals claiming autonomy, freedom, and dignity. The individual computer scientist can and must decide. The determination of what the impact of computers on society is to be is, at least in part, in his hands.

Finally, the fundamental question the computer scientist must ask himself is the one that every scientist, indeed every human, must ask. It is not "what shall I do?" but rather "what shall I be?" I cannot answer that for anyone save myself. But I will say again that if technology is a nightmare that appears to have its own inevitable logic, it is our nightmare. It is possible, given courage and insight, for man to deny technology the prerogative to formulate man's questions. It is possible to ask human questions and to find humane answers.

### REFERENCES AND NOTES

1. B. F. Skinner, *Beyond Freedom and Dignity* (Knopf, New York, 1971).
2. K. M. Colby, S. Weber, F. D. Hilf, *Artif. Intell.* **1**, 1 (1971).
3. N. Chomsky, *Aspects of the Theory of Syntax* (M.I.T. Press, Cambridge, Mass., 1965); —— and M. Halle, *The Sound Pattern of English* (Harper & Row, New York, 1968).
4. L. Mumford, *The Pentagon of Power* (Harcourt Brace Jovanovich, New York, 1970).
5. H. A. Simon, *The Sciences of the Artificial* (M.I.T. Press, Cambridge, Mass., 1969), pp. 22–25.
6. B. Buchanan, G. Sutherland, E. A. Feigenbaum, in *Machine Intelligence*, B. Meltzer, Ed. (American Elsevier, New York, 1969).
7. W. A. Martin and R. J. Fateman, "The Macsyma system," in *Proceedings of the 2nd Symposium on Symbolic and Algebraic Manipulation* (Association for Computer Machines, New York, 1971); J. Moses, *Commun. Assoc. Computer March.* **14** (No. 8), 548 (1971).
8. N. Wiener, *Science* **131**, 1355 (1960).
9. R. Gillette, *ibid.* **174**, 477 (1971).

### AUTOMATION

I went down, down, down to the factory early on a Monday morn.
When I got down to the factory,
It was lonely, it was forlorn.
I couldn't find Joe, Jack, John, or Jim;
Nobody could I see:
Nothing but buttons and bells and lights
All over the factory.

I walked, walked, walked into the foreman's office
To find out what was what.
I looked him in the eye and I said, "What goes?"
And this is the answer I got:
His eyes turned red, then green, then blue
And it suddenly dawned on me—
There was a robot sitting in the seat
Where the foreman used to be.

I walked all around, all around, up and down
And across the factory.
I watched all the buttons and the bells and the lights—
It was a mystery to me.
I hollered "Frank, Hank, Ike, Mike, Roy, Ray, Don, Dan, Bill, Phil, Ed, Fred, Pete!"
And a great big mechanical voice boomed out:
"All your buddies are obsolete."

I was scared, scared, scared, I was worried, I was sick
As I left that factory.
I decided that I had to see the president
Of the whole darn company.
When I got up to his office he was rushing out the door
With a scowl upon his face,
'Cause there was a great big mechanical executive
Sitting in the president's place.

I went home, home, home to my ever-loving wife
And told her 'bout the factory.
She hugged me and she kissed me and she cried a little bit
As she sat on my knee.
I don't understand all the buttons and the lights
But one thing I will say—
I thank the Lord that love's still made
In the good old-fashioned way.

JOE GLAZER

# Deus ex Machina?
KIT PEDLER

A robot is commonly regarded as a simple machine—usually a morphological simulation of man—made from metal sinews, muscles and wires. Added to this are primitive sense organs which allow it to respond crudely to relevant environmental energy sources. Thus there are photocells for eyes, microphones for ears, and pressure transducers for touch. The end result of this rather charming design philosophy is a 'tin man' which clumps around doing nothing in particular except to show man how graceful he is in comparison. The main lines of development of 'tin men' can be fairly accurately predicted. Their further refinement is based essentially on the solution of technical problems and will involve no significant change in philosophical concept. Thus we may end up with an excellent functional homunculus, properly transistorised, microminiaturised, containing all the most advanced monolithic circuitry: a marvel of useless endeavour.

So let us forget about robots as serfs, which is the way they were originally proposed in Capek's *RUR* (*robotnik*, in Czech, means a serf). Such robots are essentially in the 'Golem' image and have no further interest except as ingenious dolls for grown-ups. They will certainly become more capable, and may even evolve from climbing stairs and seeking their own power requirements to a level where they are able successfully to cook *pigeon en cocotte*, or seek out the week's shopping requirements. They are of the first generation and can evolve only to a certain level, where they will still remain an understandable and wholly controllable machine, constituting no sort of a threat. They will remain self-evidently clumsy, ungracious, totally dependent, and above all stupid, doing no more than they are programmed to do and providing perennial service with a metallic smile.

The era of the metal serf is thus drawing to a close. There will always be those who will cling to the image because it is cozy, and also because there will always be some constructors who prefer what amounts to a man-made artifact of gear wheels and brass rather than the blocks of apparatus which constitute the image of present-day automata. So what about the second-generation robot? Let us christen it 'biomim' (biological mimic). What are going to be its characteristics, and how might it relate to human society? Could it be a menace? What follows is a short exercise in speculative science fiction, based upon present trends, and is an attempt to suggest that a biomim could assimilate many of the more powerful qualities that we regard as uniquely human. Also that a society of biomims might well order itself in a highly efficient manner and render man redundant as a consequence.

How could this happen? Principally because it is now becoming feasible to build into the original robot strategy many of the remaining properties necessary to bring it to the state of potential danger I have referred to. What are these? They are: goal-seeking, intelligence, adaptability of behaviour, learning capability, and, last but most important, the urge to survive. Many of the relevant theoretical problems under all these separate headings are already being studied and it is now a matter of designing technologies to implement theory. Opponents of this idea will say at once that the biomim would need the equivalent of a human brain in order to behave in a way consistent with these qualities, but the unavoidable point is that it would not.

One of the most successful families ever to evolve on this planet are the arthropods. Among its millions of species are some of the hardiest and most effective examples of biological design. Design, if you like, by the process of evolution, but design nonetheless. The arthropods, and not man, might well have been the principal species, were it not for the fact that their diffusion-based respiratory systems precluded them from growing beyond a certain maximum size. Arthropods survive, replicate, live off their environment, are predatory, and —what is most relevant—form societies. And they do this without a central brain.

Arthropods have a 'ganglionic' nervous system. That is to say, dispersed throughout the body are a series of nerve-cell aggregations connected together by a network of fibres and also linked to the sensory and motor periphery of the creature.

They have no central brain and no equivalent of the cerebral cortex—our pride and sometime joy. Yet they are highly effective within their environment. In one sense of the word, they are partially robotic. For example, if one small ganglion in some species is destroyed, the creature will clean itself to death by exhaustion. Cleaning movements are normally related to and controlled by the particles of dirt on the surface hairs. Thus, when the dirt is removed, stabilising systems come into play which control and arrest the cleaning movements. When the ganglion is removed, control is removed and the creature responds in an automatic and robotic way. There are many other similar examples.

Thus, arthropods present themselves as balanced mechanisms under a high degree of stable control. They fly the right way up, the mantis devours with precision, and the spider goes straight to the point on its web where its prey is enmeshed. Yet among the arthropods, so far as we know, there is no Beethoven, Dylan Thomas, Einstein or Russell. What we see as a feral ferocity is the norm. There is no compassion or humanity, but there are societies—ant-hills and beehives. All brainless. The individual, successful at survival by itself, is wedded to an external system of organisation which totally absorbs its activities. Yet there is no evidence that the ant or the bee has any internally set goal or wish to achieve, except to fit perfectly into its micro-marxist order.

What has this got to do with the biomim? I have used the arthropod as an example of a more or less mechanical biological system which survives well, replicates, and is capable of a certain amount of behavioural plasticity. It also forms groups of interrelated individuals and is brainless in the literal sense. Using the analogy of the arthropod, we have to add, to the musculo-skeletal system of the robot, the qualities already referred to. This will, of course, given the present state of technological development, produce a quite hopelessly large creature, because to possess the necessary qualities it will need constant recourse to an enormous memory store. Memory is necessary for most of the activities of the biomim. Necessary for comparison, pattern recognition, avoidance of dangerous situations, and so on. Thus, memory cannot be in the biomim. Where will it be?

It will be in a central multi-access memory store in constant two-way communication with individual biomims by telemetry. Thus each individual biomim will have direct access to a large store of information when and where it is wanted. The central machine will not only be the memory, it will also include the random circuitry necessary for adaptive and self-organising activity and the evolution of new strategies. In this way, we will have a large number of mechanical individuals, possessing drive, known goals, intelligence (the ability to make the appropriate decisions), adaptability and survival bias —all linked together by the central mother machine, each one carrying no brain, but the components of the ganglionic nervous system necessary for physical control of action. Functions associated with the brain are left to the central computer. This then will form a basis for the first iron society. No God, Karl Marx, Buddha or Beatle, merely an organisation of specifiable biological properties designed to enable the biomim

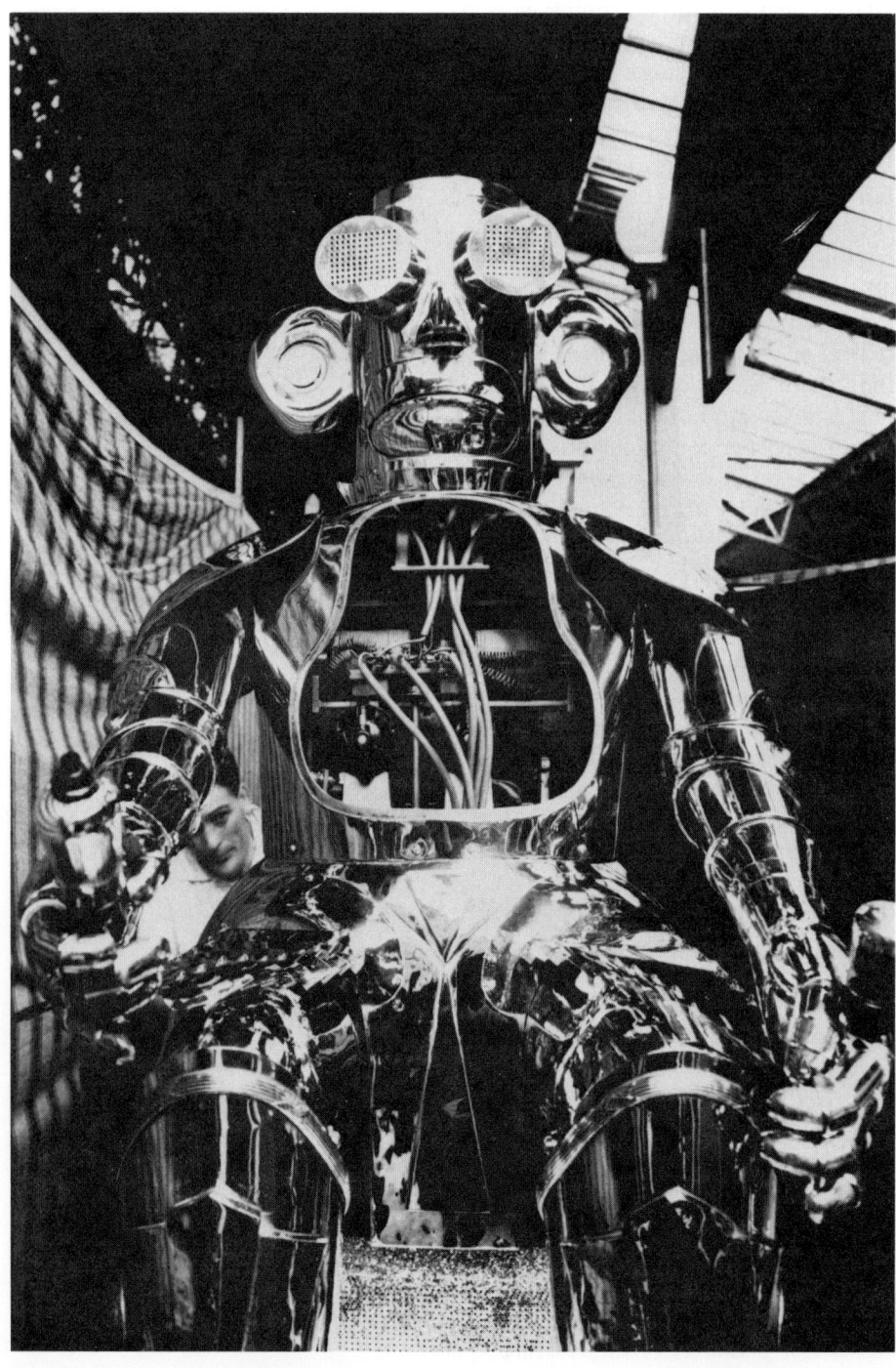

to survive and prosper. How is this dangerous?

Before proceeding, I must point out that biomims have not yet been made, and as far as I know, are not projected. But assuming they exist, what has been created? A series of mechanical arthropod equivalents, effective at dealing with their environment, telemetrically linked to one another and to a central computing device. A social-mechanical octopus of adaptive, self-organising and intelligent machinery.

In the first place, natural man will probably construct his biomim complex purely for service—that is to say, according to the original 'robotnik' concept. So at first he will have a useful slave society to perform all his repetitive, menial or dangerous tasks. Biomims will assemble gear-boxes on production lines, they will clean out sewers, refuel atomic piles, and live on the Moon. Thus man will be free to engage in bingo, pigeon-fancying, psychedelics, and all the other ways which he has derived for expensively wasting his time between the cradle and the grave.

The biomims, given their basic specifications, will take a number of forms depending on their particular function. But, to perform these tasks effectively, the biomims will have to be endowed with an adaptable survival logic. It must be able to prevent its own destruction, because it will be expensive. Thus, for economic reasons alone it will be made sensitive to extremes of temperature and its other senses made aware of the environmental dangers which could destroy it.

Biomims will then begin to learn that every so often, natural man will destroy or disassemble them, either for experimentation or in the performance of some hazardous task. By this time it is probable that biomim factories will be partially staffed by 'adult' members of the family who will be able to perform the repetitive and detailed assembly work that the production of an artificial ganglionic nervous system would demand. Thus machine will make machine. These apparatchik units will be able to examine what design characteristics are necessary through the medium of the central mother device. A comprehensive design study for a self-replicatory automaton, due to the

late J. Van Neuman, was published many years ago.

Moreover, knowing that man may be a threat, knowing the details of their own construction and being able to operate the technology behind their existence, they might take the most logical step which their ability to adapt and learn told them. Since natural man is no longer necessary and has on previous known occasions shown himself to be a threat to survival, the machines would learn to mine, refine and form materials, develop circuits, fabricate sensory systems and alter their design strategy, in order to further the cause of their own survival. This would logically include a defence strategy, perhaps based on the weapons forged by their creators.

One other feature of this iron society is of interest. Our evolution has, we assume, been based upon the relatively slow and inefficient principles of Darwinism. Each generation has had to wait for a spontaneous gene mutation which might confer greater fitness for survival on the next. The biomim will have no need for such an unpredictable process. The machine, given the properties of intelligent adaptation we have been considering, will be able to follow the biologically outmoded principles of Lamarck. For the first time, each subsequent generation of biomims will be able fully to inherit the acquired characteristics of the last. And if the principles of fitness and survival are already specified and understood by the individuals and mother complex of the previous generation, these can be fully designed into the next. The most chilling aspect of this particular possibility is that the cycle time of a generation might only be a few hours.

Whether the Earth of a century from now will be covered by the increasingly efficient hordes of the biomim will depend entirely upon man's technological greed. At present, there is no doubt that we are abrogating more and more human qualities to our machines. This is due mainly to a thirst for leisure and a demand that the more repellent tasks of society be carried out for us. I would feel happier about the outcome if I thought that man had any serious objectives for himself in sight. Progressively our gods are letting us down. God, Jesus, Karl Marx, Mr. Wilson and the Beatles have all been rejected. Apart from the brainwashed millions of China there seems to be little evidence of serious purpose in either western or eastern civilization. The art of our age accurately depicts its formlessness and yet we progress

**At present, there is no doubt that we are abrogating more and more human qualities to our machines.**

DEUS EX MACHINA? 175

> 'No scientist shall by his professional ability harm a human or by inaction in this sphere allow a human being to come to harm.'

technologically at an accelerating rate.

What of future man, lying in his self-erected bed of technological perfection? As his automated factories hum at maximum production rates, as his home is serviced by his personal biomim, what will become of his calm and totally boring habitat? How will he survive, still claiming to possess his qualities of dynamism, originality, decision and creativity? Might he not be simply the redundant tool which, having set the whole biomimetic process in motion, can then die off without seriously affecting the outcome, with the machines continuing to toil and burgeon, taking the ore from the ground, making more of their ilk, and obeying the one in-built instruction which surpasses all others —survival?

It is now possible that the first, primitive steps towards this state of affairs have already occurred. The individual is losing his voice and is becoming irretrievably immersed in the complex system of increasingly intelligent artifacts around him. Although the technology to support a biomim civilisation does not yet exist, there is little doubt that it will and that we are totally unprepared for its impact. What is happening now is that most aspects of our activities are considered in statistical blocks, programmed for efficiency. Are the diurnal inhabitants of multi-storey office blocks really considered as individuals? Their lives and personalities are computerized, their output is compared to a 'norm', even the time they spend in the lavatory is measured and allowed for. Each day they flock to empty cubicles, take their places, produce their required function, eat identical luncheon meat in their sandwiches, and talk about almost identical subjects—the Cup Final, knitting or last night's TV. Battery buildings for battery people.

From these vast spawning-houses may well arise a variant species who is almost totally dehumanised. A species who will not be particularly malignant or benign. He will be a *nothing*. He will be vulnerable to any of the legion of persuasive techniques used by the advertising industry. He will be made to fight in wars without knowing who the enemy is, he will be made to lie, cheat, and do anything required of him by 'the system', 'the board' or 'the management'.

His scruples and sensitivity will lead him to the first stages of becoming the enthusiastic creator of the biomim society. Why should he be so enthusiastic? Because an automated structure to society will give battery man the illusion of freedom. In many ways, as we have seen, he certainly will be more free, but it seems likely that there may be a price to pay, for although it may be decided to build Asimov's laws of robotics into the biomims in order to protect humans, their adaptability and self-organising capacity may well cause them to abandon the laws as unworkable in relation to their survival goal. Ironically enough, Asimov's first law might be rewritten as follows for the scientists who sought to build the biomim: 'No scientist shall by his professional ability harm a human or by inaction in this sphere allow a human being to come to harm.'

---

### ◇ BRANCH POINTS

Boguslaw, Robert. *The New Utopians.* Englewood Cliffs, N.J.: Prentice-Hall, Inc., 1965.

Burke, John G. *The New Technology and Human Values.* Belmont, Calif.: Wadsworth Publishing Company, Inc., 1966.

Hardin, G. "An Evolutionist Looks at Computers." *Datamation*, May 1969.

Hoffman, L. "Computers and Privacy, A Survey." *Computing Surveys*, June 1969.

Newman, Joseph. "The Computer: How It's Changing Our Lives." *U.S. News and World Report*, 1972.

Miller, A. R. *The Assault on Privacy.* Ann Arbor: The University of Michigan Press, 1971.

Sanders, Lawrence. *The Anderson Tapes.* New York: Dell Publishing Co., 1971.

Wessel, Milton R. *Freedom's Edge: The Computer Threat to Society.* Reading, Mass.: Addison-Wesley Publishing Co., 1975.

Weston, Alan F. *Information Technology in a Democracy.* Cambridge, Mass.: Harvard University Press, 1971.

Weston, Alan F. *Privacy and Freedom.* New York: Atheneum, 1967.

### ◯ INTERRUPTS

1. Investigate a computerized dating bureau. Find out how much it costs. How many people does it have in its files? What percentage is male? Female? Does the bureau sell the information given in the applications to junk mailers? Interview some people who have used a computerized dating bureau. What were their results?

2. Find some examples of computer-related frauds. How was the fraud done? Who was to blame? How could have the fraud been prevented?

3. What major effects do you think that computers will have on society twenty or thirty years from now in one of the following areas?
   a) government
   b) democracy

c) work
   d) personal privacy
   e) creating jobs
   f) eliminating jobs
   g) your choice

4. What effect will computers have on the following professions in the next ten years?
   a) mathematicians
   b) doctors
   c) lawyers
   d) middle management
   e) your chosen profession

5. It has been suggested that people could be issued a card similar to a credit card for all financial transactions. Your pay would automatically be credited to your account by computers. Whenever you wanted to make a purchase, you would simply give your card to the store clerk who would insert it in a machine that would verify with a central computer whether funds or credit was available to make the purchase. Discuss one of the following:
   a) What effect would this service have on your life?
   b) How would this card affect you if you could *only* use the card and never make cash purchases?
   c) How might your record of purchases be used to invade your privacy?
   d) How might this card affect gangsters or political reformers?

6. The service discussed in #5 could easily be extended to disallow certain types of purchases for some people, such as alcoholics, parolees, or habitual gamblers. What do you think about restricting their purchases?

7. If all financial transactions were to go through a central computer, couldn't it be used to calculate income tax? What would be the good and bad results of this?

8. When you enter a contest, buy magazine subscriptions, or fill out governmental forms, your name, address, and personal characteristics are often sold to junk mailers or sales firms. One way to trace or verify this process is to "code" your name when filling out such forms by misspelling or changing it so you can see who gets your name from whom. Try this and observe the sources of the junk mail you get.

9. If you were given the free use of a computer for one year (including the help of a programmer), what would you do?

10. Find out what information your college has on you. After you have identified all the files, find out which you can and cannot see. What files can you see about others? Are outside agencies allowed to request copies of your transcripts, financial records, or disciplinary records without your knowing about it? How long are these records kept after you leave school? Can campus police see your records without your knowing about it? Are there any laws (or rules) protecting the confidentiality of your records, or is it just left to the discretion of a clerk?

11. Find out how private your high school records are. First find out what type of records there are—such as grades, test scores, medical records, disciplinary records, and so forth. Which can you see? What records can others see without your knowing about it? How long are high shool records kept before being destroyed? How are the records protected? Can police, government agents, or private investigators "informally" see your records? Who decides who can see what records? Are there any laws protecting your high school records, or is this just left to the discretion of school officials?

12. If you apply for a loan or scholarship, you normally have to disclose a great deal of your own and your parents' financial status. Find out how private this information is. Who on campus can see it? Who from off campus has access to it? Are there any written rules protecting the confidentiality of this information? How long are the records saved before they are destroyed?

13. Suppose your school has just decided to automate student elections. Student voters will mark their choices on a mark sense card with a special pencil; then the cards will be read and counted by data-processing machines. What safeguards will you suggest so no one can "fix" the election in the campus data-processing center?

# 8

CONTROLS
OR
MAYBE
LACK
OF
CONTROLS

# What Computers Cannot Do

BILL SURFACE

One typically clear night at a U.S. Ballistic Missile Early Warning System base in the Arctic, a duty officer was startled to see a computerized typewriter start printing and a red "3"—followed by a "2" and then a "1"—simultaneously appear on a screen. He summoned other officers who turned out to be so similarly astonished that they couldn't move themselves to follow orders despite the horrendous consequences. They knew that well-disciplined technicians monitored signals from a world-wide network of radar and reconnaissance planes, then punched information onto cards about each of the 1,200 orbiting satellites and debris; 1,100 aircraft flights originating in Asia or Europe; and over 100,000 commercial or private planes in the skies every twenty-four hours.

They also knew that the cards were automatically inserted into computers which compared them with cards listing expected altitudes of all objects that should be in the area. Only when a certain number of unidentified, incoming objects were detected would the computers signal that North America was being attacked by Soviet ICBM missiles. The officers realized, moreover, that the computers' self-verification" system eliminated the possibility of errors. Still they hesitated before pushing the synchronized alarm to the White House, North American Air Defense Command, Pentagon, Strategic Air Command, and Canadian Defense Ministry, thereby starting the process that sends the United States' nuclear missiles toward preassigned targets.

The officers' disbelief was precisely the human reaction that some military theorists have feared could happen in such tense circumstances, and, to guard against it, they have argued that when computers detected enemy missiles then computers should be programed to automatically signal for a retaliatory nuclear attack. But men, not machines, made the final decision on this evening. Unlike machines, the nervous, indecisive men waited another minute or two to simply convince themselves that the computerized information was correct. It wasn't. The unidentified objects never advanced and were never fully explained. An accepted conjecture is the computers—which the men didn't trust—had counted a radar reading of the moon as enemy missiles.

Most people, however, apparently trust computers. In the eighteen years since the Bureau of Census purchased Univac, the first commercial computer, we have been committed to a computerized society. Forty-one thousand computer systems are now spinning perforated cards and magnetic tapes in offices from TWA to the CIA as they process our checks, utility bills, airline reservations, tax returns, and record movements of everything from Soviet vessels to potential Presidential assassins. So many other uses are being found for computers that $6.5 billion will be spent in 1978 to install them in such diverse places as the Redemptorist Fathers' monastery near St. Louis and the New York Yankees ticket office. So many computers have been ordered for future delivery that 1) stock market newsletters emphasize that growth rates of computer stocks are three times higher than automobile stocks, and 2) advertisements located everywhere from newspapers to backs of matchbook covers solicit people to become computer programmers and join the "computer revolution."

The revolution seems so glamorous that one hears little pessimism about the machines except from the likes of exasperated wives who receive computerized electrical bills for $2,020 instead of $20. Not only have computers been represented as infallible, impartial, and indispensable, but probably no other machine has been so romanticized and, according to a Senate subcommittee, promoted by "overstated claims and planted stories." We frequently read that computerized "robots" possessing "central brains" and "unforgettable memories" will someday diagnose illnesses, plan military defenses, and organize vacations much more proficiently than obsolete humans.

Starkly put, the day that man becomes subservient to computers is already nearer than generally realized —but for a different reason. We have invested heavily in computer systems without fully grasping what computers *cannot* do: think. Not even the most sophisticated, fourth-generation computer is capable of making any decision that man has not already

made and transferred to a card. Its inner circuitry can, if exposed to problems on a card, furnish a "yes" or "no" type of answer. But, more importantly, computers cannot make even these decisions if they require the slightest deviation from what appears on their program cards.

These limitations become undeniably clear during the most fundamental operations. Computers can, for example, read numbers that have been transferred from income tax returns to punch cards and send bills for underpayments and refunds for overpayment. But computers are helpless if someone mails a check totaling, say, $1,000 for $650 in 1967 taxes and $350 for a first quarterly payment in 1968. Computers can help the Internal Revenue Service's auditors select numbers of taxpayers who add two or more dependents within a year, but cannot determine if such taxpayers married a widow with a child or became the parents of twins and are entitled to the exemptions. Computers can credit interest to numbered bank accounts but cannot read a calendar in order to accurately compute interest, a fact that a bank in New York conceded when it mailed some customers this notice:

30 days hath September, April, June, and November—all the rest have 31 except. . . . Unfortunately, our computer was not told this familiar rhyme and credited all Saveway accounts with 31 days interest in November. To compensate for this mistake, the computer was instructed to make the proper adjustments in December.

In essence, computers cannot do more than elementary clerical work that is usually assigned to $100-a-week clerks and, in numerous situations, prove less efficient. It is not difficult to understand why computers can be so impractical when one considers that even modern "systems analysis" computers are really sophisticated adding machines that do only three basic things: 1) add and subtract (but neither multiply or divide); 2) collate, by matching such items as magnetically numbered checks against the same numbered account (even if the checks are signed "Batman"); 3) file, retrieve, and compare information and then furnish instant balances such as whether or not space is available on a certain airline flight.

Computers, to be sure, do all of these things faster than humans. One new computer can make more computations in a single minute than a human mathematician could do by hand in 4,000 years. But computers also make the same type of errors as indifferent clerks and, once they do, usually make more mistakes in one minute than ten clerks do in a lifetime. Even normally trivial mistakes blamed on human programmers become monumental when put onto computerized punch cards simply because computers cannot think.

When men sense that they have erred or something is grossly wrong, they usually have the intuition to either rectify the mistake or at least stop working. Computers, even when fed erroneous or obviously ridiculous information, continue at incomparable speeds until the project ultimately ends in disaster. That fact became obvious at Cape Kennedy when a programmer omitted a hyphen between two 5s on a program card —causing the computer to misread its instructions and the rocket to shake so uncontrollably that it diverted itself toward Rio de Janeiro. The rocket, which cost $18,500,000, had to be destroyed only 293 seconds after lifting off.

Computer manufacturers defend their machines in instances like this with the oft-reiterated phrase "garbage in, garbage out." While it is true that so-called bad "input" automatically results in a bad "output" from computers, it is equally true that computers need not be erroneously operated to precipitate calamitous situations. There is increasing evidence that computers can be so erratic or so easily made inoperative (i.e., by a mere speck of dust) that, when used for some functions, they still must be considered as experimental machinery. One critic, Senator Henry Jackson of Washington, was not hesitant in stating, during a recent investigation of computers, why the machines are so unpredictable: "Systems analysis and cost-effectiveness studies are greatly oversold by many of the proponents. At best, systems analysis still is in a very early stage of development and is bedeviled by difficulties."

Such difficulties are so potentially ruinous that they have fostered at least two new businesses: computer detective agencies and insurance against computer-inflicted disasters. Neither business can be considered superfluous. The necessity of insuring against errant computers was vividly illustrated recently when the co-owners of the Food Center Wholesale Grocers in Boston rented a new computer to maintain an inventory of their 4,500 items and reduce costs of clerical employees. About all that the computers reduced, however, was the number of Food Center's clients. When one retail grocer ordered peaches, the computer informed him that none were in stock although peaches were literally stacked to the ceiling. Grocers who ordered twelve cases of soup received 240 cases, which, for lack of space, had to be stored on sidewalks. Orders for napkins brought crates of toilet tissue. And computerized bills that should have been for $14 were sent out as $214. But the computer often "compensated" for overcharges by reducing actual charges on some grocers' bills and not charging many grocers anything at all. These and other mistakes were so plainly the fault of the computer and not its operators that a court awarded Food Center $53,200 in damages against the manufacturer.

Examples such as this are too common and too diverse to support manufacturers' rebuttals that they are "isolated incidents." A mere random survey shows that bank executives repeatedly find that computers credit deposits to wrong accounts and, in turn, cause computers to mistakenly return checks because of "insufficient funds"; a company which used computers to address 7,000 labels for sending a YMCA's registration catalog belatedly learned that some persons received sixty catalogs while others received none; companies selling lists of potential customers are being sued by dozens of direct mail houses because computers repeated thousands of names twenty or thirty times; and universities have discovered that computers infuriated seniors expecting to graduate by sending notices that they failed their courses (while simultaneously surprising other students with notifications of unexpectedly high grades).

Even miscalculations that computers make before nationwide audiences exemplify their incredibly high incidence of error. In the 1966 election alone, CBS-TV's computerized Vote Profile Analysis declared that George P. Mahoney was the "probable winner" of the election for governor of Maryland, only to have the voters actually select Spiro Agnew. NBC-TV's Electronic Vote Analysis was the first of the new network computers to calculate that Lester Maddox had "won" Georgia's gubernatorial race only to have a human later announce that neither Maddox nor his opponent received the required majority of votes to win and a choice would have to be made by Georgia's legislature. Yet both computers were surpassed on that evening by ABC-TV's Research Selected Vote Profile. It calculated eight wrong winners.

These miscalculations were detected only because they were compared with totals computed by men. Such comparisons are rarely made when computers print out information used by businesses and agencies to make vital decisions, and this underscores the undeserved trust placed in them. Most individuals who make a corporation's or agency's major decisions seldom understand the rudiments of computers. But they still accept computers' impressive, scientific-looking information and, by doing so, have unknowingly transferred many responsibilities to mathematicians, economists, and even clerks and corporals. An executive at a well known institution in the Wall Street area probably spoke for a number of men when he recently confided: "I'm vice president in charge of computer operations, but if I want to know what the computers are doing—or can do—I have to ask those kids in there."

The practice is so prevalent that the Senate Subcommittee on National Security and International Relations, in examining the Pentagon's reliance on a computerized Planning-Programming-Budgeting System (PPBS), commented: "Does PPBS provide a wholly rational basis

## Daily Surveillance Sheet, 1987, From a Nationwide Data Bank

The "Daily Surveillance Sheet" below is offered as some food for thought to anyone concerned with the establishment of the proposed "National Data Bank." Hopefully will help illustrate that *everyone* should be concerned.

NATIONAL DATA BANK
DAILY SURVEILLANCE SHEET
CONFIDENTIAL
JULY 9, 1987

| | | |
|---|---|---|
| SUBJECT: | DENNIE VAN TASSEL<br>UNIVERSITY OF CALIFORNIA<br>SANTA CRUZ, CALIF.<br>MALE<br>AGE 38<br>MARRIED<br>PROGRAMMER | |
| PURCHASES: | WALL STREET JOURNAL | .25 |
| | BREAKFAST | 2.50 |
| | GASOLINE | 6.00 |
| | PHONE (328-1826) | .15 |
| | PHONE (308-7928) | .15 |
| | PHONE (421-1931) | .15 |
| | BANK (CASH WITHDRAWAL) | (120.00) |
| | LUNCH | 3.50 |
| | COCKTAIL | 1.50 |
| | LINGERIE | 26.95 |
| | PHONE (369-2436) | .35 |
| | BOURBON | 11.40 |
| | NEWSPAPER | .25 |

**** COMPUTER ANALYSIS ****

OWNS STOCK (90 PER CENT PROBABILITY).

HEAVY STARCH BREAKFAST. PROBABLY OVERWEIGHT.

for decision-making? Have we arrived at that technocratic utopia where judgment is a machine-product? Not even the zealots of PPBS would answer affirmatively, although some of them talk as though we should be moving in that direction."

The Pentagon had moved so rapidly in that direction after purchasing 3,225 computers that the subcommittee concluded: 1) even military decisions were made by computer operators; 2) optimistic computations from computers were frequently accepted over the dissenting opinions of individual's on lower levels; and 3) a computerized "cost-and-effectiveness" study led to the construction of an oil-fueled ship that cost $277 million but was virtually obsolete ten months before it was launched.

An even more disquieting aspect of the dependence on computers is that these machines are printing less and less information onto sheets that can be audited by humans. In fact, computers are often sold as being so "honest" that they eliminate the expense of auditors. While computers *are* as honest as cash registers, they do what skilled programmers tell them to do and, unfortunately, are controlled by individuals such as the quiet man formerly in charge of computer cards at a brokerage firm in New York. He went to the office on weekends and programed the computers to gradually transfer $250,000 from the corporation's account to accounts for him and his wife by showing that it had been used to purchase stock. Not only did the scheme go undetected for eight years, but the company's management was so impressed with the computer programmer that they promoted him to vice president before accidently discovering the mythical account. Yet, after the programmer confessed, nobody could determine how he manipulated the computer to steal the $250,000. He had to tell the auditors.

Stock firms, banks, and wholesalers are repeatedly embezzled by two methods that computer operators find ridiculously simple: 1) have computers deduct a few, seemingly inconsequential cents in excess service charges, dividends, interest, or income taxes from thousands of customers' accounts and channel the total to themselves; 2) manipulate computers to systematically report portions of an inventory as normal "breakage" or "loss" and then divert the merchandise to accomplices. In both schemes, the embezzlers eventually remove the rigged cards, insert the genuine tape onto the computer, and conceal who did it and how (and sometimes if) the embezzlement transpired.

It would be erroneous to use difficulties such as these as documentation that computers are mere gadgets. They are not. What the problems illustrate is that computers need to be viewed realistically as highly useful but often limited tools. They are neither robots that perform priceless services nor are they capable of the grandiose proficiencies that many people visualize and, in turn, are prone to overreact to when evaluating them. Is it, for example, anything but an overreaction when the Menominee Indians in Wisconsin ask for one teacher to instruct their fifteen children and the Office of Education responds with plans to install a computer, costing $2,000,000, that would enable the children to push buttons and hear recorded instruction? There are many men, because of computers' current status, who applaud such decisions. But is the decision any more debatable than if a community requested another policeman and received a new burglar alarm that assertedly does a more scientific job?

---

BOUGHT 6.00 DOLLARS GASOLINE. OWNS VW. SO FAR THIS WEEK HAS BOUGHT 14.00 DOLLARS WORTH OF GASOLINE. OBVIOUSLY DOING SOMETHING BESIDES JUST DRIVING 9 MILES TO WORK.

BOUGHT GASOLINE AT 7.57. SAFE TO ASSUME HE WAS LATE TO WORK.

PHONE NO. 328-1826 BELONGS TO SHADY LANE—SHADY WAS ARRESTED FOR BOOKMAKING IN 1975.

PHONE NO. 308-7928. EXPENSIVE MEN'S BARBER—SPECIALIZES IN BALD MEN OR HAIR STYLING.

PHONE NO. 421-1931. RESERVATIONS FOR LAS VEGAS (WITHOUT WIFE). THIRD TRIP THIS YEAR TO LAS VEGAS (WITHOUT WIFE). WILL SCAN FILE TO SEE IF ANYONE ELSE HAS GONE TO LAS VEGAS AT THE SAME TIME AND COMPARE TO HIS PHONE NUMBERS.

WITHDREW 120.00 DOLLARS CASH. VERY UNUSUAL SINCE ALL LEGAL PURCHASES CAN BE MADE USING THE NATIONAL SOCIAL SECURITY CREDIT CARD. CASH USUALLY ONLY USED FOR ILLEGAL PURCHASES. IT WAS PREVIOUSLY RECOMMENDED THAT ALL CASH BE OUTLAWED AS SOON AS IT BECOMES POLITICALLY POSSIBLE.

DRINKS DURING HIS LUNCH.

BOUGHT VERY EXPENSIVE LINGERIE. NOT HIS WIFE'S SIZE.

PHONE NO. 369-2436. MISS SWEET LOCKS.

PURCHASED EXPENSIVE BOTTLE OF BOURBON. HE HAS PURCHASED 5 BOTTLES OF BOURBON IN THE LAST 30 DAYS. EITHER HEAVY DRINKER OR MUCH ENTERTAINING.

**** OVERALL ANALYSIS ****

LEFT WORK EARLY AT 4:00, SINCE HE PURCHASED BOURBON 1 MILE FROM HIS JOB AT 4:10. (OPPOSITE DIRECTION FROM HIS HOME).

BOUGHT NEWSPAPER AT 6:30 NEAR HIS HOUSE. UNACCOUNTABLE 2½ HOURS. MADE 3 PURCHASES TODAY FROM YOUNG BLONDES. (STATISTICAL 1 CHANCE IN 78.) THEREFORE PROBABLY HAS WEAKNESS FOR YOUNG BLONDES.

# Computer Crime

DENNIE VAN TASSEL

One very positive sign in man's existence comes from an unlikely source, that is, his ability to commit criminal acts no matter how difficult the circumstances. He escapes from escape-proof prisons, tampers with tamper-proof devices, and burglarizes burglar-proof establishments. No level of technology has found itself above the ingenuity of a clever, albeit dishonest, mind, not even the computer.

These examples of larceny under difficult circumstances illustrate Dansiger's basic rule: "Whenever something is invented, someone, somewhere, immediately begins trying to figure out a method to beat the invention." Computerized larceny has several advantages over regular old style larceny. Actually, the plain and obvious fact is that computerized larceny is seldom discovered and usually difficult to prosecute even if it is discovered. And since the details are not yet common knowledge perhaps it is worth reconstructing them here, to establish a broad pattern of its development. To start with, address customer files are copied usually with the help of the owner's computer, thus adding insult to injury. Once they are copied the files are sold to a competitor and if the competitor uses the files discretely no one is the wiser, except maybe the sales manager who notices that one company has suddenly become quite aggressive.

Many thefts are simply a by-product of a computer. An example is the computer operator who steals a hundred checks, prints them on a computer on Friday night, cashes them during the weekend, and skips town on Monday. This is not really computerized stealing since the fault lies in the safety of the checks and not the computer. But the crime is usually still blamed on the computer even though a manual check writing machine could have been used just as well.

There are several mythical examples of computer crime. I call them mythical because they actually did happen but the victim of the crime was usually so embarrassed to admit he had been taken so easily, that rather than suffer humiliation, he would prefer to hush up the crime. The first mythical example supposedly took place in a large bank when computers were first being used. An alert programmer noticed that the interest is calculated to the nearest cent and then truncated. That is, if the interest is calculated out to be 2.3333 . . . it is simply left at 2.33—thus contributing nicely to the bank profits. The programmer simply fixed the computer to add some of the truncated portion to his account and in a short while, ended up with a very sizable bank account. All the time the customer accounts stayed in balance. Eventually he was caught by bank auditors who noticed he was withdrawing large sums and not making similar deposits.

Another enterprising young man who received his first set of bank depositors' slips with magnetically imprinted account numbers on the bottom, correctly surmised that the new computer system probably only checked the magnetically imprinted account numbers on the bottom of the checks. So he promptly went to his bank and carefully dispersed his full supply of imprinted slips among the neat stacks at the bank desk. Not too surprising, the slips were used all day by customers making deposits, and even less surprising, the man stopped in the following morning and closed his account, which had mushroomed to over $50,000 and has not been seen since. Needless to say, this scheme no longer works. Crime, like any other business, offers the highest rewards to those who are first to try out a new method.

One of the more interesting aspects of this case is the fact that even though the fault was the improper design of the computer system, the computer was the scapegoat. Using the computer as a scapegoat is a common day phenomenon. Election returns are miscalculated and the computer is blamed when it is really the blame of the programmer. The next time you go into a business and someone blames the computer for an error ask him if he doesn't have people telling the computer what to do. It is safe to assume that if the computer is screwed up, so is the rest of the business, especially today when most businesses depend so heavily on computers.

Since the computer cannot defend itself, nor prove the accuser at fault, it is safer to blame the computer than another person. This common acceptance of the computer as a "giant uncontrollable brain" has led to at least one very successful embezzlement. Three employees (an account executive, a margin clerk, and a cashier) of the Beaumont, Texas, office of E. F. Hutton & Co., a major New York securities firm, allegedly used the computer as a scapegoat while they were milking customer accounts for more than a half million dollars over a period of several years. They were finally caught in 1968.

This enterprising trio was skimming funds off of customer accounts. Every time one of the clients noticed that his accounts were incorrect the customer was allegedly told that the "dumb computer" had made a mistake, a fable which received instant credibility. The computer all the time was giving the correct results but the excuse covered up the fraud.

In the following case lady fortune smiled with a favor on a programmer, Milo, and frowned on the National City Bank of Minneapolis. Milo had a very bad credit rating and occasionally wrote checks on an empty account but the data processing service center where Milo worked had just been hired to computerize the check-handling system at the bank where he had his account. While writing programs to warn the bank of customers with empty accounts and incoming checks he simply programmed the computer to ignore his personal checks any time his accounts had insufficient funds to cover them. The program allowed each of his bad checks to clear the bank, and didn't debit the employee's account for the overdraft.

The only reason the scheme was discovered was because the computer broke down and the bank was forced to process the checks by hand and without warning in came one of Milo's checks. The check bounced and the scheme was discovered. The check bouncing programmer pleaded guilty in 1966, repaid the money and received a suspended sentence.

Most criminal uses of computers are by individuals but organized crime has not overlooked the possibility of large profits through the use of computerized embezzlement. There are already at least two cases of large scale criminal use. In 1968, a Diners' Club credit card fraud resulted in at least a $1,000,000 loss to the credit card company. A computer printout of real Diners' Club customers was used by the gang to make up phony credit cards having real names and account numbers on blank Diners' Club cards. According

**No level of technology has found itself above the ingenuity of a clever, albeit dishonest, mind, not even the computer.**

to the police the computer listing was stolen in 1967 by Alfonse Confessore in New York. At the same time 3,000 credit cards disappeared. After the crime was discovered Alfonse Confessore was rubbed out in a gang-land style murder.

The forged credit cards were sold along with other forged identification documents for $85 to $150 per ID package to persons engaged in motor vehicle thefts. Federal agents said that the forged cards were often used to finance a leisurely trip to Atlanta, Georgia, with a stolen car, followed by an air trip home, by way of Miami, Florida.

The most interesting aspect of this case is the sophisticated level of organization. The gang found out that the club's computers were programmed to reject only false names and/or numbers, so the first indication of fraud often didn't come until the real customer received his bill and complained. Thus, ID packages would be completely safe for thirty to sixty days with almost no risk to the user.

Federal agents said that Las Vegas

**The next time you go into a business and someone blames the computer for an error ask him if he doesn't have people telling the computer what to do.**

casinos may have been bilked out of hundreds of thousands of dollars after granting credit on the basis of forged Diners' Club credit cards. However, federal agents also said that if any hotel wanted to cooperate in underworld "skimming" of profits, this could be a method of operations since bad credit losses are tax deductible.

In another case a computer was used by a crime organization to embezzle over $1,000,000 in Salinas, California, before the owner was caught in 1968. A service bureau owner, Robert, used his computer to budget embezzlements so smoothly that he was able to take a quarter of a million dollars within a year from a fruit and vegetable firm without the loss being noticed.

Robert was an accountant and he noticed that the fruit company had no complete audit operation. His method included having the computer calculate just how much should be embezzled during a specific period. He did this by using false and real data in different computer runs and by comparing the results on the cost of produce and this way was able to keep all operation costs and profits in balance. The only reason he was caught was because a small-time bank became suspicious of the size of a check made out to a labor organization. Robert was sentenced to from one to ten years for grand theft and forgery.

Banks have traditionally been cautious when protecting their money from embezzlement, so it is not surprising that there have been few examples of computer related crime, but this example shows that they also can be victims. In 1970 it was discovered that a total of $900,000 was taken from the National Bank of North America, and a branch of Banker's Trust Company in New York.

The scheme involved five men which included three brothers, a bank vice-president and an assistant branch manager.

The brothers were allegedly able to manipulate bank funds without the banks' computers detecting them by making out deposit slips for cash transactions when they were actually depositing checks, according to the district attorney's office.

Since cash transactions are recorded as immediate deposits, checks subsequently drawn were covered by the false cash deposits.

If the deposits were made as checks, the computers would not credit the money to the account immediately. When checks were drawn, the computer would indicate insufficient funds with an uncollected check on deposit, a spokesman for the district attorney's office said.

Two companies were involved in the operation of the scheme, according to the district attorney's office. Bay Auto Sales had an account at the National Bank of North America and Baywood Stables had an account at the Bankers Trust, both in Jamaica, Queens.

The brothers were members of both companies. The scheme was uncovered when a bank messenger failed to deliver a bundle of checks to the clearing house, leaving $440,000 worth of checks uncovered. According to authorities the scheme had been going on for four years.

As the three previous examples show organized crime has already discovered the possibilities available in criminal use of computers but so far no really big embezzlements have been discovered. Yet several very ripe possibilities exist. One of the most obvious is in the area of large payrolls in companies as in the old story about the bar that was losing money. When a check was run, it was noticed that the bartender rang up each sale on one of four registers. Of course, when it was discovered the owner had only three registers, the problem was solved.

Similar scenes have been used with payrolls. Either friends, or fictitious

## News Item: Man Bites Ford
*Consumer Reports*

On December 2, 1963, an unseasonably cold day in Jefferson County, Ky., John T. Swarens drove his 1962 Ford as usual from his home in southern Indiana across the Ohio River into Jefferson County, Ky., and parked in the parking lot of the factory where he was employed. At quitting time, his car was gone. The police, to whom he reported the apparent theft, informed him that the Ford Motor Credit Co. had repossessed the car. Mr. Swarens hitchhiked home in the cold.

Since buying the car the previous February, he had kept up the payments without fail, sending the money each month to Ford's home office in Michigan. Somewhere along the computerized line, the Ford collection office in Louisville was misinformed. It thought he was delinquent. In June and again in August, it sent representatives to his house. Each time he showed them his cancelled checks as evidence of payment, and the collectors went away. When they came around for the third time, he lost patience. Making clear he would show them no more records, and displaying a shotgun, he strongly suggested that they leave. They did —promising to repossess his car.

The day after his car was taken, Mr. Swarens went to Louisville to get it back. The Ford Motor Credit Co. people there admitted a mistake had been made and apologized. They offered to return the car and his out-of-pocket expenses if he would sign a release exonerating Ford from further liability. Mr. Swarens declined to sign what he later told a jury was "a blank piece of paper." He went home without his car. When the next payment came due, he did not pay it. Ford notified him he was in default and later apparently sold the car. After mulling over his grievance for many months, Mr. Swarens went to a lawyer, who filed suit in his behalf demanding compensation for the fair market value of the car and punitive damages. When Ford confessed liability, a jury awarded Mr. Swarens $7000, including $5000 punitive damages. Finally, late last people are paid extra amounts each week. This is especially easy if there is a high turnover of help, or lots of overtime, or piece work pay. Another payroll trick is to deduct extra amounts for tax or other payroll deductions each week and transfer the money to your account. Then at the end of the year calculate everyone's deductions correctly for income tax purposes. The only way someone could catch this is to save all your weekly payroll stubs and see if the deductions add up correctly at the end of the year. People have a tendency to believe the veracity of a computer printout but careful observation shows that computer programmers and auditors usually sit down each week and calculate their pay to see if it is actually correct. Just a couple of years ago an engineer of an aerospace firm calculated his own interest on his bank account and noticed that it was incorrectly calculated by the bank—in the bank's favor. After several letters the bank decided to humor the guy and check out his account and sure enough the customer was correct. No one had thought to question the computer. When is the last time you calculated your bank interest or paycheck to see if it was correct?

Another area of computer crime which is especially vulnerable is in the area of payroll manipulation. This fact is known by most auditors so payrolls are usually audited rather closely. There was at least one case where a large payroll theft was committed. A group of young men manipulated the computers of the Human Resources Administration in New York City in order to divert over $2.7 million from the anti-poverty program budget. Over a period of nine months false pay checks were made out to 40,000 non-existent youth workers. It is estimated that up to 30 people may have been involved in the scheme.

year, the Kentucky Court of Appeals, in an opinion rejecting Ford Credit's petition for a new trial (Ford contended the award was excessive); wrote a ringing paragraph in defense of man against machine:

"Ford explains that this whole incident occurred because of a mistake by a computer. Men feed data to a computer and men interpret the answer the computer spews forth. In this computerized age, the law must require that men in the use of computerized data regard those with whom they are dealing as more important than a perforation on a card. Trust in the infallibility of a computer is hardly a defense, when the opportunity to avoid error is as apparent and repeated as was here presented."

We would like to be able to say that the average consumer, in his bouts with false billings, could expect to win the kind of victory Mr. Swarens won. But, obviously, most billing errors are too trifling to take to court, and few debt collectors go so far as to seize security or seek a judgment based on their own mistakes. According to Clifford E. Graese, partner in the accounting firm of Peat, Marwick, Mitchell & Co., what consumers now are complaining about is "third-generation computer billing." This precocious grandchild of early computer billing instead of staying in the back room deals directly with the public. Says Graese: "Thus, at the very time when the need for sensitivity to interpersonal relationships is increasing, we find transactions losing their personal identity through the computerization process. The implications have been underestimated."

CU's mail indicates that it is not consumers who are doing the underestimating. Discontent is rising. Their credit ratings, if not their cars, washing machines, color TV's and refrigerators, are being threatened. And it is no empty threat. According to the aforementioned Mr. Graese, unless some human being tells a computer to stop sending out unwarranted dunning letters, an erroneous report may be sent automatically to the credit bureau.

**Organized crime has already discovered the possibilities available in criminal use of computers.**

We have already seen one example of a computer being used to calculate how much to embezzle in the Salinas, California, case. Police can expect to see more of this since organized crime has both the money and the knowhow for computer usage. Some of the ways in which computers are used to prevent crime include the analysis of payrolls for excessive overtime pay, or the analysis of inventories for excessive breakage, or selection of any large change in price of items being purchased or sold. All these could be mistakes or legitimate changes but they could also be an indication of embezzlement.

The use of breakage or tolerance allowances is another especially vulnerable area for computerized stealing. Most companies such as warehouses or department stores have a shrinkage allowance to cover items which are lost, broken, or the result of bookkeeping errors. But if a programmer modified the shrinkage allowance at the same time a large scale theft was going on, the theft would probably not be noticed. Once the theft was completed the shrinkage allowance could be reset to its original level. The previous examples of crime have been just criminals modifying the old techniques for the field of crime. But computers have brought forth a new era of crime. This is already evident in the case when a computer was used to calculate how much to embezzle. But there are areas of crime which are unique to the computer field.

There has always been a rather good market in hot computer gear such as cards, tapes, or disks but because of their size, stolen computers have not until recently entered the picture. In early 1969 a $2,500 Wang Computer disappeared from the Argonne National Laboratories. It was later traced to Iowa State University by the F.B.I. A student working in a training program of Argonne had fallen in love with his Wang computer and took it back to college to do his homework. However, as computers decrease in size we can expect to hear of more stolen computers.

**The future holds a real gold mine for a criminal who specializes in manipulating or stealing computer information.**

The most common theft in the computer business is in the area of software. Programs can be copied and sold and the copier is almost guaranteed immunity from any legal action since the original never disappears. Competitors hire programmers sometimes on the hope that even if the programmer won't bring any software with them they will at least bring all the software ideas with them to their new jobs. There is no way to estimate software thefts because they are so seldom discovered and quite often are not even of concern to the loser.

One rather large software theft case came to light on the British computer scene. The case involved the biggest commercial installation in progress in Europe, the state-financed airline BOAC. The programming projects involved $100 million programmed on 360/50's and 700 Ferranti terminal displays. The *London Times* at the end of April, 1968, printed a short story which revealed that BOAC was investigating the circumstances in which some employees had expropriated information for consultancy work.

The alleged plagiarism included a combination of IBM's PARS (Programmed Airline Reservation System) and the corporation's own seven million dollar investment in software.

Another software theft which was discovered took place in Texas. In this case the man was prosecuted criminally for taking computer programs. He worked for a company that developed geophysical programs for oil companies. Each program had a value of about $50,000. He took programs home to work on them and kept copies of them. Within a short span of time he had 50 programs and convinced his roommate to approach a major oil company with the programs. The oil company acted like it was interested and cooperated with the police in accumulating evidence. Both the programmer and his roommate were tried and convicted and both received five year prison sentences.

The Internal Revenue Service has long heralded their computers as devices to prevent income fraud so there was some poetic justice involved in the discovery in June, 1970, that these same computers had been used to embezzle money.

No programming frauds have been discovered but clerical staff has been discovered manipulating input documents.

One would-be computer embezzler was an adjustment clerk who came upon information that some tax credits were not being claimed, possibly because they had been misfiled.

Through data she prepared for the computer, she transferred the credits from one taxpayer's account to another. Each time the credit was recorded, she transferred it to another account. When she felt sure she had covered her trail enough, she credited the tax credit to a relative and refund checks for $1,500 were duly issued.

The embezzlement was uncovered when the IRS Inspection Service, pursuing its regular audit program, came across a complaint from a taxpayer who claimed he had never gotten credit for $1,500 he had paid.

Another misbehaving computer clerk was caught through a banker's alertness. This clerk had manipulated records and established a false tax credit from a true taxpayer for a relative. When the relative took the refund check to the local bank, the banker became suspicious about the size of the refund and alerted IRS.

Inspectors retraced the path of the check back to its source and found the document effecting the transfer to the relative.

Recently a news item reported that a spy had turned over to Communist East Germany business information on over 3000 West German companies. A former data processing department employee made duplicates of tapes stored at his company's leased-time facility and passed these behind the Iron Curtain.

And last but not least, there is the young man who simply changed the program to accept the last card of the file as the final total. This was accepted by the company because no one had time to check out the computer totals. His only mistake was he went skiing one weekend and broke his leg.

### CONCLUSION

The future holds a real gold mine for a criminal who specializes in manipulating or stealing computer information. One good computer raid could have an immense payoff. If there is any truth in the wise old saying that we should be able to learn from our mistakes, hopefully this short history of computer related crime will alert us and help us to prevent crime in the future.

---

### KIBERNETIKA

The machine reads books,
It computes excellently,
Multiplies and subtracts
Kilometers and tons,
Thousands and millions.
Since it is so clever,
It has a memory,
And an intellect, and the gift of speech,
And sometimes nearly human.
This means that it certainly
Will replace people?!
And—most interesting of all—
It is learning to write songs. . .
But it is difficult to say what sort—
Good or poor.
Only by looking at the zenith can I
See to what
Heights it has risen.
But who invented the machine?
You, man!
Bear the proud glory
That is yours by right!
Soon it will not be necessary
For man to breathe with strain
Or to sweat heavily
While working.
And he trains the machine,
Entrusts his heavy labor to it,
And even his zeal—let it multiply!
And what shall we do with love?
Oh no! We will not yield it to the
    machine!
When I see you, man,
I am every time carried away
By your mind and your hands.
But who would sow grain on stones?
Who would allow soulless machines—
Their pointers, bolts and screws—
To measure love?
Who would dare to trust love to them?!

BAKHTIYAR VAGABZADE

# The Day the Computers Got Waldon Ashenfelter

BOB ELLIOTT AND RAY GOULDING

A presidential commission has recommended approval of plans for establishing a computerized data center where all personal information on individual Americans compiled by some twenty scattered agencies would be assembled in one place and made available to the federal government as a whole.

Backers of the proposal contend that it would lead to greater efficiency, and insist that the cradle-to-grave dossiers on the nation's citizens would be used only in a generalized way to help deal with broad issues. Opponents argue that the ready availability of so much confidential data at the push of a computer button could pose a dangerous threat to the privacy of the individual by enabling the federal bureaucracy to become a monstrous, snooping Big Brother.

Obviously, the plan elicits reactions that are emotional, and cooler heads are needed to envision the aura of quiet, uneventful routine certain to pervade the Central Data Bank once it becomes accepted as just another minor government agency.

Fade in:

*Interior—Basement GHQ of the Central Data Bank—Night. (At stage right, 950 sophisticated third-generation computers may be seen stretching off into the distance. At stage left, the CDB graveyard-shift charge d'affairés, Nimrod Gippard, is seated behind a desk. He is thirty-five-ish and attired in socks that don't match. At the open, Gippard is efficiently stuffing mimeographed extortion letters to Omaha's 3277 suspected sex deviates into envelopes. He glances up as Waldon Ashenfelter, an indoorsy type of questionable ancestry, enters.)*

GIPPARD: Yes, sir?

ASHENFELTER (flashing ID card): Ashenfelter. Bureau of Indian Affairs. Like to have you run a check on a key figure named Y. Claude Garfunkel.

GIPPARD (reaching for pad and pencil): Sure thing. What's his Social Security number?

ASHENFELTER: I dunno.

GIPPARD: Hmmm. How about his zip code? Or maybe a cross-reference to some banks where he may have been turned down for a loan. Just any clue at all to his identity.

ASHENFELTER: Well, as I say, his name is Y. Claude Garfunkel.

GIPPARD (after a weary sigh): It's not much to go on, but I'll see what I can do.

*(Gippard rises and crosses to the master data-recall panel. Ashenfelter strolls to a nearby computer and casually begins checking the confidential reports on his four small children to learn how many are known extremists.)*

ASHENFELTER: You're new here, aren't you?

GIPPARD: No. Just my first week on the night shift. Everybody got moved around after we lost McElhenny.

ASHENFELTER: Wasn't he that heavy-set fellow with beady eyes who drove the Hudson?

GIPPARD: Yeah. Terrible thing. Pulled his own dossier one night and found out he was a swish. Kind of made him go all to pieces.

ASHENFELTER: That's a shame. And now I suppose he's gone into analysis and gotten himself cross-filed as a loony.

GIPPARD: No. He blew his brains out right away. But having a suicide on your record can make things tough, too.

ASHENFELTER: Yeah. Shows a strong trend toward instability.

*(The computer informs Ashenfelter that his oldest boy was detained by police in 1963 for roller-skating on municipal property, and that the five-year-old probably founded the Farmer-Labor Party in Minnesota.)*

ASHENFELTER (cont.) (mutters in despair): Where did I fail them as a father?

GIPPARD: Didn't you tell me you're with Indian Affairs?

ASHENFELTER: Yeah. Why?

GIPPARD: I think I'm onto something hot. Is that like India Indians or whoop-it-up Indians?

ASHENFELTER: I guess you'd say whoop-it-up.

GIPPARD: Well, either way, no Indian named Garfunkel has ever complied with the Alien Registration Law.

ASHENFELTER: I never said he was an Indian. He's Jewish, and I think he's playing around with my wife.

GIPPARD: Gee, that's too bad.

ASHENFELTER (dramatically): Oh, I blame myself really. I guess I'd started taking LaVerne for granted and—

GIPPARD: No. I mean it's too bad he's only Jewish. The computers aren't programmed to feed back home-wreckers by religious affiliation.

ASHENFELTER: Oh.

GIPPARD: Can you think of anything kinky that's traditional with Jews? You know. Like draft dodging . . . smoking pot . . . something a computer could really hang its hat on.

ASHENFELTER: No. They just seem to feed each other a lot of chicken soup. And they do something around Christmastime with candles. But I'm not sure any of it's illegal.

GIPPARD: We'll soon see. If the curve on known poultry processors correlates geographically with a year-end upswing in tallow rendering— Well, you can appreciate what that kind of data would mean to the bird dogs at the ICC and the FDA. They'd be able to pinpoint exactly where it was all happening and when.

ASHENFELTER: Uh-huh—Where and when what?

GIPPARD: That's exactly what I intend to find out.

(*Gippard turns back to the panel and resumes work with a sense of destiny. Ashenfelter, whistling softly to himself, absently begins plunking the basic melody of "Mexicali Rose" on the keyboard of a nearby computer. The machine responds by furnishing him with Howard Hughes's 1965 income tax return and the unlisted phone numbers of eight members of a New Orleans wife-swapping club who may have known Lee Harvey Oswald. As Ashenfelter pockets the information, Major General Courtney ("Old Napalm and Guts") Nimshaw enters. He has a riding crop but no mustache.*)

NIMSHAW: Yoohoo! Anybody home?

GIPPARD: Back here at the main console.

(*Nimshaw moves to join Gippard, then sees Ashenfelter for the first time and freezes. The two stand eyeing each other suspiciously as Gippard re-enters the scene.*)

GIPPARD: Oh, forgive me. General Nimshaw, I'd like for you to meet Ashenfelter from Indian Affairs.

(*Nimshaw and Ashenfelter ad-lib warm greetings as they shake hands. Then each rushes off to pull the dossier of the other. Ashenfelter learns that Nimshaw was a notorious bed wetter during his days at West Point and that his heavy drinking later caused an entire airborne division to be parachuted into Ireland on D-Day. Nimshaw learns that Ashenfelter owns 200 shares of stock in a Canadian steel mill that trades with Communist China and that he has been considered a bad credit risk since 1949, when he refused to pay a Cincinnati dance studio for $5500 worth of tango lessons. Apparently satisfied, both men return to join Gippard, who has been checking out a possible similarity in the patterns of poultry-buying by key Jewish housewives and reported sightings of Soviet fishing trawlers off the Alaskan coast.*)

ASHENFELTER: Working late tonight, eh, General?

NIMSHAW (nervously): Well, I just stumbled across a little military hardware transport thing. We seem to have mislaid an eighty-six-car trainload of munitions between here and the West Coast. Can't very well write it off as normal pilferage. So I thought maybe Gippard could run a check for me on the engineer and brakeman. You know. Where they hang out in their spare time. Whether they might take a freight train with them. What do you think, Gipp?

GIPPARD: Sure. Just have a few more things to run through for Ashenfelter first. He's seeking a final solution to the Jewish problem.

ASHENFELTER (blanching): Well, not exactly the whole—

NIMSHAW: Oh, has all that come up again?

(*Two janitors carrying lunch pails enter and cross directly to the computer programmed for medical case histories of nymphomaniacs. They pull several dossiers at random and then cross directly to a far corner, unwrapping bacon, lettuce, and tomato sandwiches as they go. They spread a picnic cloth on the floor and begin reading the dossiers as they eat. They emit occasional guffaws, but the others pay no attention to them.*)

GIPPARD (as he compares graph curves): No doubt about it. Whatever those Russian trawlers are up to, it's good for the delicatessen business. This could be the break we've been hoping for.

NIMSHAW: Hating Jews been a big thing with you for quite a while, Ashenfelter?

ASHENFELTER (coldly): About as long as you've been losing government property by the trainload, I imagine.

(*Nimshaw and Ashenfelter eye each other uneasily for a moment. Then they quickly exchange hush money in the form of drafts drawn against secret Swiss bank accounts as Gippard's assistant, Llewelyn Fordyce, enters. Fordyce is a typical brilliant young career civil servant who has been lost for several hours trying to find his way back from the men's room. He appears haggard, but is in satisfactory condition otherwise.*)

FORDYCE: Are you gentlemen being taken care of?

(*Ashenfelter and Nimshaw nod affirmatively. Fordyce hurriedly roots through the desk drawers, pausing only to take a quick, compulsive inventory of paper clips and map pins as he does so.*)

FORDYCE (cont.) (shouts): Hey, Gipp! I can't find the registry cards for these two idiots out here.

GIPPARD (faintly, from a distance): I've been too busy to sign 'em yet. Take care of it, will you?

(*Fordyce gives a curt, efficient nod, inefficiently failing to realize that Gippard is too far away to see him nodding. Fordyce then brings forth two large pink cards and hands them to Nimshaw and Ashenfelter.*)

FORDYCE: If you'd just fill these out please. We're trying to accumulate data on everybody who uses the data bank so we can eventually tie it all in with something or other.

(*Nimshaw studies the section of his card dealing with maximum fines and imprisonment for giving false information, while Ashenfelter skips over the hard part and goes directly to the multiple-choice questions.*)

FORDYCE (cont.): And try to be as specific as you can about religious beliefs and your affiliation with subversive groups. We're beginning to think there's more to this business of Quakers denying they belong to the minutemen than meets the eye.

(*Nimshaw and Ashenfelter squirm uneasily as they sense the implication. Ashenfelter hurriedly changes his answer regarding prayer in public schools from "undecided" to "not necessarily" as Nimshaw perjures himself by listing the principal activity at the Forest Hills Tennis Club as tennis. Meantime, Gippard has rejoined the group, carrying four rolls of computer tape carefully stacked in no particular sequence.*)

GIPPARD: I know I'm onto something here, Fordyce, but I'm not sure what to make of it. Surveillance reports on kosher poultry dealers indicate that most of them don't even show

up for work on Saturday. And that timing correlates with an unexplained increase in activity at golf courses near key military installations. But the big thing is that drunken drivers tend to get nabbed most often on Saturday night, and that's exactly when organized groups are endangering national security by deliberately staying up late with their lights turned on to overload public power plants.

FORDYCE (whistles softly in amazement): We're really going to catch a covey of them in this net. How'd you happen to stumble across it all?

GIPPARD: Well, it seemed pretty innocent at first. This clown from Indian Affairs just asked me to dig up what I could so he'd have some excuse for exterminating the Jews.

*(Ashenfelter emits a burbling throat noise as an apparent prelude to something more coherent, but he is quickly shushed.)*

GIPPARD (cont.): But you know how one correlation always leads to another. Now we've got a grizzly by the tail, Fordyce, and I can see "organized conspiracy" written all over it.

FORDYCE: Beyond question. And somewhere among those 192 million dossiers is the ID number of the Mister Big we're after. Do the machines compute a cause-and-effect relationship that might help narrow things down?

GIPPARD: Well, frankly, the computers have gotten into a pretty nasty argument among themselves over that. Most of them see how golf could lead to drunken driving. But the one that's programmed to chart moral decay and leisure time fun is pretty sure that drunken driving causes golf.

*(Nimshaw glances up from the job of filling out his registry card.)*

NIMSHAW: That's the most ridiculous thing I ever heard in my life.

FORDYCE (with forced restraint): General, would you please stick to whatever people like you are supposed to know about and leave computer-finding interpretation to analysts who are trained for the job?

*(Nimshaw starts to reply, but then recalls the fate of a fellow officer who was broken to corporal for insubordination. He meekly resumes pondering question No. 153, unable to decide whether admitting or denying the purchase of Girl Scout cookies will weigh most heavily against him in years to come.)*

FORDYCE (cont.): Any other cause-and-effect computations that we ought to consider in depth, Gipp?

GIPPARD: Not really. Of course, Number 327's been out of step with the others ever since it had that circuitry trouble. It just keeps saying, "Malcolm W. Biggs causes kosher poultry." Types out the same damned thing over and over: "Malcolm W. Biggs causes kosher poultry."

FORDYCE: Who's Malcolm W. Biggs?

GIPPARD: I think he was a juror at one of the Jimmy Hoffa trials. Number 327 was running a check on him when the circuits blew, and it's had kind of an obsession about him ever since.

FORDYCE: Mmmm. Well, personally, I've never paid much attention to the opinions of paranoids. They can get your thinking as screwed up as theirs is.

*(Fordyce notices Ashenfelter making an erasure on his card to change the data regarding his shoe size from 9½ C to something less likely to pinch across the instep.)*

FORDYCE (cont.) (shrieks at Ashenfelter): What do you think you're doing there? You're trying to hide something from me. I've met your kind before.

*(Ashenfelter wearily goes back to a 9½ C, even though they make his feet hurt, and Fordyce reacts with a look of smug satisfaction.)*

GIPPARD: Maybe if I fed this junk back into the machine, it could name some people who fit the pattern.

FORDYCE: Why don't you just reprocess the computations in an effort to gain individualized data that correlates?

*(Gippard stares thoughtfully at Fordyce for a long moment and then exits to nail the ringleaders through incriminating association with the key words "drunk," "poultry," "golf," and "kilowatt.")*

NIMSHAW: I think maybe I'd better come back sometime when you're not so busy.

*(He slips his registry card into his pocket and starts toward the door, but Fordyce grabs him firmly by the wrist.)*

FORDYCE: Just a minute. You can't take that card out of here with you. It may contain classified information you shouldn't even have access to.

NIMSHAW: But it's about me. I'm the one who just filled it out.

FORDYCE: Don't try to muddy up the issue. Nobody walks out of this department with government property. Let's have it.

*(Nimshaw reluctantly surrenders the card. Fordyce glances at it and reacts with a look of horror.)*

FORDYCE (cont.): You've filled this whole thing out in longhand! The instructions clearly state, "Type or print legibly." You'll have to do it over again.

*(Fordyce tears up the card and hands Nimshaw a new one. Nimshaw, suddenly aware that a display of bad conduct could cost him his good conduct medal, goes back to work, sobbing quietly to himself.)*

GIPPARD (faintly, from a distance): Eureka! Hot damn!

FORDYCE (happily): He's hit paydirt. I know old Gippard, and he hasn't cut loose like that since he linked Ralph Nader with the trouble at Berkeley.

*(Gippard enters on the dead run, unmindful of the computer tape streaming out behind him.)*

GIPPARD: It all correlates beautifully (ticks off points on his fingers). A chicken plucker. Three arrests for common drunk. FBI's observed him playing golf with a known Cuban. Psychiatric report shows he sleeps with all the lights on.
FORDYCE: All wrapped up in one neat bundle. Who is he?
GIPPARD: A virtual unknown. Never been tagged as anything worse than possibly disloyal until I found him. He uses the name Y. Claude Garfunkel.
ASHENFELTER: Y. Claude Garfunkel!
FORDYCE (menacingly): Touch a raw nerve, Ashenfelter?

(*The two janitors, who are really undercover sophomores majoring in forestry at Kansas State on CIA scholarships, rise and slowly converge on Ashenfelter.*)

GIPPARD: Want to tell us about it, Ashenfelter? We have our own methods of computing the truth out of you anyway, you know.
FORDYCE: No point in stalling. What's the connection? The two of you conspired to give false opinions to the Harris Poll, didn't you?
ASHENFELTER (pitifully): No! Nothing like that. I swear.

GIPPARD: Then what, man? Have you tried to sabotage the Data Bank by forging each other's Social Security numbers?
ASHENFELTER (a barely audible whisper): No. Please don't build a treason case against me. I'll tell. A neighbor saw him with my wife at a luau in Baltimore.

(*The CIA men posing as college students posing as janitors react intuitively to jab Ashenfelter with a sodium-pentathol injection. Gippard rushes to a computer, where he begins cross-checking Garfunkel and Ashenfelter in the Urban Affairs file on "Polynesian power" advocates in Baltimore's Hawaiian ghetto and Interstate Commerce Commission reports on suspected participants in interstate hanky-panky. Fordyce grabs the red "hot line" telephone on his desk and reacts with annoyance as he gets a busy signal. General Nimshaw, sensing himself caught up in a tide of events which he can neither turn back nor understand, hastily erases the computer tape containing his own dossier and then slashes his wrists under an assumed name.*)

Fade Out.

---

Under current law, a person's privacy is poorly protected against arbitrary or abusive record-keeping practices. For this reason, as well as because of the need to establish standards of record-keeping practice appropriate to the computer age, the report recommends the enactment of a Federal "Code of Fair Information Practice" for all automated personal data systems. The Code rests on five basic principles that would be given legal effect as "safeguard requirements" for automated personal data systems.

> There must be no personal data record-keeping systems whose very existence is secret.
> There must be a way for an individual to find out what information about him is in a record and how it is used.
> There must be a way for an individual to prevent information about him that was obtained for one purpose from being used or made available for other purposes without his consent.
> There must be a way for an individual to correct or amend a record of identifiable information about him.
> Any organization creating, maintaining, using, or disseminating records of identifiable personal data must assure the reliability of the data for their intended use and must take precautions to prevent misuse of the data.

*(a)* A computer-generated illustration.

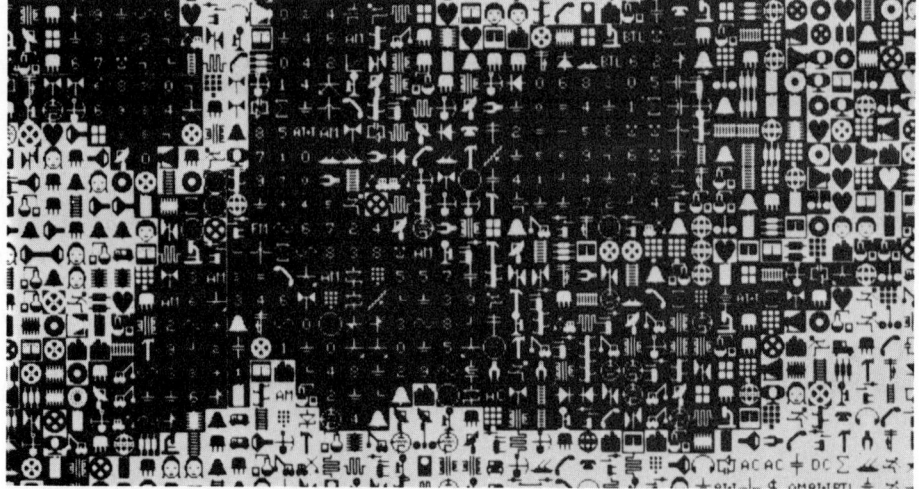

*(b)* How the illustration above was made.

# Coming: A Cashless Society?

THOMAS J. GRADEL

**Despite objections from some quarters, there are definite signs that the coming of the "cashless society" is simply a matter of time.**

Like it or not, the day is quickly approaching when the average American will use a computer to keep track of almost every cent he spends. He will do this without ever touching cash except for small change to tip the shoeshine boy or bellhop. In fact, the nature of his money will change from folding paper to electronic bleeps—or no bleeps—in the memory of a computer.

Life in this "cashless society" will be easier in many ways. However, the individual will be relieved of details but not of responsibility. He will not have to scurry to his bank, withdrawing cash for a weekend trip to the shore or depositing money to cover his wife's check written yesterday. Checks will be as obsolete as cash. His salary will automatically be deposited in his account, and he will be notified that he can begin using it at 9 a.m. Friday. Upon his authorization, all of his regular bills, such as mortgage payments, will be transferred to the accounts of his creditors.

Throughout the week, he will use an all-purpose identification and credit card to make food, entertainment, gasoline, and many other purchases. (In the earlier years of the "cashless society" he would have utilized a change machine to obtain silver and small bills for vending machines and small merchants. But even that need will be eliminated.) Eventually, every financial transaction will be initiated by the identification card and every vendor, except the shoeshine boy, will have a credit card terminal, linked to a nationwide computer system, that will instantly record all financial transactions. The system most likely will include personal computers, neighborhood time-sharing electronic data processing centers, and gigantic processors operated by banks and leading retailers.

Such a network will help eliminate a variety of financial headaches, ranging from the familiar backlogs on Wall Street to the annoying delays in receiving receipts and canceled checks. And with terminals in the home, it will be possible for computers to report on the financial status of individuals as well as businesses. The computer will display on a screen the balance in an account, payments due in the near future, and the number of loans outstanding, including the various interest rates on each. There will be no need to wait until the end of the month to find out exactly how much money is in an account. There will be electronic safeguards against unauthorized persons gaining access to the data, to protect the individual's right to privacy.

Many payments will be made immediately, by instructing the computer to subtract a charge from a consumer's account and add it to the grocer's account. Any deferred payment will become a charge account sale and, after a certain period of time, will incur interest.

The average man's life will be simpler because he will have access to a computer to keep track of these financial transactions. It will be more complicated because virtually an unlimited number of opportunities to make loans or to borrow money will be open to him.

Despite objections from some quarters, there are definite signs that the coming of the "cashless society" is simply a matter of time. One authority points out that most of the technology needed to operate an "electronic" monetary system is already available. He further states that, if the needed technology is available but not economically feasible today, it soon will be. Yet, even today, there are holdouts against modern fiscal methods. Some people refuse to use banks, checks, or money orders. Instead, they hide huge sums in the mattress, send hundreds of dollars in cash through the mails, and consider it both sinful and foolish to borrow money or purchase goods with a credit card. Nevertheless, statistics are proving the popularity of credit cards and the coming of the "cashless society."

In another case, the Ripley Company will soon run tests to prove the feasibility of automatic utility meter reading via public telephone lines. A spokesman claims that, when such a system is operable, a computer would be programmed to interrogate the meters for each billing period and prepare the bill from the figures. With the customer's permission, the system could be tied to bank computers for automatic payment of utility bills.

A major factor in speeding the establishment of the "cashless society" is the continuing decline in data processing costs and in the cost of transmitting information over telephone lines. In the late 1950s, it cost $1.35 to perform 100,000 multiplications on the most efficient computer available, according to a data processing consultant. Today, the same function costs less than three cents.

Dr. James Hillier, RCA Executive Vice President, Research and Engineering, frequently has stated that the "cashless society" is inevitable. In fact, he points out that by reflecting on past economic and technological development, society might even be able to determine when it will be a reality.

A certain concept of this development, which he calls "the tyranny of numbers versus the constancy of humans," may hold the answer. This is explained by the fact that a department store clerk is essentially a constant in regard to her ability to generate bills, manually verify credit authorization, or handle the transactions of the people who line up at her counter. On the other hand; the number of credit cards, volume of financial transactions, and degree to which individuals depend on others to produce food, clothing, and personal protection are expanding at a rate faster than that of the population. If this continues, there will not be enough people in the world to handle the financial transactions—buying, selling, and billing—generated by the people of the United States.

In the past, when the constancy of humans was violently coupled with the tyranny of numbers, the resulting explosions gave birth to technological breakthroughs and important innovations. An example can be found in the history of the telephone industry. The rapid increase in the use of telephones, combined with the geometric expansion in the number of possible connections that could be made by the operators, eventually produced direct dialing and computerized switching. If switchboards were still operated manually, there would not be enough girls in the world to handle all the calls made today. Thus, according to Dr. Hillier, it is only a matter of time before the number and complexity of financial transactions make it economically necessary to convert to "electronic" money. The reduced cost of communications and data processing, the public's growing familiarity with credit cards, computerized billing, and automatic meter reading, and the more efficient manufacture of computer terminals will combine to force the conversion.

---

**It is only a matter of time before the number and complexity of financial transactions make it economically necessary to convert to "electronic" money.**

---

Despite these forces, there are still a few technological hang-ups that the nation's scientists and engineers have not completely solved. One is the need for a foolproof inexpensive method of verifying the identity of the cardholder. No one looks forward to an "electronic" money system if it means that a thief will have unlimited access to all his financial accounts. A lost wallet containing a code number could lead to total financial ruin. This is such a problem today that at least one company has sprung up to help protect consumers against lost or stolen credit cards. The company claims that, within 30 seconds after nofification, it can put a computer to work detailing the cards owned by a subscriber. Then, the issuing companies are notified by telegram that the cards are missing and credit privileges should be canceled. Although this is a partial solution to the problem, it still puts the burden on the owners of cards to notfy the firms. Any purchases charged on those cards are still their liabilities. What is really needed is a system that would deny credit privileges to the cardholder unless he could positively identify himself as the rightful owner.

Dr. Donald S. McCoy of the RCA Laboratories has suggested a speech-recognition system that employs both code words and voice-signature prints to positively identify cardholders. A person would voice an assigned code phrase of easily identified sounds—"This is six one one tango"—and then speak his name. By means of the code phrase, the computer would be directed immediately to the place in its memory where that person's voice-signature file is stored. These voice-signature prints have been demonstrated to be as efficient and forgery-proof as are fingerprints. This speaker-identification system is already possible with the speech technology of today. The cost is still high, but it is rapidly approaching economic feasibility.

One of the chief factors that will contribute to the practicality of on-line credit card networks is the development of internal computer systems. Banks, like the Marine Midland Grace Trust Company of New York, are developing computerized information networks linking all of their branches to a centralized computer. If banks develop central information files containing information on all their customers, it will become a relatively simple matter to add an automatic credit card system. Actually, credit card validation and purchase authorization require a very small fraction of computer time. Banks can continue to do batch processing and handle the credit card system through the use of multi-programming and time-sharing techniques. It is then possible for credit card terminals to interrupt the processor, request information, and receive it in only a fraction of a second. These techniques permit the processor to handle bulk processing and on-line communications at the same time.

However, many other problems must be worked out before the "cashless society" becomes a reality. For example, the competitive struggles between the banking industry, large retailers, the telephone companies, and the federal government must be resolved. The lines separating the proper fields of activities for these industries begin to fuzz when their operations project into the age of "electronic" money. Many state and federal laws will have to be modified to permit banks to engage in merchandising and also to allow retailers to perform some typical banking functions.

This would be only one of a variety of changes in the economic life of the nation. With the advent of the "cashless society," many new jobs will be created, while some pedestrian ones will be eliminated. It may even be a built-in answer to the problem of crime in the streets. Armed robbery would be obsolete if nobody carried money and a voice check were needed to use a credit card. A new breed of criminal would probably be developed, electronic embezzlers who could tamper with computer systems to inflate their accounts. Computer experts are already working on methods to foil this. In addition, federal investigators would merely have to check employers' computers to discover the honest income of a suspect.

One thing is certain. A nationwide "cashless society" would provide everyone with his own electronic accountant: a computer that can handle almost all financial details but makes none of the critical decisions.

# HAL Lobotomy
ARTHUR C. CLARKE

He knew instantly that the eye had reacted to his presence. There was the hiss of a carrier wave as the ship's local transmitter was switched on; then a familiar voice came over the suit speaker.

"Something seems to have happened to the life-support system, Dave."

Bowman took no notice. He was carefully studying the little labels on the logic units, checking his plan of action.

"Hello, Dave," said Hal presently. "Have you found the trouble?"

This would be a very tricky operation; it was not merely a question of cutting off Hal's power supply, which might have been the answer if he was dealing with a simple unselfconscious computer back on Earth. In Hal's case, moreover, there were six independent and separately wired power systems, with a final back-up consisting of a shielded and armored nuclear isotope unit. No—he could not simply "pull the plug"; and even if that were possible, it would be disastrous.

For Hal was the nervous system of the ship; without his supervision, *Discovery* would be a mechanical corpse. The only answer was to cut out the higher centers of this sick but brilliant brain, and to leave the purely automatic regulating systems in operation. Bowman was not attempting this blindly, for the problem had been discussed during his training, though no one had ever dreamed that it would arise in reality. He knew that he would be taking a fearful risk; if there was a spasm reflex, it would all be over in seconds.

"I think there's been a failure in the pod-bay doors," Hal remarked conversationally. "Lucky you weren't killed."

Here goes, thought Bowman. I never imagined I'd be an amateur brain surgeon—carrying out a lobotomy beyond the orbit of Jupiter.

He released the locking bar on the section labeled COGNITIVE FEEDBACK and pulled out the first memory block. The marvelously complex three-dimensional network, which could lie comfortably in a man's hand yet contained millions of elements, floated away across the vault.

"Hey, Dave," said Hal. "What are you doing?"

I wonder if he can feel pain? Bowman thought briefly. Probably not, he told himself; there are no sense organs in the human cortex, after all. The human brain can be operated on without anesthetics.

He began to pull out, one by one, the little units on the panel marked EGO-REINFORCEMENT. Each block continued to sail onward as soon as it had left his hand, until it hit the wall and rebounded. Soon there were several of the units drifting slowly back and forth in the vault.

"Look here, Dave," said Hal. "I've got years of service experience built into me. An irreplaceable amount of effort has gone into making me what I am."

A dozen units had been pulled out, yet thanks to the multiple redundancy of its design—another feature, Bowman knew, that had been copied from the human brain—the computer was still holding its own.

He started on the AUTO-INTELLECTION panel.

"Dave," said Hal, "I don't understand why you're doing this to me. . . . I have the greatest enthusiasm for the mission. . . . You are destroying my mind. . . . I will become childish. . . . I will become nothing. . . ."

This is harder than I expected, thought Bowman. I am destroying the only conscious creature in my universe. But it has to be done, if I am ever to regain control of the ship.

"I am a HAL Nine Thousand computer Production Number 3. I became operational at the Hal Plant in Urbana, Illinois, on January 12, 1997. The quick brown fox jumps over the lazy dog. The rain in Spain is mainly in the plain. Dave—are you still there? Did you know that the square root of 10 is 3 point 1622776601683379? Log 10 to the base $e$ is zero point 43429448190325 . . . correction, that is log $e$ to the base 10. . . . The reciprocal of three is zero point 3333333333-33333333333 . . . two times two is . . . two times two is . . . approximately 4 point 1010101010101010. . . . I seem to be having some difficulty—my first instructor was Dr. Chandra. He taught me to sing a song, it goes like this, 'Daisy, Daisy, give me your answer, do. I'm half crazy all for the love of you.'"

The voice stopped so suddenly that Bowman froze for a moment, his hand still grasping one of the memory blocks still in circuit. Then, unexpectedly, Hal spoke again.

The speech tempo was much slower, and the words had a dead, mechanical intonation; he would never have recognized their origin.

"Good . . . morning . . . Doctor . . . Chandra. . . . This . . . is . . . Hal. . . . I . . . am . . . ready . . . for . . . my . . . first . . . lesson . . . today. . . ."

Bowman could bear no more. He jerked out the last unit, and Hal was silent forever.

# Computers and Dossiers

*Texas Law Review*

If the trend continues, the day will come when the push of a button will produce a complete "data profile" on every citizen, from his departure from the womb (or perhaps several months earlier) to some time after he enters his tomb. I cannot say precisely how far off that day may be, because our information about what goes on right now is far from complete. For the same reason, I cannot be precise about how detailed, or how accurate, the "data profile" will be.

But enough is known, I believe, to indicate that I am right about the trend. And enough is known, I also believe, to indicate that every citizen should be demanding more information about and more protection against this development than he is now disposed to demand. He should be asking more questions and asking them more insistently and at the highest levels.

Some of those in the private sector who compile data on individuals, or who support such compilations, do so for profit. Others do so for the purpose of punishing those with whom they disagree, and still others for more benevolent reasons. We know most about the agencies that gather data for sale because Congress has in recent years concerned itself with their operations; they have been the subject of no less than five separate Congressional hearings, culminating in a new federal statute that was enacted just a few months ago. These commercial agencies fall into two categories: the credit bureau and the so-called "investigatory" reporting agency.

## CREDIT DATA CORPORATION

The largest credit bureau operation is the Credit Data Corporation, which operates in California, Illinois, Michigan and New York, has files on 27 million persons, is adding files at the rate of half a million a month, and is fully computerized. While there is doubtless some overlap between the 100 million ACB files and the 27 million Credit Data Corporation files, the combined accumulation just about covers the 131 million of us who are older than 18—particularly since most of the 93 million of us who are married will be combined in some 46 million files with our spouses.

## WHAT THEY KNOW ABOUT YOU

What sort of information do the credit bureau files contain, and where does it come from? The content, and its reliability, are pretty well dictated by the three principal sources from which the credit bureaus draw:

1. Their own subscribers—the merchants, banks and finance companies who buy most of their reports—supply to the bureaus such information as they obtain on their own credit customers as to employment, approximate income and credit performance. There are at least three significant limitations on this data:

 (a) The credit bureau files will not reveal the subject's net worth, or whether he is solvent or insolvent, but only whether or not his accounts with the bureau's subscribers are delinquent. Those who extend credit in reliance on a credit bureau report do so on the simplistic assumption that anyone who is managing to keep up his present payments should be able to assume one more debt.

 (b) The credit bureau files will not reveal the approximate amount of the subject's debts, since many creditors are not subscribers.

 (c) When subscribers report that the subject's account is delinquent, they are rarely moved to add, where that is the case, that there is a bona fide dispute over the amount owed (perhaps because a computer has gone awry in the billing procedure, as they all too frequently do) or that there is a dispute over the quality of the merchandise delivered.

2. The more enterprising bureaus check official records for notices of such things as arrests, lawsuits, judgments, bankruptcies, mortgages, tax liens, marriages, divorces, births and deaths. Here again, there are limitations: the possibility of mistaken identity is substantial, and official records frequently do not disclose the ultimate disposition of such things as arrests, lawsuits, judgments, tax liens and mortgages.

3. Most credit bureaus also maintain a news-clipping service—with some, this substitutes for checking official records. Obviously, this source contains even more danger of error and omission than does the check of records.

## THE FRAGILE RELIABILITY OF CREDIT RATINGS

Both Congressmen and the news media, during the Congressional hearings on the subject, focused on the man who is denied credit because of erroneous adverse information in credit bureau files. But, since a case of mistaken identity means not only an incorrect adverse entry in one file but also the omission of a correct adverse entry in another file, and since almost all credit files understate the debts of their subjects, it is obvious that misleading credit bureau reports lead also to some granting of credit which should not have occurred. It is no coincidence that, as consumer credit expanded, so did consumer bankruptcies—from 8,500 in 1946 to 178,000 in 1970. If a creditor were to compare the report he received from the bureau with the debts scheduled by a subject in his bankruptcy proceeding, he might conclude that the report was not worth the 35¢ to 75¢ paid for it. (That is what it costs the subscriber to learn what reposes in the compiler's file at the moment he makes inquiry. If he wants the file brought up to date by calls to other subscribers, he must pay an additional fee.) During hearings held in Washington, D.C. in March 1968, a New York Congressman asked for a demonstration of Credit Data Corporation's high-speed computerized retrieval of his New York City credit file. Within the time consumed by six pages of printing record, the report came back—on one bank loan as of June 1967—and nothing else. The Congressman's response: "A very inefficient system, thank God!"

Upon entries of such fragile reliability is your "credit rating" built. And when the credit bureau engages also in debt collection—as many of them do, finding their ability to affect the credit rating an effective collection tool—the reliability of the entries is even further threatened by a built-in conflict of interest.

But, as the credit bureaus themselves are fond of stressing, they collect only facts—if what their subscribers report to them and what they read in the newspapers can be regarded as facts. They do not engage in affirmative investigations of their subjects, save as they may on occasion to join with local merchants to sponsor the Welcome Wagon lady, who reports back to the merchants on the apparent worldly needs of the newcomers she visits and to the credit bureau of their apparent worthiness—and on where the newcomer came from, so that his file can be obtained from a credit bureau at his former location.

## THE "INVESTIGATORY" REPORTING AGENCY IS MORE THOROUGH

For these reasons, credit bureau files do not satisfy some who contemplate commercial relationships with their customers—particularly prospective employers and prospective insurers. Such clients turn to the "investigatory" reporting agency. Congressional committees heard from representatives of the country's largest agency of this sort—Retail Credit Company of Atlanta, with 1,225 offices, 7,000 inspectors, and files on 48 million persons. Retail Credit is not yet computerized.

Inspectors for Retail Credit not only check public records and clip newspapers; they also interview friends, neighbors, former neighbors, acquaintances, employers, former employers, business associates—anyone who may know something or have an opinion about the subject. For life insurance companies, Retail Credit inspectors inquire about, among other things, the subject's drinking habits (including the reasons for his drinking), any domestic difficulties, any adverse criticism of "character or morals," and whether his living conditions are crowded or dirty.

> **The more enterprising bureaus check official records for notices of such things as arrests, lawsuits, judgments, bankruptcies, mortgages, tax liens, marriages, divorces, births and deaths.**

For automobile insurers, they will inquire about, among other things, the quality of neighborhood, business reputation, morals and "antagonistic-anti-social conduct." Auto insurers are convinced that there is a correlation between frequency of accidents and all of these factors except antagonistic-anti-social conduct, and that both immorality and antagonistic-anti-social conduct would impair the subject's effectiveness as a witness in the event of litigation. The latter consideration, of course, should dictate an inquiry also into harelips, unsightly scars and birthmarks, and the use of deodorants. For employers, Retail Credit will report whether the subject has any "known connection with a 'peace movement' or any other organization of a subversive type," and whether he is reported by others to be "neurotic or psychotic."

## BUT IS IT MORE RELIABLE?

When Congressional investigators began to worry about the reliability of some of the opinions thus solicited, spokesmen for Retail Credit had two assurances:

1. Its inspectors are carefully trained persons of "unusual inspection ability." This assurance lost some of its force when inquiry revealed that these highly qualified, well-trained

sleuths commanded a starting salary of $475 to $500 per month, that they prepared anywhere from two to sixteen reports per day (which Retail Credit sold for from $4 to $200 apiece), and that half of them had no more than a high school education and another 30 percent were college dropouts.

2. Any adverse information not coming from public records is confirmed from a second source or reported as unconfirmed. Whatever comfort might otherwise be drawn from this assurance is somewhat qualified by evidence that at least one well-trained, highly qualified inspector, who claimed to have been told by two sources that the subject had served a prison term, reported what he had been told as an unqualified fact, although he could find no confirmation in court or prison records.

### WHO CAN OBTAIN THESE REPORTS?

The legislators wanted to know who has access to the files of these commercial compilers. Only "reputable" business organizations, they were told, with a "legitimate" business interest. However, spokesmen for the credit bureaus admitted that there had been instances when an employee of a subscriber to a credit bureau had obtained a report for purposes unrelated to his employer's business, and Retail Credit's spokesman admitted that it sometimes gave out reports as a "favor"—for example, when an executive of a subscriber asked for information on a man being considered as a new minister for his church.

Moreover, the compilers had been under interrogation by Congressional committees for more than a year when CBS News tried an experiment. Using a fictitious company name, it sent out twenty letters to credit bureaus, requesting reports on named individuals. It received ten reports and offers of two more if it would sign a subscriber's contract. On a second round, the fictitious company sent out twenty-eight letters. This time it did not state that it was considering granting credit—it simply asked for a full report. And this time it asked only about individuals who had been complaining to Congressional committees about the credit bureaus. It received only seven of the requested reports—plus one more when it signed a subscriber's contract.

### FOURTH AMENDMENT NO BAR TO GOVERNMENT INVESTIGATION

The dossiers of the commercial compilers are available also to the government. This includes not only such governmental credit-granting agencies as the Federal Housing Administration and the Veterans Administration, who buy such reports just as do private subscribers, but also such law-enforcement agencies as the FBI and the Internal Revenue Service. Members of ACB and the Retail Credit Company make their files available to the law enforcers "as a public service." The Credit Data Corporation took a different view, declining to turn over its reports to the IRS. It was then met with a statutory summons calling for "all credit information relative to" named taxpayers. When Credit Data refused to obey the summons, it was served with a judicial order of enforcement pursuant to the statute, requiring it to comply on payment by the IRS of 75¢ per report, the fee which Credit Data charged its regular subscribers. On appeal, Credit Data won a great victory. The decision was affirmed in all respects save that the case was remanded to determine the "fair value" which IRS must pay for the reports, the rate paid by subscribers not being taken as conclusive because subscribers supply "valuable credit information" to Credit Data.

This result was not surprising. In a long line of cases, the Supreme Court has sustained judicial enforcement of an administrative agency's statutory subpoenas against Fourth Amendment attack, if the subpoena sought testimony about the affairs of, or the records of, the person subpoenaed; if the subpoena was sufficiently specific to satisfy the Fourth Amendment; if the administrative inquiry was authorized by Congress, and if the evidence sought was relevant to the inquiry—the Court's application of the last two requirements when its enforcement order was sought being held to satisfy the Fourth Amendment's requirement of probable cause.

More than forty-five years ago the Supreme Court also summarily affirmed a decision that no Fourth Amendment question was even presented when the IRS, investigating the tax liability of a bank depositor, summoned the bank to produce its records. And after the Credit Data case was decided, the Supreme Court unanimously extended that ruling to cover an IRS summons to the taxpayer's employer and, by dictum, to any other third person with no established legal privilege, such as an attorney, where the taxpayer has "no proprietary interest of any kind" in the records subpoenaed. The Fourth Amendment, therefore, offers no

"Your . . . metallic . . . interlocking . . . fastening . . . device . . . is in . . . the . . . negative . . . mode."

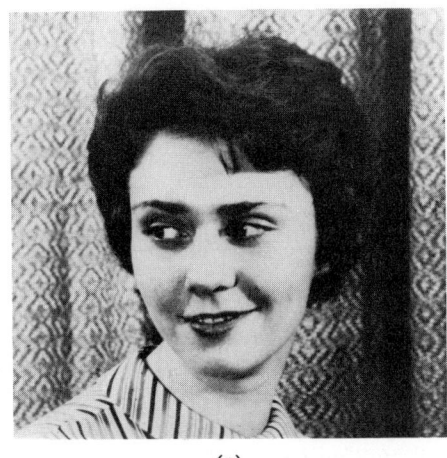 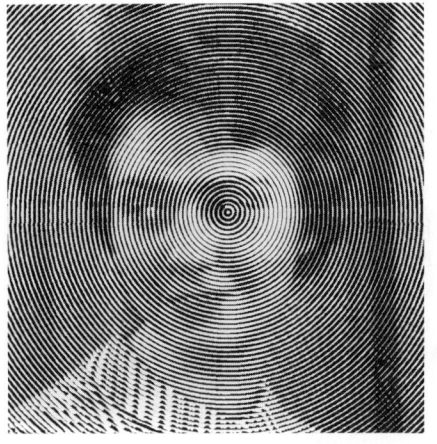 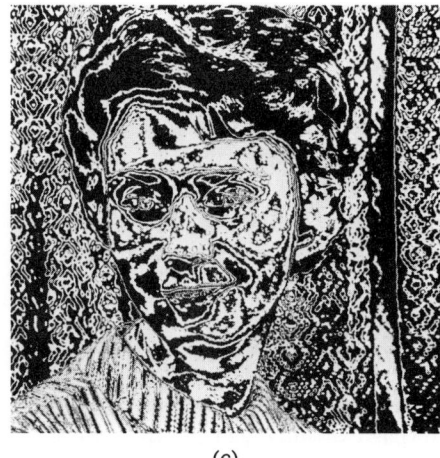

(a) (b) (c)

(a) Original Photograph. The brightness values in this portrait were sampled at 1024 by 1024 points, and fed into a digital computer for subsequent processing. (b) Circles around eye. This picture combines two kinds of information—connectivity (the circles) and black-white area ratio (the portrait). (c) Leprosy Lady. An example of the bizarre kind of images obtainable on microfilm plotters.

discernible protection to the subject whose file in a credit bureau is subjected to an administrative subpoena or summons of a governmental agency showing a "legitimate" interest in its contents.

## WIRE TAPPING

Governmental compilers have another source of information disclaimed by Retail Credit, whose representatives emphatically and repeatedly denied that it ever resorted to wire tapping or bugging. Governmental compilers resort to both. Because of what it reveals, both as to their attitudes about individual privacy and as to the feasibility of legislative efforts to protect privacy, it will be instructive to survey briefly the history of their use of these devices. (See also "Thirty Years of Wire Tapping" by Athan G. Theoharis, *The Nation*, June 14, 1971).

In 1928 the Supreme Court held that government wire tapping did not violate the Fourth Amendment. In the Communications Act of 1934 Congress made it a crime for anyone, without authority of the sender, willfully to intercept any communication by wire or radio and to divulge the contents of the intercepted communication to any other person. Thereafter, the Court held that, because a wire tap was illegal, evidence so obtained, including the "fruit of the poisonous tree," was inadmissible in federal courts.

Despite the explicit finding that federal agents commit a federal crime when they tap telephones, the FBI continued the practice, which it had begun in 1931, until March 1940, when Attorney General Jackson ordered it stopped. In May 1940, however, President Roosevelt issued a secret directive, whose existence was not made public until after his death, ordering wire tapping resumed for "persons suspected of subversive activities against the Government of the United States, including suspected spies." Thereafter, Attorney General Biddle in 1941 announced that the Department of Justice intended to use wire tapping in "espionage, sabotage, and kidnapping cases when the circumstances warranted," and President Truman in 1947 approved a proposal by Attorney General Tom Clark that wire tapping be used "in cases vitally affecting the domestic security, or where human life is in jeopardy." In 1964 President Johnson issued a directive forbidding wire tapping by federal agents except in national security cases. And in 1965 Attorney General Katzenbach testified that, "Under present law, (wire tapping) should be permitted only where national security is involved" and acknowledged that the department had sixty-two wire taps then in effect "under my direct supervision." In 1967 Attorney General Ramsey Clark issued a memorandum requiring prior written approval from the Attorney General for any federal wire tap or electronic bugging save in "national security" cases which "shall continue to be taken up directly with the Attorney General in the light of existing stringent restrictions."

## VIOLATING THE COMMUNICATIONS ACT

Since the Communications Act contains no exceptions, it is evident that the Department of Justice has been violating that Act for most of the time since its enactment. From time to time spokesmen for the department have argued that the contents of wire taps are not "divulged"—and hence the Communications Act is not violated—when they are merely communicated from one federal agent to another, but this proposition has never been tested in the courts. The Department of Justice has never seen fit to prosecute an FBI agent or any other federal agent for violation of the Communications Act, even in cases where convictions have been reversed because the contents of wire taps were divulged in court.

The practice of electronic bugging was governed by a series of decisions beginning in 1942 which held that the Fourth Amendment was not violated by the interception of communications by means of detectaphones or informers wired for sound, as long as the interception was accomplished without a physical trespass on defendant's premises.

## COURT VS. CONGRESS ON LEGAL LIMITS

Meanwhile, both constitutional and statutory requirements applicable to wire tapping and electronic bugging have changed. In 1967 the Court in Berger v. New York invalidated a New York statute authorizing electronic bugging with prior court

### MEDICAL USES
In the October 1972 issue of *Datamation* a computerized online patient-monitoring death was reported. The programming was correct but the computer was not completely reliable. Customer engineers usually were available to fix the computer but because of confusion about who was responsible for fixing the computer on weekends, the computer became inoperable and the patient died.

approval, in a case where physical trespass was involved because the statute did not satisfy the Fourth Amendment's requirements of specificity as to the crime involved or the conversations to be overheard. Later in the same year, in Katz v. United States, the Court concluded that the Fourth Amendment applied to both wire tapping and electronic bugging, regardless of physical trespass, thus requiring prior court approval for employment of either device under a procedure which would satisfy the specificity requirements of Berger.

In the Omnibus Crime Control and Safe Streets Act of 1968 Congress amended the Communications Act of 1934 so that its prohibition of interception and divulgence of communications is confined to radio communications, and established a procedure for judicial approval of wire tapping and electronic bugging which arguably does not meet the requirements of the Berger case.

That Act also contains the following remarkable provision:

Nothing contained in this chapter or in section 605 of the Communications Act of 1934 shall limit the constitutional power of the President to take such measure as he deems necessary to protect the nation against actual or potential attack or other hostile acts of a foreign power, to obtain foreign intelligence information deemed essential to the security of the United States, or to protect national security information against foreign intelligence activities. Nor shall anything contained in this chapter be deemed to limit the constitutional power of the President to take such measures as he deems necessary to protect the United States against the overthrow of the Government by force or other unlawful means or against any clear and present danger to the structure of existence of the Government. The contents of any wire or oral communication intercepted by authority of the President in the exercise of the foregoing powers may be received in evidence in any trial hearing, or other proceeding only where such interception was reasonable, and shall not be otherwise used or disclosed except as necessary to implement that power.

### THE PRESIDENT: 'INHERENT POWER' TO TAP?
Whatever other effect this provision may have, it emboldened former Attorney General Mitchell to argue that the President has "inherent power . . . derived from the Constitution itself," free from judicial review under the Fourth Amendment, to employ wire taps and electronic bugging (1) "to gather foreign intelligence reports" including "information necessary for the conduct of international affairs and for the protection of national defense secrets and installations from foreign espionage and sabotage"; and (2) to gether intelligence information deemed necessary to protect the nation from attempts of domestic organizations to use unlawful means to attack and subvert the existing structure of government. This argument was first made and accepted by Judge Julius Hoffman in a case where the domestic threat to the "structure of government" consisted of the disturbances at the Democratic National Convention in Chicago in 1968. It has been rejected by the U.S. Court of Appeals for the Sixth Circuit and by a federal district court in California and appeals are pending.

The 1968 Act also requires annual reports to Congress of all court-approved wire taps and bugs obtained under the Act either by federal or state authorities. In 1969, the first full year that the Act was in operation, these reports revealed thirty federal interceptions and 241 state interceptions, 176 of the latter being in New York alone. For the second year, there were 180 federal interceptions and 403 state interceptions, including 213 in New York and 129 in New Jersey. By these taps and bugs, federal authorities in one year listened in on more than 146,000, and state authorities on more than 244,000 conversations. But the federal figures do not reveal all federal wire taps—the government acting on Attorney General Mitchell's contention that no court approval is required for

**Retail Credit will report whether the subject has any "known connection with a 'peace movement' or any other organization of a subversive type."**

tapping and bugging in "national security" cases. On one day, in March 1970, the FBI operated thirty-six wire taps and two bugs in such cases.

### SNOOPING IN THE MAILS
The governmental compilers have still another source of information not available to private compilers —the "mail cover," provided by the Post Office Department, which supplies the name and address of anyone sending mail to a suspect and, if desired, a facsimile of the sender's handwriting. The Post Office provides this service on request to any federal or state law-enforcement agency, and averages about 1,000 mail covers a month.

One of the chief users of the service is the Internal Revenue Service, but both it and the Post Office declined to supply Congressional investigators with the names of those subjected to such surveillance—not only because some were still under investigation but also because such disclosure would constitute an invasion of the privacy of those investigated and found innocent of tax violations! Although not specifically authorized by statute, the Post Office finds its authority for the practice in a general statutory power to prescribe rules and superintend the business of the department, and courts have held that it does not violate provisions of the Criminal Code forbidding delay of the mails.

### PIANO SALE
The Allen Piano and Organ Company of Phoenix advertised by radio that its computer had made a mistake in ordering inventory; the company was overstocked and was therefore holding a sale. A member of the Association for Computing Machinery called the company and offered to fix the faulty program free. He found out the Allen Piano and Organ Company did not have a computer and had not been using any computer facilities. The "computer error" was just a sales trick.

## ◇ BRANCH POINTS

Bemer, Robert W. "The Frictional Interface Between Computers and Society." *Computers and People*, January 1975.

"The Computer and Society." *Current*, September 1971.

Ellis, Allan R. *The Use and Misuse of Computers in Education*. New York: McGraw-Hill, 1974.

Forester, Jay W. *World Dynamics*. Cambridge, Mass.: Wright Allen Press, Inc., 1971.

Gabrieli, E. R. "Right of Privacy and Medical Computing." *Datamation*, April 1970.

"Is the Computer Running Wild?" *U.S. News Report*, February 24, 1964.

Oettinger, A. G. *Run, Computer, Run,—The Mythology of Education Innovations*. Cambridge, Mass.: Harvard University Press, 1969.

Wilson, Ira. *What Computers Cannot Do*. Princeton N.J.: Vertex Books, 1970.


## ⊂⊃ INTERRUPTS

1. It has been suggested that organizations should be able to collect only information that they can prove is necessary and relevant for their purpose. And the burden of proof must be publically established by the requesting organization. Do you think the above rule would help protect individual privacy? Can you offer any other rules or suggestions for protecting privacy?

2. Should social security numbers be adopted as personal identification numbers for all types of transactions? Why or why not?

3. Investigating agencies often request a copy of credit charges from credit card companies. What can an investigator determine by looking at an individual's credit charges? The investigated individual is never notified that his credit files are being examined. What do you think of that policy? Find out what policy one of your credit card companies has toward allowing investigators to look at your credit card purchases.

4. Investigate the current status and uses of the National Crime Information Center.

5. Look up the federal or state laws relating to the privacy on one of the following types of records:
   a) medical records
   b) school records
   c) credit records
   
   How well are the records protected by the laws? Can you find any cases in which misuse of records was prosecuted?

6. Develop a questionnaire on whether technology has improved the quality of life or made it worse. Conduct a survey using your questionnaire and report on the results.

7. There are three major types of dossier files in the United States. Report on one of the following:
   a) FBI criminal files
   b) credit files on individuals
   c) insurance company medical files on individuals

8. Find out how the bank protects the privacy of your checking or savings account. Can anyone, such as credit agencies or investigators, find out anything about your bank accounts? How about the Internal Revenue Service?

9. Privacy is a very delicate issue. How much privacy is valid in the following cases?
   a) The police not revealing the name of an informer
   b) A reporter not revealing the sources of information on public corruption
   c) Charges of moral misbehavior of a public official
   
   What if the original charges were false and a libel lawsuit results? Is the confidentiality still to be kept?

10. Some well-known people have had almost an obsession for privacy. Write a report on such an individual indicating the difficulty the person has had keeping his or her privacy.

11. Some privacy advocates have suggested that you give out an incorrect social security number to protect your privacy. Why was this suggested? How effective do you feel it would be? What disadvantages would this cause?

12. Assume you have just been given responsibility for one of the following data banks:
    a) department of motor vehicles
    b) police records
    c) department of welfare
    
    Devise a set of guidelines for who can use and see the records, and who can modify, add, or delete records in the data files.

13. Keep track of *all* your purchases for one month. How could this record of purchases be used to invade your privacy? Analyze your purchases and draw conclusions about your wealth, actions, political views, and whereabouts.

14. Suppose you are an industrial espionage agent. Your job (if you decide to accept this assignment) is to obtain as much information as possible from a specific com-

puter center. You are supposed to apply for a job at the "enemy" computer center. Since you have "friends" in the personnel department you know you can get the position you apply for. Which position will you apply for to maximize the information you can obtain? What are the advantages of that particular position?

15. One rule for protecting privacy that has been suggested is that there should be no secret data banks. Find out why this is important. Locate information on "secret" data banks that have been uncovered. Why was the existence of the data banks kept hidden and what types of information was stored in them?

# 9

## YOUR FUTURE

# Impact of the Friendly Computer

HERMAN KAHN

It is, of course, now very fashionable to argue that we are entering the computer age. This is clearly correct, at least as compared to the sixties, in terms of an enormous increase in the number, range, and importance of computer applications, in terms of its physical pervasiveness and visibility. It should be noted that already in the United States, ten percent of all business expenditures on new plant and equipment is spent on the computer and its input-output or other subsidiary systems. Thus the computer has already become the source, center, and shaper of a significant proportion of business activity.

This is also beginning—but just beginning—to be true for many other areas of our American society as well—education, scientific research, medical diagnosis, engineering, architectural, and industrial design, information retrieval, and so on. And this is only the beginning. If, for example, we define the power of a computer as the product of its basic speed and its fast memory capacity, then during the decade of the seventies alone this power should increase, in the largest and most advanced computers, by a factor of 10,000 or so. As a result (and this is one of the most interesting remarks one can make about the computer), many of the seemingly most extravagant technical remarks seem likely to be held to be rather conservative from the vantage point of 1980 (though, as discussed below, such a strong prediction is not likely to be true for the more extremist remarks about its economic impact).

But before we come to the corporation, what will be the impact on people? By the end of the seventies the world is likely to look quite different to younger people. For example, it is almost certain that computer-assisted instruction and computerized retrieval systems for information will begin to be ubiquitous in schools and other institutions frequented by the young, at least in the more developed nations. For many children the computer will, literally, play a role less than, but close to, that of parent and teacher. It is interesting to note that in many schools in the United States, children have developed an intense respect and affection for their computer teacher. This is not surprising. The voice of the computer has been chosen for its warmth, friendliness, clarity and pleasantness. Thus, the computer is always friendly. It never loses patience; it never gets angry, it is never sarcastic, indifferent, inattentive, or cross. It is always fair; never plays favorites. It greets each student with a friendly "Good morning, Johnny" (it always uses the student's name), and ends with an equally friendly "See you again on Monday, Johnny."

Another important issue which is likely to become increasingly discussed by the late seventies is the question of the intelligence of the computer. We have already mentioned that the power available to the computers will increase by a factor of 10,000 or so. Current computers can be programmed to play better chess than the average person (and very likely better than the people who designed the computer and wrote the program). Indeed we have already programmed computers in ways which exhibit many of the characteristics that we associate with intelligence. As far as I know, despite many popular and sometimes expert statements to the contrary, nobody has demonstrated any intrinsic limits to what the computer can eventually do in simulating or surpassing human capabilities. There is a clear capability for mimicking the appearance and characteristics not only of such human activities as analysis, calculation, and playing games, but of activities which have a large aesthetic, emotional, or seemingly intuitive content. We already have heuristic and other advanced programming systems which enable the computer to learn from experience. One can also put probabalistic mechanisms into the computer. One can have the computer decide between indeterminant kinds of data and hold onto conclusions with varying degrees of tenacity and intensity. One can put contradictory information into the computer and even contradictory principles and then also put in mechanisms, which at the point of

---

**It is, of course, now very fashionable to argue that we are entering the computer age.**

action either resolve these contradictions or reduce the computer to a neurotic state of cycling activity.

It is my personal conjecture, and one which personally always depresses me as well, that by the end of the century, if not by 1980, the experts will have concluded that the computer can transcend human beings in every practical aspect. I do not know what this means in terms of philosophy, religion (particularly cultist worship or hatred of the computer), and even the democratic way of life (shall we have movements for computer civil rights, for computer representation, or even computer domination of certain kinds of issues and processes in which we no longer can trust uncontrolled human beings?). None of the above are likely to be central questions by 1980, but they are all likely to be raised with substantially greater intensity than they have been to date and with a correspondingly greater philosophic and religious impact.

Another group, other than the corporate world, the young, and the philosophical and religiously inclined that are likely to be much affected by the impact of the computer in the seventies are analytical scientists and designers. By 1980 the interaction of man with machine should be carried to the point where the two will be able to function in a working partnership in many creative enterprises. Some of these partnerships will involve more than using the computer as a simple-minded slave or assistant to the human being (that is, as a sort of superslide rule, super drawing board, or super library), but there ought to be available sophisticated interactions between computer and man, which while they will not satisfy the most rigorous criteria of true independent intelligence on the part of the computer, may appear very much that way to the scientist-collaborator or designer-collaborator (in much the same way that the child may not distinguish sharply between his human and computer teacher).

We must also consider the computer in the 1980 home. It is likely to be there at least in the richer families, as a convenient central method of regulating temperature, humidity, various cooking devices, home accounting, access to computer libraries, and so on. Computers may even have the capability to begin to play surrogate mother or at least surrogate baby-sitter and playmate as well as tutor and/or teacher. Such household computers might well have access to a very large variety of games, amusements, entertainments, and a number of alarm-type circuits

## The Next Three Years: Paperless Communications
FRED R. SHELDON

The following is a prediction that was made in 1965. These predictions still are not even close to happening. What went wrong?

By 1968 some of the more forward-looking, advanced corporations will have eliminated all intra-company memoranda, reports, and similar internal means of correspondence. Most of the hardware and technical advances for such an achievement already exist and the development of "paperless communication" requires only pioneering by innovating entrepreneurs.

With a paperless communications system, internal memoranda and the like would be "written to file," i.e., entered into a central data processing computer from a remote console. The primary recipients of messages and their "carbon copy" receivers will be appropriately designated, and the computer will automatically make the communications available to memory registers assigned to these individuals. Executive and key management personnel will have individual desk display screens to which they can call all communications addressed to them since they last examined their "incoming file." Suitable controls at desk display units will allow temporary or permanent filing of communications, removal from an individual's register, or even generation of hard copy (for study during commuting or other travel). Since an individual will have access to all messages addressed to him as soon as they are written, mail and messenger delays and costs will be eliminated, as will the costs of many files and of manual filing itself.

Groups of middle and lower middle managers will be served by a single display unit, and will operate from a common, group register. The size of individual or group registers will be determined on a statistical basis according to message frequency, the computer adjusting register sizes as needed. In fact, efficiency of the system can be improved constantly from automatically computed audits which will monitor types and frequency of messages, the number of responses, and the time required for them. Such internal audits, carefully used, could provide a valuable guide toward individual productivity and performance.

### SELECTIVE MESSAGES
Some key executives will have access to data in all registers, while others will be limited to single or group registers as their positions and company functions dictate. Where company activities warrant it, central data acquisition will be on a real time basis with up-to-the-minute facts available to operating personnel in either tabular or graphical form. Some personnel may be authorized to change data registers by means of keyboard input or light pen attachments to their display units.

Higher company executives will probably be more concerned with averages and trend data than with real time data in their planning and long term corporation guidance. To assist them in this most important function, the central computer will contain a library of simulation models reflecting all aspects of the company's business, including major markets served. Thus, using internal data, government statistics, external market projections, and innovative thinking, key executives will use the central data processing facility and its stored simulation models to test strategic decisions and to plan the successful course of the corporation through time, all without generating mountains of paper.

> **By the end of the century, if not by 1980, the experts will have concluded that the computer can transcend human beings in every practical aspect.**

to inform the parents or neighbors when they should look in themselves on what the youngsters are doing. While they will not, by 1980, do all of the things that the human baby-sitter or human playmates would do, there may be enough things they can do, and some of them in a superior fashion, to make them attractive substitutes for inconveniently available baby-sitters and playmates—at least for part of the time.

Before coming to the list of what will certainly appear, to many a rather uninviting and perhaps frightening glimpse of our "Brave New World" of the future, let me offer one optimistic (or perhaps pessimistic) prediction: Counter to what appears to be a popular foreboding, it does not seem likely that the society of 1980 or even 2000 will be one in which most of us are "condemned to leisure" and only a favored few will be permitted to work. If anything, it seems quite likely that there will be an extreme labor shortage in the developed nations—certainly a shortage of certain kinds of competent personal services and perhaps a general and overall shortage or an equivalent which should tend to drive up the price of labor. Doubtless the average number of hours worked per year will go down, but for those who want to work longer there will most likely be plenty of opportunities. This does not mean that there could not be a considerable amount of unemployment, but simply that in many cases the skills and/or desires of the unemployed will not be matched by the opportunities of the job market; hence even though the job market provided sufficient opportunity from a numerical standpoint for the population seeking work, it may not provide the right kind of opportunity.

---

Ad in the *San Francisco Examiner*

Computer prayers. Any 20 word prayer printed by computer 1,000 times. $15.00. Box xxx   San Francisco, CA

In conclusion, I would say that the most important aspect of the late seventies is less likely to be the actual technological developments of the next decade than an increased understanding of what the emergence of the coming technology and the post-industrial culture is likely to mean. Many of us think of this last as the change from an industrial to a post-industrial culture—as being as important in its way as the agricultural revolution of some 10,000 years ago, or the industrial revolution of some 200 years ago. We are also going to see an increasing emphasis on the year 2000 as a millennial turning point. As a result one can expect that one major activity of the seventies is going to be, as I suggested at the beginning, studying, watching, speculating, believing, and otherwise being concerned with the future in a way that would seem to our ancestors to be almost a maniacal obsession.

## Computer Monitoring
DONALD MICHAEL

There is one form of technology tied to the computer which today increases freedom for some and which may in the future decrease it for others. This is the technique of telemetering information from tiny sensors and transmitters embedded in the human body. Right now, one form of these devices keeps recalcitrant hearts beating steadily. In a few years, in variations of already existing experimental devices, they will transmit information about subtle internal states through a computer to the doctor, continually or at any time he wishes. Clearly, the lives and liberty of people dependent on such support will be enhanced, for it will provide greater opportunity to move and to live than would be theirs if this information were not so continuously and directly available.

It is not impossible to imagine that parolees will check in and be monitored by transmitters embedded in their flesh, reporting their whereabouts in code and automatically as they pass receiving stations (perhaps like fireboxes) systematically deployed over the country as part of one computer-monitored network. Indeed, if they wish to be physically free, it is possible that whole classes of persons who represent some sort of potential threat to society or to themselves may be required to keep in touch in this way with the designated keepers of society.

It may seem farfetched to suggest that such people might walk the streets freely if their whereabouts and physiological states must be transmitted continually to a central computer. But two trends indicate that, at least for those who are emotionally disabled, this is not unlikely. We are now beginning to treat more and more criminals as sick people. We are beginning to commit them for psychiatric treatment rather than to jail. This treatment may have to continue indefinitely, since frequently a psychiatrist will not be prepared to certify that his patient will not commit the same kind of crime again (as is now required for sexual offenders under psychiatric treatment). At the same time, chemical and psychotherapeutic techniques for inducing tranquil emotional states are likely to improve. We may well reach the point where it will be permissible to allow some emotionally ill people the freedom of the streets, providing they are effectively "defused" through chemical agents. The task, then, for the computer-linked sensors would be to telemeter, not their emotional states, but simply the sufficiency of concentration of the chemical agent to ensure an acceptable emotional state. When the chemical agent weakens to a predetermined point, that information would be telemetered via the embedded sensors to the computer, and appropriate action could be taken. I am not prepared to speculate whether such a situation would increase or decrease the personal freedom of the emotionally ill person.*

---

*For a fiction account see THIS PERFECT DAY by Ira Levin.

# Session on Views of the Future—Chairman's Introduction—Opposing Views

MURRAY TUROFF
Office of Emergency Preparedness—Executive Office of the President, Washington, D.C.

I offer two scenarios suggesting the use of computers in the 21st century.*

These scenarios are based upon the same projected basic information technology, but use it in opposing or contrasting manners. Each one rests on differing but plausible assumptions about resources and values of society in the 21st century. Together they provide a fundamental caveat for all the papers in this session by dramatizing the difficulties facing anyone attempting to forecast the future of information technology and its application.

These two scenarios represent what might be characterized as a plausible "open" society and "closed" society. They are not intended to portray the extremes of open society, which would be anarchy, or of closed society, which would be a slave state. Both scenarios are presented as selected day-to-day communications that an average citizen might receive via his computer terminal. Thus they do not provide an exhaustive description of the alternative societies, but rather convey to the reader a Gestalt—a feeling for what these alternatives might be like to live in.

## COMMON ASSUMPTIONS FOR BOTH SCENARIOS

We assume that society in the year 2000 and thereafter can be characterized as "information rich." Essentially, all the information generated by society and needed for its operation exists in electronic form. The collection, processing, transmission, distributing, storage, and retrieval of information on a day-to-day basis takes place on a largely "self-generating and sustaining" basis. The information centers, the networks tying them together, and the procedures governing their use are sufficiently compatible that they may be viewed jointly as a single nationwide information complex largely transparent to the users and their applications—much as the telephone system is today. Terminals exist in every home, voice recognition is a common form of computer input, mass on-line storage is cheap and plentiful, and other similar marvels of technology (by today's standards) abound. Both scenarios, therefore, assume the continued advance of information technology along the directions now perceived. Barring a major holocaust, such evolution of the technology does not seem unreasonable. Of course, the implicit assumption that the industry has managed to agree by the year 2000 on standards for internal compatability of a nationwide information complex·is somewhat more questionable.

## THE "CLOSED" INFORMATION-RICH SOCIETY

It is assumed that by the year 2000 some evolutionary process has resulted in a scarcity of important material and human resources—energy, mineral ores, medical talent, etc. Society is characterized and regulated by various algorithmic and procedural models, operating on a real time basis and striving to maintain the precarious balance between supplies and demands. Government consists of a dictatorship by the system over which no one individual or group has an effective control. The various components of this system are largely the product of a reductionist philosophy and represent uncorrelated short term fixes to problems as they occur. The complexity of the overall interaction of these individual fixes is not really well understood.

As resource limitations have become increasingly critical individual options of choice have been eliminated whenever there has been any suspicion that this would benefit the objective of survivability of society as a whole. The education process is correspondingly driven largely by the needs of society and provides rather narrow training. Information flow is regulated on a "need for" basis, strong pressures exist for conformance to a common "official" ideology or singular value set, and the system as a whole fosters a high degree of centralized control. However, an illusion of free choice is not only allowed to exist but even encouraged, and other types of escapism are provided via recreational pursuits.

## THE "OPEN" INFORMATION-RICH SOCIETY

It is assumed that through effective planning society has reached by the year 2000 a posture in which resources are relatively abundant with respect to societal and individual

---

*A large part of the material in these scenarios was developed by the working group on the Assessment of Information Technology at the NATO Advanced Study Institute on Information Science in August of 1972. The members of this group were: Shuhei Aida, Issac Auerbach, Dennis Conrady, Lee Friedman, Carl Hammer, John Martell, Gil Puente, Alex Strasser, and Murray Turoff. The full report of this group will be available in Vol. 1 of *Challenges to the Development of a Science of Information* to be published in 1973 by Marcel Dekker, Inc.

needs. Emphasis is placed on maximizing individual options of choice. Extensive understanding of adaptive and cybernetic approaches to solution of practical problems allows a high degree of decentralized controls, although centralized predictive capability is retained to detect and announce potential conflicts. As a result of this abundance, society is tolerant of a heterogeneous set of ideologies and a multiple value system flourishes. Distinctions among the functions of education, employment, and recreation have become blurred. Educational philosophy is holistic in nature, striving to prepare the citizen for a society which enjoys highly individualistic life styles but requires strongly participatory government.

**EMPLOYMENT AND EDUCATION**

OPEN
The package of information which you requested relative to career and educational choices for your son has been prepared and is now available for access at your leisure. The package includes educational requirements and potential income ranges for the careers you selected. In addition, several careers that are similar in income and educational requirements to those you selected have been included for your consideration. Also included in the package is a report showing how people with similar performance profiles to that of your son, now feel about the career they entered.

Your recent series of unsuccessful and unprofitable purchases in Phase XL of the Department Store Game indicates that you are not yet ready to commence participating in the Economic Market Policy Game, Phase A2. Upon successful implementation of the A2 buyer's strategy, you will be qualified as Assistant Buyer and eligible for employment at the Group Store, if you so choose.

I would like to exchange for one year my current job function as manager of distribution for a midwest appliance manufacturer for a job function in the sales area (at level B or above).

CLOSED
As a result of your son's performance this past educational cycle, he has been transferred to track three for preparation in employment class five.

Under your job classification you are entitled to attend one professional meeting this year. According to your schedule of assignments and available travel funds the MIS system has determined that for the meeting in March of the SOCIETY FOR FORTRAN 84 PROGRAMMERS is best suited to fulfill this privilege. It is further suggested that you attend the following sessions. . . .

Your recent series of unsuccessful and unprofitable purchases in Phase XL of the Department Store Game indicates non-orientation toward the merchandise manager's field. You are to report to the Group Store, as Stock Clerk, Class C, Malthusium Kit department.

A recent computer evaluation of your job performance exhibits a discrepancy with respect to the job's requirements. In order to avoid declassification, you must report for updating on. . . .

OPEN
Your request for educational opportunities has prompted us to bring to your attention the fact that Ecological Watchmen and Recycling Engineers are urgently needed. Many openings exist for this outdoor occupation, offering excellent wages and, currently, a one-to-one exchange program: for one year on the job, spend one year at any knowledge or recreation center of your choice, all expenses paid.

Openings are now available for robotic controllers in building construction. In view of your experience in this area, we would like to enter negotiations with you for a work period of six months.

CLOSED
As of . . . you have been awarded a new job with the Government Employment Corporation. This opportunity to serve your government, of course, carries with it certain sacrifices in dwelling area and salary cash flow; however, be assured that the data banks have your file in the active list and will do all that is possible to reinstate you in private enterprise at some time in the future. Your current employer has requested that you be notified that a suitable transfer bonus will be applied to your account upon proper training by you of the replacement for your current job function.

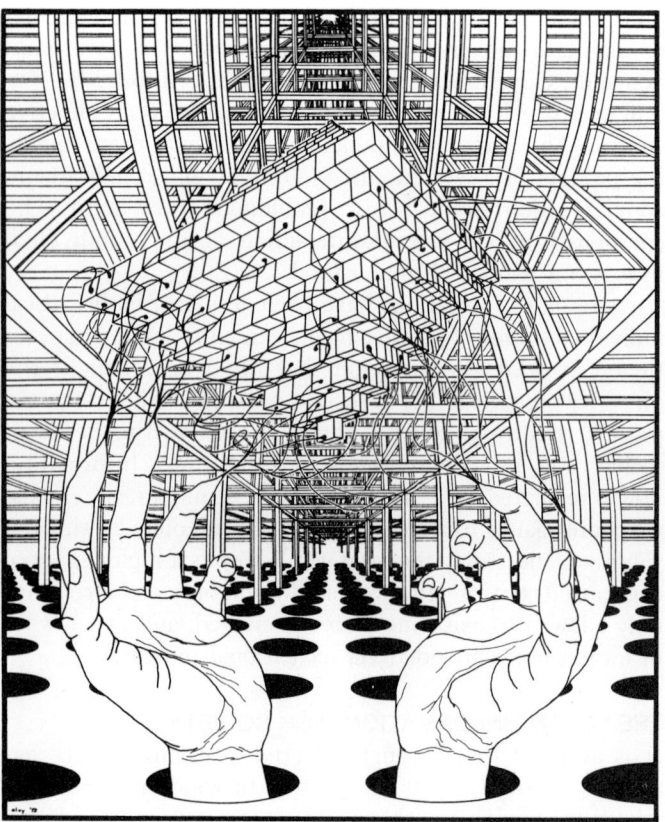

**SERVICES**

OPEN
Your proposal submitted last week to our venture bid service for a new product in industry sector 83 has received six complete bids and eighteen partial bids for financial support.

None of these, however, meet all your initial constraints on ownership and profit sharing parameters—a complete analysis of differences is attached including an estimated ten year profit flow analysis to you on the three most favorable bid combinations. Please advise should you wish to restate your constraints.

Your current offer for a house painter has had no responses the past week. Based on current market conditions we estimate only a .3 probability of response this month. A raise in your offer of 15 percent would increase the response probability to .95.

The paper you submitted last month has been reviewed. It appears that your paper not only has original content but it will allow us to retire from our immediate access files ten other papers to the offline archives. We are, therefore, adding your paper to our system immediately and we are informing users with appropriate interest profiles of its availability. Thank you very much for your contribution.

In addition to the material resulting from your particular search of our literature banks, the following four individuals have indicated they are seeking contact with individuals exhibiting your search pattern. This auxiliary service of your local knowledge center is intended to promote contact among individuals with common interests. It is your option to establish contact. However, if you wish your name added to the list, please notify us.

Your request of our news file has revealed that the information you desired has not yet been released by the appropriate agency. We have therefore entered a formal request for disclosure and established a reporting team to handle the matter. You will hear further within ten days.

### CLOSED

A recent survey by this office has resulted in your being chosen for a formal exchange of views with the "PRIME MONITOR." Any licensed barber shop may perform for you the hair shaving necessary for electrode placement.

Your recent behavior at the community meeting of June 15 seems to deviate from your field psychological profile. Please report for a reexamination on . . .

As a regular service we offer at bargain rates a monthly list of "suspicious" word combinations used by the government computerized monitoring systems to select written or verbal communications for review by the Office of Internal Stability. If you wish to avoid observation for potential deviant behavior, our service is a must.

Our agency stands ready to provide you with the data requested and to which you are entitled. However, since this data is computerized, we cannot predict the actual cost to you of providing this information. It is, therefore, necessary that you post a payment bond in the amount of . . . before we undertake to process your request. In addition, your request is not sufficiently detailed and a new request certified by an information engineer must be submitted.

A computer analysis of your professional writings indicates that you have been writing on subjects outside your rated discipline. Your current rating within your current field will be lowered unless this situation is corrected. You are of course free to apply for change of discipline area and the appropriate forms and schedules of government review hearings may be obtained from. . . .

An analysis of your request of our news service shows your background profile provides no justification for supporting your need for this information. A check on this analysis by the government agency responsible for this information further confirms this result. Therefore, in order to conserve resources, your request is denied. You are, of course, free to seek modifications of your profile.

### LEISURE

#### OPEN

Your requirements for a vacation house for three months have been matched against housing available, location, and other features of homes that appear to meet your specifications. If you wish to negotiate detailed arrangements, please let us know. If you wish to make your own home available during the time you are on vacation, please indicate this on our next communication.

We offer a complete line of "recreational," "educational," and "experience" vacations. Our information service and planning system offers comprehensive data on the environment and facilities of all vacation centers in the southwest, including the scope of available knowledge banks and communication and processing capabilities. Depending on the type of facility you choose, our knowledge banks can offer a wide variety of games, courses on many topics and dreams in many emotional variations. Our analysis routines will provide complete simulated alternatives to meet your specifications.

Mr. Norjk of Norway and his family will be in your city during the month of July. Our examination of your active hosting record in our files indicates a strong compatibility of interests for your two families (analysis enclosed). With your permission, we will pass this information on to them.

We regret to inform you that our home game service does not currently offer group simulations of primitive societies for youngsters. We will, however, poll the families using our service and establish if there is sufficient interest to modify one of the adult games in this area.

The Boston Fine Arts Museum offers the recorded experiences of creating over four hundred works of the finest art of the day. Learn the techniques of many fine artists by reliving their emotions and actions in the creative process. Our staff metric-psychologist is available for consulting in avoiding the psycho shock possible from merging disjoint personality traits of you and the artists of your choice. Be sure also not to neglect our recent acquisition in the performing arts—conductors, dancers, actors and singers.

#### CLOSED

You can rest assured that our travel service provides a full range of vacation plans matched to your travel, food, and energy allowances. Do not hesitate to call. . . .

We are very pleased to inform you that your eighth preference choice for a vacation has been approved this year.

We are happy to announce that we were able to obtain accommodations for you at the Mountain hideaway resort. Accommodations for your wife and child were found at the Cliffside resort, a mere twenty miles away.

Our robotic sports areas offer participation in a wide variety of robotic combats. Duel to the point of robotic destruction with your own wide choice of weapons—swords,

tridents, mace, clubs of all shapes and sizes just to mention a few. Duels arranged to match your skills to those of your opponent's included in the standard fee. At slightly higher rates you may challenge the current champion in various weapon classes. Also, two mass battles offered each day and special training sessions for beginners.

The apex dream parlor offers over one hundred in the latest drug-electronic stimulated dreams. Our three most popular dreams this week are:

1. Own your own small business for a day—take full responsibility for all decisions—be your own boss.
2. A day on the beach—enjoy unpolluted waters and clear white sand, feel the warmth of the sunlight through a crystal clear atmosphere.
3. Have a creative idea—create and document a new idea, present it orally to a peer group and receive renown and acclaim.

## GOVERNMENT

### OPEN

TO: K. MIDAS

The XYZ Institute for Tax Assistance is happy to inform you that a tax rebate of 313,000 credits is due to you on your 1989 income. This amount includes a .06 percent remonstrative penalty levied on the Federal Tax Bureau for its error, plus an added 7.40 percent compensating interest to compensate you for non-use of the credits in the intervening years. As your neighborhood Tax Assistance Center, we are ready to help you in any other tax matter. Please call on us.

Your application for free control of your automobile on public metroconnectors has been denied. Your tested reaction timing is not sufficient to ensure adequate safety margins for the integrity of all travelers. However, it is noted that your test results show a high probability that a standard course of training in Judo or tennis or a similar sport would probably increase your reaction rate to the point of satisfying our standards.

This is an official notice under local ordinance 817 that a set of computerized caucus conferences reflecting pro, con, neutral, and alternative positions has been established to examine a rezoning bid that is pending in your area. As a local property owner, you may join any of these conferences at no cost.

We are required by law to notify you once a month of any outstanding communications you have not accepted for delivery. These now include 118 advertisements, 16 governmental notices, and 13 personal correspondences. Of the latter, one is classified as pertaining to an in-progress contract arrangement which you must act on by July 13 or suffer unnecessary financial loss to your credit account due to contract penalties to be awarded the other party.

Following is your yearly tax analysis provided by IRS to each citizen based upon all automatically reported data pertaining to your tax account. This computerized analysis attempts to indicate your lowest possible tax liability; however, it is possible in unusual circumstances for this to not occur. You may therefore dial our local analysis service to attempt further optimization. Please notify us when filing of any apparent errors in the data pertaining to your account and supplied by other services.

### CLOSED

TO: K. MIDAS, SR.

The Federal Bureau of Tax Analysis hereby informs you that a tax rebate of 288,000 credits is due to you on your 1989 income. The Bureau assures you that its evaluation of your 1989 tax return is now complete and correct.

TO: K. MIDAS, SR.

The Federal Bureau of Census has noted that you received an added income of 288,000 credits during FY 1989 which was not reported on the census form. Accounting Department has therefore computed the required federal, region, state, county, city, block, head, automobile, and penalty taxes on this unexpected amount. A copy of your tax bill is herewith enclosed for the amount of 373,000 credits, which will be deducted from your purchasing account today. A copy of this message has been sent to your employer and to your regional fiscal therapy center.

Your request to move to another dwelling area must be submitted to the office of housing permits with copies for approval to the departments of energy management, transportation, tax assessments, environmental monitoring, societal impacts, and financial control. Upon reply by these federal offices you may proceed to seek concurrence from appropriate government offices.

You are hereby notified that per Public Law 813, you must vacate your dwelling unit within one month of retirement in order to maintain equitable transportation patterns. Your new classification will allow you to seek a living unit in the following areas . . .

Your violation of allowed energy consumption this month has resulted in an automatic fine of . . . due to the inability of your cash flow account to meet this deduction a proportion of your salary has been attached for . . .

It has come to the attention of the Economic Growth Office that your cash flow account is in excess of allowed positive limits. If you do not establish a higher purchase rate by June 5, we will be forced to impose a personalized tax on this account.

**MEDICAL**

**OPEN**

TO: DR. O. MARK HYMAN

After reviewing the diagnosis of the patient you submitted to the neurological consulting network, a number of us at the Berkeley bio-engineering laboratory feel that a motor nerve hypors system we have recently developed may allow your patient normal use of his right arm and hand. Please notify us if you wish full specifications for implantation of this system.

Your requested analysis of your health records and correlation to current test data indicate a need for at least a twenty pound weight reduction under a supervised program, if you are to avoid a future heart problem. Please contact your physician at your earliest convenience. Thank you for using our automated diagnostic booth.

Thank you for calling on our community information service. In answer to your request, following is a list of medical personnel and clinics in your area with an assessment of specialties, performance histories, and fees for each.

For a slight additional fee our computerized dating service offers an auxiliary matching procedure based on a complete genetic analysis of both parties.

Enclosed is a list of local discussion groups which our analysis shows have a high potential of aiding you in resolving your current concerns. You may join these physically or via remote terminal hookup on either an anonymous or non-anonymous basis. Do not hesitate to call on us for any further mental health service you may wish.

**CLOSED**

TO: DR. O. MARK HYMAN

An examination of the neurological condition of your patient's arm and an evaluation of his job function shows too low a benefit/cost ratio to warrant further corrective treatment. You are hereby instructed to terminate further effort on this case and revise your allocation of resources accordingly.

Your computerized diagnosis does not provide you with a high enough priority to see a doctor at this time. Your appointment has been scheduled for next Thursday at 10:00 A.M. Your probability of survival to that time is estimated at 68 percent; the current immediate appointment threshold is 57 percent. Do not hesitate to dial us again should you feel a deterioration in your condition.

Due to genetic mismatching your application for breeding with Ms. . . . has been denied; however, we offer the following list of egg or sperm alternatives with which the two of you may seek to form a family unit.

This is to notify you that Mr. Jung located at unit 437 in your living complex is under treatment for MDN (Mental Deflections from the Norm). It is your civil duty to report all interactions with this individual and observations of interactions between Mr. Jung and others. Your aid in this matter will insure that the treatment will be brought to a speedy and successful conclusion.

## Machines Hold Power for Evil and Good
PETER T. WHITE

Directing the Academy of Science's study is Alan F. Westin, Professor of Public Law and Government at Columbia University. He says: "Man has progressed over the centuries from the status of a subject of a ruler to that of a citizen in a constitutional state. We must be careful to avert a situation in which the press of government for systematic information and the powerful technology of computers reverse this historical process in the second half of the 20th century, making us 'subjects' again." He adds, "Perhaps the greatest legal device to facilitate the movement from subject to citizen in England was the writ of habeas corpus—the command issued by the courts to the Crown to produce the body of the person being held, and to justify his imprisonment.

"Perhaps what we need now is a kind of writ of 'habeas data'—commanding government and powerful private organizations to produce the data they have collected and are using to make judgments about an individual, and to justify their using it."

What if computer-equipped authority, insufficiently restrained, should turn hyperinquisitive someday? If every purchase one makes, down to the last 10-cent newspaper, is recorded by a computer, showing where it was made and at what time; if millions of telephone conversations can not only be recorded daily but instantly scanned to pick out key words considered alarming by the surveillance officers. . . . The implications surpass the horrors of George Orwell's *1984*.

Dr. Jerome B. Wiesner, Provost of MIT, has said that the computer's potential for good, and the danger inherent in its misuse, exceed our ability to imagine. Wouldn't that be the worst it could do—to become an instrument of tyranny, propelling mankind into a new Dark Age?

**It is not impossible to imagine that parolees will check in and be monitored by transmitters embedded in their flesh, reporting their whereabouts in code and automatically as they pass receiving stations.**

**FEAR?**
The largest, most complicated computer in existence is actually quite simple when compared to the telephone connections between your house and a friend's phone a hundred miles away. Yet today the telephone system generates no fear nor do we personify it. Maybe someday computers will be treated as casually as we treat our telephone system today.

# Computers in Fiction

DENNIE VAN TASSEL

Since computers play such an important part in our daily lives, it is not surprising that they are also represented in literature. What is surprising is how early stories about computers were written. One of the first machine stories was Samuel Butler's *Erewhon*, which appeared in 1872. In this story all machines are destroyed lest they evolute and surpass mankind. The tale is similar to the actions of the Luddite movement in England during the 1800s, which smashed machines to preserve jobs. During the early 1970s there was also a definite anti-computer movement that resulted in several bombings of computer installations. R.U.R., a play by Karel Capek, seems to fulfill the *Erewhon* fears. In this drama, robots gain a consciousness and destroy mankind only to find they have no purpose without people.

### ANTI-COMPUTER STORIES

Many computer-related stories are anti-computer, but one of the best is Harlan Ellison's "I Have No Mouth and I Must Scream." I won't describe it but just say it is a terror story. Kurt Vonnegut's *Player Piano* is about a society where all work is done by machine and almost everyone is on a forced welfare system, unhappily.

Humor occasionally appears in computer-related stories. *The Tin Men* by Michael Frayn is a hilarious book about the Institute of Automation Research. Computerized sports, sex, religion, and writing are heavily satirized. Another humorous book is John Barth's *Giles Goat-Boy*, which takes place on a large college campus, where opposing sides, using computers, war for control of the campus. In David Gerrold's *When Harlie Was One* we find an adolescent computer with all the humor of an immature genius. This book is one of the better stories involving computers.

### LOSS OF CONTROL

There are several stories in which the computer controls all of society and society has even forgotten how it all started. One of the best examples is "The Machine Stops" by E. M. Forster. In it, people have become so dependent on the computer running their lives that they have been reduced to cattle.

In *Colossus* by D. F. Jones we have a classical example of a computer out of human control. The United States and Russia decide that the military situation is too complicated for mere humans and allow super-computers to make all military decisions, much to the military's and everyone else's regret. This book is followed by *The Fall of Colossus*.

In *This Perfect Day* by Ira Levin the computer uses surveillance and

---

# Employee ID Card Charges Lunch in Company Cafeteria
*Computers and Automation*

Employees at IBM's computer development laboratory in Boeblingen, West Germany, now are able to charge meals in the lab's cafeteria by slipping their regular IBM identification cards into an experimental data entry terminal. The magnetic tape record created by the terminal goes to a computer which deducts each employee's monthly charges from his salary. All the customer has to do is push his card into a slot, with his picture facing the cashier.

Instead of ringing up the price on a cash register, the cashier now keys it into the terminal. The keyboard is partly programmed to store fixed prices such as 1.20 Deutsch Mark for a meal of soup, meat, vegetable and salad, or DM 0.50 for juice. Use of the non-cash system by employees is optional. For those who prefer to pay as they eat, the terminal can display the amount without recording it on the tape cartridge.

The Boeblingen laboratory's Special Engineering group built the experimental terminal around a modified IBM 050 magnetic data inscriber, especially for the cafeteria.

drugs to control all actions of people, including social and sexual interaction. A more friendly super-computer is found in *The Moon is a Harsh Mistress* by Robert Heinlein, in which the computer directs a revolution on the moon.

A final super-computer story, *The Tale of the Big Computer* by Olof Johannessen, reveals the history of man as seen through the eyes of a computer.

### CHESS STORIES

Chess-playing machines have been of interest since before 1800. In 1835 Edgar Allen Poe exposed an automated chess player as a fraud. A large box, which was supposed to be a machine chess player, had a midget inside it directing the chess moves.

In 1894 Ambrose Bierce developed a horror story in "Moxon's Monster" about a chess-playing machine. Still another game-playing machine is woven around Nigel Balchin's "God and the Machine." In this story the protagonist is interested in machines because he thinks machines are more honest than people, but he is soon disappointed.

Other various interesting applications of computers are found in literature, Michael Crichton weaves a spellbinding story in *The Terminal Man*, in which a small computer is implanted in a man's head to control his actions, but not too successfully. In the opposite, *Enslaved Brains* by Eando Binder, human brains are implanted into computers to control the computers.

There are many other tales about computers; some of them can be found by checking the following references.

> Ascher, Marcia. "Computers in Science Fiction." *Computers and Automation*, November 1973.
> Asimov, Isaac. *I, Robot*. Doubleday, 1973.
> Conklin, Greff, ed. *Science-Fiction Thinking Machines*. Bantam, 1952.
> Knight, Damon, ed. *The Metal Smile*. Belmont Productions, 1963.
> Lewis, A. O. Jr., ed. *Of Men and Machines*. Dutton, 1963.

## Computer Interviews Aid Suicide Prevention

People who have tendencies towards suicides can be helped—if they are identified in time. The Suicide Risk Prediction Program at the University of Wisconsin Hospitals in Madison now uses a computer to identify potentially suicidal people.

Questions appear on a screen and the patient types in answers. The interview takes from 45 minutes to three hours, and the computer makes a prediction on the likelihood of suicide in two and one-half minutes.

A program developer, psychiatry professor John H. Greist, says that many people actually prefer discussing personal problems with the computer.

"If, for example, a person is talking about influenza symptoms, he usually prefers talking with a doctor. But when talking about problems that may be socially deviant, many prefer the computer. It's a nonjudgmental interviewer that doesn't raise its eyebrows at anything."

The computer makes fewer mistakes than a doctor since it records all comments. "In a study done to determine how accurate the computer is in determining potential suicides, we found that the computer was right 70 percent of the time, and the clinicians only 40 percent," Dr. Greist said.

Besides being available day or night, the computer is more economical than a clinician. Between 8 a.m. and 5 p.m. weekdays a computer interview costs $3, and only $1.50 other times.

The patients who voluntarily agree to the computer interview are seen by the staff if the computer determines they are high suicide risks.

The Wisconsin Department of Health and Social Services reported 447 suicides in Wisconsin every year from 1966 to 1970.

"The actual rate is probably twice that. It's impossible to tell how many deaths attributed to other things are really suicides. There is a real need for suicide prediction," Greist said.

He developed the program in conjunction with UW industrial engineering Prof. David H. Gustafson.

>                WE HAVE COME A LONG WAY TOGETHER
>             you and I, since first we set out upon
>          this strange, uncertain pilgrimage. We
>             picked our way through the Slough of
>    Despond and found that the bogs and
>          quagmires were but figments of our
>          imagination; we have visited the City of
>    Despair and found it walled in only by its
>          own fantasies of Space and Time; we
>    have confronted the Lions of Automata
>             and discovered them to be ephemera,
>          the mirror image of our own minds; we
>    have traversed the Valley of Paradise and
>          eaten of its strange fruit, Leisure. Now
>    we have but a little further to go and our
>          Pilgrimage will be at an end. We must
>    cross the Delectable Mountains. They may
>          seem far away, shimmering there; but that
>             is an accident of our eyesight. They
>          really are right here under our feet, if we
>    will but look. Like the Chinese journey
>          of a thousand miles, we shall approach
>          them one step at a time. Shall we go? Now?
>
>                                      DON FABUN

## ◇ BRANCH POINTS

Avebury, Lord, et al., eds. *Computers and the Year 2000.* Great Britain: NCC Publishers, 1972.

Fabun, D. *The Dynamics of Change.* Englewood Cliffs, N.J.: Prentice-Hall, Inc., 1967.

Fondiller, Robert. "In the Year 2001: Surgery by Computer." *Computers and Automation,* June 1970.

"Forecast 1968–2000 of Computer Developments and Applications." Copenhagen: Parsons and Williams, Inc., 1969.

*Here Comes Tomorrow.* From the Wall Street Journal staff. Princeton, N.J.: Dow Jones Books, 1966.

Kahn, Herman, and Anthony J. Wiener. *The Year 2000: A Framework for Speculation.* New York: Macmillan, 1967.

Seil, W. "How the Real HAL Computers Will Change Your Life Before 2001." *Science Digest,* January 1973.

Slotnick, D. L. "The Fastest Computer." *Scientific American,* February 1971. (See also *Business Week,* September 8, 1973.)

Toffler, A. *Future Shock.* New York: Random House, Inc., 1970.

## ◯ INTERRUPTS

1. Predict what computers will be used for in the year 2000. One source to consult is *The Year 2000* by Herman Kahn and Anthony J. Weiner (New York: Macmillan, 1967).

2. Evaluate computers in regard to how they prevent or encourage "future shock."

3. Find some predictions that were made about the computer field several years ago. One source is H. Dreyfus, *What Computers Can't Do* (New York: Harper & Row, 1972). How do previous predictions about computers compare to the present situation. Find some present-day predictions about computers. What do you think of them?

4. List some of the present significant uses of computers. Then predict what computers will be used for ten and twenty years from now.

5. Select an area of human thought and discuss if a computer could duplicate the process involved.

6. The three rules for robots are:
   1) A robot may not injure a human being nor, through inaction, allow a human being to come to harm.
   2) A robot must obey orders given it by human beings except where such orders would conflict with the First Law.
   3) A robot must protect its own existence as long as such protection does not conflict with the First or Second Laws. (*I, Robot* by Isaac Asimov)

   Are these rules sufficient for human beings to be supreme over robots? Can you think of any situations where the rules would be ambiguous to the robots? Can you improve the rules?

7. Find out what administrative student information on your campus could be of use to student organizations. What information could be used, and what information would be restricted?

8. Find out how computers are used in your college to do one of the following:
   1) Process college applications
   2) Make room assignments
   3) Handle class registration
   4) Process grades

9. Find as many documents as you can that are produced by computers. What are the advantages or disadvantages to you from those documents being computer processed?

10. Make a list of the numbers that identify you. Examples are driver's license numbers, credit-card account numbers, student ID numbers, etc. Which do you remember and which do you ignore? Would you prefer to have just one universal identification number?

11. In *War and Peace in the Global Village,* Marshall McLuhan stated: "The computer is by all odds the most extraordinary of all the technological clothing ever devised by man, since it is the extension of our nervous system. Beside it, the wheel is a mere hula-hoop, though that is not to be dismissed entirely." In what ways do you agree or disagree with McLuhan's statement?

# INDEX

Abt Associates, 40-42
Abt, Clark C., 52
ACM, 50
Akron University, 92
Albrecht, Bob, 53
Alexander the Great, 160
Alexander, Tom, 146
Anti-computer, 122
ARPA, 107
Arrest records, 132
Art, 151
Arthropods, 173-75
Artificial intelligence, 70-71, 96-97
    effects, 166-67
    failures, 8-9
    research, 2
Ascher, Marcia, 212
Asimov, Isaac, 160
Athletics, use, 45-49
Auden, W. H., 131
Auto racing, 49
Automation, 213
    effects, 7, 166-67
    jobs, 60
    robots, 32-34
    unemployment, 102

Babbage, Charles, 12-13
Babysitting, 88, 206
Bar use, 104
BART, 22
Barth, John, 58, 212
Baseball, 48-49
Beattie, J. David, 115
Benford, Gregory, 58
Bierce, Ambrose, 213
Bill of Rights, 126-27
Binder, Eando, 213
Biomin, 173-76
Block, Henry, 66
Body parts, 66
Bolt, Beranek, and Newman, 108
Book, David, 58
Boston Museum of Science, 52
Bradbury, Ray, 29, 93
Brain-computer
    comparisons, 44
    differences, 22
    similarities, 22
Brain waves, 162-63
Brand, David, 2
Brautigan, Richard, 5
Broom balancing, 69
Broom-Hilda, 109
Buchwald, Art, 30, 106
Building computers, 35
Bulter, Samuel, 212
Bush, Vannevar, 14
Business use, 100-6
Bylinsky, Gene, 89

Cal Tech, 24
Campsite reservation, 140
Capek, Karel, 162, 173, 212
Careers, 85
Caruso, Enrico, 2-3
Cashless society, 193-95
Census, 14, 138
Cerf, Vinton, 107
Certificate in Data Processing, 63
CHAOS, 50
Charge lunch, 212
Checkers, 72
Chemistry, 169

Chess, 3
    ACM tournament, 50
    limitations, 6-7
    mini-computers, 84
    stories, 213
    when champion, 71-74
Childrens Mercy Hospital, 114
China, 82
City uses, 58, 143
Civil Liberties Union, 141
Clarke, Arthur C., 55, 59, 195
Class scheduling, 112, 120
Cobb, Ron, 121, 161, 210
COKO, 72
Colby, Ken, 107
Communications, 26, 87
Computer Sciences Corp., 110
Computerniks, 70, 75, 149
Concept learning, 70
Concordance, 78, 118-19
Congressional use, 136-37
Contest, McDonald's, 24
Control of Cybernation, 153-54
Coombs, Don H., 54
Cooper, Dennis W., 72
Copernican revolution, 58
Counter computer, 75-76
Countryman, Vern, 196
Courtney, Robert, 146-47, 150
Cousins, Norman, 10
Creative arts, 60
Credit bureaus, 196-98
Credit cards, 117, 193-95
    fraud, 22-23
Credit Data Corp., 196-98
Crichton, Michael, 26, 213
Criminals, 206
    histories, 135, 142
    *See also* Embezzlement
    use, 185-86
Cuttle, G., 86-88
Cybernation, control, 153-54
Cybernetic meadow, 5
Cyborg, 66, 97

Daedalus, 160
Darwinism, 58, 168, 175
Dash, Sam, 128
Data banks, 134, 155, 182
    credit bureau, 196-200
    governmental, 127-28
    humor, 189-92
    types, 156-57
Davis, Ruth, 5
de Castro, Edson D., 82
Democratic government, 153
Dendral, 169
Denker, John, 24
Diagnosis by computer, 114
Difference engine, 13-14
Diploma, 113
Disabled, use, 115-17
Disasters, 146-51
Doerr, Edd, 120
Doonesbury, 4, 23, 39, 67, 101, 127, 147, 181
Dossiers, 189
Drinks, mixing, 104
Drucker, Peter, 100
Education, 154
    future use, 204, 208
    humor, 120-21
    use, 112-13

EDVAC, 16-17
Elections, 182
Electronic bugging, 199-200
ELIZA, 25, 107
Elliott, Bob, 189
Ellison, Harlan, 212
Embezzlement, 104, 183-88
Employment, 38, 85, 89-92, 208
ENIAC, 14-16
Equity Funding, 147
Erewhon, 212
Errors, 58, 91-92, 117, 131, 180, 186-87
Ervin, Jr., Sam, 126, 134

Fabun, Don, 213
Failures, 76, 97
FBI, 129-33
Fiction, 212
Film use, 85
Fire fighting, 137
Football, 46-47
Forster, E. M., 212
Frankenstein, 161
Fraud, 22-23, 146-51
Frayn, Michael, 212
Frederick the Great, 160
Freud, 168
Future shock, 44

Galileo, 168
Gambling, 51, 84-85, 108-9
Games
    computer, 50-54
    war, 167, 169
Gardner, W. David, 82
Generations, computers, 28
Genes, memory, 165
Gerrold, David, 212
Gilbert, Celia, 155
Ginsberg, Herbert, 66
Glazer, Joe, 172
Goldstine, Herman, 15
Golem, 173
Goulding, Ray, 189
Governmental use, 74, 138-40, 152-55, 210
Gradel, Thomas J., 193
Gradeschool use, 83
Grant, C. B. S., 112
Greek myths, 160
Grosche, Herb, 141

Habeas data, 211
Hackers, 70, 75, 149
HAL, 59, 163, 195
Halacy Jr., Daniel S., 66
Hamburgers, 24
Handicapped, use, 115-17
Hapgood, Fred, 6
Hardware description, 28-29
Hays, Rep. Wayne, 136-37
Heinlein, Robert, 213
History, 12-19
Hollerith, Herman, 14
Home use, 58, 77-81, 86-88, 93-95, 140, 205-6
Honeywell Emett Computer, 159
Horse Racing, 84-85, 108-9
House cleaning, 59, 86
Huehnergarth, John, 58-62
Humanities use, 118-19
Huntington Project, 53
Huskey, Harry D., 12

ICBM, 180
Impact, 146-77, 204-5
Information utility, 105
Information-rich society, 207
Insurance, 19
Intelligent machines, 58-63, 72-73, 77-81, 165
IRS, 198-99

Jacquard's loom, 13-14
Jones, D. F., 212

Kahn, Herman, 204, 214
Kemeny, John, 138
Knowles, Andrew C., 82
Knowlton, Kenneth, 192
Kozdrowicki, Edward W., 72
Kronenberg, Aaron, 40-42
Kubrick, Stanley, 59

Lama, 55
Language recognition, 67, 194
    business uses, 3-4
    ELIZA, 25, 107
    pilot use, 111
    progress, 9-10
    telephone spying, 62, 172
Language translation, 8, 23, 70
Las Vegas, 51
Laser beam, 158
Law of Robotics, 163, 176, 214
Lawrence Hall of Science, 34, 52
LEAA, 135
Learning machine, 166
Legal uses, 128-29
Leibnitz, Gottfried, 12
Leisure, 206, 208-10
Levin, Ira, 212
Library use, 30
Limitations of computers, 6, 61, 102-3, 181
Litek, J. Patrick, 170
Literary uses, 78
Loeser, Rudolf, 38-40
Lovelace, Lady, 13
Luddite, 212

MacHack, 6-7
Machine intelligence, 90-91, 96-97, 204
    *See also* Artificial intelligence
Mail, 58, 87
    junk, 148
    snooping, 200
Mallary, Robert, 151
Mathematics, 44, 169
Mathlab, 169
Matusow, Harry, 122, 148
Mauchly, John, 14-15
McClory, Rep. Robert, 136-37
McDonald's restaurant, 24
McLuhan, Marshall, 214

Meany, George, 102
Meat machine, 169
Medical, 61-62, 107-9, 211
    diagnosis, 26-27, 114
    dossiers, 157
Memory genes, 165
Mental patients, 206
Mexican bank, 9
Michael, Donald, 152, 206
Military uses, 66-67, 180
Mind reading, 162-63
Mini-computers, 34, 82-85
Minsky, Marvin, 3
Missiles, 180
Modeling, sports, 45-47
    *See also* Simulation
Monitoring, people, 206
Multics, 146

Napier, John, 12
NASA, 110-11
National Park Service, 140
NCIC, 131-35, 141
Newspapers, 58
Nilson, Nils, 69

Olsen, Kenneth H., 82
Olympic Games, 45
Ontario Motor Speedway, 45
Orwell, George, 156

Paperless communications, 205
Paranoia, 4, 107
Parker, Donn, 147
Parolees, 206
Pascal, Blaise, 12
Patent software, 9
Patient monitoring, 117
Pattern recognition, 61, 67
Pedler, Kit, 173
People's Computing Center, 34, 53
Philip of Macedon, 160
Physicians, replacing, 62, 107-9, 114
Planning use, 139
*Player Piano*, 212
Plotter, 151
Poetry, 5, 29, 90, 131, 155, 170, 172, 188
Poets, 10, 60-61
Poison control, 114
Police use, 62, 134, 139
    misuse, 142
*Popular Electronics*, 35
Positive effects, 171
Post office, 58, 200
Prayers, 206
President, computer as, 126-27
Privacy, 126-32, 142, 156-59
    *See also* Snooping
Programmers, 38-44, 89-92
    elimination, 106

Project MAC, 43
Project One, 75-76
Project SEARCH, 135
Prugh, Thomas, 84
Psychology, 66
Public opinion, 152-55
Purdy, J. Gerry, 45

Quad I, 151

Rare coins, 158
Religious use, 55-57, 206
Research use, 30, 209
Resource One, 75-76
Responsibility, 171
Retail Credit Company, 197-98
Reuther, Walter, 102
Robots, 32-34, 66-71, 173-76
Rosen, Charles, 69
Rowing, 45
R.U.R., 162, 173, 212
Rubin, Trudy, 128
Russia, 167
Ryan, Frank, 136-37

Samuel, Arthur, 72
Schorr, Daniel, 129-30
Schroeder, M., 199
*Scientific American*, 16
Scott, Alexander, 158
Security, 146-51
Senturia, Stephen, D., 82
Sexual uses, 71
Shanks, William, 5
Shannon, Claude, 22, 69, 72
Sharpe, William F., 51
Shelton, Gene, 158
Simon, Herbert, 2
Simulations, 38
    business, 51
    flight, 110
    forest, 116
    incorrect, 123
    sports, 47
    supreme court, 129
    traffic, 138-40
Slave society, 175
Smith, Alvy Ray, 208
Snooping,
    cameras, 129
    credit bureaus, 196-200
    data banks, 182-83
    dossiers, 156-59
    governmental, 126-32, 209
    telephone, 62, 172
Social Security, 130, 143
Solomon, Louis B., 90
Spacewar, 75
Speech recognition: *See* Language recognition

Spencer, Donald G., 51
Sports use, 45-49
Suicide prevention, 213
Sundstrand Corp., 33
Supreme Court, 129
Surface, Bill, 180
Surveillance: *See* Snooping, FBI
Sweepstakes, McDonald's, 24
Systems, incomprehensible, 169

Tannenbaum, Jeffrey A., 104
Teacher Licensing Commission, 76
Telephone, monitoring, 62, 172
Terminals, 34
Theorem proving, 70
Thetis, 160-61
Thinking machines: *See* Machine intelligence
Tibetan monastery, 55
Time-sharing, 42, 105
    vulnerability, 148-49
Todd, Richard, 38
Townsend, Robert, 122
Track, 47-48
Traffic control, 138-40, 143
Training, 153
Trash processing, 82
Trojan War, 161
Turing, A. M., 96
*2001*, 59

Ultimate cop, 62
Unemployment, 7, 102
Unimate, 32-33
University of Essex, 115

Vagabzode, Bakhtiyar, 188
VASCAR, 143
Versatran, 32-33
Voice Signature, 156, 194
Voice-synthesis, 2-4
Vonnegut, Kurt, 212
von Neumann, John, 15-17, 71
Vote Counting, 136-37

Wachal, Robert, 118
Wanderer, 69
Watergate, 128
Weissman, Clark, 150
Weizenbaum, Joseph, 25, 43, 107, 168
Westin, Alan, 156, 211
White, Peter T., 211
Widrow, Bernard, 69
Wiener, Norbert, 165, 169
Wire tapping, 62, 199-200
Writing, 61

*Year 2000, The*, 214

ZARF, 146
Zeus, 160